WINDOWS® 95 AND NT 4.0 REGISTRY & CUSTOMIZATION HANDBOOK

WINDOWS® 95 AND NT 4.0 REGISTRY & CUSTOMIZATION HANDBOOK

Written by Jerry Honeycutt with

Bernard Farrell • Rich Kennelly •
Jerry Millsaps • Rob Tidrow

Windows 95 and NT 4.0 Registry & Customization Handbook

Library of Congress Catalog No.: 96-69962

ISBN: 0-7897-0842-6

99 98 97   6 5 4 3

Interpretation of the printing code: the rightmost double-digit number is the year of the book's printing; the rightmost single-digit number, the number of the book's printing. For example, a printing code of 97-1 shows that the first printing of the book occurred in 1997.

Screen reproductions in this book were created using Collage Plus from Inner Media, Inc., Hollis, NH.

Credits

PRESIDENT
Roland Elgey

PUBLISHING DIRECTOR
Brad R. Koch

TITLE MANAGER
Kathie-Jo Arnoff

ACQUISITIONS MANAGER
Elizabeth South

EDITORIAL SERVICES DIRECTOR
Elizabeth Keaffaber

MANAGING EDITOR
Michael Cunningham

DIRECTOR OF MARKETING
Lynn E. Zingraf

SENIOR PRODUCT DIRECTOR
Lisa D. Wagner

PRODUCT DIRECTOR
Kevin Kloss

EDITORS
Lori A. Lyons
Geneil Breeze
Kate Givens
Brian Sweany
Nick Zafran

STRATEGIC MARKETING MANAGER
Barry Pruett

PRODUCT MARKETING MANAGER
Kris Ankney

ASSISTANT PRODUCT MARKETING MANAGERS
Karen Hagn
Christy M. Miller

TECHNICAL EDITORS
Robert Bogue
Bill Bruns

MEDIA DEVELOPMENT SPECIALIST
David Garratt

TECHNICAL SUPPORT SPECIALIST
Nadeem Muhammed

ACQUISITIONS COORDINATOR
Tracy C. Williams

SOFTWARE RELATIONS COORDINATOR
Susan Gallagher

EDITORIAL ASSISTANT
Virginia Stoller

BOOK DESIGNER
Ruth Harvey

COVER DESIGNER
Dan Armstrong

PRODUCTION TEAM
Marcia Brizendine
Brian Grossman
Kay Hoskin
Heather Howell
Anjy Perry

INDEXERS
Tim Tate
Nadia Ibrahim

Composed in *Century Old Style* and *Franklin Gothic* by Que Corporation.

For Tanja; I hope all of your dreams come true.

About the Authors

Jerry Honeycutt provides business-oriented technical leadership to the Internet community and software development industry. He has served companies such as The Travelers, IBM, Nielsen North America, IRM, Howard Systems International, and NCR. Jerry has participated in the industry since before the days of Microsoft Windows 1.0, and is completely hooked on Windows and the Internet.

Jerry is the author of many Que books, including: *Using Microsoft Plus!*, *Using the Internet with Windows 95*, *Windows 95 Registry & Customization Handbook*, *Special Edition Using the Windows 95 Registry*, *VBScript by Example*, *Special Edition Using the Internet 3E*, and *Using the Internet 2E*.

Many of his books are sold internationally and have been translated into French, Italian, Korean, Portuguese, Russian, Spanish, and Turkish.

Jerry is also a contributing author of *Special Edition Using Windows 95*, *Special Edition Using Netscape 2*, *Platinum Edition Using Windows 95*, *Visual Basic for Applications Database Solutions*, *Special Edition Using Netscape 3*, *Windows 95 Exam Guide*, *Netscape Navigator 3 Starter Kit*, *Using Java Workshop*, *Using JScript*, and *Internet Explorer ActiveX and Plugins Companion* published by Que. He has been printed in *Computer Language* magazine and is a regular speaker at Windows World, Comdex, and other industry trade shows on topics related to software development, Windows, and the Internet.

Jerry graduated from the University of Texas at Dallas in 1992 with a B.S. degree in Computer Science. He currently lives in the Dallas suburb of Frisco, Texas with two Westies, Corky and Turbo, and a bird called Opie. Jerry is an avid golfer, and has a passion for fine photography and international travel. Feel free to contact Jerry on the Internet at **jerry@honeycutt.com** or visit his Web site at **http://rampages.onramp.net/~jerry**.

Bernard Farrell started working in computers after leaving high school in Ireland in the mid-1970's. He has moved from punched cards and core store into graphics programming on PCs and UNIX workstations. He now works as an independent computer consultant in Massachusetts, architecting, designing, and developing systems in C++, C, and Visual Basic. He's proud to be a U.S. citizen who votes. Bernard lives in Littleton, Massachusetts, with his wonderful wife Jackie, also a software warrior, and their beautiful baby daughter Nina. He also has three older kids, Eleanor, Lee, and Hayley, who are the greatest.

When not working, he likes to bake bread, take photographs, and do home renovation projects, when Jackie lets him borrow her power tools. He can be reached at **bernard@ultranet.com**.

Rich J. Kennelly has been a developer of Windows applications for more than eight years. Having earned a Bachelor of Science degree in Computer Science from Rensselaer Polytechnic Institute, he spent much of the early days dissecting real mode and RAM CRAM. Now he spends his time guiding the development of Registry applications. Rich lives happily with his wife Cindy and his son Tim in Massachussetts.

Kelly Millsaps is an applications technology aficionado. He has worked on projects with several Fortune 100 companies and the U.S. Government. Specializing in systems automation, large enterprise information distribution, and medical applications, Kelly is a candidate for a Bachelor of Science in Electrical Engineering degree at Purdue University. Cofounder of the consulting firm Binary Arts, he is a Microsoft certified Systems Engineer with certifications in Windows NT Server, Windows NT Workstation, and Windows 95, among others. Correspodence can be directed to **merlin@binarta.com**.

Rob Tidrow has been using computers for the past six years and has used Windows for the past four years. Mr. Tidrow is a technical writer and recently was the Manager of Product Development for New Riders Publishing, a division of Macmillan Computer Publishing. Rob is co-author of the best-selling *Windows for Non-Nerds*, and has co-authored several other books including *Inside the World Wide Web, New Riders' Official CompuServe Yellow Pages, Inside Microsoft Office Professional, Inside WordPerfect 6 for Windows, Riding the Internet Highway, Deluxe Edition*, and the *AutoCAD Student Workbook*. In the past, Mr. Tidrow created technical documentation and instructional programs for use in a variety of industrial settings. He has a degree in English from Indiana University. He resides in Indianapolis with his wife, Tammy, and two boys, Adam and Wesley. You can reach him on the Internet at **rtidrow@iquest.net**.

Acknowledgments

The Registry is not an easy topic about which to write. At times, it's a bit puzzling because many portions of the Registry are documented only in the minds of a programmer, who is probably hidden deep in the bowels of Microsoft. Many people participate in order to get a book like this to you. In particular, I want you know about these individuals:

- Elizabeth South put together a fine group of contributing authors in order to get this book done.

- Kevin Kloss managed to keep a 10-thousand-foot level of this book while, at the same time, occasionally getting down to the details. His vision guided this book into what you hold in your hands.

- Lori Lyons, the production editor for this book, works with demanding details and schedules, but manages to keep her head screwed on tight.

- The copy editors—Geneil Breeze, Kate Givens, Brian Sweany, and Nick Zafran—made sure that the gibberish I banged out on the keyboard was readable and conformed to some sense of English structure.

- The contributing authors—Bernard Farrell, Rich Kennelly, Jerry Millsaps, and Rob Tidrow—had to go from 0 to 60 on some pretty complicated topics.

- The Internet community contributed ideas for content and often provided solutions to problems for which I was stumped. They were often unwitting contributors as I found some pretty clever ideas by searching UseNet.

- My friends and relatives provided plenty of support and encouragement when the schedule got a bit too much to handle. In particular, I'd like to thank Charlene for our "Monday night ride."

We'd Like to Hear from You!

As part of our continuing effort to produce books of the highest possible quality, Que would like to hear your comments. To stay competitive, we *really* want you, as a computer book reader and user, to let us know what you like or dislike most about this book or other Que products.

You can mail comments, ideas, or suggestions for improving future editions to the address below, or send us a fax at (317) 581-4663. For the online inclined, Macmillan Computer Publishing has a forum on CompuServe (type **GO QUEBOOKS** at any prompt) through which our staff and authors are available for questions and comments. The address of our Internet site is **http://www.mcp.com** (World Wide Web).

In addition to exploring our forum, please feel free to contact me personally to discuss your opinions of this book: I'm **74201,1064** on CompuServe, and I'm **kkloss@que.mcp.com** on the Internet.

Thanks in advance—your comments will help us to continue publishing the best books available on computer topics in today's market.

Kevin Kloss
Product Director
Que Corporation
201 W. 103rd Street
Indianapolis, Indiana 46290
USA

N O T E Although we cannot provide general technical support, we're happy to help you resolve problems you encounter related to our books, disks, or other products. If you need such assistance, please contact our Tech Support department at 800-545-5914 ext. 3833.

To order other Que or Macmillan Computer Publishing books or products, please call our Customer Service department at 800-835-3202 ext. 666.

Contents at a Glance

Table of Contents

II | Customizing and Troubleshooting with the Registry

7 Customizing Your Windows Desktop   125

III | Administering the Windows Registry

Appendixes

Introduction

by Jerry Honeycutt

Windows 95 and Windows NT have one very important bit of common technology: the Registry. It plays a key role in Windows. In Windows 95, for example, the Registry makes Plug-and-Play possible. The Registry is the central repository for your hardware and software configuration. It makes that context-sensitive desktop possible, straightens out a lot of the confusion you experience with INI files, and makes managing networked computers in the corporate environment significantly easier.

If all that sounds too good to be true, it is. The Registry isn't as easy to understand as the disappearing INI file. It's often difficult to find the configuration item for which you're looking, and even when you do, the chances are good that you won't know what to do with it. Worse, if you're trying to get around both the Windows 95 and Windows NT Registries, you'll probably get frustrated by the subtle differences between them.

That's where *Windows NT 4.0 and 95 Registry and Customization Handbook* comes into action. It debunks some of the myths you've heard. It clarifies the role of the Registry in Windows 95 and Windows NT. It also opens the door to many of Windows' hidden secrets.

Here's what this book does for you:

- Helps you understand how the Registry works. You get the information you need in order to back up, edit, and repair your own Registry. For example, you learn about the relationships between the various parts of the Registry and the various parts of your computer so that you gain a much clearer perspective about how things work.

- Shows you how to personalize your computer using the Windows Registry. This book shows you how to remove those sometimes annoying icons from your desktop, for example. You also learn how to troubleshoot and fix a variety of problems on your computer.

- Teaches you how to program and administer Windows using the Registry. For example, you learn about the Registry API and the variety of tools you can use to administer a Windows computer. You also find plenty of examples that you can reuse, such as code that you can paste into your programs, or templates you can use to establish policies for your users. ▄

How to Use This Book

This is not a tell-all book about Windows. It doesn't cover the entire breadth and depth of Windows like *Special Edition Using Windows 95* or *Special Edition Using Windows NT Workstation 4.0* by Que. However, it does cover the Registry in more detail than you're likely to find anywhere else. It also provides many useful tips for personalizing Windows and overcoming some of Windows' more annoying quirks. In short, this book contains the secrets you're looking for.

No matter what type of user you are—programmer, administrator, or just curious—read all of Part I, "Starting Out with the Registry," before you continue with the rest of this book. The information in these chapters shows you how to protect yourself from accidents, get around the Registry, and use the Registry Editor. After you've read those chapters, take a look at the following sections to learn which parts of this book might be most valuable to you.

Programmers

So, you hack code for a living? I don't envy you. Life is harder for programmers these days. Lots more to learn. Lots of deep holes in which to fall. Holes that are hard to get out of.

One of those holes is the Registry. If you're a Windows programmer, you're going to have to deal with the Registry sooner or later. You might as well learn how to do it the right way and save yourself a lot of trouble. Part IV, "Programming the Windows Registry," can help. It shows you how to program to the standards and how to write code that works well with both the Windows 95 and Windows NT Registries. You also find a lot of sample code that you can paste right into your application.

Administrators

Sometimes, Microsoft just can't win. According to the August 26, 1996 issue of *PC Week* magazine, 55 percent of the IT managers they surveyed said that their support costs didn't decrease after deploying Windows 95. *PC Week* goes on to report that "several Windows 95 features that might reduce client support costs have been largely ignored by administrators." Only 16 percent of the managers they surveyed say that they use policies to restrict a user's privileges. Likewise, only 33 percent use the Registry to remotely administer a user's computer.

Do you want to make a difference in your organization? Help reduce support costs by learning how to remotely administer and control the computers on their desktops. You can start by diving into Part III, "Administering the Windows Registry." This part shows you how to remotely edit a user's Registry, how to work with REG and INF files, and how to use policies to control what a user can do.

Curious Users

If you're a curious user who wants to learn more about Windows, personalize or troubleshoot Windows, or protect yourself from the many problems that the Registry creates, you're reading the right book. Here are some suggestions to get you started:

- If you want to change how Windows looks, works, or performs, skim the table of contents for Part II, "Customizing and Troubleshooting with the Registry," to find a place in which to jump.
- If you're reading this book because you have a specific problem that you think you can fix using the Registry, read Chapter 9, "Troubleshooting Windows," to learn how to fix some of the more common problems that involve the Registry.
- If you're getting all sorts of strange error messages about a bad or corrupt Registry, keep your hands off that keyboard until you read Chapter 5, "Fixing a Broken Registry."

How This Book Is Organized

Windows NT 4.0 and 95 Registry and Customization Handbook covers the Windows Registry in depth. It has five parts, 20 chapters, and three appendixes. You learn the basics about the Registry in the first part of this book. Part II shows you how to customize and troubleshoot Windows using the Registry. Parts III and IV are for administrators and programmers. You find more information about how this book is organized in the rest of this section.

Part I: Starting Out with the Registry

Chapter 1, "Before You Begin," is Registry 101. You learn the basics in this chapter, such as working with the Registry files and backing up the Registry. This chapter is packed with warnings about all the things that can go wrong and how to prevent them, too.

If Chapter 1 is Registry 101, Chapter 2, "Inside the Windows Registry," is Registry 102. This chapter introduces you to how Windows organizes the Registry and what types of information you find in the Registry.

Chapter 3, "Using REGEDIT with Windows 95 and NT 4.0," shows you how to use REGEDIT, which comes with Windows 95 and Windows NT. This is by far the simplest Registry editor to use.

Chapter 4, "Using REGEDT32 with Windows NT 4.0," shows you how to use REGEDT32, which comes only with Windows NT. This editor is more difficult to use but provides additional features that you don't find in REGEDIT.

Chapter 5, "Fixing a Broken Registry," is the Registry's little instruction book. This chapter shows you how to get out of trouble when you find yourself uttering "something's not quite right with that there Registry."

Chapter 6, "File Associations," describes the largest group of entries in the Registry. File associations define the relationships between the documents on your computer and the programs that operate on them. These entries control things such as what happens when you right-click a file with your mouse.

Part II: Customizing and Troubleshooting with the Registry

Chapter 7, "Customizing Your Windows Desktop," is like the TV show *Inside Edition*—for Windows. It exposes some of Windows' deepest secrets so that you can personalize it just the way you want. For example, you learn how to use a bitmap file's image as the file's icon in Explorer.

Windows is a complex operating system. You might have problems that have annoyed you for months, and maybe even problems you don't even know about. Chapter 8, "Troubleshooting Windows," shows you how to fix them.

Chapter 9, "Using ConfigSafe to Track Down Settings," introduces you to a hot new product called ConfigSafe that helps you track changes in the Registry, among other types of changes. You learn how to use this to determine which Registry entries a program changes and how the Registry represents different settings.

You can find a lot of freeware and shareware programs that help you and the Registry live together peacefully. Chapter 10, "Free and Shareware Software to Customize Windows," shows you where to find them and how to use them.

Chapter 11, "Getting Your Windows 95 Configuration Just Right," goes beyond the Registry to show you how to get your Windows configuration just the way you want it. You learn about MS-DOS compatibility mode, the CONFIG.SYS and AUTOEXEC.BAT files, and changing how Windows starts.

Part III: Administering the Windows Registry

Chapter 12, "Securing the Windows Registry," explains why you can't secure the Windows 95 Registry and how you can secure the Windows NT 4.0 Registry.

Chapter 13, "Remotely Editing a User's Registry," shows you how to set up your network configuration so that you can remotely edit a user's Registry. This is handy if you need to tweak a user's settings or fix a problem, but you can't tear yourself away from your desk.

REG and INF files allow you to write a script for changing the Registry that you can pass around to your users—in an e-mail, perhaps. Chapter 14, "Working with REG and INF Files," shows you how to create both types of files.

Chapter 15, "Using the Policy Editor to Administer the Registry," introduces you to one of the most useful tools for administrators. Too bad that it's also the most under-utilized tool. The Policy Editor lets you specify what users can and can't do on their computers.

If you're not happy with the policies that are predefined by the Policy Editor, you can create your own. Chapter 16, "Creating Your Own Policies," shows you how.

Part IV: Programming the Windows Registry

Chapter 17, "Programming to the Standards," shows programmers how to use the Registry correctly; that is, it shows you where to store a program's settings in the Registry. It also shows you how to register a file type, how to build a context menu, and much more.

Chapter 18, "Programming with the Win32 Registry API," gives you all the nitty-gritty details about the Win32 Registry API. You learn about the functions that are available for maintaining your settings. You also learn about the key differences between the Windows 95 and Windows NT Registries.

Chapter 19, "Programming the Registry Using C++," gives you all the sample code you need to grapple with the Registry in your own C++ programs. It even contains an example program that lets a user safely make the changes described in Chapters 7 and 8. It's yours to change in anyway you like.

Chapter 20, "Programming the Registry Using Visual Basic," is similar to Chapter 19, except that it provides examples with Visual Basic. Like the C++ examples in the previous chapter, you can use the code in this chapter in your own programs.

Part V: Appendixes

Appendix A, "The Registry API," describes each function available in the Win32 Registry API. You can look up a function's parameters and return value, as well as information about what the function does.

Appendix B, "Internet Resources for Windows," describes a wealth of Internet resources (FTP, UseNet, Web, and more) that you can use to learn more about Windows 95 and Windows NT. In particular, many of the resources in this appendix are handy if you want to learn even more about the Registry.

Appendix C, "Technical Resources for Windows," describes other technical resources you can use to learn more about Windows. These resources all come from Microsoft and include things such as Microsoft Technet and Microsoft Developer network.

Other Books of Interest

This book is specialized towards the Windows 95 and NT Registries. Que also publishes other books that focus on other specific areas, as well as more general books about Windows 95 and Windows NT. Here are some you might find interesting:

- *Special Edition Using Windows 95* and *Platinum Edition Using Windows 95* covers just about every facet of Windows 95. If you can buy only one more book about Windows 95, this should be it.

- *Special Edition Using Windows NT Workstation 4.0* covers just about everything a power user or administrator needs to know about Windows NT. Like the previous book, this is the one to buy if your manager will only let you expense one book (managers are cheap these days).

- *Special Edition Using Microsoft Office Professional* provides equally wide coverage for using Microsoft Word, Excel, and PowerPoint. Que also publishes books focused on each individual part of Office, including *Special Edition Using Word for Windows 95, Special Edition Using Excel for Windows 95,* and *Special Edition Using PowerPoint for Windows 95.*

■ *Special Edition Using the Windows 95 Registry* attempts to document most of the Windows 95 Registry. The first part of the book provides an overview of the Registry. The second part of the book documents each Registry entry.

■ *Special Edition Using the Internet,* 2nd Edition, shows you how to get connected to the Internet and how to use it like a pro. It also points you to some of the more useful resources on the Internet, such as the World Wide Web, UseNet newsgroups, mailing lists, and so on.

Special Features in This Book

This book has some special features that Que has designed to help you get the information you need—fast. You find the special features described in this section.

Chapter Roadmaps

Each chapter begins with a brief introduction and a list of the topics covered. You then know what you'll be reading about before you start. You can think of the roadmap as my commitment to cover those topics in the chapter.

Registry Closeups

Registry closeups point you to interesting Registry keys. The closeups refer you to a Registry key that fits the context in which you find it. For example, if you're reading a passage about Windows NT security, you might find a Registry closeup that points you to one or more Registry entries that apply to security. Here's what a Registry closeup looks like:

```
Registry Closeup
HKEY_LOCAL_MACHINE\SOFTWARE\Microsoft\Windows
```

Internet References

You'll run across Internet references here and there. These are similar to Registry closeups except that they point you to interesting places on the Internet where you can learn more information about what you're reading. Sometimes an Internet reference contains nothing but an Internet address. Other times it also contains a brief description of what you'll find at that address. Here's what an Internet reference looks like:

ON THE WEB

http://www.microsoft.com

Notes, Tips, Cautions

Notes, tips, and cautions give you useful information that applies to the passage you're reading. A sample of each element is below. Each sample describes the type of information you'll find in that element.

N O T E Notes provide useful information that's not necessarily essential to the discussion. They usually contain more technical information, but can also contain interesting but non-vital technical or non-technical information. ■

T I P Tips enhance your experience with Windows 95 by providing hints and tricks you won't find elsewhere.

CAUTION

Cautions warn you that a particular action can cause severe harm to your configuration. Given the consequences of editing your Registry, you shouldn't skip the cautions in this book.

TROUBLESHOOTING

I need help with a particular problem. Troubleshooting elements anticipate the problems you might have and provide a solution.

This book uses cross-references to help you access related information in other parts of the book:

▶ **See** "Section Title," **p.xx**

Sidebars Are Interesting Nuggets of Information

Sidebars are detours from the main text. They usually provide background or interesting information that is relevant but not essential reading. You might find information that's a bit more technical than the surrounding text, or you might find a brief diversion into the historical aspects of the text.

Conventions

In addition to the special features that help you find what you need, this book uses some special conventions that make it easier to understand. The sections that follow describe the keyboard, mouse, and typographical conventions you find in this book.

Keyboard   The keyboard conventions you see below help you better understand what the instructions are telling you to do. For example, they help you understand the key combinations and menu commands that the instructions want you to type or choose.

Element	Convention
Hot keys	Hot keys are underlined in this book, just as they appear in Windows 95 menus. To use a hot key, press Alt and the underlined letter. The F in File is a hot key that represents the File menu, for example.
Key combinations	Key combinations that you must press together are separated by plus signs. For example, "Press Ctrl+Alt+D" means that you press and hold down the Ctrl key, then press and hold down the Alt key, and then press and release the D key. Always press and release, rather than hold, the last key in a key combination.
Menu commands	A comma is used to separate the parts of a pull-down menu command. For example, "Choose File, New" means to open the File menu and select the New option.

In most cases, special-purpose keys are referred to by the text that actually appears on them on a standard 101-key keyboard. For example, press "Esc" or press "F1" or press "Enter." Some of the keys on your keyboard don't actually have words on them. So here are the conventions used in this book for those keys:

Backspace key

Up-, down-, left-, or right-arrow key

Mouse   In this book, the following phrases tell you how to operate your mouse within Windows:

Click

Double-click

Drag

Drop

Typeface   This book also uses some special typeface conventions that make it easier to read:

Element	Convention
Italic	Italic indicates new terms. It also indicates placeholders in commands and addresses.
Bold	Bold indicates Internet addresses and text you type.
Bold Italic	Bold italic indicates placeholders in text that you type, which you substitute with appropriate text.
`Monospace`	Monospace indicates text you see on-screen and file names.

Starting Out with the Registry

Before You Begin

by Jerry Honeycutt

The Registry enables some of the most exciting technology we've seen to hit the Windows desktop in a long time, such as Plug-and-Play and user profiles. In some regards, however, the Registry is Windows' Achilles' heel—a small problem in the Registry can bring your entire system to its knees. If you make a mistake, Windows might stop working properly. If an errant program messes up the Registry, you might encounter all sorts of problems with Windows. The Registry deserves your respect.

Knowledge is power. Windows' reliance on the Registry and the Registry's volatility are precisely why you need to educate yourself about this little understood part of Windows. If I've learned anything over the last year, it's that you can't avoid the Registry. No way. For example, many of the solutions you find in Microsoft's Knowledge Base (see Appendix C, "Technical Resources for Windows") require that you change the Registry. Some of the coolest Windows hacks that you can use to customize Windows require that you change the Registry. You need to understand the Registry.

This chapter gets you off and running with the information you need to work safely with the Registry. This chapter introduces you to basic information about

Learn how Windows stores the Registry

Learn about the different files in which Windows 95 and NT stores the Registry.

Back up the Registry

Use the most common, and the safest, methods of backing up the Windows 95 and NT Registries.

Use the alternatives to editing the Registry

You don't always have to edit the Registry to make the changes you want. Learn the alternatives here.

Make a plan before changing the Registry

If you must change the Registry, use the guidelines in this chapter to safely make your changes.

backing up the Registry. It also shows you how to make a plan so that you can safely make any change you like and easily recover if something terrible goes wrong. ■

What's the Worst That Could Happen?

Oh, sure, changing the Registry is risky business. On the other hand, nothing is irrevocable if you back up the Registry using the methods in this chapter or if you stick to the plan you learn about in "Make a Plan," later in this chapter. Just to be sure, though, here's a glimpse at the types of things that can go wrong if you're not careful:

- The Registry Editor (see Chapter 3, "Using REGEDIT with Windows 95 and NT 4.0") doesn't validate your changes—period. If you enter a bad value in the Registry, the editor doesn't warn you about it.

- You can easily miss related values when changing something in the Registry. Some of the values in the Registry have siblings that you have to change, too. That is, if you change one value, you should also change the related value.

- The Registry Editor doesn't have an undo feature. You can't make a few changes, change your mind, and then exit the editor without saving your changes. Once you've made a change, it's a done deal.

The Registry Files

Both Windows 95 and Windows NT 4.0 store the contents of the Registry in files that you'll find on your hard drive. They're databases. The only reason that you should care about this is that the easiest way to back up the Registry is to simply copy these files to a safe place on your hard drive or onto a floppy disk. Otherwise, you don't have much of a reason to mess with these files.

Windows 95

Windows 95 stores the entire contents of the Registry in two files: SYSTEM.DAT and USER.DAT. These are binary files that you can't view using a text editor as you can with INI files. Windows 95 also turns on the read-only, system, and hidden attributes of SYSTEM.DAT and USER.DAT so that you can't accidentally replace, change, or delete these files. SYSTEM.DAT contains configuration data specific to the computer on which you installed Windows 95. USER.DAT contains configuration data specific to the current user. Take a look. Both files are read-only, hidden files that you find in C:\WINDOWS (see Figure 1.1).

FIG. 1.1
You sometimes find other backup copies of SYSTEM.DAT or USER.DAT that other programs create when you install them.

SYSTEM.DAO and SYSTEM.DAT

USER.DAO and USER.DAT

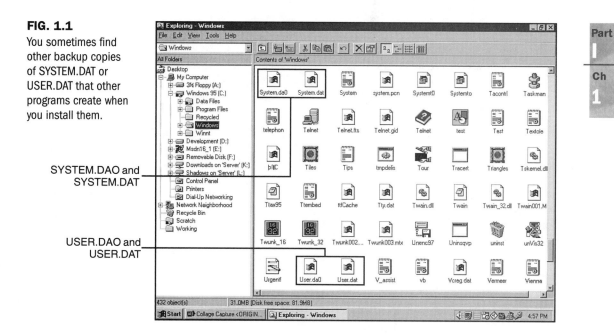

The location of USER.DAT will be different if you configure the computer to use profiles. Windows creates a new system folder called C:\WINDOWS\PROFILES, under which you'll find a folder for each user that has a profile. For example, C:\WINDOWS\ PROFILES\JERRY contains my configuration data, and C:\WINDOWS\PROFILES\ BECKY contains my wife's configuration data. Each user's profile folder contains an individual copy of USER.DAT. You'll still find a default USER.DAT in C:\WINDOWS, which is for users who don't have a profile.

N O T E Profiles allow multiple users to log onto a single computer with their own, familiar settings (Start menu, desktop, and so on). You enable profiles using the Control Panel: double-click the Passwords icon, click the User Profiles tab, select Users Can Customize Their Preferences, and click OK. Now, when new users log onto Windows 95, it asks them if they want to keep their own individual settings. ▓

Windows NT 4.0 Hives

Windows NT 4.0 isn't quite as simple as Windows 95. It doesn't neatly store the contents of the Registry in two files. It stores them in files that represent *hives* instead, each of which represents a portion of the Registry that starts at the very top of the hierarchy.

NT stores hives that are specific to the computer on which you installed it in C:\WINNT\ SYSTEM32\CONFIG (see Figure 1.2). NT stores each hive in a file without an extension.

Thus, a hive called Sam is stored in a file called SAM. Each hive has two other types of files associated with it: SAV and LOG. A hive's SAV file is a backup copy of the hive that Windows NT creates when it successfully starts. A hive's LOG file records each and every change that Windows NT makes to that hive. You learn more about what's in each hive in Chapter 2, "Inside the Windows Registry."

FIG. 1.2

The exact number and names of files you see in C:\WINNT\ SYSTEM32\CONFIG might be slightly different.

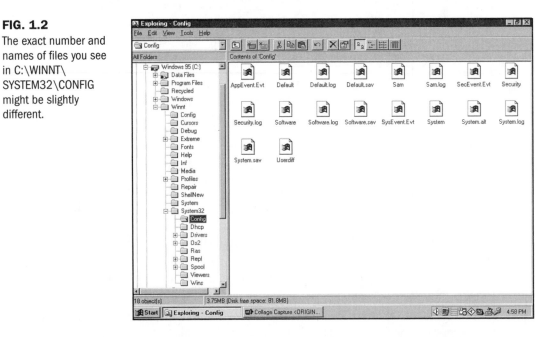

Windows NT 4.0 stores user-specific configurations in a different location, just like Windows 95 when you configure it for profiles. NT stores each user's configuration data in a profile folder under C:\WINNT\PROFILES\USERNAME, where *UserName* is the logon name of the user. Windows NT calls the file NTUSER.DAT. C:\WINNT\PROFILES\ JERRY\NTUSER.DAT contains the hive for my configuration data, for example.

You'll also notice that NT creates folders called Administrator, All Users, and Default User in C:\WINNT\PROFILES. Administrator is for you know who: the big guy. All Users contains settings that every user inherits, whereas Default User contains settings that apply to users who log onto NT without a profile.

T I P   The term *hive* comes from a tormented Microsoft engineer who thought there was a strong analogy between portions of the Registry and the structure of a beehive.

▶ **See** "What's In a Hive," **p. 49**

Backing Up the Windows 95 Registry

You'll find comfort in knowing that Windows 95 automatically backs up the Registry for you. Each time Windows 95 successfully starts, it copies SYSTEM.DAT to SYSTEM.DAO in C:\WINDOWS; and USER.DAT to USER.DAO in either C:\WINDOWS or the current user's profile folder.

You can't rely on this backup as your only protection, however. Windows 95 backs up the Registry every time it thinks that it started successfully. Your definition and Windows 95's definition of a successful start may not be the same. Thus, you can accidentally destroy your only good backup of the Registry if you restart your computer after encountering a problem. To make matters worse, Windows writes over the previous backup each time it backs up the Registry; leaving you with two copies of the same screwed up Registry files.

> **N O T E** Many of the tools in this section (ERU, Cfgsafe, and so on) come from the Windows 95 CD-ROM. If you don't have the CD-ROM, however, you're not out of luck. You can download them from Microsoft's Web site at **http://www.microsoft.com/windows/software/ cdextras.htm**. ▦

Create a Startup Disk

If you're in a pinch and can't start Windows 95, you'll be very, very glad that you created a *startup disk*. This disk gets your computer going when it won't start from the hard drive. You'll also find a handful of utilities on the disk that you might be able to use to fix your computer. Here's how to create the startup disk:

Add/Remove
Programs

1. Double-click the Add/Remove Programs icon in the Control Panel.

2. Click the Startup Disk tab after the Add/Remove Programs Properties dialog box opens.

3. Click the Create Disk button and follow the instructions you see on the screen. Windows 95 will likely ask you for your Windows 95 CD-ROM (or diskettes) and, if you've installed Microsoft Plus!, your Microsoft Plus! CD-ROM.

4. After Windows 95 finishes creating your startup disk, click OK to close the Add/Remove Programs Properties dialog box.

5. Label your Emergency Startup Disk and keep it in a safe place just in case you encounter problems starting Windows 95.

Here's what you'll find on the startup disk:

Filename	Description
ATTRIB.EXE	Change a file's attributes
CHKDSK.EXE	Scan a disk for errors (lost clusters)

continues

continued

COMMAND.COM	Command interpreter for MS-DOS
DEBUG.EXE	MS-DOS debugger
DRVSPACE.BIN	Driver for DriveSpace disk compression
EBD.SYS	Marker for "Emergency Boot Diskette"
EDIT.COM	Text file editor
FDISK.EXE	Partition a computer's hard drives
FORMAT.COM	Format a partition on a computer
IO.SYS	Core operating system
MSDOS.SYS	Empty startup configuration file
REGEDIT.EXE	Real-mode Registry Editor
SCANDISK.EXE	Scan for and fix disk errors
SCANDISK.INI	Configuration file for SCANDISK.EXE
SYS.COM	Make a disk bootable
UNINSTAL.EXE	Windows 95 uninstaller

Windows 95 doesn't put CD-ROM or network drivers on your startup disk. If you need access to either of these when you start from your startup disk, copy the 16-bit DOS drivers to the disk. Then create a CONFIG.SYS and AUTOEXEC.BAT that loads them properly.

Copy the Registry Files to a Safe Place

The absolute easiest way to back up the contents of the Registry is to copy the files that contain the Registry to a safe place. You can even do this in Windows 95 Explorer, like this:

1. Create a folder on your computer to hold the backup copy of the Registry: C:\WINDOWS\REGISTRY, for example.

2. Make sure that you can view hidden files in Windows 95 Explorer (remember that SYSTEM.DAT and USER.DAT are hidden files). Choose View, Options from the main menu, select Show All Files, and click OK.

3. Copy SYSTEM.DAT from C:\WINDOWS to the backup folder. Copy USER.DAT from C:\WINDOWS, or your profile folder, to the backup folder.

4. Don't forget to restore Windows 95 Explorer so that it hides those system files: Choose View, Options from the main menu; select Hide Files of These Types; and click OK.

If you'd rather do this more or less automatically, create a batch file that does the same thing. Then, all you have to do is double-click the batch file to copy SYSTEM.DAT and USER.DAT to a safe place.

The following batch file copies both files as well as the backup files (SYSTEM.DAO and USER.DAO). It uses the Xcopy command with the /H and /R switches. The /H switch copies files with the hidden and system attributes. You use this switch in lieu of changing the files' attributes with the attrib command. The /R switch replaces read-only files. That way, Xcopy will be able to write over previous backup copies of the Registry. %WinDir% expands to the location of your Windows folder when the batch file runs.

```
xcopy %WinDir%\system.da? %WinDir%\Registry\ /H /R
xcopy %WinDir%\user.da? %WinDir%\Registry\ /H /R
```

ON THE WEB

You can also download this batch file from my Web site at **http://rampages.onramp.net/~jerry**.

N O T E   If you configured Windows 95 to use user profiles, you'll need to tweak this batch file to make it correctly back up your USER.DAT and USER.DAO files. In particular, you need to change the second line so that it copies these files from your profile folder rather than the Windows folder. You can also enhance this batch file so that it copies USER.DAT and USER.DAO for all users on the computer by copying the second line for each user.

▶ **See** "Restore Your Copy of the Registry Files," **p. 89** ▇

Back Up Your System Using a Tape Drive

Backup

Windows 95 comes with a tape backup utility that you can use as part of your regular backup strategy. Windows 95 Setup doesn't install it by default, however. You can use the Add/Remove Programs icon in the Control Panel to install the backup utility. After you install it, choose Programs, Accessories, System Tools, Backup from the Start menu to run it. Figure 1.3 shows you what Microsoft Backup looks like.

Microsoft Backup doesn't support most of the popular tape drives on the market. For example, it doesn't support Travan TR-3 tape drives, which allow you to back up 3.2G on a single tape (compressed). So, you might need to use the Windows 95 backup software provided with your tape drive. If the tape drive you installed didn't come with Windows 95 software, contact the manufacturer for updated software. For your convenience, Table 1.1 lists the Web sites of some of the most common off-the-shelf tape drives. You can probably get updated software from these sites.

FIG. 1.3
You can also use
Microsoft System
Agent to automatically
schedule backups with
Microsoft Backup. See
Using Microsoft Plus!
by Que.

Name	Size	Type	Modified
Windows		Folder	3/17/96 7:1...
Program Files		Folder	3/17/96 7:1...
Recycled		Folder	3/17/96 7:2...
Data Files		Folder	3/17/96 8:2...
Winnt		Folder	9/8/96 10:2...
Bootlog.prv	15253	PRV File	3/31/96 12:...
Command	92870	MS-DOS Ap...	7/11/95 10:...
Suhdlog.dat	7738	DAT File	3/17/96 7:1...
Msdos.---	22	--- File	3/17/96 7:1...
Setuplog	55590	Text Docum...	3/17/96 7:2...
Bootlog	203893	Text Docum...	8/11/96 5:5...
Detlog	69371	Text Docum...	10/18/96 7:...
Netlog	3665	Text Docum...	3/17/96 7:1...
Msdos.sys	1720	System file	10/13/96 3:...
Mtmcdai.sys	14470	System file	6/20/95 2:3...
System.1st	361684	1ST File	3/17/96 7:1...
Io.sys	223148	System file	7/11/95 10:...
Drvspace.bin	64135	BIN File	7/14/95 1:0...
Dblspace.bin	64135	BIN File	7/14/95 1:0...
Logo.sys	129078	System file	7/14/95 1:0...
Scandisk.log	600	LOG File	10/26/96 2:...
.hst	219	HST File	4/2/96 11:3...

File set: Untitled   Files selected: 379   27,571 Kilobytes selected

Table 1.1 Tape Drive Manufacturers

Drive	Name	Web URL
Arcada	Seagate	**http://www.arcada.com**
Colorado	Hewlett-Packard	**http://www.hp.com/cms**
Conner	Seagate	**http://www.conner.com**
Ditto	Iomega	**http://www.iomega.com**
Wangtek	Techmar	**http://www.tecmar.com**

ON THE WEB
If you don't find your tape drive manufacturer in Table 1.1, check for it here: **http://
www.yahoo.com/Business_and_Economy/Companies/Computers/Peripherals/Storage**.

A Windows 95-compatible backup program backs up your Registry when you back up
your Windows 95 folder or even allows you to explicitly specify that you want to back up
the Registry. These backup programs usually export the Registry into a text file and then
back up the text file. When you restore files from a tape that contains the Registry, the
program usually asks you whether you want to restore the Registry. If you choose Yes, the
program restores the text file and imports it back into the Registry.

TROUBLESHOOTING

Can I use my Windows 3.1 or DOS backup software with Windows 95? Absolutely not. The Windows 3.1 or DOS backup utilities don't back up the Registry or long file names correctly. You may not be able to restore your computer in the event that something goes wrong.

I backed up my computer a few weeks ago using Microsoft Backup. I restored a file to my Windows folder, and now Windows 95 seems to have forgotten many of its settings. Microsoft Backup doesn't ask you whether you want to restore the Registry when you restore files from a tape—it just does it. The safest way to restore a file into your Windows folder is to restore it into a temporary folder and then copy it into your Windows folder by hand.

Normally, Microsoft Backup only backs up the Registry when using the Full Backup Set. Can I back up the Registry using a backup set other than the Full Backup Set provided with Microsoft Backup? Yes. Copy the Registry files to a temporary folder, as described in "Copy the Registry Files to a Safe Place," earlier in this chapter and then select that temporary folder in your own backup set. To restore the Registry files, use Microsoft Backup to restore them to the temporary folder, and them copy them over the current Registry files as described in Chapter 5, "Fixing a Broken Registry."

▶ **See** "Restore Your System from a Tape Drive," **p. 90**

Export the Registry Using the Registry Editor

You can export the entire contents of the Registry into a REG file. A REG file is a text file that looks very similar to an INI file (you know, from Windows 3.1). Chapter 3, "Using REGEDIT with Windows 95 and NT 4.0," shows you how to export all or part of the Registry.

> **CAUTION**
>
> Don't rely on an exported copy of the Registry as your only backup. Microsoft has recorded problems restoring a backup using this method, such as Windows 95 not correctly updating all Registry data.

▶ **See** "Importing and Exporting Registry Entries," **p. 66**
▶ **See** "Import an Exported Copy of the Registry," **p. 90**

Use the Emergency Repair Utility

The Emergency Repair Utility (ERU) is a tool that you can use to back up your important configuration files. You can back up those files to a floppy disk or to another folder on your computer. Microsoft preconfigured it to back up your most important configuration files, including:

AUTOEXEC.BAT

COMMAND.COM

CONFIG.SYS

IO.SYS

MSDOS.SYS

PROTOCOL.INI

SYSTEM.DAT

SYSTEM.INI

USER.DAT

WIN.INI

You'll find ERU on your Windows 95 CD-ROM in \OTHER\MISC\ERU. Copy ERU.EXE and ERU.INI to your computer; then, add a shortcut to your Start menu by dragging ERU.EXE and dropping it on the Start button. After you've copied it to your computer, use these steps to back up your configuration files, including the Registry:

1. Start ERU by choosing it from the Start menu or double-clicking ERU.EXE in Windows 95 Explorer.

2. Click Next after ERU pops up. As a result, you see the dialog box shown in Figure 1.4, which lets you choose between backing up to a floppy or to another folder.

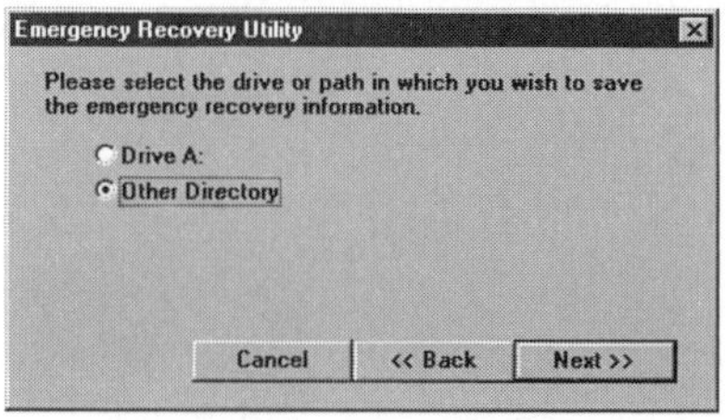

FIG. 1.4

If your Registry is very large, save the emergency recovery information to your hard drive rather than drive A.

3. Choose Drive A: if you want to back up your configuration files to disk, or choose Other Directory to back up your configuration files to another folder on your hard drive. Click Next to continue.

4. If you're backing up your configuration files to another folder on your computer, type the path of the folder in the space provided. Then, click Next to continue. Otherwise, insert a formatted disk in drive A, and click OK to continue.

5. Click Next, and ERU backs up your configuration files into the destination you chose. Note that you can change which files ERU backs up by clicking Custom.

6. ERU displays a dialog box that explains how to restore your configurations in the event that something bad happens to them. Click OK to close it.

TROUBLESHOOTING

I have some very important configuration files that ERU doesn't back up. You can add files to the list that ERU backs up. Open ERU.INI in your favorite text editor (Notepad, perhaps) and follow the instructions that you see at the top of the file. To make ERU back up C:\MYFOLDER\ MYFILE.INI, for example, add a section called **[MyFolder]** and an item under that section called **MyFile.ini**.

▶ **See** "Use the Emergency Repair Utility," **p. 90**

Back Up the Registry with Cfgback

Like Emergency Repair Utility, CfgBack is a configuration backup utility that you'll find on the Windows 95 CD-ROM. It allows you to make up to nine different backups of your Registry and restore any one of them when you need to. This utility is on the Windows 95 CD-ROM in the \OTHER\MISC\CFGBACK folder. Copy the files to your hard drive and drag a shortcut to CFGBACK.EXE to your Start menu or desktop.

NOTE I don't recommend that you use Cfgback to back up your Registry files. Neither does Microsoft. Cfgback has a defect that can cause it to trash your configuration when you attempt to restore a copy of the Registry.

▶ **See** "Restore a Backup from CfgBack," **p. 91** ▦

Backing Up the Windows NT 4.0 Registry

Like Windows 95, Windows NT 4.0 backs up the Registry each time it successfully starts. It copies each hive into a SAV file. Then, it logs each change to that hive in the corresponding LOG file. (Not sure what I'm talking about? See "Windows NT 4.0 Hives," earlier in this chapter.) If anything bad happens while you're starting Windows NT, it can easily reconstruct the hive from its SAV and LOG files for each hive.

NOTE Windows NT 4.0 handles the System hive differently from the other hives. NT can't reconstruct that hive from the SAV and LOG files while starting. Thus, NT stores each change in both SYSTEM and SYSTEM.ALT so that it can quickly copy SYSTEM.ALT over SYSTEM if it needs to. ▦

Windows NT 4.0 doesn't have nearly as many options for backing up the Registry as does Windows 95. The reason is that NT is a very secure operating system (you should feel good about this). You can't just copy the Registry's files around like you can in Windows 95 because NT protects the hives. You can't export and import the Registry, either, because NT's Registry Editor can't replace keys that are open by the system or another program.

Update the Repair Information Frequently

The Repair Disk Utility that comes with Windows NT 4.0 updates the repair information stored on your hard drive in C:\WINNT\REPAIR. It also creates a repair disk that you can use to restore your Windows NT configuration in the event of catastrophic failure (that is, it "doesn't work"). Note that this utility only makes it possible to recover a bootable system if something terrible happens to your configuration. Microsoft recommends that you don't rely on this tool as a means of backing up your configuration or your system.

To run the Repair Disk Utility, choose Run from the Start menu, type **RDISK**, and click OK. Then, click one of the buttons described here:

Update Repair Info   This button updates the repair information stored in C:\WINNT\REPAIR and, optionally, creates a new repair disk from that information.

Create Repair Disk   This option creates a new repair disk from the information currently stored in C:\WINNT\REPAIR.

Start in DOS and Copy the Registry Files

Because Windows NT is very persnickety about security, you can't just copy the Registry files around all willy-nilly (you'll get a sharing violation). You have to boot into another operating system, such as MS-DOS, before you can copy those files. This only works if you're using FAT partitions, however, not NTFS partitions.

Start your computer using an MS-DOS formatted system disk. Then copy all the files you find in C:\WINNT\SYSTEM32\CONFIG to a backup folder that you create, such as C:\WINNT\REGISTRY. Alternatively, you can use a batch file similar to the one you learned about in "Copy the Registry Files to a Safe Place," earlier in this chapter. Remember that the Xcopy command with the /H and /R switches copies system and hidden files to the destination while overwriting read-only files. Line two of the following example copies all the profiles to the backup folder using the /S switch to copy all subfolders, too. Here's what it looks like:

```
xcopy %WinDir%\System32\Config\*.* %WinDir%\Registry\*.* /H /R
xcopy %WinDir%\Profiles\*.* %WinDir%\Registry\Profiles\*.* /S /H /R
```

ON THE WEB

You can also download this batch file from my Web site at **http://rampages.onramp.net/~jerry**.

Back Up Your System Using a Tape Drive

Ntbackup

Windows NT 4.0 comes with a tape backup utility that you can use as part of your regular backup strategy. NT Setup installs it by default. Choose Programs, Administrative Tools (Common), Backup from the Start menu to run it, as shown in Figure 1.5.

FIG. 1.5

Backup is a bit archaic. If the manufacturer of your tape drive provides backup software, you're better off.

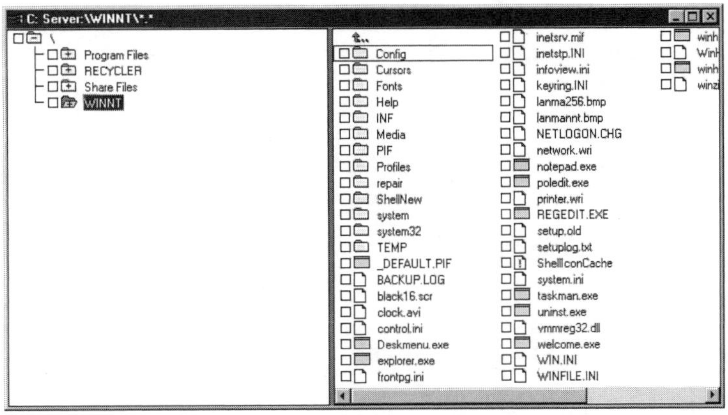

Backup doesn't support all the popular tape drives on the market. So, you might need to use the Windows NT backup software provided with your tape drive. If the tape drive you installed didn't come with a Windows NT driver, contact the manufacturer for updated software. Table 1.1, earlier in this chapter, provides the Web address of many popular tape drive manufacturers. In most cases, you can get Windows NT backup software or tape drivers from those sites.

Backup backs up your Registry only when you tell it to. Make sure that you select Backup Local Registry in the Backup Information dialog box. Likewise, make sure that you select Restore Local Registry in the Restore Information dialog box to restore an archived copy of the Registry from tape.

T I P You can schedule backups using the AT command.

Back Up the Registry with REGBACK

REGBACK is a utility that Microsoft provides as part of the Windows NT 4.0 Resource kit. You use it to back up individual Registry hives to a file or all open Registry hives to a directory. When you install the NT Resource Kit, the setup program copies REGBACK.EXE to the installation folder. It doesn't add a shortcut to the Start menu. You can run this program from a DOS prompt, however, or choose <u>R</u>un from the Start menu, type the REGBACK command line, and press Enter.

REGBACK has three different command lines:

> **regback.** Displays help for REGBACK.
>
> **regback *directory*.** Backs up all of the Registry hives to the named directory. Note that REGBACK backs up only those Registry hives which Windows NT 4.0 has open.
>
> **Regback *filename hivetype hivename*.** Backs up a specific hive to a file. *Hivetype* must be either **machine** or **user**, corresponding to HKEY_LOCAL_MACHINE and HKEY_USERS, respectively. *Filename* is the name of the file into which you want to backup the hive, and *hivename* is the name of the hive that you want to backup (system, for example).
>
> ▶ **See** "Restore the Registry with REGREST," **p. 93**

Look for a Better Way

I'm going to tempt you. Tempt you a lot. You're going to learn all sorts of secrets about the Registry in this book. How to change file associations, personalize your desktop, change your hardware configuration, and much more.

It's one thing to know how a parachute works; it's another thing to actually jump out of a plane. Likewise, you need to know how the Registry works; but, if at all possible, you should steer clear of making changes to the Registry. In many cases, you can use a safe alternative to make the change you want.

The sections that follow describe some of the more useful alternatives that are a part of Windows. You can also use a variety of freeware and shareware programs to safely change the Registry (see Chapter 10, "Free and Shareware Software to Customize Windows").

Windows Explorer

Almost two-thirds of the data in the Registry is for file extensions, file associations, and so on. You can change all of this Registry data using Windows Explorer. Choose <u>V</u>iew, <u>O</u>ptions from Explorer's main menu and click the File Types tab. You see a dialog box similar to Figure 1.6, which you can use to change the file types defined on your computer.

FIG. 1.6
Chapter 2 describes how Windows organizes file extensions and types in the Registry.

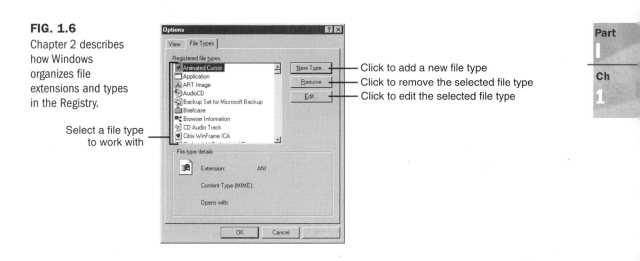

Click to add a new file type
Click to remove the selected file type
Click to edit the selected file type

Select a file type to work with

Policy Editor

Poledit

Windows comes with a Policy Editor that administrators can use to change most of the settings that are interesting to them. You learn more about policies in Chapter 15, "Using the Policy Editor to Administer the Registry." Figure 1.7 shows you what it looks like.

FIG. 1.7
You can create your own policies, too. Check out Chapter 16, "Creating Your Own Policies."

Control Panel

Don't reconfigure your hardware using the Registry. You can change any useful settings using the Control Panel. For example, you can use Windows 95's Add New Hardware or System icons in the Control Panel to change your hardware configuration. You can change your network configuration using the Network icon.

REG and INF Files

If you find an interesting Registry hack that you would like to try, look for a REG or INF file that will make all the changes for you—safely. Likewise, if you're instructing someone on how to do something in the Registry, give them an REG or INF file that does it for them automatically. You learn how to create REG and INF files in Chapter 14, "Working with REG and INF Files."

Windows NT Diagnostics

Windows NT Diagnostics displays numerous Registry settings in a format that's easy to understand. From the Start menu, choose Programs, Administrative Tools (Common), Windows NT Diagnostics, and you'll see a dialog box similar to Figure 1.8.

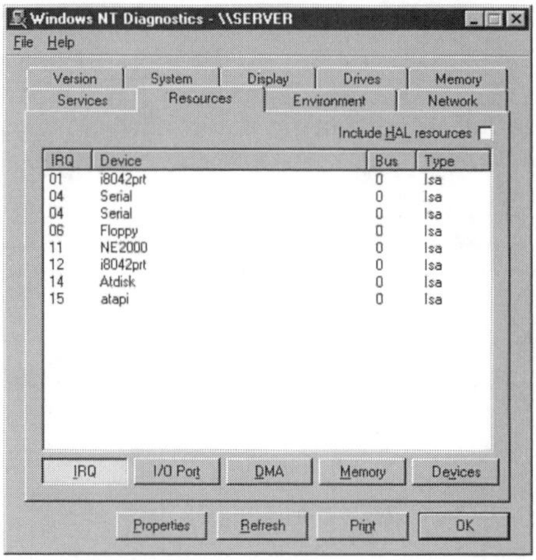

FIG. 1.8
You can use Windows NT Diagnostics to view and print many of your settings, but you can't use it to change settings.

As you can see, Windows NT Diagnostics displays a lot of information. Here's what you'll find on each tab:

Tab	Description
Version	Information about the version of Windows NT, the serial number, and person to whom it's registered.
System	Information about the computer's BIOS and CPU.
Display	Information about the computer's video adapter including its BIOS, resolution, scan rate, memory, chip type, and device drivers.
Drives	A list of the drives installed on your computer.

Tab	Description
Memory	Information about the physical memory installed on your computer and the size of page file. It also contains a variety of performance information.
Services	Information about each program, service, or device running on your computer.
Resources	Information about each device installed on your computer, including its IRQ, I/O address, DMA channel, and memory range.
Environment	A list of each environment variable defined on your computer.
Network	A list that describes your access rights, workgroup, and any other machines logged onto yours.

Make a Plan

Here's the part of the program where you learn how to make any change you want to the Registry without risking anything—well, almost. You can safely experiment with the Registry. I've written three books on the Registry and, throughout all my endless tinkering, have only made one change that I couldn't safely recover from (I deserve an OSHA safety award or something). You can make sure that your experience with the Registry is just as good by making a plan before you strike out and start making changes. To that end, here's a go at a plan, which you can change to suit your own needs:

- Back up the Registry before you make any change. You learned many techniques for backing up the Registry in this chapter. Most of them are quick and painless.

- Make only one change at a time, seriously. If you make too many different changes in one sitting, you're not as likely to figure out what went wrong if Windows fails.

- Don't delete data from the Registry until you're absolutely sure of the impact. Rename data so as to hide it from Windows—the same effect as deleting it. When you're sure that everything is okay, delete the key.

- Don't make changes to a Registry setting until you're sure about the impact it will have. Make a copy of the setting in a new, temporary entry; then make your change. If everything works out okay, remove the temporary value. If nothing else, write down the original value so that you can easily recall it if things don't work out.

Just in case you're the act-first-plan-later type of person, I'll remind you about these suggestions from time to time. In Chapter 3, for example, you learn how to use the Registry Editor for Windows 95 and NT 4.0. You'll find tips for following through on the suggestions scattered about this chapter.

You wouldn't think that the Registry is in peril when you install a new program, because you don't change any Registry settings yourself. Regardless, experience suggests that you should back up the Registry before you install programs with which you're unfamiliar so that you can easily recover from a wayward Setup program's faux pas.

Inside the Windows Registry

by Jerry Honeycutt

Young companies start out with very little organization—Anarchy. As organizations grow, however, they introduce a certain amount of hierarchy into their otherwise flat organization. At the top, you have the president. The president may have a few vice-presidents (in some cases, entirely too many). Each vice-president may have a few mid-level managers, and so on until you reach the worker-bees.

And so it is with Windows. Windows originally stored its configuration in a few INI files: SYSTEM.INI and WIN.INI. Over time, Windows' configurations grew much more complex, requiring many INI files—files for Windows, private files for each application, and more. Yet, the organization remained fairly flat. Now, Windows has grown up. The flat organization of configuration data can't do the job anymore.

That's what the Registry brings to Windows. It introduces the hierarchy that Windows needs to manage such a complex system. The Registry is the central repository for all the software and hardware configuration in Windows (well, almost all). The Registry is much more complicated than INI files

What's in the Registry

Windows stores configuration data in named value entries. Learn about them in this chapter.

How the Registry is organized

Windows organizes the Registry hierarchically. This chapter unravels the Registry so that you can better understand how to navigate through it.

What types of configuration data are in the Registry

This chapter describes the variety of configuration data that Windows stashes in the Registry, including hardware and software settings.

The difference between Windows 95 and NT 4.0

You find a variety of subtle differences between the Windows 95 and NT 4.0 Registries, including such areas as security and structure. This chapter demystifies those differences.

ever were; but, it also adds significantly more power and flexibility. Technology, such as Plug and Play, is possible because of the Registry's power and flexibility. The Registry also makes Windows 95's document-centricity possible by providing a more intimate link between documents and their applications. The list of technology that the Registry enables goes on and on. ▨

Understanding Registry Entries

To better understand what you find in the Registry, you should recall what's inside an INI file. Then relate those concepts to the information you find in the Registry. Here's what you learn:

- ▨ Registry keys are similar to sections in an INI file. They store related groups of configuration data.

- ▨ Value entries are similar to individual named items within an INI file's section. They have a name and a value.

Tripping Through INI Files

INI files provide persistent storage of configuration data; that is, Windows permanently saves configuration data from session to session. Recalling this configuration data is easy, too, because it's stored in plain, old text files that are separated into sections. Each section contains a number of entries, each on an individual line. For example, Figure 2.1 shows my WIN.INI file.

All a program has to do to get a bit of configuration data is ask Windows for it. The program has to be specific about what it wants, though. It gives Windows the name of the INI file, the section name, and the entry name. Windows replies with the value of that particular entry. In the example shown in Figure 2.1, a program that asks for a value from WINI.INI that's in section [Mail], and has the entry name MAPI, would receive a value of 1 from Windows.

FIG. 2.1
Windows 95 keeps
WIN.INI up-to-date
primarily for compat-
ibility with 16-bit
applications.

Section Name
Entry Name
Entry Value

Skipping Through the Windows Registry

Just like INI files, the Registry stores persistent configuration data. It does the job a bit
differently, however. Instead of storing configuration data in flat, text files, the Registry
stores configuration in a hierarchical fashion. Remember the organization of a company
with presidents, vice-presidents, and so on?

The files in which Windows stores the Registry (see Chapter 1, "Before You Begin")
aren't text files, either. They're binary files that you can't open in your favorite text editor.
You have to use the Registry Editor to get at them. Windows 95 users use REGEDIT
(Chapter 3, "Using REGEDIT with Windows 95 and NT 4.0") and NT 4.0 users use
REGEDT32 (Chapter 4, "Using REGEDT32 with Windows NT 4.0").

▶ **See** "The Registry Files," **p. 14**

INI Files versus the Registry

INI files aren't without their drawbacks. Otherwise, Microsoft's engineers (a clever bunch)
wouldn't have created the Registry. The following table describes some of the INI file's short-
comings the Registry overcomes:

INI Files Don't Do	The Registry Provides
Administration	A single location for all configuration data that's much easier to administer remotely.

continues

continued

Organization	A hierarchical organization for which Microsoft has defined where programs store configuration data.
Central Interface	A single user interface (Registry Editor) for access to all configuration data on the user's computer.
Relationships	A more intimate relationship between documents and associated programs.
Binary Data	Support for multiple types of string and binary data.
Files > 64K	Support for an unlimited amount of configuration data.

N O T E On the downside, programming the Windows Registry is much more complicated than programming INI files. For full information about programming the Registry, see Part IV, "Programming the Windows Registry." It describes the Registry API (Application Programming Interface) and shows you how to program for the Registry using Visual Basic and Visual C++. ■

Keys and Subkeys   Take a look at Figure 2.2. This Figure shows you what the Windows 95 Registry looks like in the Registry Editor. In the left pane, you see all of the Registry's keys. On the right side, you see all of the configuration data for the selected key. You call each group of configuration data in the Registry a key. Keys are very much like sections in INI files. They have names and can contain one or more bits of configuration data. Key names can be any combination of alphabetical, numeric, and symbol characters, as well as spaces.

The most important difference between the Registry's keys and an INI file's sections is that a key can contain other keys. That's where the Registry's hierarchy comes from. You can think of it as stuffing a bunch of file folders inside of another file folder. At the top of Figure 2.2, you see My Computer. This just represents the computer whose Registry you're viewing (you can view more than one). Below My Computer, you see a handful of *root keys*. Each root key contains a number of *subkeys*.

Another obvious analogy is the Windows file system. If you open Windows Explorer, you see all of your computer's folders in the left side of the window. In the right side of the window, you see all of the files contained in the selected folder. Registry keys are very much like folders in Explorer. They contain things. They can contain other keys (folders), and they can contain configuration data (files).

T I P   I use the terms key and subkey interchangeably. In particular, when I'm referring to a child key, or key underneath the key I'm discussing, I call it a subkey.

FIG. 2.2

Relax. You'll learn more than you ever wanted to know about the Registry Editor in the next chapter.

Registry keys —

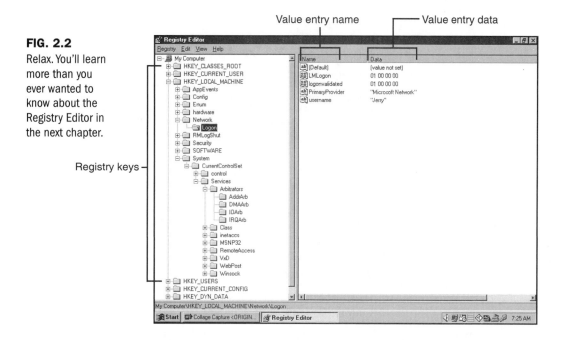

Value Entries   That leads me to value entries, where Windows stores the actual configuration data. Each key can contain one or more value entries. Each value entry has three parts:

- Value entries, just like items in an INI file, have names. Each name can be any combination of alphabetical, numerical, and symbol characters, including spaces. The name uniquely identifies the value entry within a key. That is, you might find the same name used in different Registry keys.

- Value entries have a data type. Whereas INI files only store string configuration data, the Registry stores a variety of different types in a value entry. Table 2.1 describes the types of data that you find in the Windows 95 and NT 4.0 Registries.

- Value entries might also contain data, also called *value data*, which can be up to 64K in size in Windows 95 and 1M in Windows NT 4.0. An important concept you need to understand is that of an empty value entry. No such animal. If Windows or some other program has never assigned a value to a value entry, the value entry contains the *null* value, indicating that it's empty. This is very different from assigning an empty string to a value entry, which is a string of characters that just happens to be of zero length.

Table 2.1   Windows 95 and NT 4.0 Data Types

Type	Description
Windows 95	
String	Text. Words. Phrases. The Registry always encloses strings in quotes.
Binary	Binary values of unlimited size represented as hexadecimal. They're similar to DWORDs except they're not limited to four bytes.
DWORD	32-bit binary values in hexadecimal format (double words). The Registry displays DWORDs as an 8-digit (four bytes) hexadecimal number.
Windows NT 4.0	
REG_BINARY	Binary values of unlimited size represented as hexadecimal. They're the same as Binary values in Windows 95.
REG_DWORD	32-bit binary values in hexadecimal format. The NT 4.0 Registry displays DWORDS as hexadecimal numbers. They're the same as Windows 95 DWORD values.
REG_EXPAND_SZ	Expandable strings. These are string values that contain values which NT replaces when used by a program (%SystemRoot%).
REG_MULTI_SZ	Multiple strings. These are value entries that contain a number of individual strings separated by null characters (0).
REG_SZ	Text. Words. Phrases. REG_SZ is the same as Windows 95's String data type.

N O T E   Every key contains at least one value entry, called (`Default`). In this book, I just call it the default value entry for a key. The default value entry is always a string value. Windows provides it for compatibility with the Windows 3.1 Registry and older 16-bit applications. In many cases, the default value entry doesn't contain anything at all. In other cases, when a program needs to store only one value, the default value entry is the only data stored in that key. ■

INI Files Are Alive and Well

Indeed; they are. To demonstrate that INI files are certainly not gone, I counted them on my Windows 95 computer. You can do it, too. Choose Find, Files or Folders from the Start menu. Type ***.ini** in Named, and click Find Now. After Find finishes searching your computer, you see in the status bar the total number of files it found.

So, what did Find say about my computer? It reported 144 file(s) found. I have 144 INI files on my computer despite the fact that I have almost no 16-bit applications installed on it. Yep. The INI file is alive and well. How many do you have on your computer?

Incidentally, I found very few INI files on my Windows NT 4.0 computer.

Starting at the Top

You now understand what you find in the Registry. Keys. Subkeys. Value entries. You know that value entries have a name, a type, and data. But how is all this organized in the Registry? Good question; and one that I answer in this section.

You find six root keys in the Windows 95 Registry (take another look at Figure 2.2) and five in Windows NT 4.0. HKEY_LOCAL_MACHINE and HKEY_USERS are real Registry keys and the remaining are aliases. Let's look at the real keys first (we cover the aliases a bit later):

HKEY_LOCAL_MACHINE	Contains configuration data that is specific to the computer, such as the hardware configuration. The information in this key applies to all users who use the computer.
HKEY_USERS	Contains configuration data for each user that logs on to the computer. This includes software configuration data that is specific to each user.

N O T E   In this book, I use fully qualified path names to each Registry key. No shortcuts here. Fully qualified path names include the entire path to the key I'm discussing. For example, instead of referring to the Current User key, I tell you about HKEY_LOCAL_MACHINE\ System\CurrentControlSet\Control\Current User key. This helps you go directly to that key. ■

HKEY_LOCAL_MACHINE

HKEY_LOCAL_MACHINE contains configuration data that describe the hardware and software installed on the computer, such as device drivers, security data, and computer-specific software settings such as uninstall information. This information is specific to the computer itself, rather than any one user who logs on to it.

The following sections describe the contents of HKEY_LOCAL_MACHINE. Conceptually, HKEY_LOCAL_MACHINE is pretty much the same in both Windows 95 and Windows NT 4.0. You'll find many differences as you dig further down into this branch, however.

Even HKEY_LOCAL_MACHINE's immediate subkeys are different between both operating systems. Table 2.2 gives you an overview of which subkeys you find in Windows 95 and NT.

Table 2.2 HKEY_LOCAL_MACHINE Subkeys

Subkey	Windows 95	Windows NT 4.0
Config	Yes	
Enum	Yes	
Hardware	Yes	Yes
Network	Yes	
SAM		Yes
Security	Yes	Yes
Software	Yes	Yes
System	Yes	Yes

N O T E Windows NT 4.0 security prevents you from removing or changing any value in Hardware, SAM, or Security. You can only change values in Software and System. See Chapter 12, "Securing the Windows Registry," for more information. ■

Config Config is a Windows 95-specific subkey that contains information about multiple hardware configurations for the computer: hardware profiles. It contains groups of individual hardware settings from which Windows 95 may choose automatically or that you can choose when you start the computer. Each subkey under HKEY_LOCAL_MACHINE\Config (numbered 0001, 0002, and so on) represents an individual hardware profile. HKEY_LOCAL_MACHINE\System\ CurrentControlSet\Control\IDConfigDB contains the name and identifier of the hardware profile that Windows 95 is currently using.

The really interesting subkey under each hardware profile is Enum. The structure of this key resembles the structure of HKEY_LOCAL_MACHINE\Enum. It only contains subkeys for the devices that are explicitly in the hardware profile, however. Windows 95 uses this structure to find the device in HKEY_LOCAL_MACHINE\Enum. It uses the CSConfigFlags value entry to determine how the device participates in the hardware profile.

TIP HKEY_CURRENT_CONFIG is an alias for the current hardware configuration in HKEY_LOCAL_MACHINE\Config. In most cases, it links to the 0001 subkey.

Enum   HKEY_LOCAL_MACHINE\Enum is another Windows 95-specific Registry key. It is the branch of the Registry that contains information about each device that has been installed on the computer. It doesn't matter if the device is in use or not. That is, even if the user has excluded a device using a hardware profile, you still find that device in this branch.

Each subkey under HKEY_LOCAL_MACHINE\Enum represents a particular class of hardware. The following list describes each class that you typically find in the Registry. Under each hardware class, you find one or more subkeys that in turn contains additional subkeys, which identify a single piece of hardware. The organization of this branch and its contents depends largely on the devices you install on the computer and how the manufacturer organizes its settings.

- BIOS contains information about devices on a Plug and Play system, such as the timer or keyboard.
- EISA contains entries for each EISA device installed on the computer.
- ESDI contains subkeys for each ESDI hard drive installed on the computer.
- FLOP contains subkeys that contain information about the diskette drivers installed on the computer.
- ISAPNP is a subkey you see on ISA or EISA systems that contain Plug and Play devices.
- LPTENUM is a subkey you find on a system that is connected to a Plug and Play printer. It contains a subkey for each printer.
- Monitor contains a subkey for each monitor installed on the system. It contains a subkey called Default_Monitor, which is a bit special. This key contains additional subkeys that associate a particular monitor with each hardware profile.
- Network contains information about the network, but doesn't describe the network hardware. It primarily describes the bindings.
- PCI contains subkeys for each PCI device attached to the computer.
- Root contains subkeys for different types of legacy devices. Each subkey's name looks something like *PNP*XXXX*, where *XXXX* is a hexadecimal number.
- SCSI contains subkeys for each SCSI device attached to the computer. The name of each subkey usually indicates which device the subkey is for.

The Windows 95 Configuration Manager

The Configuration Manager is at the heart of Plug and Play. It is responsible for managing the configuration process on the computer. It identifies each bus on your computer, (PCI, SCSI, ISA) and all of the devices on each bus. It notes the configuration of each device, making sure that each device is using unique resources (IRQ, I/O address). As well as managing the configuration process, it also manages the reconfiguration process on the computer. That is, when the user yanks a PCMCIA modem out of the computer, the Configuration Manager is responsible for reconfiguring the system and notifying all of the applications about the change.

The Configuration Manager works with three key components to make all of this happen: bus enumerators, arbitrators, and device drivers. Here's a summary of the purpose of each component:

Bus Enumerators	Bus enumerators are responsible for building the hardware tree (the hierarchy of buses and devices you learned about earlier). They query each device or each device driver for configuration information.
Arbitrators	Arbitrators assign resources to each device in the hardware tree. That is, it doles out IRQs, I/O addresses, and such to each device.
Device Drivers	The Configuration Manager loads a device driver for each device in the hardware tree and communicates the device's configuration to the driver.

Hardware   Hardware describes the actual hardware installed in a Windows NT 4.0 computer. It also contains information about device drivers, such as which device drivers work with which bits of hardware and the resources (IRQ, and so on) that each device uses. In NT, this subkey is dynamically rebuilt by the recognizer each time NT starts. Windows 95 doesn't do much with this subkey at all. Here's a list of subkeys you find under Hardware:

Description	Contains information about the hardware database built as NT starts.
DeviceMap	Contains values that indicate where in the Registry NT you can find more driver information about a particular bit of hardware.
ResourceMap	Maps each device driver to the resources that the device uses, including IRQ, I/O port, I/O memory addresses, DMA channels, and so on.

Network   Network is a Windows 95-specific subkey that contains information about the user currently logged on to the computer. Each time a user logs on to the computer, Windows stores details about the current network session, such as the user's logon name, in HKEY_LOCAL_MACHINE\Network\Logon. The following list describes each of the value entries you find in this key:

LMLogon	To provide during AR.
logonvalidated	Indicates that a domain server validated the logon.
PrimaryProvider	Contains the name of the primary network provider as found in HKEY_LOCAL_MACHINE\System\CurrentControlSet\Services.
username	Contains the logon name of the current user; contains the previous user's name if the current user pressed Esc at the logon prompt in Windows 95.

SAM   SAM (Security Account Manager) is specific to Windows NT 4.0. It contains security information for each user and group account, as well as domains in Windows NT 4.0 Server. You normally get at this information through the User Manager or User Manager for Domains. Note that this is really an alias for HKEY_LOCAL_MACHINE\ Security\SAM, described next.

N O T E   Microsoft now calls the Security Account Manager the Directory Services Database. In this book, I continue to use the term SAM when referring to the Directory Services Database only because you're probably more familiar with that term. ◼

Security   In Windows 95, this subkey contains information about the computer's network security provider, administrative shares (for remote administration), and public shares. Windows 95 keeps track of all the open network connections other users have on your computer in HKEY_LOCAL_MACHINE\Security\Access. You find a single subkey for each connection.

In Windows NT 4.0, Security contains the local security policy—information about user rights, password policy, group membership, and so on. Like SAM, most of the configuration data in this subkey is specific to NT. You see this information in User Manager or User Manager for Domains. Note that you can't browse through this information using the Registry Editor.

▶ **See** "Setting Up Remote Administration," **p. 239**

Software   Programs store settings that are specific to the computer in Software. These programs store their settings in branches that look similar to HKEY_LOCAL_MACHINE\Software\CompanyName\ProductName\Version, where CompanyName is the name of the company, ProductName is the name of the product, and Version is the current version number of the product. You find many Windows-specific settings in this subkey, too. Here's what you find in each subkey under Software:

Classes	Associates file types to programs installed on the computer. It also contains information about COM objects, makes context menus possible, and more.

Microsoft	Contains settings for Microsoft programs, including Windows. The Windows NT\CurrentVersion subkey contains interesting settings for Windows NT 4.0. Likewise, Windows\CurrentVersion contains interesting settings for Windows 95.
Program Groups	In Windows NT 4.0, this subkey records whether or not it has converted each former program group (remember the Program Manager?) into the new Start menu folder structure.
Secure	Programs store settings that should be changed only by an administrator in this subkey. This subkey is specific to Windows NT 4.0.
Windows 3.1	Indicates whether or not Windows Migration NT 4.0 has converted the Windows Status 3.1 INI files and Registry to the Windows NT 4.0 format.

N O T E The single largest branch in the Registry is HKEY_LOCAL_MACHINE\Software\Classes. This subkey describes all of the associations between documents and programs, as well as information about COM objects, and is thus very large. You can also get to this branch through the root key HKEY_CLASSES_ROOT. ▪

System   Windows maintains control sets, each of which determines exactly which device drivers and services Windows loads and how it configures them when Windows starts. For example, a control set provides the various parameters Windows needs when it starts, such as the computer's name on the network and the current hardware profile. A control set also controls which device drivers and file systems Windows loads and provides the parameters that Windows needs in order to configure each driver.

In both Windows 95 and Windows NT 4.0, you find the control sets in HKEY_LOCAL_MACHINE\System. In Windows 95, you see only one subkey: CurrentControlSet. Thus, HKEY_LOCAL_MACHINE\System\CurrentControlSet contains all of the configuration data required to start your computer in Windows 95. Windows NT 4.0 uses multiple control sets. Here are the subkeys you find under System in NT:

- ▪ Clone. Contains the last known control set used to start Windows NT 4.0.
- ▪ ControlSet*nnn*. Each control set, number 000 through 003, contains the actual configuration data that Windows requires when it starts.
- ▪ CurrentControlSet. Contains the control set that Windows is currently using.
- ▪ Select. Contains values that determine how Windows is using the control sets such as the number of the current control set, the default control set, and so on.

■ Setup. Contains settings used by the Windows NT 4.0 setup program.

Under each control set, you find two additional subkeys.

■ Control. Control contains a variety of parameters which Windows uses to start the computer. The following list describes some of the subkeys you might find under Control:

ComputerName	The computer's name on the network
Filesystem	File system configuration
IDConfigDB	Hardware profile selection and names
Keyboard layouts	DLLs for each keyboard language
MediaResources	Driver information for multimedia
NetworkProvider	List of network providers
Nls	National language configuration
PerfStats	Items System Monitor can track
Print	Configuration and drivers for printers
SessionManager	Compatibility information for Windows
TimeZoneInformation	Information about chosen time zone
Update	Indicates if Windows 95 is an update
VMM32Files	VxD files combined into VMM32.VXD

■ Services. Services determines which device drivers and services Windows loads and how it configures them. The following list describes some of the subkeys you find under Services:

Arbitrators	Helps arbitrators determine free resources
Class	Describes all device classes Windows supports
MSNP32	Configuration data for a Microsoft network
NWNP32	Configuration data for a NetWare network
VxD	Configuration data for all virtual drivers

TIP When Windows NT 4.0 starts, you can choose the control set you want to use. For example, if your computer won't start under a particular control set, you can start with a different one. Press the Space key when you see the Boot Loader command prompt.

HKEY_USERS

HKEY_USERS contains all of the user-specific configuration data for the computer. That is, Windows stores configuration data for each user that logs on to the computer in a subkey under HKEY_USERS. The following sections describe what you find under each subkey under HKEY_USERS, such as those in Table 2.3, which describes which subkeys you find in each operating system.

Table 2.3   HKEY_USERS/*UserName* Subkeys

Subkey	Windows 95	Windows NT 4.0
AppEvents	Yes	Yes
Console		Yes
Control Panel	Yes	Yes
Environment		Yes
InstallLocationsMRU	Yes	
Keyboard Layout	Yes	Yes
Network	Yes	Yes
Printers		Yes
RemoteAccess	Yes	
Software	Yes	Yes
Windows 3.1 Migration Status		Yes

N O T E   Wonder where in the world the HKEY_ comes from? Microsoft uses this notation to indicate that the key is a handle used by a program. In Windows, handles uniquely identify a resource. See Part IV, "Programming the Windows Registry," for more information. ■

AppEvents   AppEvents contains associations between the sounds Windows produces and events generated by Windows and other programs. Chapter 7, "Customizing Your Windows Desktop," shows you how to add your own custom events to this branch. You find two subkeys called EventLabels and Schemes\Apps:

■ EventLabels contains a subkey for each sound event. The default value entry for each subkey is the description of the event. These subkeys don't actually define the sound generated for each event, however; that's up to the next key.

■ Schemes\Apps contains a subkey for each sound event, just like EventLabels. These subkeys define the sounds associated with each event, however. For example, an event called AppGPFault contains additional subkeys, one for each scheme installed in Windows. Regardless of which themes you've installed, all the subkeys under Schemes contain the .Current and .Default subkeys. .Current is the current sound associated with that event. .Default is the default sound associated with that event.

Console   Console is unique to Windows NT 4.0. It defines options used for character-based applications (CHUI, pronounced chewy). This includes settings such as window size, font, color, and so on.

Control Panel   Control Panel contains settings that the user can change using the Control Panel, such as Display and Accessibility Options. Many of the settings in Control Panel are migrated from the Windows 3.1 WIN.INI and CONTROL.INI files. The following list describes the types of settings you find in this key:

Accessibility	Contains settings from the Accessibility Control Panel applet, including StickyKeys and MouseKeys.
Appearance	Contains all of the color schemes found in Display properties.
Colors	Contains all of the active colors used for windows, such as the background and caption bar colors.
Cursors	Contains all of the mouse pointer schemes found in the Control Panel's Mouse applet.
Desktop	Contains various information about the user interface, such as screen saver settings, window sizes, and the wallpaper.
International	Indicates the current locale.
Mouse	Contains mouse settings such as the double-click rate or sensitivity.

Environment   Environment is unique to Windows NT 4.0. It contains the values of all the user's environment variables, such as TEMP and PATH. You set environment variables in both the AUTOEXEC.BAT file and the System icon in the Control Panel.

InstallLocationsMRU   This itty-bitty subkey contains the last several paths from which you've installed Windows extensions. That is, every time you double-click the Add/Remove Programs icon in the Control and click the Have Disk of the Windows Setup tab to install an extension, Windows 95 records the path of the INF file in InstallLocationsMRU. Note that this subkey is specific to Windows 95.

Keyboard Layout   Keyboard Layout defines the language used for the current keyboard layout. You change these values in the Keyboard icon in the Control Panel.

Network   Windows 95 stores persistent network connections in HKEY_CURRENT_ USER\Network\Persistent. Each subkey represents a mapped drive letter (D, E, F, and so on). Under each driver letter's subkey, you find a handful of value entries, as shown in this list:

Provider Name	Contains the name of the network provider defined in HKEY_LOCAL_MACHINE\System\CurrentControlSet\Services.
RemotePath	Contains the UNC path of the resource on the remote computer (\\Server\Downloads, for example).
UserName	Contains the name of the user who mapped this resource.

Windows 95 stores non-persistent connections in HKEY_CURRENT_USER\Network\Recent. You find the same type of information under this key as you found under the Persistent key; Windows organizes it a bit differently, however. Instead of creating a subkey for each mapped drive letter (non-persistent connections don't have a drive letter), Windows creates a subkey that takes its name from the UNC of the network resource. You must remember, though, that you can't put backslashes (\) in a key's name. So Windows handles this by using a period and forward slash (./) in place of each backslash.

Windows NT 4.0 doesn't use Network. Previous versions of Windows NT stored information about persistent connections in this subkey. Windows NT 4.0 keeps the Network subkey for compatibility purposes, but it doesn't store information about persistent connections in it. NT now stores information about persistent connections in HKEY_CURRENT_USER\Software\Microsoft\Windows NT\CurrentVersion\Network\ Persistent Connections.

Software   Software is by far the most interesting subkey in this branch. It contains software settings that are specific to each user. Windows stores each user's desktop preferences under this subkey. Each program installed on the computer installs user-specific preferences in this subkey. This subkey is organized just like the similar subkey in HKEY_LOCAL_MACHINE.

Windows 3.1 Migration Status   Windows 3.1 Migration Status contains values that indicate whether or not NT has converted any Windows 3.1 INI files and the program groups to the Windows NT 4.0 format. This subkey isn't present if you didn't upgrade Windows 3.1 to Windows NT 4.0.

N O T E The Registry has an order of precedence. Often, Windows or other programs stores duplicate data in both HKEY_USERS and HKEY_LOCAL_MACHINE. In these cases, the configuration data stored in HKEY_USERS has precedence over the data stored in HKEY_LOCAL_MACHINE. Windows does this so that individual user preferences override computer-specific settings. ▣

Aliases

Even though the Registry Editor does show six root keys, there are really only two: HKEY_LOCAL_MACHINE and HKEY_USERS. The remaining root keys are really just aliases that refer to *branches* (entire portions of the Registry beginning with a particular key) within the other two root keys. In other words, aliases are a bit like shortcuts in Explorer: if you change a value in one of the aliases, that value is actually changed in either HKEY_LOCAL_MACHINE or HKEY_USERS.

You learn about the following aliases in this section:

> HKEY_CLASSES_ROOT
>
> HKEY_CURRENT_USER
>
> HKEY_CURRENT_CONFIG
>
> HKEY_DYN_DATA

N O T E When you export the Registry to a REG file (see Chapter 3, "Using REGEDIT with Windows 95 and NT 4.0"), the file contains entries found only in HKEY_LOCAL_MACHINE and HKEY_USERS. That's because it is redundant to export the aliases. ▣

HKEY_CLASSES_ROOT HKEY_CLASSES_ROOT is an alias for a branch in HKEY_LOCAL_MACHINE that contains the associations between file types and programs. See "Software," in the "HKEY_LOCAL_MACHINE" section earlier in this chapter.

HKEY_CURRENT_USER HKEY_CURRENT_USER is an alias for a branch in HKEY_USERS that contains the configuration data for the currently logged on user. See "HKEY_USERS," earlier in this chapter.

N O T E In most cases, I use HKEY_CURRENT_USER to refer to the contents of any one of the subkeys under HKEY_USERS. For example, when I'm discussing the general contents and organization of HKEY_USERS*Subkey*, I use HKEY_CURRENT_USER. ▣

HKEY_CURRENT_CONFIG   HKEY_CURRENT_CONFIG is an alias for HKEY_LOCAL_MACHINE\Config\Profile, where Profile is one of 0001, 0002, etc. It contains the current hardware configuration for the computer. See the section "HKEY_LOCAL_MACHINE," earlier in this chapter, for more information.

HKEY_DYN_DATA   HKEY_DYN_DATA contains dynamic information about the current status of the computer. This isn't really an alias, but is totally dynamic and not stored permanently on disk. The Windows NT 4.0 Registry doesn't contain this key. The following list describes the contents of HKEY_DYN_DATA:

Config Manager	Describes the hardware actually loaded on the computer, including status information. Each subkey under Enum contains a value entry called HardWareKey that indicates the path relative to HKEY_LOCAL_MACHINE\Enum which contains information about that device.
PerfStats	Contains performance measurements.
Security	Contains information about the network security provider.

Abbreviations for Root Keys

You frequently see abbreviations for the root keys used in many publications (but not this one). The following table describes the abbreviations used for each root key:

Abbreviation	Root Key
HKCR	HKEY_CLASSES_ROOT
HKCU	HKEY_CURRENT_USER
HKLM	HKEY_LOCAL_MACHINE
HKU	HKEY_USERS
HKCC	HKEY_CURRENT_CONFIG
HKDD	HKEY_DYN_DATA

Comparing the Windows 95 and NT 4.0 Registries

The Windows 95 and Windows NT 4.0 Registries, in many ways, are very similar—particularly if you look at HKEY_CLASSES_ROOT and HKEY_USERS. There are some pretty huge differences between these two Registries, however, that you should be aware of:

- Windows NT 4.0 stores the Registry in hives, which you'll learn about in a moment, whereas Windows 95 stores the Registry in two binary files.
- Windows NT 4.0 implements full security for the Registry hives and for each individual key in the Registry. Windows 95 provides little security.
- The structure of HKEY_LOCAL_MACHINE\System is very different in Windows 95 and Windows NT 4.0.
- Windows NT 4.0 provides an additional Registry Editor that takes advantage of security and the different types of data you can store in a value.

What's in a Hive

Windows 95 makes everything simple. It stores the Registry in two binary files: SYSTEM.DAT and USER.DAT. The only bit of complexity is that if you configure the computer to use profiles, you find a copy of USER.DAT in each user's profile folder. Other than that, they're just plain old binary files that you can copy around at will, edit with the Registry Editor, and so on.

Windows NT 4.0 makes things a bit more difficult, however. It uses hives. *Hives* are branches that start at the top of the NT Registry hierarchy. A hive is persistent. That is, it's stored permanently on disk and isn't created dynamically. Each subkey under HKEY_LOCAL_MACHINE, except for Hardware, and HKEY_USERS is a hive. Hardware isn't a hive because NT builds it dynamically as NT starts. The following two sections describe both groups of hives individually.

T I P The term hive comes from a tortured Microsoft engineer who thought there was a strong analogy between portions of the Registry and the structure of a beehive. Must be inside humor, because I just don't get it.

HKEY_LOCAL_MACHINE Windows NT 4.0 stores each hive for HKEY_LOCAL_MACHINE in its own set of binary files. You find four types of files in C:\WINNT\System32\Config. Table 2.4 describes the purpose of each type of file in this folder.

Table 2.4 Files Used for Hive Files

Extension	Description
None	Contains a current copy of a hive.
.Alt	Contains a backup copy of a hive.
.Log	Contains a log of all changes to a hive.
.Sav	Contains a backup copy of the hive at the end of the text mode portion of setup.

Part
I

Ch
2

Go ahead, take a look. Figure 2.3 shows the relationship between the Registry's hives in the Registry Editor and the files in which they're stored in Windows NT Explorer.

FIG. 2.3
Each hive has a corresponding hive file, SAV file, and LOG file in C:\WINNT\ System32\Config.

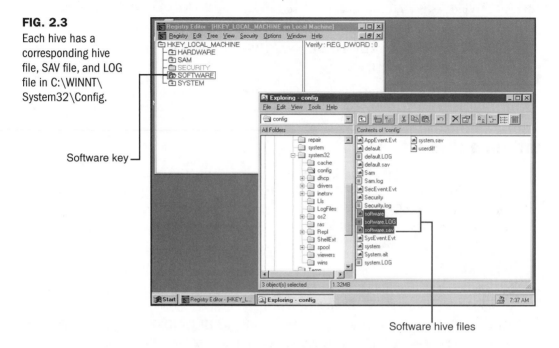

Software key

Software hive files

Table 2.5 relates each hive to its binary files. HKEY_LOCAL_MACHINE\Hardware isn't in this table because Windows NT 4.0 rebuilds it every time NT starts. It's dynamic. Each hive is stored in a file that doesn't have a file extension. NT makes a backup copy of each hive into a SAV file after the text mode portion of setup. NT also logs each change to a hive in a corresponding LOG file. If anything bad happens while you're starting your computer, NT can easily reconstruct the hive from the SAV and LOG files for each hive.

Table 2.5   Hives and Their Binary Files

Hive	ALT	LOG	SAV
SAM		Sam.log	Sam.sav
Security		Security.log	Security.sav
Software		Software.log	Software.sav
System	System.alt	System.log	System.sav

The System hive is special. Windows NT 4.0 can't reconstruct the System hive from the SAV and LOG files while starting. Thus, NT stores each change in both System and System.alt so that it can quickly copy System.alt over System if it needs to. System.alt isn't a log file like System.log. It's a duplicate copy of System.

HKEY_USERS Windows NT 4.0 doesn't store HKEY_USERS's hives in the same place as HKEY_LOCAL_MACHINE's hives. Each user's hive is stored in his own profile folder under C:\WINNT\PROFILES*USERNAME*, where *USERNAME* is the logon name of the user. The file is called NTUSER.DAT. C:\WINNT\PROFILES\JERRY\NTUSER.DAT contains the hive for my configuration data, for example. NT also logs changes to NTUSER.DAT in NTUSER.DAT.LOG.

N O T E When a file name has two periods (.) in its name like NTUSER.DAT.LOG does, the last portion of the name is the extension. The first period is actually part of the base file name. Thus, NTUSER.DAT.LOG is a file called NTUSER.DAT whose file extension is .LOG. Don't let this throw you when viewing a profile folder in Windows NT 4.0. You'll see two files that appear to be called NTUSER.DAT. ▣

Figure 2.4 shows the relationship between the Registry's user hives in the Registry Editor and the files in which they're stored in Windows NT Explorer.

FIG. 2.4
Default User is the profile that Windows NT 4.0 uses for all users who log on without a profile.

Registry branch for
Administrator

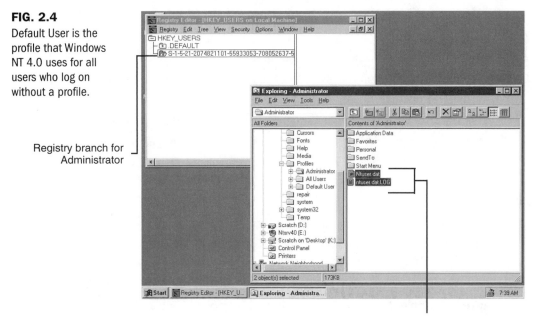

Hive files for Administrator

HKEY_USERS\.DEFAULT is an exception to this rule. This is the system default profile. When Windows NT 4.0 is running without any logged on users, you see the infamous Ctrl+Alt+Del logon window bouncing around the screen. The system default profile controls all aspects of this screen, including its color and wallpaper. NT doesn't store HKEY_USERS\.DEFAULT in C:\WINNT\PROFILES and doesn't call its hive file NTUSER.DAT. Instead, NT stores the default system profile in C:\WINNT\System32\ config and names the hive file DEFAULT. NT names the LOG and SAV files DEFAULT.LOG and DEFAULT.SAV, respectively.

N O T E In C:\WINNT\SYSTEM32\CONFIG you find two interesting files called USERDIFF and USERDIFF.LOG. These are hive-type files which aren't actually loaded into the Registry. Windows NT 4.0 uses these files to upgrade any user from a previous version of Windows NT to Windows NT 4.0 the first time they log on to the computer. ▪

Security

Windows 95 doesn't implement any sort of Registry security. Windows NT 4.0 does. In fact, Windows NT 4.0 lets you choose who can and can't access a branch or particular Registry key. It lets you determine what each user's rights to each key are (full access, read only, and so on). It also lets you audit activities on individual keys. Chapter 12, "Securing the Windows Registry," describes in detail how to take full advantage of Registry security in NT, including:

- ▪ How to totally block a user's access to the Registry through the Registry Editor.
- ▪ How to control what users can and can't do with an individual Registry key or an entire branch.
- ▪ How to audit what happens to an individual Registry key or an entire branch.
- ▪ How to control who can remotely edit the computer's Registry using remote administration.

Structure

In many cases, the Windows 95 and Windows NT 4.0 Registries are very similar. HKEY_USERS and HKEY_LOCAL_MACHINE\SOFTWARE reflect this similarity. Structurally they're the same but can contain very different information.

There are so many differences between these two Registries, however, that I can't say they're compatible. They're not. You should already have an idea of that after reading "Starting at the Top," earlier in this chapter. You learned about a number of Registry keys that Windows NT 4.0 has which Windows 95 is still only dreaming about.

In other cases, both operating system may have similar keys, but Windows structures them very differently. This is where some of the biggest incompatibilities come from. It's not at all possible to document every difference down to the subkey and value entry level. I have documented a handful of differences that you observe in these two beasts, however, if not just to illustrate the point. Take a look:

- Windows 95 stores its settings in user-specific windows settings in HKEY_CURRENT_USER\Software\Microsoft\Windows\CurrentVersion and computer-specific settings in HKEY_LOCAL_MACHINE\Software\Microsoft\Windows\CurrentVersion. Windows NT 4.0 stores user-specific windows settings in HKEY_CURRENT_USER\Software\Microsoft\Windows NT\CurrentVersion and HKEY_LOCAL_MACHINE\Software\Microsoft\Windows NT\CurrentVersion.

- Windows 95 stores information about hardware profiles in HKEY_LOCAL_MACHINE\Config. Windows NT 4.0 stores information about hardware profiles in HKEY_LOCAL_MACHINE\System\CurrentControlSet\Hardware Profiles.

- HKEY_LOCAL_MACHINE\System\Services is organized very differently in Windows 95 that in Windows NT 4.0. In NT, it contains subkeys for each system service you see in the Device Manager, while in Windows 95, it contains information about arbitrators, virtual device drivers, device classes, and more.

- Windows NT 4.0 stores information about device classes in HKEY_LOCAL_MACHINE\System\CurrentControlSet\Control\Class. Windows 95 stores the same type of information in HKEY_LOCAL_MACHINE\System\CurrentControlSet\Services\Class.

- Windows 95 stores the results of bus enumeration in HKEY_LOCAL_MACHINE\Enum. Windows NT 4.0 stores the results of bus enumeration in HKEY_LOCAL_MACHINE\System\Enum.

REGEDIT versus REGEDT32

REGEDIT (provided with Windows 95 and Windows NT 4.0) is a very simple Registry Editor. It has a few basic menu commands. You can add and remove keys; add, remove, and change value entries and connect to a remote Registry. It supports the string, DWORD, and binary data types. That's about it. Figure 2.5 shows you what REGEDIT looks like. You actually learn how to use REGEDIT in Chapter 3, "Using REGEDIT with Windows 95 and NT 4.0."

Part

I

Ch

2

FIG. 2.5

Although you can view the Windows NT 4.0 Registry with REGEDIT, you shouldn't try to change any values in the NT Registry with it.

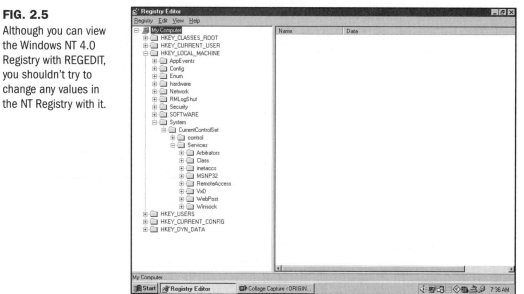

REGEDT32 (provided only with Windows NT 4.0) is a much more complex Registry Editor. It does everything that REGEDIT does and more. It supports Registry security so that you can control access to individual keys or entire branches of the Registry. It works with different data types—REG_MULTI_SZ and REG_EXPLAND_SZ, for example. It works more closely with NT's Registry hives. Figure 2.6 shows you what REGEDT 32 looks like. You actually learn how to use REGEDT32 in Chapter 4, "Using REGEDT 32 with Windows NT 4.0."

For your convenience, Table 2.6 describes the differences between REGEDIT and REGEDT 32.

Table 2.6 Differences between REGEDIT and REGEDT32

Feature	Windows 95	Windows NT 4.0
Add Keys/Values	Yes	Yes
Auditing		Yes
Automatically Refresh		Yes
Change Permissions		Yes
Change Values	Yes	Yes
Import/Export	Yes	Yes
Load/Unload NT Hives		Yes

Print	Yes	Yes
REG_BINARY	Yes	Yes
REG_DWORD	Yes	Yes
REG_EXPAND_SZ		Yes
REG_MULTI_SZ		Yes
REG_SZ	Yes	Yes
Remote Edit	Yes	Yes
Remove Keys/Values	Yes	Yes
Rename Keys/Values	Yes	
Search Keys	Yes	Yes
Search Value Entries	Yes	
Take Key Ownership		Yes

Part

I

Ch

2

FIG. 2.6
REGEDT32 supports Registry security and works more closely with Windows NT 4.0's hives than REGEDIT.

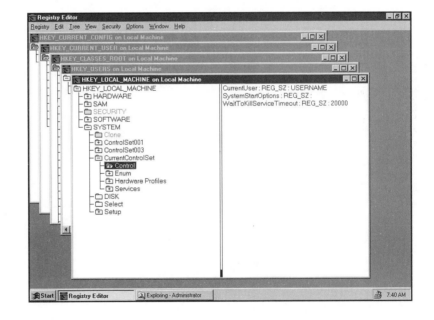

Using REGEDIT with Windows 95 and NT 4.0

by Jerry Honeycutt

Microsoft's philosophy about the Windows 95 and NT 4.0 Registry Editor (REGEDIT from now on) is that if you never had it, you'll never miss it. It is not installed in your Start menu when you install Windows 95, and Microsoft doesn't tell you much about it, either. Probably just as well, too. Microsoft wants to prevent inexperienced users from accidentally breaking their computer system by tampering with the Registry. But you have this book now, and you'll learn how to do it safely, right?

REGEDIT is your window into the Windows Registry. Even though REGEDIT is powerful, it is a simple program. It doesn't have a toolbar; its menus are fairly straightforward, too. It displays the organization of the Registry on the left side of the window and the actual data on the right side—not too complicated. You learn about using REGEDIT in this chapter, including tips that come from my agonizing experiences. ■

Learn how to install and get around REGEDIT

REGEDIT is a simple program that's hiding on your computer, ready to use. Learn how to start it.

Work with Registry keys and value entries

You use REGEDIT to search for, rename, change, create, and delete keys and value entries.

Export and import any portion of the Registry

REGEDIT makes it easy to export the Registry to a text file and import it from a text file.

Use the REGEDIT command line

REGEDIT provides some useful command-line parameters to simplify its usage.

> **CAUTION**
>
> REGEDIT.EXE is identical in both Windows 95 and NT 4.0. NT provides a more advanced Registry Editor called REGEDT32.EXE, however, which you learn about in Chapter 4, "Using REGEDT32. with Windows NT 4.0." Microsoft recommends that you don't use REGEDIT.EXE in NT because it incorrectly handles some of the data types unique to the NT Registry (REG_EXPAND_SZ and REG_MULTI_SZ). Thus, in NT, you should only use REGEDIT.EXE to search the Registry; don't change values with it.

Starting REGEDIT

Regedit

REGEDIT may not be on your Start menu, but it is probably in your Windows folder (C:\WINDOWS in Windows 95 or C:\WINNT in Windows NT 4.0). The file name is REGEDIT.EXE. Choose Programs, Run from the Start menu, type **regedit**, and then click OK. The REGEDIT window pops up. You can also drag REGEDIT.EXE from your Windows folder to the Uvart button to create a shortcut to it.

◆ **TROUBLESHOOTING**

I see REGEDIT.EXE in my Windows folder, but I can't run it, or it won't let me change anything in the Registry. If you're using a computer in a networked environment, your system administrator may have disabled it. You'll have to plead your case to the system administrator for access to REGEDIT.EXE. Note that the system administrator can also prevent REGEDIT.EXE from being installed on your computer if you're installing Windows from the network or a custom installation.

> **CAUTION**
>
> In Chapter 15, "Using the Policy Editor to Administer the Registry," you learn how to prevent user access to the Registry Editor. This policy requires the cooperation of the program that the user is using to edit the Registry. REGEDIT cooperates. Other programs probably don't. Thus, in Windows 95, you can't be sure that a user doesn't have access to the Registry.

Getting Around REGEDIT

Figure 3.1 shows you what REGEDIT looks like when you open it on your desktop. You see two panes, which REGEDIT separates by a divider that you can drag left or right to change the size of each pane. The following sections describe the contents of each pane.

Registry hierarchy   Value entries for selected key

FIG. 3.1

The left pane of REGEDIT works similarly to the left pane of Windows Explorer.

Key

Subkeys

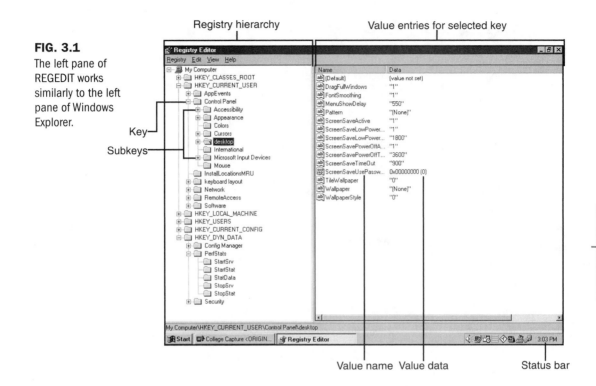

Value name   Value data   Status bar

Left Pane: Registry Organization

The left pane shows the organization of the Registry—the hierarchy. Even though the Registry is physically stored in two or more files, REGEDIT displays the entire Registry as one logical unit. When you update a key in REGEDIT, it automatically updates the appropriate Registry file.

The first entry is My Computer (unless you're remotely administering another user's Registry as described in Chapter 13, "Remotely Editing a User's Registry"). It contains several root keys that REGEDIT represents as folders. Each root key can contain subkeys (also represented by folders); each subkey can contain more subkeys; and so on. Click a plus sign (+) to open a folder, or click a minus sign (-) to close a folder.

Mouse challenged? You can also use the keystrokes you see in Table 3.1 to move around REGEDIT. These keys are often the quickest way to get around because you don't have to flop around with the mouse, trying to hit those tiny plus and minus signs.

Part

I

Ch

3

Table 3.1   REGEDIT Keystrokes

Key	Description
Keypad +	Expands the selected folder one level
Keypad -	Collapses the selected folder one level
Keypad *	Expands all levels of the selected folder
Up-arrow	Moves up the list one key
Down-arrow	Moves down the list one key
Right-arrow	Expands the selected folder if collapsed; otherwise, moves to its first subkey
Left-arrow	Collapses the selected folder if expanded; otherwise, moves to the parent key
Home	Moves to the first key in the list
End	Moves to the last key in the list
Page Up	Moves up one screen in the list
Page Down	Moves down one screen in the list
Tab	Moves the highlight to the right pane

 TIP If you don't want REGEDIT to "remember" which subkeys were open below a folder after you collapse it, press F5 to refresh the window.

Right Pane: Value Entries for Selected Key

The right pane shows the value entries for the key you've selected in the left pane. Each row in the right pane represents a single value entry. The Name column contains the value name of each entry. The Data column contains the actual value data for each entry.

The first value entry is always (Default). This is a string value entry that represents the default value for that Registry key. All Registry keys contain this value entry, but some keys don't contain any additional value entries. Aside from (Default), each key can contain zero or more value entries that have both a name and data.

Notice that different value entries in the right pane of the REGEDIT window have different icons. These icons represent different types of data that the Registry can store, as described in Table 3.2.

Table 3.2 Icons Representing Data Types	
Type	**Description**
[ab]	Strings values that you can read (text)
[010/110]	Binary values (hexadecimal strings or DWORDS)

Working with Keys and Value Entries

The following sections show you how to use REGEDIT to search for, add, change, and delete keys and value entries. You find tips for doing all those things as safely as possible. Also, some of these sections contain examples that you can use to flex your muscles. You learn how to rename the Recycle Bin, for example. Go ahead and try them.

Before you learn how to edit the Registry, however, remember the advice you I gave you in Chapter 1, "Before You Begin":

- Back up the Registry before you change it.
- Make sure that you have a plan for safely making changes so that you can fix any problems that you encounter.

Searching for Keys and Value Entries

When you search the Registry, REGEDIT looks for keys, value names, and value data that match the text you specify. That is, it searches using the name of each key, the name of each value entry, and the actual data from each value entry. You can use the search feature to find entries relating to a specific product, find all the entries that contain a reference to a file on your computer, or locate entries related to a particular hardware device.

To search the Registry, follow these steps:

1. Choose Edit, Find from the main menu, and REGEDIT displays the dialog box shown in Figure 3.2.

TIP If you select anywhere in REGEDIT's left pane and start typing the name of a Registry key, REGEDIT selects the key that best matches what you've typed thus far. For example, expand HKEY_CLASSES_ROOT. Then press **.**, and REGEDIT selects .386; press **b**, and REGEDIT selects .bat; press **m**, and REGEDIT selects .bmp. Note that if you pause between keystrokes, REGEDIT starts your *incremental search* over with the next key.

FIG. 3.2
Deselect the parts of the Registry in which you don't want REGEDIT to search: Keys, Values, or Data.

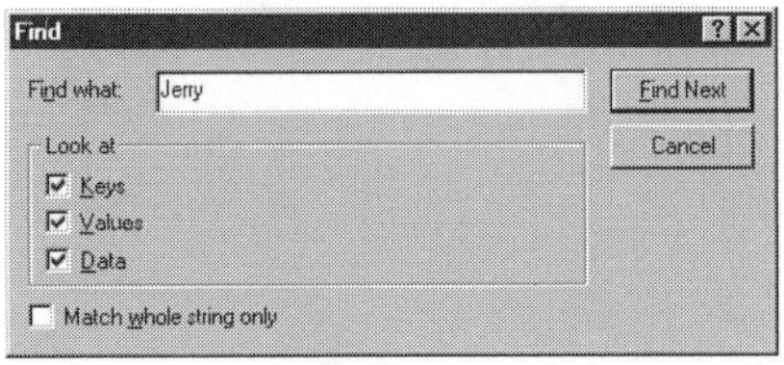

2. Type the text you want to search for. If you're searching for a number, try both the decimal and hexadecimal notations, because both formats are common in the Registry.

3. Click Find Next, and REGEDIT searches for a match. This can sometimes take quite a while—up to a few minutes on slower machines. If REGEDIT finds a matching key, it selects that key in the left pane. If REGEDIT finds a matching value entry, it opens the key that contains it in the left pane and selects the value entry in the right pane.

4. If the result isn't exactly what you had in mind, press F3 to repeat the search. When REGEDIT reaches the bottom of the Registry, it displays a dialog box telling you that it has finished searching.

T I P If the left pane isn't big enough to easily tell which key REGEDIT found, look at REGEDIT's status bar to see the fully qualified name of the key. You can also drag the divider to the right to make more space in the left pane.

Renaming a Key or Value Entry

You have a really good reason to rename a key or value entry; and that is to hide an entry from Windows while you test out a change. It's easy. Renaming a key or value entry in REGEDIT works similarly to renaming a file in Windows Explorer, except that you can't rename it by clicking once on the name. Instead, select the key or value entry that you want to rename; choose Edit, Rename from the main menu; type over the name or change it; and press Enter.

T I P You can also rename a key or value entry by selecting it and pressing F2.

Changing an Entry's Value

As a user, changing a value entry's setting is probably the number one activity you'll do with REGEDIT. You might want to personalize your desktop, for example, or you might need to adjust a TCP/IP setting to work better with your network. Chapter 7, "Customizing Your Windows Desktop," and Chapter 8, "Troubleshooting Windows," are loaded with Registry entries that you can change. To change a value entry, just follow these steps:

1. Double-click a value entry in the right pane to open the Edit dialog box. Remember that each value entry can be a string, DWORD, or binary data (see Chapter 2, "Inside the Windows Registry"). This dialog box will be different depending on the type of data stored in the value. Figures 3.3, 3.4, and 3.5 show you what each dialog box looks like.

2. Change the value, and click OK to save your changes.

Part

I

Ch

3

FIG. 3.3
The Edit String dialog box shows you the original data before you start editing.

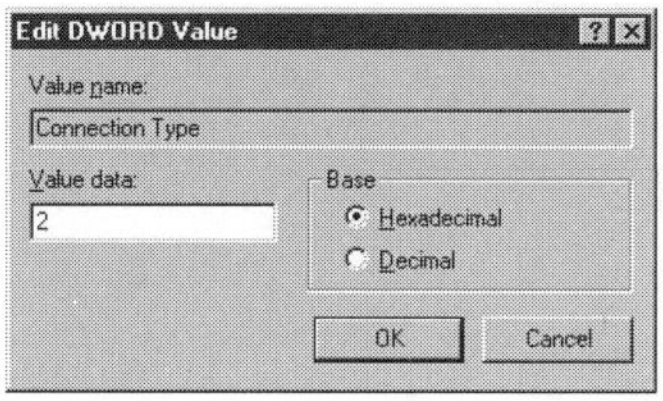

FIG. 3.4
Choose Decimal if your hexadecimal math is a bit rusty.

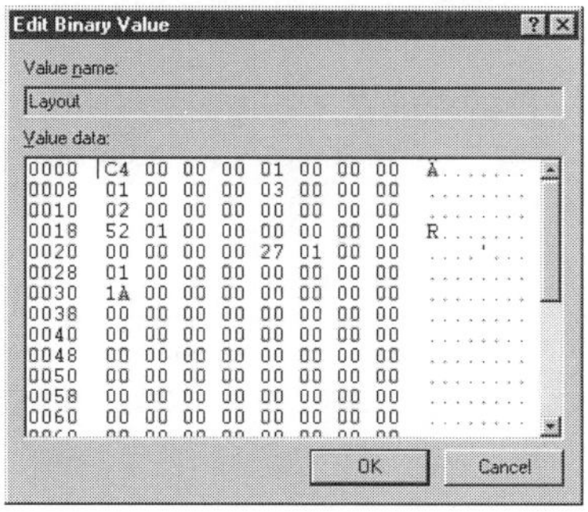

FIG. 3.5
You can use the Windows calculator (in Scientific mode) to convert decimal values to hexadecimal values for use with this dialog box.

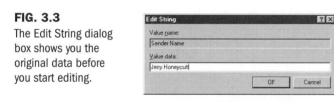

T I P Protect yourself when changing value data. Note the name of the value entry that you want to change and then rename it to some obscure name that Windows won't recognize such as **MyValue**. Then, create a new Registry key with the name you noted, as described in "Creating a New Key or Value Entry," later in this chapter and set its value as you like. This way, you can always restore the original setting by deleting the value entry you created and renaming the value entry you saved to the original name.

Are you interested in trying a real example? Of course you are. Use this example to change the text you see below the Recycle Bin icon on your desktop. You can make it a bit more personal, for example, by changing it to something like "Jerry's Trash." Here's how:

1. Open HKEY_CLASSES_ROOT\CLSID\{645FF040-5081-101B-9F08-00AA002F954E} in REGEDIT.

2. In the right pane, double-click the default value entry, which is called (Default).

3. In the Edit String dialog box, type the text you want to see below the Recycle Bin icon on your desktop.

4. Click OK to save your changes and minimize REGEDIT so that you can see the desktop.

5. Click once on any open area of the desktop and press F5. You must do this to cause the desktop to refresh itself. Figure 3.6 shows you the result.

FIG. 3.6
You can also change the actual icon and names of all the desktop icons.

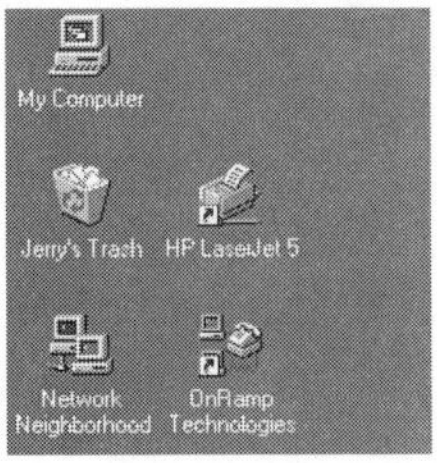

N O T E   Changes that you make to the Registry may not be reflected immediately in Windows or the programs that are currently running. The only way to make sure is to restart Windows after closing REGEDIT or restart the affected program.

You can restart Windows 95 (not Windows NT) quickly by choosing Shut Down from the Start menu. Then select Restart the Computer in the Shut Down Windows dialog box and hold down the Shift key while you click Yes. Windows 95 restarts without rebooting your computer. ▨

Creating a New Key or Value Entry

Creating a new key or value entry is generally harmless and equally as useless—unless, of course, you know for sure that either Windows or another program will use your new key. For example, the Microsoft Knowledge Base (see Appendix C, "Technical Resources for Windows") might instruct you to create a new Registry key to fix a problem. That's useful. Creating a new key out of thin air is pretty useless, however. To create one or the other, do the following:

- *New Key.* Select an existing key under which you want your new subkey to appear. Choose Edit, New, Key from the main menu; type the name of your key; and press Enter.

- *New Value Entry.* Select an existing key under which you want your new value entry to appear. Choose Edit, New from the main menu and choose either String Value, Binary Value, or DWORD Value from the menu. Type the name of your new value entry and press Enter.

Part
I

Ch
3

Deleting a Key or Value Entry

Be very careful about deleting keys and value entries from your Registry. You'll likely prevent Windows from working properly if you carelessly delete keys or value entries from the Registry. If you don't know for sure what will happen, or you haven't been instructed to do so, *don't do it*. Otherwise, use these steps:

1. Highlight the key or value entry you want to delete.
2. Press Delete, and REGEDIT asks you to confirm that you want to delete it.
3. Click Yes to delete the key or value entry.

TIP Before deleting a key, rename it to some obscure name such as **MyNukedKey**. This hides it from Windows and your applications. Restart your computer and test it out. If everything works okay, go ahead and delete the key.

Importing and Exporting Registry Entries

There are two ways you can work with the Registry. You can work with it in its current form (SYSTEM.DAT and USER.DAT in Windows 95) using REGEDIT. You can also export it to a text file (REG files) and edit it with your favorite text editor, such as WordPad (the file is too big for Notepad). If you export your Registry to a text file, you can use your editor's search-and-replace features to make massive changes to it. Be careful doing this, however, because you can inadvertently change a value you don't mean to change.

Aside from editing the Registry with a text editor, exporting the Registry to a text file has a more practical purpose. You're not limited to exporting your entire Registry. You can export a specific key and all its subkeys and value entries (branch). Thus, you can export a tiny part of the Registry for the following purposes:

■ *Backup.* You can export a branch of the Registry in which you're making many changes. If you get confused or things get out of hand, you can import that file back into the Registry to restore your settings.

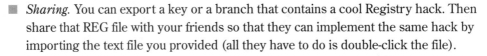

■ *Sharing.* You can export a key or a branch that contains a cool Registry hack. Then share that REG file with your friends so that they can implement the same hack by importing the text file you provided (all they have to do is double-click the file).

To export your entire Registry or just a specific branch, perform the following steps:

1. Select the key that represents the branch you want to export in the left pane of the window. (If you're exporting the entire Registry, you can skip this step.)

2. Choose <u>R</u>egistry, <u>E</u>xport Registry File from the main menu. REGEDIT displays the dialog box shown in Figure 3.7.

FIG. 3.7
If you don't type a file extension, REGEDIT uses the default file extension (REG).

3. If you're exporting the entire Registry, select <u>A</u>ll. Otherwise, select S<u>e</u>lected Branch. REGEDIT automatically fills in the key you selected in step 1.

4. Type the file name into which you want to export the Registry in File <u>N</u>ame, and click <u>S</u>ave.

The resulting file looks very much like a classic INI file. Open it in Notepad: right-click the REG file and choose <u>E</u>dit (Notepad will offer to open the file in Wordpad if it's larger than 64K). The first line always contains REGEDIT4, which identifies the file as a REGEDIT file. The remainder of the file contains the keys and value entries REGEDIT exported. Figure 3.8 shows what exported Registry entries look like in a text file.

FIG. 3.8
A Registry export file looks similar to an INI file.

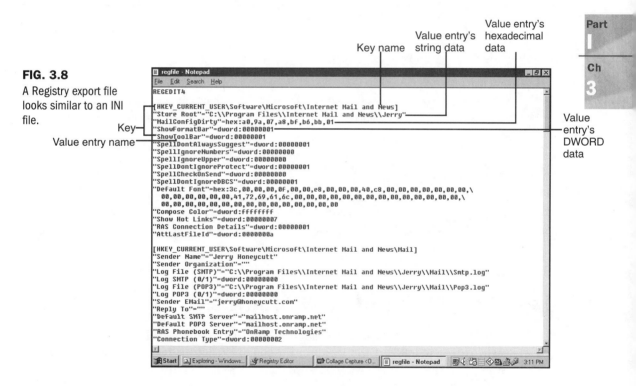

Part
I
Ch
3

CAUTION
REGEDIT puts REGEDIT4 at the top of REG files created in both Windows 95 and Windows NT 4.0. You can't rely on this identifier to prevent you from importing a Windows 95 REG file into NT. Be careful, because importing a REG file into Windows NT that you created in Windows 95, or vice versa, can really foul things up.

The file is split into multiple sections, with each Registry key in its own section. The name of the key is given between two brackets, and it is the fully qualified name of that key in the Registry file. That is, you see the entire name of the branch including the name of the root key. Each value entry for a key is listed in that key's section. The value entry's name is quoted, except for default value entries that REGEDIT represents with the at-sign (@). The value entry's data looks different depending on its type, as shown in Table 3.3.

Table 3.3   Formats for String, DWORD, and HEX Data

Type	Example
String	"This is a string value"
DWORD	DWORD:00000001
HEX	HEX:FF 00 FF 00 FF 00 FF 00 FF 00 FF 00

After you've made changes to your exported file, you may want to import it back into the Registry. In Windows Explorer, right-click an exported Registry file and choose Merge. Windows updates your Registry.

CAUTION

Don't accidentally double-click a REG file. Windows automatically merges it with the Registry because merge is the default action for the REG file type. Note that you can change the default action associated with this file type, as described in Chapter 7, "Customizing Your Windows Desktop."

Useful Command Line Parameters

REGEDIT has a few command line options that you may find useful. For example, you can create a shortcut to REGEDIT that uses the command line options to automatically export a portion of your Registry—easy backups. You can also use the command line options with REGEDIT in real-mode (MS-DOS) so that you can recover a backup copy of the Registry that you previously exported (see Chapter 5, "Fixing a Broken Registry").

To use the command line options, choose Run from the Start menu, type **regedit** followed by any of the options you want to use, and press Enter. You can also use the command line options when you run REGEDIT in real-mode. That is, you can use REGEDIT with these command line options when you boot to MS-DOS, instead of booting to Windows 95 (doesn't apply to Windows NT 4.0). Note that if you type **regedit.exe** and press Enter at the command line in a Windows 95 MS-DOS window, MS-DOS will start REGEDIT in protected-mode (Windows 95).

REGEDIT's command line has three different forms. You learn about each in the sections that follow.

N O T E In Windows NT 4.0, REGEDIT supports the command line parameters that you learn about in this section. You can't rely on REGEDIT to import a REG file because it can't replace keys that the system or other programs have open while NT is running. ▪

regedit [/L:*system*] [/R:*user*] *file1.reg, file2.reg...*

Use this form of REGEDIT's command line to import one or more REG files into the Registry. /L specifies the location of SYSTEM.DAT, and /R specifies the location of USER.DAT. (I'm not sure why Microsoft picked L and R rather than S and U.) REGEDIT imports each of the files it finds on the remainder of the command line.

For example, to import EXPORT1.REG and EXPORT2.REG, use the following command line (specifying the location of SYSTEM.DAT and USER.DAT is optional, but I include it here for completeness):

```
regedit /L:c:\windows\system.dat /R:c:\windows\user.dat export1.reg
export2.reg
```

regedit [/L:*system*] [/R:*user*] /e *file.reg [regkey]*

Use this form of REGEDIT's command line to export the entire Registry or just a specific branch of the Registry to a REG file. /L and /R work as you read in the previous section. /e specifies the name of the file into which you want to export the Registry. *regkey* is the name of the key that you want to export, including all its subkeys. If you want to export the entire Registry, leave out *regkey*.

For example, to export HKEY_LOCAL_MACHINE\SOFTWARE into MyExport.reg, use this command line (without /L and /R this time):

```
regedit /e MyExport.reg HKEY_LOCAL_MACHINE\SOFTWARE
```

T I P Create a shortcut that contains the previous command line so that you can back up a portion of the Registry by double-clicking the shortcut. You'll want to change the name of the REG file and branch to something useful, though.

regedit [/L:*system*] [/R:*user*] /c *file.reg*

This is the scariest form of REGEDIT's command line. /c replaces the entire contents of the Registry with the contents of *file.reg*. This is handy, however, if you've exported the entire Registry as a backup and need to restore it using REGEDIT in real-mode. (See Chapter 5, "Fixing a Broken Registry.")

Part
I

Ch
3

Here's an example of a command line that restores the Registry from a file called BACKUP.REG:

```
regedit /L:c:\windows\system.dat /R:c:\windows\user.dat /c backup.reg
```

Compact Your Windows 95 Registry

You can sometimes recover a lot of space from the Registry. As you, Windows 95, or various other programs remove Registry keys, Windows 95 doesn't recover the space that those keys occupied. Use these steps to compact that wasted space out of SYSTEM.DAT and USER.DAT:

1. Start your computer in MS-DOS mode (don't try this from within the Windows 95 graphical user interface).

2. Export the entire contents of the Registry into a temporary REG file by typing **regedit /e temp.reg** at the DOS prompt. If you're using profiles, you must use the /R switch to specify the location of USER.DAT.

3. Make a backup copy of SYSTEM.DAT and USER.DAT by copying both files to a safe place on your hard drive.

4. Delete both SYSTEM.DAT and USER.DAT. Make sure to delete USER.DAT from your profile folder if you're using profiles.

5. Rebuild the Registry from the REG file by typing regedit /c temp.reg at the DOS prompt. If you're using profiles, you must use the /R switch to specify the location of USER.DAT.

6. Restart your computer.

If for any reason whatsoever REGEDIT can't rebuild your Registry, restore the backup copy you made in step 3.

TROUBLESHOOTING

I tried to import a REG file using the /c switch, but REGEDIT reports an error that says "Error accessing the registry: The file may not be complete or Unable to open registry (14) - System.dat." Due to a bug in real-mode REGEDIT, you might get this error message when you try to import very large REG files using the /c switch. Microsoft acknowledges this bug but hasn't provided a solution yet. Use REGEDIT in protected-mode, instead.

CHAPTER 4

Using REGEDT32 with Windows NT 4.0

by Jerry Honeycutt

Microsoft isn't as particular about editing the Windows NT 4.0 Registry as they are about the Windows 95 Registry. Why? Many times administrators have to rely on the Registry Editor to make changes to the Registry. For example, many of the fixes that you find in Microsoft's Knowledge Base require that you edit the Registry. A lot of suggestions that you find in the NT resource kits also require that you edit the Registry. Thus, the Registry is just one of the many tools that is available to administrators for diagnosing and fixing problems.

REGEDT32 is your window into the Windows NT 4.0 Registry. Even though REGEDT32 is very powerful, it is a very simple program. It doesn't have a toolbar. Its menus are fairly straightforward. It displays each root key in its own MDI (Multiple Document Interface) window. Within each window, it displays the organization of the Registry on the left-hand side of the window and the actual data on the right-hand side—not too complicated. You learn about using REGEDT32 in this chapter, including tips for getting around some of REGEDT32's limitations.

Learn how to start and navigate REGEDT32

REGEDT32 isn't on your Start menu, but it's easy to find. This chapter shows you how to run REGEDT32 and how to navigate its windows and menus.

Work with Registry keys and value entries

This chapter shows you how to search for, add, change, and remove keys and value entries from the Registry. You also find tips for getting around REGEDT32's limitations.

Save and restore branches of the Registry

You learn all about REGEDT32's features that let you save a branch of the Registry, work with it as a separate subkey, and also restore it.

Export Registry keys to text files

This chapter shows you how to export a Registry key to a text file so that you can inspect it in your favorite text editor.

N O T E   There are many things that you can't do in REGEDT32. For example, you can't rename keys or value entries. You can't search value entry names or data, either. These are all, however, activities that you can safely do with REGEDIT, as described in Chapter 3, "Using REGEDIT with Windows 95 and NT 4.0." ▧

Starting REGEDT32

REGEDT32 may not be on your Start menu, but it is on your computer in C:\WINNT\System32. The file name is REGEDT32.EXE. Choose Programs, Run from the Start menu, type **REGEDT32**, and then click OK. The REGEDT32 window pops up. You can also drag REGEDT32.EXE from C:\WINNT\System32 folder to the Start button to create a shortcut to it.

TROUBLESHOOTING

I see REGEDT32.EXE in my Windows folder, but I can't run it or it won't let me change anything in the Registry. If you're using a computer in a network environment, your system administrator may have disabled it. You'll have to plead your case to the system administrator for access to REGEDT32.EXE. Note that the system administrator can also prevent REGEDT32.EXE from being installed on your computer if you're installing Windows from the network or a custom installation.

Getting Around REGEDT32

Figure 4.1 shows you what REGEDT32 looks like when you open it on your desktop. You see one MDI window for each root key in the Registry. In each window, you see two panes, which REGEDT32 separates by a divider that you can drag left or right to change the size of each pane. The following sections describe the contents of each pane.

Left-hand Pane: Registry Organization

The left-hand pane of each root key's window shows the organization of that key—the hierarchy. Even though a key is physically stored in multiple hives, REGEDT32 displays the entire key as one logical unit. When you update a key in REGEDT32, it automatically updates the appropriate hive.

Value entries for selected key

FIG. 4.1

The left-hand pane of REGEDT32 works similarly to the left-hand pane of Windows Explorer.

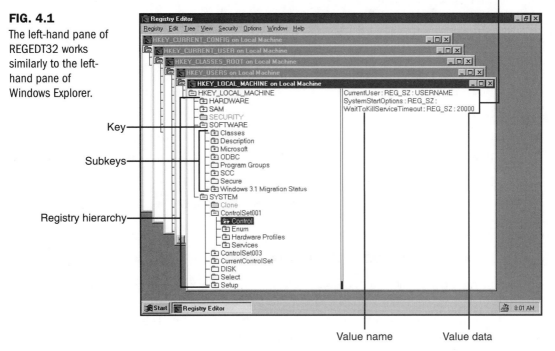

Key

Subkeys

Registry hierarchy

Value name   Value data

 The title bar of each window indicates the name of the root key and the computer which contains the Registry you're editing (you can remotely edit another computer's Registry as described in Chapter 13, "Remotely Editing a User's Registry"). It contains several subkeys that REGEDT32 represents as folders. Each subkey can contain more subkeys (also represented by folders), and each of those subkeys can contain more subkeys. Double-click a folder that contains a plus sign (+) to open it, or double-click a folder that contains a minus sign (–) to close it.

Mouse challenged? You can also use the keystrokes shown in Table 4.1 to move around REGEDT32. These keys are often the quickest way to maneuver because you don't have to stumble around with the mouse, trying to hit those tiny folder icons.

Table 4.1   REGEDT32 Keystrokes

Key	Description
Keypad +	Expands the selected folder one level
Keypad –	Collapses the selected folder one level

continues

Part

I

Ch

4

Table 4.1   Continued

Key	Description
Keypad *	Expands all levels of the selected folder
Up-arrow	Moves up the list one key
Down-arrow	Moves down the list one key
Home	Moves to the first key in the list
End	Moves to the last key in the list
Page Up	Moves up one screen in the list
Page Down	Moves down one screen in the list
Tab	Moves the highlight to the right-hand pane

Right-hand Pane: Value Entries for Selected Key

The right-hand pane shows the value entries for the key you select in the left-hand pane. Each row in the right-hand pane represents a single value entry and looks something like Name : Type : Value. *Name* is the value entry name, *Type* is the value entry type (REG_SZ, and so on), and *Value* is the value entry data. REGEDT32 separates each part with a colon (:). Texas : REG_SZ : "Howdy" is a REG_SZ value entry called Text that contains the word Howdy. Easy stuff.

Within some keys, you'll notice a value entry called (No Name). This shows up as (Default) in REGEDIT. This is a string value entry that represents the default value for that Registry key. All Registry keys contain this value entry, but some keys don't contain any additional value entries. REGEDT32 also doesn't show default value entries that haven't yet been assigned a value. Aside from (No Name), each key can contain zero or more value entries that have both a name and data.

T I P You can make REGEDT32 read only so that you can't accidentally mess up any settings while you're getting used to it. Choose Options, Read Only Mode. Now, REGEDT32 won't allow you to make any changes to the Registry. Choose Options, Read Only Mode again to be able to make changes.

Working with Keys and Value Entries

The sections that follow show you how to use REGEDT32 to search for, add, change, and delete keys and value entries. You'll find tips for doing all those things as safely as possible.

Before you learn how to edit the Registry, however, remember the advice you were given in Chapter 1, "Before You Begin." First, back up the Registry before you change it. Second, make sure you have a plan for safely making changes so that you can fix any problems that you encounter.

Searching for Keys

When you search the Registry, REGEDT32 looks for keys that match the text you specify. You can't use REGEDT32 to search for value entry names or value data, though, which makes this feature somewhat useless (you'll usually want to search for names and paths in value entries). Here's how to search the Registry for matching keys:

1. Choose View, Find Key; REGEDT32 displays the Find dialog box shown in Figure 4.2.

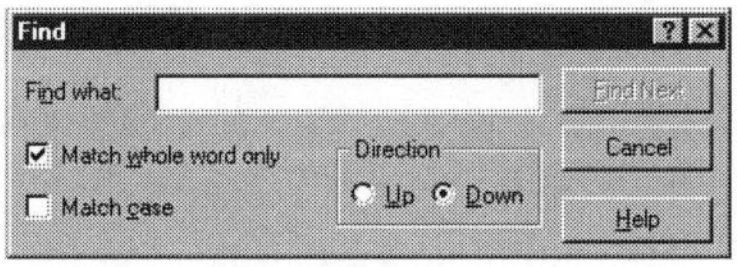

FIG. 4.2
Make sure that you deselect Match Whole Word Only if you want to find partial matches.

2. Type the text for which you want to search. If you're searching for a number, try both the decimal and hexadecimal notations because both formats are common in the Registry.
3. Click Find Next, and REGEDT32 searches for a match. This can sometimes take quite a while—up to a few minutes on slower machines. If REGEDT32 finds a matching key, it selects that key in the left-hand pane.
4. If the result isn't exactly what you had in mind, click Find Next again to repeat the search. When REGEDT32 reaches the bottom of the Registry, it displays a dialog box telling you that it can't find the requested key.
5. Click Cancel to close the Find dialog box.

Part
I

Ch
4

> **TIP**   If you need to search for value entry names and data, use REGEDIT as described in Chapter 3, "Using REGEDIT with Windows 95 and NT 4.0."

> **NOTE**   If you select any Registry key in the left-hand pane of a window and press a key on the keyboard, REGEDT32 selects the first Registry key that starts with that character. Press the same key again, and REGEDT32 selects the next Registry key that starts with that character. ■

Renaming a Key or Value Entry

In REGEDT32, you can't rename a key or value entry. If you need to rename a key or value entry, use REGEDIT. See Chapter 3, "Using REGEDIT with Windows 95 and NT 4.0," for more information.

> **NOTE**   REGEDT32 doesn't provide a feature to rename keys, but you can work around this. You can save a key and its subkeys to a temporary hive as described in "Saving and Restoring Keys" later in this chapter. Then, you can restore that temporary hive into a new subkey with a different name and remove the original key. ■

Changing an Entry's Value

As a user, changing a value entry's setting is probably the number one activity you'll do with REGEDT32. You might want to personalize your desktop, for example, or you might need to adjust a TCP/IP setting to work better with your network. Chapter 7, "Customizing Your Windows Desktop," and Chapter 8, "Troubleshooting Windows," are loaded with Registry entries that you can change. It's easy, if you have the appropriate permissions (see Chapter 12, "Securing the Windows Registry"). Here's how:

1. Double-click a value entry in the right-hand pane to open the editor. Remember that each value entry can be a REG_SZ, REG_MULTI_SZ, REG_EXPAND_SZ, REG_DWORD, or REG_BINARY (see Chapter 2, "Inside the Windows Registry"). This dialog box will be different, depending on the type of data stored in the value. Figures 4.3, 4.4, 4.5, 4.6, and 4.7 show you what each dialog box looks like.

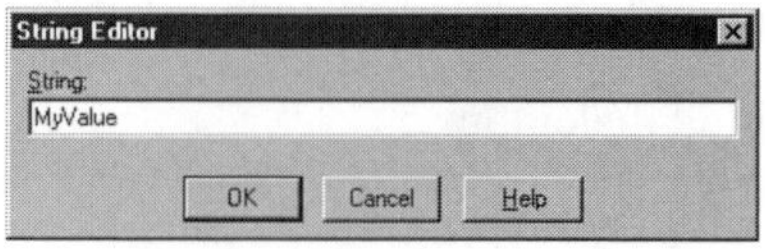

FIG. 4.3

The String Editor dialog box shows you the original data before you start editing.

FIG. 4.4
Each line in this window represents a separate string in REG_MULTI_SZ.

FIG. 4.5
The editor for REG_EXPAND_SZ looks just like the editor for REG_SZ (String Editor).

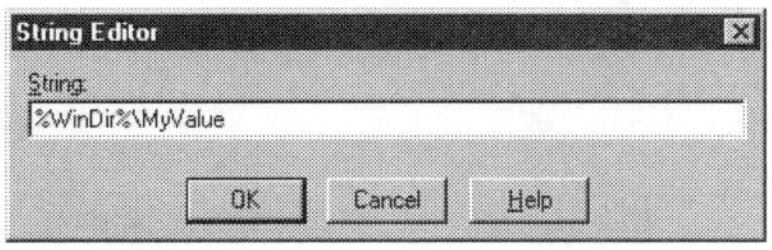

FIG. 4.6
Choose Decimal if your hexadecimal math is a bit rusty.

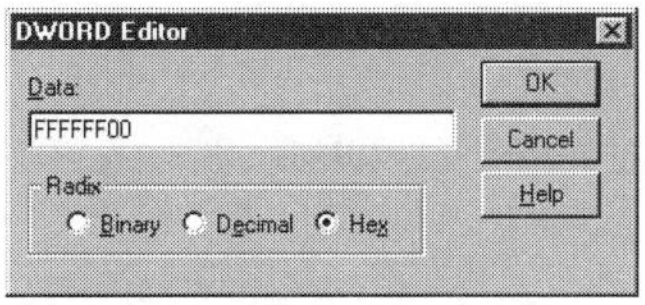

FIG. 4.7
You can use the Windows calculator (in Scientific mode) to convert decimal values to hexadecimal values for use with this dialog box.

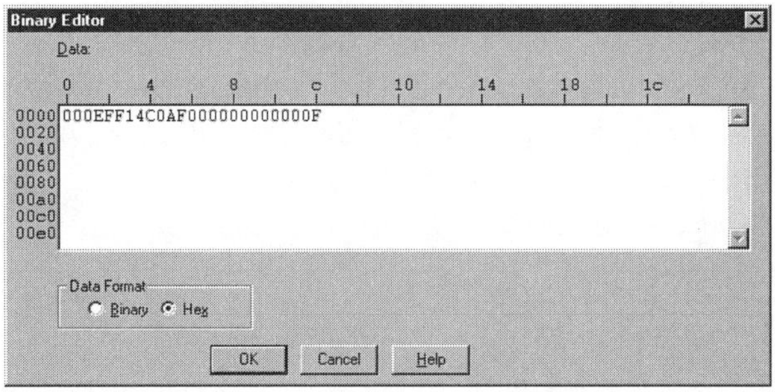

Part

I

Ch

4

2. Change the value, and click OK to save your changes.

TIP Protect yourself when changing value data. Save the Registry key that you're changing to disk, as described in "Saving and Restoring Keys" later in this chapter. This way, if something goes terribly wrong, you can always restore the original key as described in the same section.

NOTE Changes that you make to the Registry may not be reflected immediately in Windows or the programs that are currently running. The only way to make sure is to restart Windows after closing REGEDT32 or restart the affected program. ▦

Creating a New Key or Value Entry

Creating a new key or value entry is generally harmless, and equally as useless—unless, of course, you know for sure that either Windows or another program will use your new key. For example, the Microsoft Knowledge Base (see Appendix C, "Technical Resources for Windows") might instruct you to create a new Registry key to fix a problem. That's useful. Creating a new key out of thin air is pretty useless, however. To create one or the other, do the following:

- *New Key*. Select an existing key under which you want your new subkey to appear. Choose Edit, Add Key, type the name of your key in Key Name, leave Class blank (REGEDT32 doesn't use it), and press Enter.

- *New Value Entry*. Select an existing key under which you want your new value entry to appear. Choose Edit, Add Value from the menu. Type the name of your new value entry in Value Name, select the type of value entry from Data Type, and press Enter. REGEDT32 pops open the appropriate editor for the type of value entry you created.

> **TIP** To quickly add a value entry, move the highlight to the right-hand pane by pressing the Tab key, and then press the Insert key.

Deleting a Key or Value Entry

Be very careful about deleting keys and value entries from your Registry. You'll likely prevent Windows from working properly if you carelessly delete keys or value entries from the Registry. If you don't know for sure what will happen, or you haven't been instructed to do so, *don't do it*. Otherwise, use these steps:

1. Highlight the key or value entry you want to delete. Make sure that the highlight is on the key or value entry you intend to delete.
2. Press Delete, and REGEDT32 asks you to confirm that you want to delete it.
3. Click Yes to delete the key or value entry.

> **TIP** Before deleting a key, save it to disk as described in "Saving and Restoring Keys" later in this chapter. Then, if something goes wrong, you can restore it as described in the same section.

> **NOTE** If you mess up badly while working in HKEY_LOCAL_MACHINE\System\ CurrentControlSet, you can easily recover. Restart the computer, press the Spacebar when you see `Press spacebar to invoke Hardware Profile/Last Known Good Menu`.

Saving and Restoring Keys

You can save a key, all of its subkeys, and all of its value entries to disk as a hive. This is a hive separate from the other hives you find in C:\WINNT\System32\Config. Hives you create by saving a key use the same format as the system hives, however. Think of these as a temporary hive. You have to be a member of the Administrators group with Backup permission, though. This is very valuable, for a number of reasons:

- You can save a key as a hive and restore it into a new key with a different name. This has the effect of renaming the key.

- You can save a key as a hive and load the hive on a remote computer to work with it. Then, after you're finished working with it, you can restore the hive into its original key.

- You can save a key from a working computer as a hive and restore that hive on a broken computer. In that way, you can fix a computer's broken Registry by using a portion of a working computer's Registry.

Saving a Key, Its Subkeys, and Value Entries   To save a key, as well as all of its subkeys and value entries, as a hive, use these steps:

1. Select the key that you want to save to a hive in the left-hand pane of a root key's window. REGEDT32 saves all of its subkeys and value entries, too.

2. Choose Registry, Save Key from the main menu, and REGEDT32 displays the Save Key dialog box, which works exactly like every other Save As dialog box in Windows NT 4.0.

3. Type the name of the hive (preferably without an extension as that's how Windows NT 4.0 likes to see hives) into which you want to save the key, and click Save.

Restoring a Hive into a Key   Restoring a hive into a key replaces all of that key's subkeys and value entries with the contents of the hive. To restore a hive that you saved as described in "Saving a Key, Its Subkeys, and Value Entries," use these steps:

1. Select the key into which you want to restore a hive that you saved. The hive replaces the contents of this key.

2. Choose Registry, Restore; REGEDT32 displays the Restore Key dialog box.

3. Select the hive and click Open.

N O T E   You can't load a REG file created by REGEDIT using REGEDT32. Likewise, you can't load a file created by REGEDT32 using REGEDIT. REGEDIT exports keys into text files (REG files), while REGEDT32 saves keys in binary files.

Part
I

Ch
4

Loading and Unloading Hives

Loading a hive is very different from restoring a hive. When you restore a hive, the contents of the hive replaces the key in which you restore it. When you load a hive, REGEDT32 loads that hive in its own space. That is, you get a new subkey under HKEY_LOCAL_MACHINE or HKEY_USERS. Loading a hive doesn't replace anything. Like saving and restoring hives, loading hives has a good purpose. Here's why:

- You can load a hive from a computer which isn't working properly so that you can fix the problem.
- You can load a user's NTUSER.DAT, if he or she isn't logged onto the computer, so that you can fix problems or make other changes.

Loading a Hive into a Temporary Workspace   In order to load or unload a hive, you must have administrator privileges with Restore and Backup permissions. Here's how:

1. Select either the HKEY_USERS or HKEY_LOCAL_MACHINE window. You can only load hives into one of these two root keys.
2. Choose Registry, Load Hive; you'll see the Load Hive dialog box.
3. Select the hive that you want to load, and click Open. REGEDT32 opens another Load Hive dialog box in which you specify the name of the key in the Registry.
4. Type the name of the key into which you want to load the hive, and click OK. REGEDT32 creates a new subkey by that name under the root key you chose in step 1.

N O T E   You can't load a hive that contains a key that Windows NT 4.0 or another program is currently using. For example, if you want to load the System hive from a remote computer, you must first save a copy of that hive to another file. Then you can load the copy in REGEDT32.

Unloading a Temporary Hive   After you've made any changes you like to the hive you loaded earlier, use these steps to unload it:

1. Choose the hive in the Registry that you want to unload. You can only unload a hive which you loaded using the steps from the previous section.
2. Choose Registry, Unload Hive. REGEDT32 removes that subkey from the Registry. Any changes you made are saved to the hive on disk, however.

Exporting a Key to a Text File

You can export the contents of a Registry key to a human-readable text file. Unlike REGEDIT, however, you can't import the file back into the Registry with REGEDT32. Here's how:

1. Select the key that you want to export into a text file.

2. Choose Registry, Save Subtree As. You see the same old Save As dialog box.

3. Type the name of the text file into which you want to save the key, and click Save.

Figure 4.8 shows what this text file looks like in Notepad. It doesn't use the same format as REGEDIT when it exports a key into a REG file. In fact, REGEDT32 only exports the selected key; it doesn't export any subkeys.

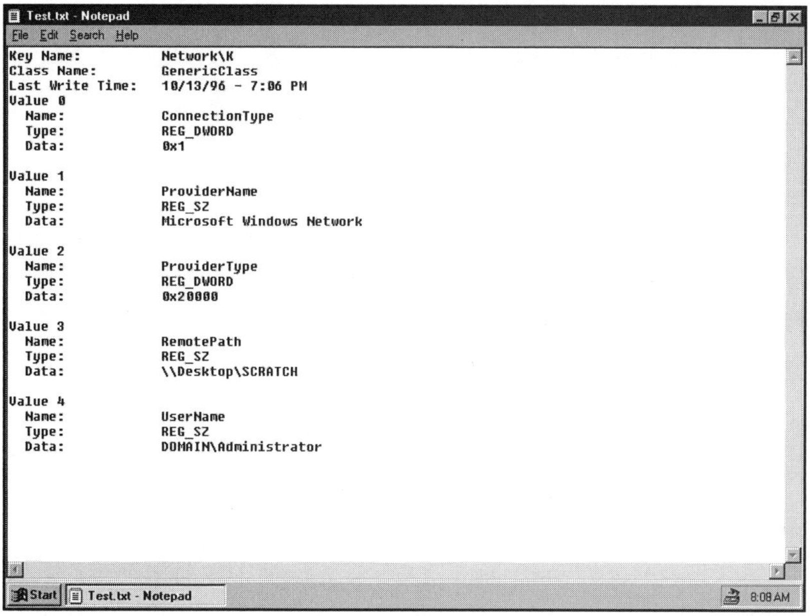

FIG. 4.8
You can save keys such as HKEY_LOCAL_MACHINE\ Hardware to a text file, even though you can't save them as a hive.

Part

I

Ch

4

CHAPTER 5

Fixing a Broken Registry

by Jerry Honeycutt

In Chapter 1, "Before You Begin," you learned about several methods you can use to back up the Registry. Backing up the Registry without learning how to restore it is like spending thousands of dollars on tools at an automotive center, without ever actually fixing your car yourself. This chapter shows you how to restore the backups that you made in Chapter 1.

This chapter goes far beyond restoring backups. It also shows you how to repair the Windows Registry by brute force. You're not going to whack it around. You're going to use all the tricks you can muster to figure out what's wrong in the Registry and fix it. It's not as difficult as it sounds if you have the right tools and information at hand. ■

Starting Windows 95 in Safe Mode

Learn how to start Windows 95 in Safe Mode, and exactly what this means for you.

Restoring Your Windows 95 Registry from a Backup

You have been making regular backups, right? This chapter shows you how to restore those backups to your Windows 95 Registry.

Restoring Your Windows NT 4.0 Registry from a Backup

Discover how to restore the Windows NT 4.0 Registry—a bit more difficult than its Windows 95 counterpart—from a backup.

Repairing the Windows Registry

In addition to restoring a backup, learn how to easily fix the Windows Registry.

Starting in Safe Mode (Windows 95 Only)

Safe Mode is a special boot option that causes Windows 95 to load without most of its device driver support loaded. It uses the standard VGA, mouse, and keyboard drivers only. If you're experiencing a problem starting Windows 95, you can usually start in Safe Mode to fix it.

When you start Windows 95 in Safe Mode, you won't have networking support. Many other devices won't work either because Windows 95 loads the bare minimum needed to start properly. Here's how to start Windows 95 in Safe Mode:

1. Restart your computer.
2. When you see `Starting Windows 95`, press F8. If this message doesn't stay on your computer very long, you can anticipate when the message will appear, and press F8 just prior to that moment. You'll see a boot menu.
3. Choose Safe Mode from the boot menu and Windows will start in Safe Mode. You'll see the words `Safe Mode` in the four corners of your display.

T I P You can start Windows 95 in Safe Mode with networking enabled by choosing Safe Mode with Network Support from the boot menu.

N O T E When you boot Windows 95 in Safe Mode, it doesn't make a backup copy of the Registry files. That is, Windows 95 doesn't copy `SYSTEM.DAT` to `SYSTEM.DA0` or `USER.DAT` to `USER.DA0`. This is good to know, because if you're having problems with Windows 95 that you think relate to the Registry, you don't want Windows replacing the backup copies of the Registry with the loused up copies. ■

▶ **See** "Configuring Your Boot Options," **p. 193**

Letting Windows Fix the Registry

In most cases, you don't have to use the Registry Editor to repair the Registry. You can let Windows do it for you. In fact, Windows will fix some errors before you even know there are any.

The following sections discuss four techniques you can use to repair the Registry automatically:

   ▪ Redetect the hardware in your computer.
   ▪ Reinstall a program on your computer.

- Reassociate a file extension to a file type.
- Use the Registry Editor to repair an error.

Redetect Your Hardware (Windows 95 Only)

If your hardware configuration is mysteriously messed up, you won't be able to fix it using the Registry Editor. The hardware entries in the Registry are just too complicated. Figure 5.1 proves the point.

FIG. 5.1
The Registry Editor displays the complicated hardware configuration.

Chapter 2, "Inside the Windows Registry," describes the Registry branches that contain hardware information. The simplest way to fix your hardware configuration is to use the Add New Hardware Wizard in the Control Panel. Here's how:

Add New Hardware

1. Double-click the Add New Hardware Wizard in the Control Panel.
2. Click Next.
3. Select Yes to let Windows 95 automatically detect the hardware that is installed in your computer.
4. Click Next, and Windows 95 detects your computer's hardware. After it's finished, you'll see the Add New Hardware Wizard dialog box shown in Figure 5.2.

FIG. 5.2
You might want to click
Details to see a list of
the hardware that
Windows 95 detected.

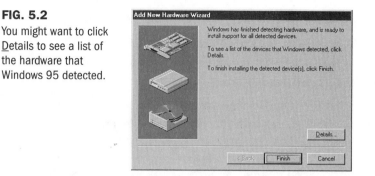

5. Click Finish, and Windows 95 installs the drivers it needs for the hardware it detected. If Windows 95 asks for your disks or CD-ROM, follow the instructions.

6. Click Yes if Windows 95 asks you to restart Windows 95.

N O T E   If the Add New Hardware Wizard doesn't fix the problem, you'll need to remove the device from the Device Manager first, and then try the wizard again. Double-click the Control Panel's System icon, and click the Device Manager tab. Delete the device from the list, and click OK to save your changes. After you've removed the device, repeat steps 1 through 6. ▨

Reinstall an Offending Program

If a program's settings get too messed up, it's often easier to reinstall the program. You don't have to remove the program first—just install right over it. You'll replace the program's files on the hard drive and the program's settings in the Registry. Be careful to make sure that you install over the same folder, otherwise you'll end up wasting drive space.

Some of the smarter programs know enough to leave your preferences alone, while they correctly fix other Registry settings. If you reinstall Netscape Navigator, for example, it preserves all your server settings while it resets all of the program's settings in HKEY_CLASSES_ROOT.

T I P   Many programs use REG files to create their settings in the Registry. You may be able to use the REG file again to restore the damaged settings without reinstalling the program. Look in the program's installation folders for a REG file and inspect it by right-clicking the file and choosing Open. If it looks like it will fix your problem, double-click the file to merge its settings with the Registry.

Reassociate a File Extension

The order in which you install programs on your computer affects a file extension's association with a file type. Last come, first served—if you install Microsoft Word first and install the Microsoft Word Viewer second, the DOC file extension is associated with the Microsoft Word Viewer program.

Some programs, such as Internet Explorer and WinZip, automatically detect that they are no longer associated with a particular file type. In these cases, you can let the program fix the problem automatically.

In other cases, you'll have to manually reassociate a file extension with a particular file type by following these steps:

Explorer

1. Open Explorer, and select a file with the extension that you want to reassociate with a different file type.

2. Hold down the Shift key and right-click the file. Choose Open With. You'll see the Open With dialog box shown in Figure 5.3.

FIG. 5.3
This list shows the programs associated with the open action of each file type in HKEY_CLASSES_ROOT.

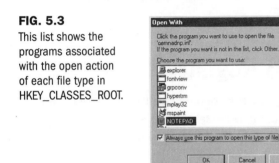

Part
I

Ch
5

3. Choose the program you want to associate with this file extension, select Always Use This Program to Open This Type of File, and click OK.

The next time you double-click a file with the same extension, the program you chose in step 3 will be used to open it.

Use REGEDIT to Rebuild the Registry (Windows 95 Only)

If Windows 95 reports that the Registry is corrupted, the Registry is damaged, or Registry access failed, it's probably because information is missing from the Registry or the structure of the Registry is messed up. The Registry is only partially damaged, however, so Windows 95 still starts. But some of your hardware or programs may not work correctly.

You can use the Registry Editor to reconstruct the Registry. This must be done at the Safe Mode command prompt, however, with the Registry Editor in real mode. Here's how:

1. Restart the computer, and when it displays Starting Windows 95, press F8.

2. Choose Safe Mode Command Prompt Only from the Windows 95 Startup menu. You'll see the old, familiar MS-DOS prompt after Windows 95 loads.

3. Type **regedit /e registry.reg**, and press Enter. The Registry Editor exports the entire contents of the Registry into a text file called REGISTRY.REG. Ignore messages about missing or invalid data.

4. Type **regedit /c registry.reg**, and press Enter. The Registry Editor imports the entire context of the REGISTRY.REG text file back into the Registry.

5. Press Ctrl+Alt+Delete to restart your computer.

> **CAUTION**
>
> You'll lose any settings that are in damaged portions of the Registry. You won't know exactly which settings you lost, either. It may be necessary to reinstall some of your hardware or software.

Restoring the Windows 95 Registry

You can use a variety of methods to back up and restore the Registry. You can copy the files, use a tape drive, use a utility, and so on. My personal favorite is to just copy the Registry files to a safe place, particularly while I'm tinkering around with the Registry.

The sections that follow describe different ways to restore the Registry. Their organization reflects the same organization you saw in Chapter 1.

Here's what you'll find in the remainder of this section:

Restore a copy of the files

Restore your system from a tape

Import an exported copy of the Registry

Use the Emergency Repair Utility

Restore a backup from CfgBack

Restore SYSTEM.1ST

Restore Your Copy of the Registry Files

Did you make a backup copy of SYSTEM.DAT and USER.DAT? If so, you can easily restore these files and continue on with business by following these steps:

1. Make sure that you can view hidden files in Windows 95 Explorer. Choose View, Options from the main menu, select Show all files, and click OK.

2. Copy your backup copy of SYSTEM.DAT to your C:\Windows. Copy USER.DAT to C:\Windows or your profile folder (see Chapter 1, "Before You Begin," if you're not familiar with how profiles work).

3. Don't forget to restore Windows 95 Explorer so that it hides those system files: Choose View, Options from the main menu, select Hide Files of These Types, and click OK.

4. Restart your computer.

N O T E If you're convinced that SYSTEM.DA0 and USER.DA0 contain a good copy of the Registry, you can copy these files to SYSTEM.DAT and USER.DAT. ▮

You can create a batch file that automatically restores your backup copies of SYSTEM.DAT and USER.DAT. Then, all you have to do is double-click the batch file to restore them.

The following batch file restores your backup files. It uses the Xcopy command with the /H and /R switches. The /H switch copies hidden and system files. The /R switch replaces read-only files. That way, Xcopy will be able to overwrite the current copy of SYSTEM.DAT and USER.DAT. %WinDir% expands to the location of your Windows folder when the batch file runs.

```
Xcopy %WinDir%\Registry\System.dat %WinDir%\System.dat /R /H
Xcopy %WinDir%\Registry\User.dat %WinDir%\User.dat /R /H
```

ON THE WEB

You can also download this batch file from the author's Web site at
http://rampages.onramp.net/~jerry.

N O T E If you configured Windows 95 to use user profiles, you'll need to tweak this batch file to make it correctly restore USER.DAT. In particular, you need to change the second line so that it restores the backup copy into your profile folder. ▮

▶ **See** "Copy the Registry Files to a Safe Place" **p. 18**

Part
I
Ch
5

Restore Your System from a Tape Drive

If you used the Windows 95 tape backup utility (Microsoft Backup) to back up the Registry, you can easily (if not quickly) restore the Registry to its state when you last backed up your computer using the Full System Backup file set. The only way to get Microsoft Backup to restore the Registry is to restore a file that's in C:\Windows, however. You can also restore an innocuous file such as README.TXT or TIPS.TXT to C:\Windows in order to restore the Registry.

You can also restore the Registry using a Windows 95-compatible backup program from another vendor. In most cases, the backup program will ask you if you want to restore the Registry. In other cases, the backup program will ask you if you want to restore the Registry after it has restored one or more files to your computer or to C:\Windows. This is very dependent on the manufacturer. For example, you could use Conner Backup Exec, which asks you if you want to restore the Registry after you restore any file to your computer—regardless of its location.

▶ **See** "Backup Your System Using a Tape Drive," **p. 19**

Import an Exported Copy of the Registry

Chapter 1 also shows you how to export the Registry into a REG file. You can't import this file while Windows 95 is running, however, because the Registry Editor can't replace keys that are open. You need to start your computer to the DOS prompt, and then use the Registry Editor in real mode to import the Registry. Chapter 3, "Using REGEDIT with Windows 95 and NT 4.0," shows you how to import a REG file, replacing the entire contents of the Registry.

▶ **See** "Export the Registry Using the Registry Editor," **p. 21**
▶ **See** "Useful Command Line Parameters," **p. 68**

Use the Emergency Repair Utility

The Emergency Repair Utility (ERU) is a tool that backs up all of your important configuration files, including the Registry. Like the other backup methods in this chapter, Chapter 1 shows you how to use it. You can use it to back up your configuration files to a diskette or a folder on your hard drive. Either way, here's how to restore your configuration files from the backup:

1. Start your computer to the DOS prompt.

2. Change to the folder to which you backed up your configuration files. If you backed up your configuration files to a diskette, put that diskette in the drive, and change to it.

3. Run ERD.EXE. It's mixed in with all the backup copies of your configuration files.

4. Select the files that you want to recover. Highlight a configuration file using the arrow keys, and press the Enter key to select it.

5. Once you've selected the configuration files you want to recover, select Start Recovery, and press the Enter key.

▶ **See** "Use the Emergency Repair Utility," **p. 21**

Restore a Backup from CfgBack

CfgBack is a utility that is very similar to the Emergency Repair Utility. Chapter 1 shows you how to use it. It's not recommended that you use this utility, however, because of numerous problems that Microsoft and other users have reported with it.

Regardless, here's how to restore a backup using CfgBack:

Cfgback

1. Start CfgBack, and you'll see the Configuration Backup window shown in Figure 5.4.

FIG. 5.4
CfgBack can store up to nine different backup copies of the Registry.

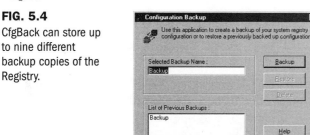

Part

I

Ch

5

2. Choose the backup you want to restore in List of Previous Backups.

3. Click Restore to restore the Registry using the chosen backup. CfgBack extracts the backup copy and merges it into the Registry.

◆ TROUBLESHOOTING

When I restore a backup copy of the Registry using CfgBack, it says You are about to backup over a previous backup. Do you want to proceed? This is a known bug in the CfgBack utility. You can safely ignore this message, and click OK to restore the Registry.

I restored a backup copy of the Registry using CfgBack, but all my settings were not restored. This is another known bug in the CfgBack utility. It doesn't always restore all the settings in the Registry. You won't lose your settings, however, because it leaves the settings that are already in the Registry alone.

▶ **See** "Backup the Registry with CfgBack," **p. 23**

Restore SYSTEM.1ST

If all else fails, you'll find one more backup copy of the Registry on your computer. SYSTEM.1ST is a read-only, hidden, system file in the root folder of your boot drive. This is a backup copy of SYSTEM.DAT that Windows 95 made after you successfully installed and started Windows 95. It doesn't contain any custom settings, nor does it include any information added by the programs that you've installed. The only thing this file does for you is get your machine running again if nothing else works.

Here's how to restore SYSTEM.1ST:

1. Start your computer to the DOS prompt.

2. Copy your C:\SYSTEM.DAT to your C:\Windows\SYSTEM.DAT. At the DOS prompt, type **Xcopy C:\system.1st C:\windows\system.dat /H /R**, and press Enter.

3. Restart your computer.

Restoring the Windows NT 4.0 Registry

Restoring the Windows NT 4.0 Registry isn't as easy as restoring the Windows 95 Registry. For example, it prevents you from copying hives while NT is running. Regardless, you do have a few alternatives with which to work, such as these:

- Restore a copy of the Registry files.
- Restore your system from a tape drive.
- Restore the Registry with REGREST.
- Borrow a key from a working computer.

Restore Your Copy of the Registry Files

You can't copy your backup files over Windows NT 4.0's hives. You'll get a sharing violation if you try. You have to start in another operating system, such as MS-DOS, before you can restore those files. You can't use this method if you're using NTFS.

Start your computer using an MS-DOS formatted system diskette. Then, copy all of the files you backed up in Chapter 1 into C:\WINNT\System32. You can also use the following batch file to restore your backup copies of these files. Remember that Xcopy with /H and /R copies hidden and system files, while overwriting read-only files. Line two of the following example restores all of the profile folders using the /S switch to copy all sub-folders. Here's what the batch file looks like:

```
xcopy %WinDir%\Registry\*.* %WinDir%\System32\Config\*.* /H /R
xcopy %WinDir%\Registry\Profiles\*.* %WinDir%\Profiles\*.* /S /H /R
```

ON THE WEB

You can also download this batch file from the author's Web site at

http://rampages.onramp.net/~jerry.

▶ **See** "Start in DOS and Copy the Registry Files," **p. 24**

Restore Your System from a Tape Drive

In Chapter 1, you learned how to use Windows NT 4.0's tape backup utility to back up the Registry. You have to explicitly tell NT's backup utility to restore the Registry; make sure that you select Restore Local Registry in the Restore Information dialog box.

▶ **See** "Backup Your System Using a Tape Drive," **p. 19**

Restore the Registry with REGREST

REGREST is a utility that Microsoft provides as part of the Windows NT 4.0 Resource kit. You use it to restore Registry hives that you backed up using REGBACK, as described in Chapter 1, in the section "Backup the Registry with REGBACK." When you install the NT Resource Kit, the setup program copies REGREST.EXE to the installation folder. It doesn't add a shortcut to the Start menu. You can run this program from a DOS prompt, however, or choose Run from the Start menu, type the REGREST command line, and press Enter.

REGREST has three different command lines. The following list describes each:

- **regrest**. Displays help for REGREST.
- **regrest** *BackupDir SaveDir*. For each hive in the Registry, REGREST looks for a similarly named file in BackupDir and restores that file to the \Config folder. It saves a copy of the existing file to SaveDir before replacing it, however.
- *regrest Filename SaveFilename hivetype hivename*. Restores the hive in Filename to the \Config folder. REGREST saves a copy of the original hive file to SaveFilename first, though. Hivetype must be either Machine or User, corresponding to HKEY_LOCAL_MACHINE and HKEY_USERS, respectively. hivename is the name of the hive that you want to backup (machine or users).

▶ **See** "Back Up the Registry with REGBACK," **p. 25**

Part
I

Ch
5

Borrow a Key from a Working Computer

This section is for those who didn't make a backup copy of the Registry. You know who you are. If all seems lost, you can try borrowing a key from another computer that is working or from another installation of NT on the same computer; that is, if you know for sure which key in your Registry is damaged, you can replace that key with the same key from another computer.

Of course, there are a few cautions. You can't borrow a key that contains information so specific to the other computer that it has no place in your computer. HKEY_LOCAL_MACHINE\System is probably a poor candidate. However, if HKEY_LOCAL_MACHINE\Software\Classes is broken on your computer, and you're completely without a backup, you might consider borrowing that key from another computer. Just follow these steps:

regedt32

1. Open REGEDT32 on the computer that contains the key you want to swipe.
2. Save that key, all of its subkeys, and its value entries to a hive as described in Chapter 4, "Using REGEDT32 with Windows NT 4.0."
3. Open REGEDT32 on your computer.
4. Restore the hive file you created in step 2 into the key you're replacing.
5. Close REGEDT32, and restart your computer.

N O T E This is risky business. Before restoring the borrowed key, go ahead and make a backup copy using one of the techniques you learned about in Chapter 1. ■

▶ **See** "Saving and Restoring Keys," **p. 79**

Using ConfigSafe to Restore Settings

Chapter 9, "Using ConfigSafe to Track Down Settings," describes a handy utility that you can use to protect your settings. It takes periodic snapshots of your configuration files, including the Registry. It also takes a snapshot of the computer's hardware configuration and the files on your hard drive.

You can restore your configuration to any one of the snapshots it takes. If your configuration goes bad, you can use ConfigSafe to load a previous version of your configuration. You can also use the DOS version of ConfigSafe. In some cases, you won't be able to start Windows at all. The DOS version of ConfigSafe can restore your configuration to a previous version that you know worked well.

Removing a Program from the Registry Manually

The way most programs use the Registry is rather predictable. They all store the same types of information in the same types of places. You can use this fact to help you successfully remove a program from the Registry.

T I P   Before you begin, back up the Registry. You'll be making some heavy-duty changes to the Registry. It's comforting to know you have a way out if things get out of hand.

Delete all the program's installation folders. Most Windows 95 programs are installed in C:\PROGRAM FILES. Highlight the program's folder, and press the Delete key. Confirm that you want to delete these files.

Regedit

After you've removed the program's files, open the Registry Editor. Search the Registry for any entry that belongs to that program, and remove it. Here are some suggestions for the types of things you should search for:

- Search the Registry for each of the program's installation paths. If the program has two paths called C:\PROGRAM FILES\PROGRAM and C:\PROGRAM FILES\COMPANY\PROGRAM, search for both of these paths in the Registry. Delete any keys or value entries that contain this path.

- Search the Registry for the program's name. If you're removing a program called "Elvis Lives for Windows 95," search the Registry for any key or value entry containing "Elvis" or "Elvis Lives." Delete any keys or value entries that contain the name of the program.

T I P   If you've found a key whose default value entry contains the name or path of the program you're removing, it's probably safe to remove the entire key, even if it has subkeys.

- Some programs name their DLLs and EXE files with the same few starting characters. HiJaak 95 DLL files all begin with the letters HJ. Search the Registry for these characters. After verifying that the DLL files belong to the program you're removing by finding that file in the program's installation folder or looking at the file with Quick View, delete the key or value entry containing the letters.

Part
I
Ch
5

◆ **TROUBLESHOOTING**

I installed a new program on my computer, and now I can't start Windows 95. Help!

The program is loading shell extensions, drivers, or other files when Windows 95 starts, and these files are causing it to crash. Restart your computer, and press F8 when Windows 95 displays "Starting Windows 95." Choose Command Prompt Only from the Startup menu. Then, completely delete the program's installation folder and subfolders (normally found under C:\Program Files). Restart Windows 95. You'll see a few messages about missing files, but Windows 95 will successfully start. Remove the program's Registry entries using the steps in this section. After you remove the program's Registry entries, you won't see the messages about missing files.

CHAPTER 6

File Associations

by Rob Tidrow

Among various other system settings that are stored in the Registry, Windows 95 and Windows NT store information about file associations. These file associations enable you to launch applications by double-clicking a desktop shortcut icon for that application. Or, you can double-click a document in the Windows Explorer that is associated with an application. In addition, one application can launch another application via an OLE (Object Linking and Embedding) or DDE (Dynamic Data Exchange) instruction. All of these events require that Windows 95 or Windows NT store instructions on these actions in the Registry.

You can find information about file extensions and OLE instructions in the HKEY_CLASSES_ROOT Registry subkey. ■

How file extensions are listed in the Registry

When you double-click on a file in the Windows Explorer, Windows 95 and Windows NT must know what application is associated with that file. The Windows Registry stores file extension information and related associations for each file type.

What class-definition subkeys comprise

Class-definition subkeys tell Windows the type of file that is defined by a file extension. The file extension TXT, for instance, is usually associated with text files.

What class identifiers (CLSIDS) are

A CLSID subkey contains the class identifier for a file type. Every type of Windows OLE (Object Linking and Embedding) object has a unique class identifier, or CLSID, recorded in this section. The CLSIDs help Windows to organize various OLE objects, including DLLs, EXE files, Windows functions, and file types.

Understanding File Extension Information in the Registry

For Windows to know what to do with a file when you double-click it, you must associate that file with a file extension. Further, Windows needs a way to know what certain file extensions mean. These meanings are stored in the Registry so that each time Windows, an application, or a service encounters a file with an extension, the Registry can be searched to reveal what should be done with that file. In some cases, the file extension may point to an application that runs, which is the case for files that have the extensions EXE, COM, and BAT, for instance. Other files may be document files that point to a specific application to launch and display that file, such as in the case of DOC files for Word for Windows. Still, other extensions may point to dynamic link libraries (DLLs) that are to be accessed when a file with a specific file extension is encountered.

File extension information is stored in the Registry under the HKEY_CLASSES_ROOT subkey, which is shown in Figure 6.1. Every type of file extension setup on your machine needs to have a file extension setting in the Registry. These settings include a separate subkey for each extension, beginning with a period, such as .TXT, .BMP, and so on. The HKEY_CLASSES_ROOT subkey also contains class-definition subkeys and CLSID subkeys (class identifiers).

FIG. 6.1

The Registry stores file extension information in the HKEY_CLASSES_ROOT subkey.

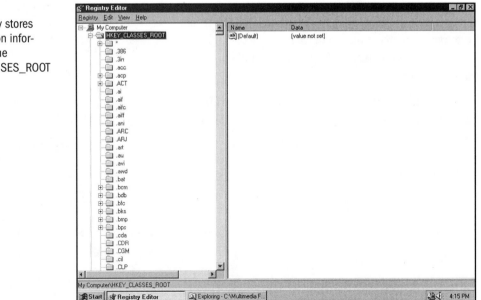

TIP The HKEY_CLASSES_ROOT subkey is cross-linked to the HKEY_LOCAL_MACHINE\Software\ Classes subkey in the Registry. The same information stored in the HKEY_CLASSES_ROOT subkey is stored in the HKEY_LOCAL_MACHINE\Software\Classes subkey. The reason HKEY_CLASSES_ROOT even exists is so that some Windows 3.1 applications can locate OLE information there.

You can edit either the HKEY_CLASSES_ROOT or HKEY_LOCAL_MACHINE\Software\Classes subkey. When changes are made in one subkey, they are automatically made in the other subkey.

Within the file extension subkeys, there are typically three types of data. There can be data that points to class-definitions of a file extension, sometimes referred to as *application identifiers*. You also can have information within a file extension subkey that instructs Windows how to open and print a file. In addition, some file extension subkeys instruct Windows on the class-definition of a file extension, plus additional information on how to create new files with a specific file extension. These three types of data are discussed in the next three sections.

File Extensions with Class-Definition Subkeys

File extension subkeys that contain pointers to class-definition subkeys include subkeys and/or value entries that specify the file type associated with an extension. A file extension of TXT, for example, is associated with a text file. A file extension of BMP, on the other hand, is associated with a bitmap file. The pointers in the file extension subkeys do not actually specify what should be done (such as activating an application or running a DLL) with a file, they just point to another subkey in the Registry that instructs Windows how to handle the file. To make things easy to locate, Windows stores these subkeys in the same HKEY_CLASSES_ROOT subkey that stores file extension data.

When a file is activated in the Windows Explorer or on the desktop (such as from a shortcut), Windows looks in the Registry for the file extension subkey that corresponds to the file activated. Next, Windows retrieves the class-definition for that file and locates the class-definition subkey for that file type. Within the class-definition subkey are instructions on how Windows should handle that file.

A typical Registry entry for a JPG file, for example, might include the following value entries:

```
(Default) "jpegfile"
ContentType "image/jpeg"
```

The (Default) "jpegfile" value entry lists the file type associated with a file that has a .JPG extension. The ContentType "image/jpeg" value entry shows the MIME, or *Multipurpose Internet Mail Extensions*, type associated with that file extension. If you scroll down the HKEY_CLASSES_ROOT subkey window, you see a long list of file extension

Part
I

Ch
6

entries, followed by class-definition subkeys. Locate the subkey that matches the name in the (Default) value entry, in this case jpegfile, to determine the class-definition of the file extension. Within the jpegfile class-definition subkey are specific instructions on how Windows should display files of this type, as well as what the default icon is for JPG files and how to print JPG files.

You can tell where file extension subkeys end and class-definition subkeys begin by looking for subkeys without periods at the beginning of them. In Figure 6.2, for example, you can see that file extension subkeys end with the .ZIP subkey, and the class-definition subkeys begin at the 3INFile subkey. Your particular settings may differ from these, but this gives you an idea of the differences between file extension subkey names and class-definition subkey names. For more information on class-definition subkeys, see the section "Understanding Class-Definition Subkeys" later in this chapter.

FIG. 6.2
Class-definition subkeys do not have to start with periods, but file association subkeys do.

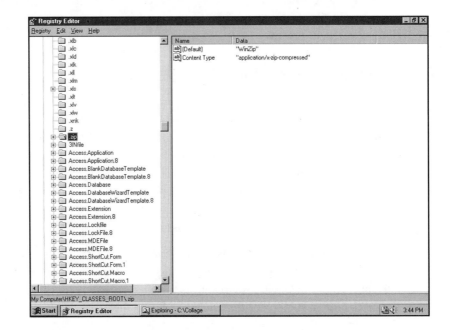

File Extensions Without Class-Definition Subkeys

Some file extension subkeys do not include class-definition value entries. Instead, they contain information instructing Windows 95 or Windows NT how to open or print a file. In Figure 6.3, for instance, the .gif file extension subkey contains a few subkeys as follows: \shell\open\command. (In this example, there is not a subkey for printing a file with a .gif extension.) The instruction Windows uses to open a file with a .gif extension is located under the \command subkey, which is C:\SPRY\BIN\imagevw.exe %1 in this case. This means that the imagevw.exe application (which is the Spry Image Viewer application distributed with CompuServe's WinCim 2.01 product) launches and displays a selected file. The %1 value is a variable that instructs the viewer to display the selected file.

FIG. 6.3

An example of a file extension subkey that does not contain class-definition information.

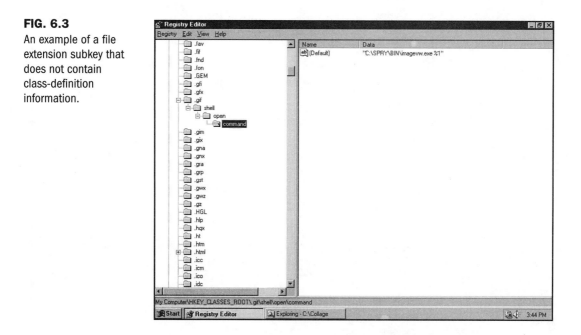

To see how this works in real terms, a file with the name KEYBAR.GIF is shown in the Windows Explorer in Figure 6.4. When this file is double-clicked, Windows locates the .gif file extension subkey in the Registry, reads the value entry in the \shell\open\command subkey, and launches Image Viewer, with KEYBAR.GIF displayed (see Figure 6.5)

File Extensions with Class-Definitions Plus Additional Instructions

Some file extension subkeys contain class-definition value entries, as well as additional information. These additional instructions usually tell Windows how to create a new file of the selected type. For instance, when you right-click the desktop and choose the New command, you can choose from a list of file types to create (see Figure 6.6). The context-menu items are placed there by ShellNew subkey entries in the Registry.

Part
I
Ch
6

FIG. 6.4
The KEYBAR.GIF as displayed in the Windows Explorer.

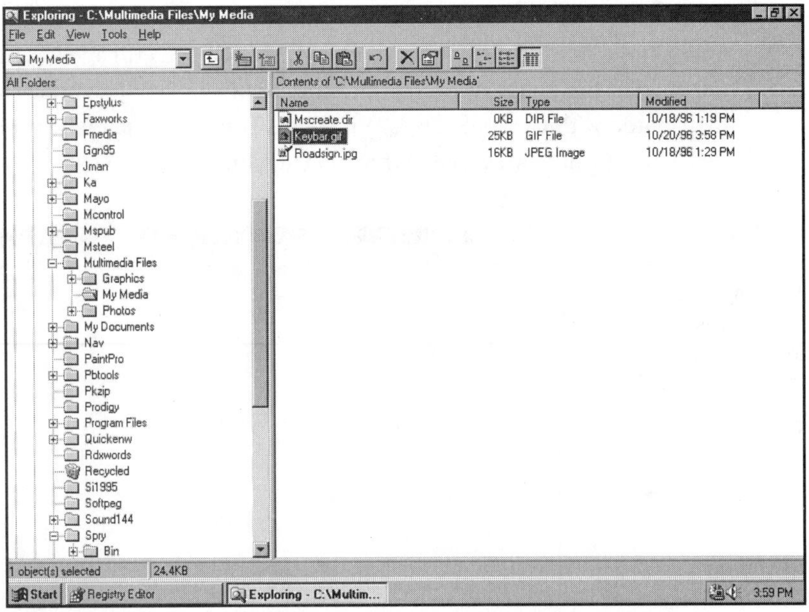

FIG. 6.5
The results of double-clicking the KEYBAR.GIF file in the Windows Explorer.

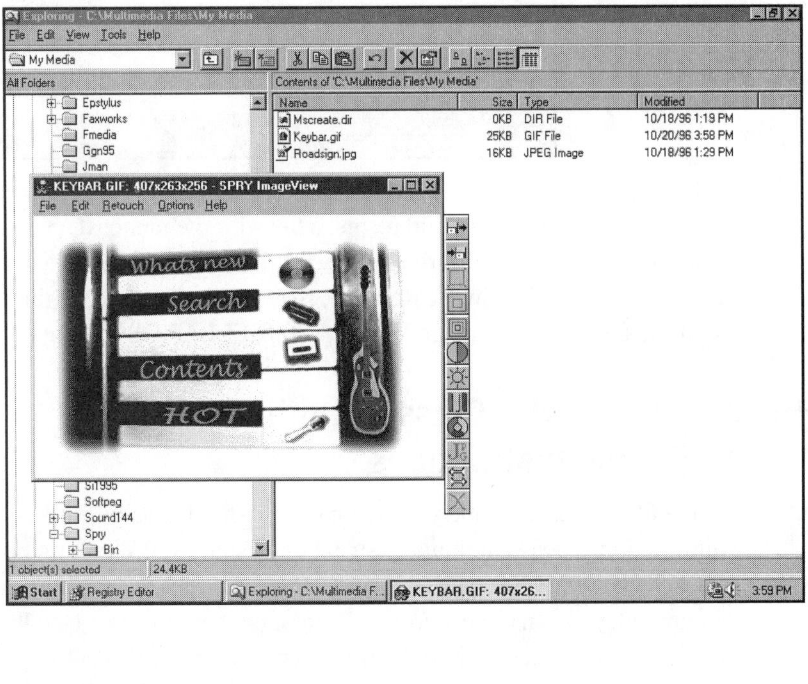

FIG. 6.6

A context-menu with new file types you can create.

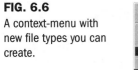

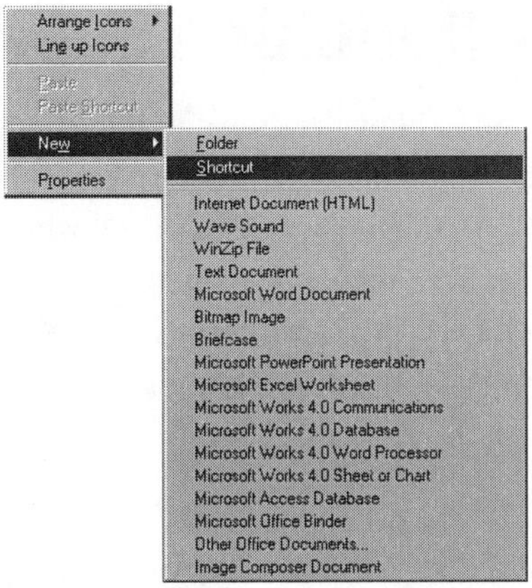

As shown in Figure 6.7, for instance, the .lnk file extension subkey contains a class-definition entry ("lnkfile") and a \ShellNew subkey. (Lnkfile file types are shortcut files.) Under the \ShellNew subkey is a Command value entry that instructs Windows what to do when a user clicks on the Shortcut selection on the desktop context menu. In this case, the Command value entry is "C:\Windows\rundll32.exe AppWiz.Cpl,NewLinkHere %1", which instructs Windows to launch the Create Shortcut wizard contained in the runddl32.exe file.

FIG. 6.7

The .lnk file extension subkey includes class-definition information and ShellNew information.

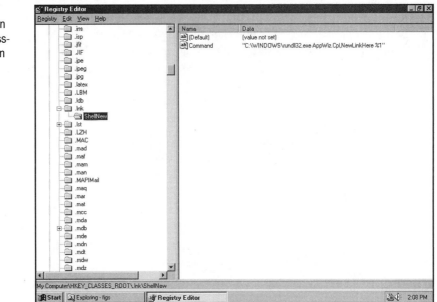

Part

I

Ch

6

Understanding Class-Definition Subkeys

You read earlier how class-definition subkeys are used to tell Windows how to handle files when they are encountered and the associated applications for the files. Class-definition subkeys also tell Windows the icon to display for that file and whether the Quick View application can be used for that file. The following sections describe how class-definition subkeys are used, how default icons are listed, and how Quick View settings are used.

How Class-Definition Subkeys Are Used

The reason Windows 95 and Windows NT use the format of providing a pointer from a file extension subkey to a class-definition subkey is to give the system some flexibility. Windows could easily store all the information about a file type, including its file extension and commands on how to handle the file, in one Registry subkey. By doing this, however, the Registry would be full of duplicate information when a single class-definition can handle two or more file extension types, or when a single application can handle multiple file types. A couple of examples can clarify this.

Because Windows now supports long file names, file extensions can be longer than three characters. Files with the extension .jpg and .jpeg are the same type of image file and can be handled by the same application. In the Registry, both .jpg and .jpeg file extension subkeys are present and have class-definition information pointing to jpegfile types. Figure 6.8 illustrates this point. In this situation, the same data file has more than one file extension; therefore, only one class-definition is needed. If the Registry did not support this type of pointing, both the .jpg and .jpeg subkeys would have to duplicate the information located in the jpegfile subkey, increasing the size of the Registry unnecessarily.

FIG. 6.8
Two different file extensions can point to the same class-definition subkey in the Registry.

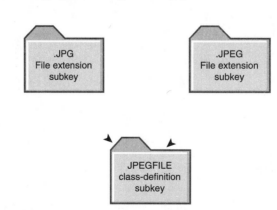

Another reason to enable this pointing is so that the same application can handle multiple file types. You can, for instance, display different types of files in a word processor, such as Word for Windows. Word can be set up to handle ASCII text files (TXT), document files (DOC), hypertext documents (HTM and HTML), document template files (DOT), and others. The Word application can assign each of these file extensions a single class-definition of WordDocument (for Word for Windows 2.0) or Word.Document.6 (for Word for Windows 95). When Windows needs to open these file types, it searches the Registry, finds the class-definition to point to Word, and displays the file in Word for Windows (see Figure 6.9). If you need to change the way Word handles files or if the path for Word changes, only one subkey needs to be modified instead of five different ones.

N O T E When you install Microsoft Office 97, new class-definitions for Office applications are used. For instance, in Word for Windows documents, the class-definition is Word.Document.8. ▨

N O T E When Windows is instructed to open a file, this does not always mean the same thing to different applications. One application, for instance, may display the file in the application window. This is the case for documents, image files, and so on. But Windows does not govern how these files are opened. The open command is used by the Windows ShellExecute function to look for application parameters in the HKEY_CLASSES_ROOT\class-def\shell\open\command subkey to see how the file should be handled. Then, the application takes over and handles the file as specified by the parameters listed in the preceding subkey. A file of type REG, for instance, is a registration file. When you double-click a REG file, the file does not launch the Registry Editor, which may be the action many think it would do. Instead, the contents of the REG file are merged or imported to the Registry database as a background task. ▨

FIG. 6.9
The Registry enables one application to handle multiple file types.

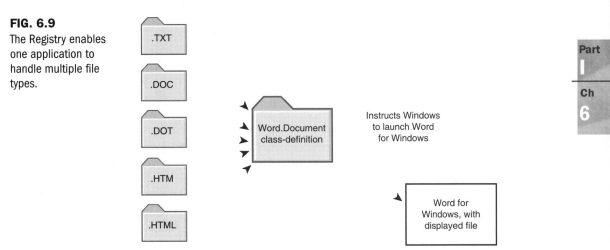

One downside to the way file types are handled by Windows is that multiple applications cannot display the same file type. In the preceding example, for instance, you may want to display small text files in Notepad, which is much quicker than Word for Windows, but large text files in Word, which can handle very large documents. Windows doesn't "think" like this. One way around this is to change the way in which Windows opens a file on a per-use method. To do this, use the following steps:

1. In Windows Explorer, click the file you want to open.

2. Hold down the Shift key and right-click the file.

3. Select Open With from the context menu.

4. From the Open With dialog box (see Figure 6.10), select the application you want to use to display the file. This is the same dialog box that displays when a file type is not registered in the Registry and you double-click it.

   The application you select must be one that can handle the file type selected. For instance, for a TXT file, select Notepad, WordPad, or a similar text editor. If, on the other hand, you try to open a GIF file in Notepad, the result is a bunch of ASCII characters or an error message (if the GIF file is larger than 64K in size) reporting that the selected application cannot read the file. In the case of Notepad, for instance, you are given the option of opening the file in WordPad, which in turn displays a bunch of ASCII characters.

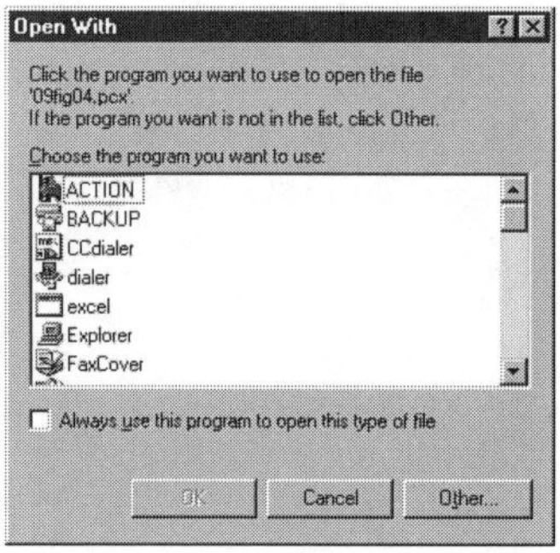

FIG. 6.10
You can select the program you want to open a file with in the Open With dialog box.

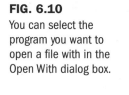

TIP If an application you want to use is not listed in the Open With dialog box, click the Other button and select the application from the Open With dialog box, as shown in Figure 6.11. Choose Open after you select the application. Using this method is handy if you want to use an application located on the network or CD-ROM.

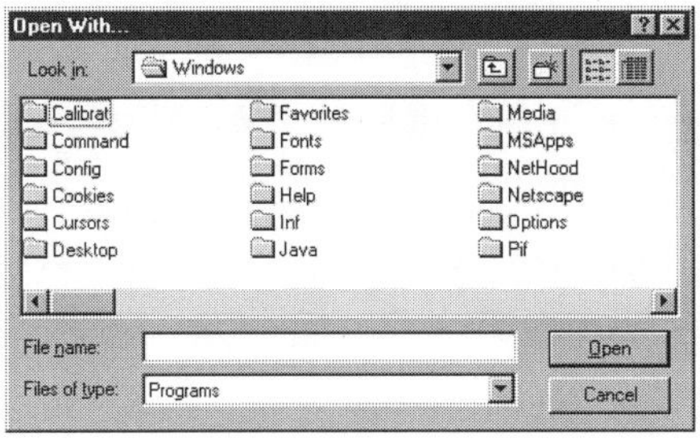

FIG. 6.11

Use the Open With dialog box to locate a program you want to use to open a selected file.

5. Click the Always Use This Program To Open This Type Of File check box only if you want Windows to always use this application to open this file type. When you choose this option, Windows modifies the class-definition subkey for the selected file type in the Registry to point to the new application. If you don't want to change the class-definition permanently, leave the check box cleared and Windows will use the selected application only for this instance. The next time you double-click the selected file, the original application is used to open it.

6. Click OK. Windows displays the selected file in the application you pick in step 4.

The applications that display in the Open With dialog box are all the ones that Windows finds when it enumerates the HKEY_CLASSES_ROOT\class-def \shell\open\command subkey. Because the \command subkey points to the actual executable file (such as IEXPLORER.EXE) for a program and not to its common name (such as Internet Explorer 3.0), the Open With dialog box displays program names that may be difficult to distinguish.

Some application developers do not want their applications to display in the Open With dialog box. To achieve this, the developers simply name the \open subkey something other than open. This is seen with a file that is of an unknown file type. File types that are not registered in the Registry use the HKEY_CLASSES_ROOT\Unknown subkey to direct how these files should be handled. Because it would be worthless to the user to have an entry called Unknown in the Open With dialog box, the \Unknown subkey has the subkey \shell\openas under it. The openas subkey still has instructions on how to handle files of unknown type (see the section "Understanding How the Registry Handles Unknown File Types" later in this chapter), but users are not given the option of selecting Unknown from the Open With dialog box. (In fact, if they did have this option, the Open With dialog box would display again, because that is the default instruction on how to handle unknown file types.)

Part

I

Ch

6

How Default File Type Icons Are Registered

Class-definition subkeys also list the default icons Windows should display. These icons are used by Windows in the following ways:

- As taskbar icons when you execute an application.
- As desktop icons when you add a link or shortcut to a file or application.
- As icons in the Windows Explorer.
- As icons on title bars in applications.
- As icons on the Start menu.

The Registry setting for icons in class-definition subkeys are found in the DefaultIcon subkey. You can see an example of this by locating the subkey for the registration files, as shown in Figure 6.12. In this example, the DefaultIcon subkey points to the file C:\Windows\regedit.exe,1, which instructs Windows to use the second icon in the REGEDIT.EXE file. If Windows is to use the first icon in a file, the number at the end of the value entry should be set to 0.

FIG. 6.12

The icon used by the Registry Editor is set by the DefaultIcon subkey.

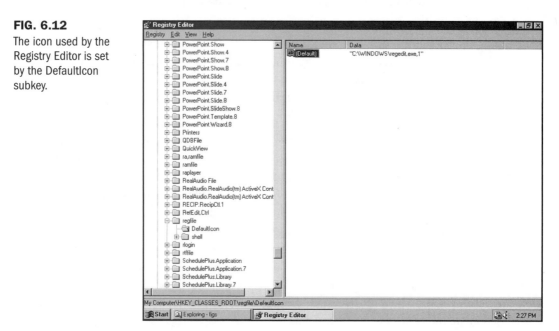

Windows can store the following four types of values in the DefaultIcon subkey:

- By specifying a path and filename of an executable file (EXE) or dynamic link library file (DLL) that contain icons. Along with the path, you need to specify the ordinal position of the icon you want to use, with the offset starting from zero.

So, if you want to specify the first icon in the file, use ordinal position 0, for the second icon in the file, use position 1, and so on. The example illustrated in the preceding paragraph is an example of specifying an icon in this manner.

■ By specifying a path and filename of an executable file or DLL that includes icons, a minus sign, and the resource identifier for the selected icon resource. To use this method, you must be able to extract the icon resource by using a tool such as Microsoft Developer Studio. An example of using this method is as follows

    C:\Windows\System\shell32.dll,-155

This is the default icon Windows uses to denote a font file. It uses the icon specified by resource ID 155 in the SHELL32.DLL file.

■ By specifying the path and filename of an image file that Windows can display as an icon. You can use any of the following types of files:

BMP	Bitmap image file
ICO	Icon image file
CUR	Cursor file
SCR	Screen save file
ANI	Animated cursor file
RLE	Windows run-length encoded bitmap

■ Including the string %1 to instruct Windows to use an icon handler to specify an icon for a specific file type. Files that are applications (EXE) use this method. This way, the same icon file is not used for all EXE files. Instead, Windows displays the icon specified in an application's IconHandler subkey if one exists. The IconHandler points to an icon in the application's EXE file. If an IconHandler subkey is not present for an application, then Windows uses the default icon handler for the SHELL32.DLL. This is also the method many applications use to display application-specific icons for desktop shortcuts.

N O T E   Icons in Windows 95 and Windows NT can be large (32x32 pixels) and small (16x16 pixels). For files you specify that are not sized to these settings, Windows automatically sizes the file to fit these specifications. In some cases, the image may not look that great, such as when you specify screen saver files and some BMP files. ■

How Quick View Settings Are Used

Windows 95 and Windows NT 4.0 include Quick View, a utility that enables you to view selected files without opening the application that created it. In Figure 6.13, for instance, a DOC document is displayed in Quick View instead of launching Word for Windows. This enables you to quickly read or view a file. When a file is configured to support Quick View, a menu item called Quick View displays on the context menu when you right-click a file.

FIG. 6.13
QuickView lets you read or view a file's contents without opening the application that created the file.

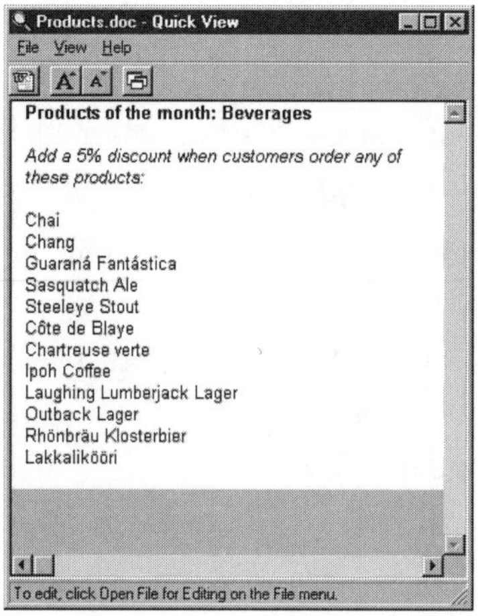

T I P You must specify during Windows Setup if you want Quick View installed. If it is not installed on your system, double-click the Add/Remove Programs icon in Control Panel, click the Windows NT (or Windows 95) Setup tab, and select the Accessories component. Click Details and select Quick View. Click OK twice for Windows to copy the Quick View files from your Setup disks or CD.

You can determine if a file type supports Quick View by looking under the HKEY_CLASSES_ROOT\QuickView subkey (see Figure 6.14). Listed in this subkey is the class definition of the file type (for example, Windows Bitmap Graphics File for BMP file type) and a subkey that lists the class identifier (CLSID) for the file viewer. (See "Understanding Class Identifiers (CLSID)" earlier in this chapter for more information on CLSIDs.)

By viewing the value entry for the file viewer (open the subkey with the long string name), you can find out the name of the viewer used. You can quickly tell which file types use the same Quick Viewer by expanding all the subkeys in the \QuickView subkey and scanning the CLSIDs for each file type and their value entries. In most cases, the CLSID is F0F08735-0C36-101B-B086-0020AF07D0F4 (see Figure 6.15) with a value entry of SCC Quick Viewer, which is the System Compatibility Corporation's Quick Viewer application included withWindows.

FIG. 6.14
The HKEY_CLASSES_ ROOT\QuickView subkey.

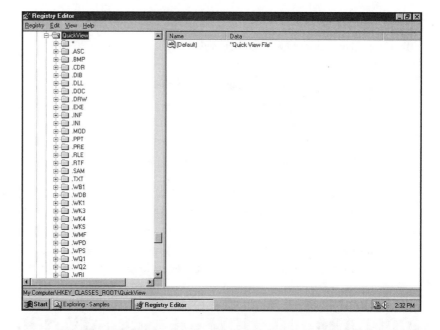

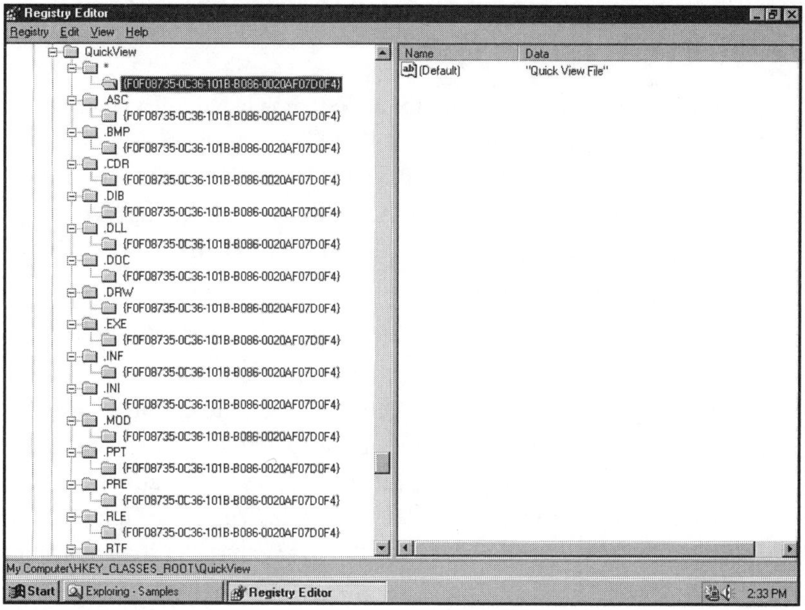

FIG. 6.15
The same CLSID and Quick Viewer application is used by most files that support Quick View.

Part

I

Ch

6

ON THE WEB

For a more advanced version of QuickView, you can download a 30-day evaluation copy of Quick View Plus from the World Wide Web at

http://www.inso.com/consumer/qvp/demo.htm

Quick View Plus enables you to access and view file types of over 200 applications, including databases, spreadsheets, and word processing files. The full version of Quick View Plus is also available from the Inso site for $49.00. Point your Web browser to

http://www.inso.com/consumer/qvp/order.htm

The HKEY_CLASSES_ROOT\QuickView\Shell subkey is used to instruct Windows on what to do when a user selects the Quick View command for a file. Windows looks in this subkey and enumerates the open\command entry. In many cases, the value entry for this subkey looks like C:\Windows\System\Viewers\quickview.exe, which tells Windows to execute the QUICKVIEW.EXE application found in your Windows\System\Viewers folder.

Understanding How the Registry Handles Unknown File Types

Sometimes you may encounter a file that is listed in Explorer as an unknown file type. This means that the file type for that file is not registered in the Registry. A common time for this to occur is when you download a file from the Internet that has a file type that has never been on your computer. Also, for applications that are being developed and are in the beta stage, they may have certain file types that have not been coded yet to specify file association information.

If you double-click a file of this type, Windows looks for a file extension subkey in the HKEY_CLASSES_ROOT subkey. If one is not found, Windows automatically skips to the HKEY_CLASSES_ROOT\Unknown class-definition subkey and looks in the \shell\openas\command subkey for instructions on how to handle files of unknown type (see Figure 6.16). By default, the value entry in this subkey is "C:\Windows\rundll32.exe shell32.dll,OpenAs_RunDLL %1", which instructs the Open With dialog box to display. From the Open With dialog box, the user can select the application to use to display the file.

TIP For application developers, it's always a good idea to register file types and what their default open behaviors should be. If this is not done, users may use the wrong application to open the file, causing their system or an application to become unstable.

FIG. 6.16
Windows finds out what to do with unknown file types by looking in the HKEY_CLASSES_ROOT\ Unknown\shell\ openas\command subkey.

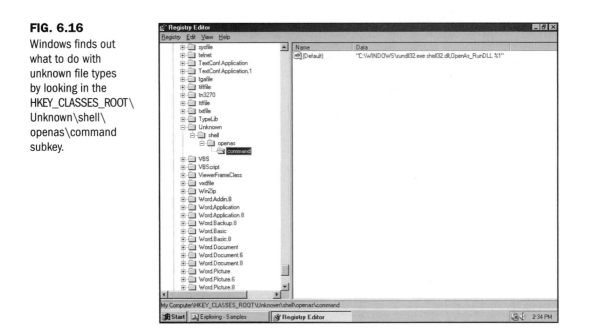

Understanding Context Menu Registry Entries

One of the most often used features of Windows 95 and Windows NT 4.0 is the right-click context menus. These menus display when you right-click a file and desktop, and change their content based on the file or resource you are clicking. For instance, if you right-click a file that supports Quick View, the Quick View menu option displays. For files that don't support Quick View, the context menu does not display this menu choice.

Another way the context menu changes is when application designers add options to the context menu based on the object you select. One common example of this is with the compression program, WinZip. When you install WinZip under Windows 95 or Windows NT 4.0, a menu option named Add to Zip is placed on the context menu (see Figure 6.17) when you select a file in the Windows Explorer.

Windows stores the information needed to control the context menus in the HKEY_CLASSES_ROOT subkey in the Registry. Windows uses the following types of context menu items:

Part

I

Ch

6

- *Static items.* These items are based on file associations and include options such as Open, Quick View, and Print.

- *Dynamic items.* These items change based on context menu handlers listed in the Registry. Context menu handlers are OLE in-process server entries that control which dynamic menu items are added to a context-menu. The Add to Zip item, for instance, is a dynamic menu item.

- *Program-defined items.* These items are maintained by the Windows Explorer and should not be modified. Some of the common menu options that fall in this category include Send To, Cut, Copy, Create Shortcut, Delete, Rename, and Properties.

The static and dynamic items are described in more detail in the following sections.

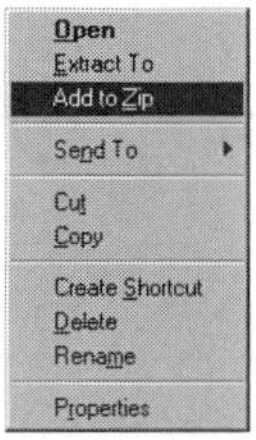

FIG. 6.17
WinZip adds an option to context menus.

Static Context Menu Items

To build the context menu, Windows first looks in the HKEY_CLASSES_ROOT*\shell subkey in the Registry to locate any static menu items. Normally, this subkey is not present, but can be added by the user or an application to list menu items that display regardless of the file type selected.

N O T E The * subkey is the first subkey in HKEY_CLASSES_ROOT. subkey and includes information on how Windows should handle default context menu items, as well as the properties dialog box. These settings affect all files. ▪

After Windows looks in this key, it searches within a specific file's class-definition subkey for the \shell subkey, such as shown in Figure 6.18. Here, files that have an extension of REG (registration files) include subkeys called \edit, \open, and \print. Windows knows how to handle default settings for several subkeys, including those shown in Table 6.1. These are known as canonical verbs (verbs are names of the subkeys listed in the shell subkey). For canonical verbs, if you do not change the value entry for these subkeys, Windows simply uses the name of these subkeys as the default menu option (see the Default Menu Option column in Table 6.1). In some cases, however, Windows does not automatically know what the option name should be. In the REG example, for instance, there is an edit subkey included, which is not a canonical verb. For this type of verb, there must be a value entry in the \edit subkey to list the menu option name. Here the entry is "&Edit" to specify that Windows should display an Edit menu option.

FIG. 6.18

Context menus gather menu items from the Registry, including the Merge, Print, and Edit menu options for the regfile file type.

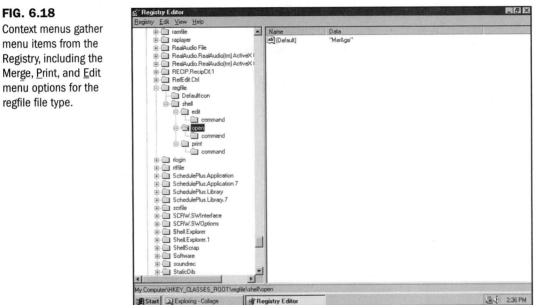

N O T E An ampersand (&) in a verb name, such as &Edit, indicates the accelerator key for that menu option. In the example shown in Figure 6.18, for instance, the "G" in Merge is shown as the accelerator key. ▩

Table 6.1	Canonical Verbs Windows Automatically Recognizes	
Name	**Default Menu Option**	**Description**
open	Open	Opens the selected file in an associated application or executes a program.
openas	Open With	Displays the Open With dialog box, enabling users to select an application in which to display the file.
print	Print	Sends the file to the default printer and prints the file.
find	Find	Enables the user to search for files using the Find dialog box.
explore	Explore	Displays files or objects within an Explorer window. You can see an example of this when you right-click a folder icon in Explorer or on the desktop.

Part

I

Ch

6

Another situation may occur when a canonical verb is changed to reflect a new menu name or a new action that the verb takes. In this case, files of regfile type do not use the open command like many other files. For a text file, for instance, the default open command can be used to instruct Windows to open the selected file in Notepad or another text editor. For REG files, however, these files must be merged or inserted directly into the Registry without any interaction from the user. To do this, Windows uses a value entry of "Mer&ge" in the \open subkey to indicate that a context menu item named Merge should appear when a file of type REG is right-clicked.

N O T E   When a user selects a static menu item from the context menu, Windows reads the information contained in the \command subkey for a specific option. For instance, if a user selects the Edit command for a REG file, Windows is instructed to launch Notepad and display the selected file. The value entry in this case is "C:\Windows\Notepad.exe %1". ■

When Windows finds all of the static menu options, it looks for all of the dynamic menu items, as discussed in the next section.

Dynamic Context Menu Items

After Windows locates the static menu options, it goes after the dynamic menu options, which are included in menu handler subkeys. As with static menu items, dynamic menu options are based on the type of file or object you right-click, but also are based on conditions of the operating system or application. An application, for instance, can be programmed to display a context menu for an application file (EXE) to ask the user if the file should be scanned for viruses. This menu option can be set up to display only for EXE, COM, and BAT files. Further, the application developer can program this menu item to display if certain conditions are met, such as if an archive bit is not set on the file.

Windows finds menu handler subkeys in the \shellex\ContextMenuHandlers subkey. A common application that many Windows users install is the Briefcase application. When a user clicks a file, there is an option to send the file to the Briefcase. The settings for this menu option are located in the HKEY_CURRENT_USER*\shellex\ContextMenuHandlers\BreifcaseMenu. Within the menu handler, there is a class ID for the DLL file that includes context menu handler information. Windows then locates the DLL name and location by searching the HKEY_CLASSES_ROOT\CLSID subkey based on the ID listed in the menu handler. The value for the DLL can be located in the \InProcServer32 subkey.

After dynamic menu items are added, Windows finishes populating the context menu with program-defined menu items. These are the menu items that appear below the first separator bar in a context menu.

Understanding Class Identifiers (CLSID)

In this chapter you've read a little about class identifiers (CLSIDs), but they haven't been discussed in detail yet. The CLSIDs section is probably the most daunting section of the HKEY_CLASSES_ROOT subkey. A CLSID subkey contains the class identifier for a file type. Every type of Windows OLE object has a unique class identifier, or CLSID, recorded in this section. The CLSIDs help Windows to organize various OLE objects, including DLLs, EXE file, Windows functions, and file types. Unfortunately, this section of HKEY_CLASSES_ROOT is organized into subkeys named after the class identifiers, which are not easily readable by humans—as you can see in Figure 6.19.

FIG. 6.19
The CLSID subkey is located in the HKEY_CLASSES_ROOT subkey.

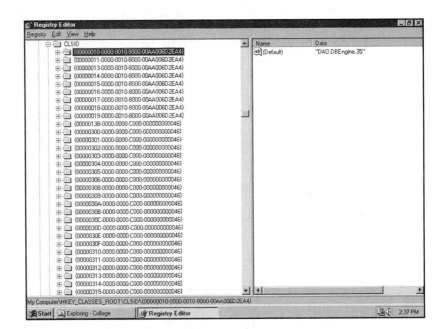

A CLSID consists of a long string of hexadecimal digits surrounded by curly brackets and separated by hyphens into a group of eight digits, three groups of four digits, and a group of twelve digits. In Figure 6.19, the CLSID {00000010-0000-0010-8000-00AA006D2EA4} is represented by the selected subkey, which bears the same incomprehensible name. To find a more readable equivalent of a CLSID, you need to select its subkey and note the string contained in the (Default) value entry. In this example, the name DAO.DBEngine.35 corresponds to the CLSID selected on the left.

N O T E CLSIDs are created by program developers when they write OLE programs. Because CLSIDs must be unique among all applications that reside on a specific computer, they must also be unique among all applications that might possibly be installed on the computer. Therefore, every Windows application must have a unique CLSID, or as it is technically called a globally unique identifier (GUID). This means that the CLSID needs to be generated by a random CLSID generator program, or a centrally established body who governs CLSIDs must hand out CLSIDs to programmers. Because the latter idea would dramatically slow down the process of writing a program (just imagine contacting Microsoft or someone else each time you want to write a new OLE application!), a generator program is used. Microsoft's GUIDGEN.EXE application bundled with Microsoft Visual C++ is one such program. It generates a very large number in hex code that, by statistics, no other application should ever have the same CLSIDs.

One or more subkeys are found under each CLSID entry. You shouldn't ever need to edit the entries here, unless you move critical DLL or EXE files to new folders. You can, however, use CLSID entries to discover more about the programs used to manage various object types.

The following are the most common subkeys found under the CLSID entries:

- *DefaultIcon.* Specifies the icon used for the CLSID's corresponding objects.
- *InprocHandler.* Points to an ObjectHandler, a DLL that works in conjunction with an EXE file to manage objects of the type defined by the CLSID.
- *InprocServer.* Contains a pointer to the object's In-Process Server, which is a DLL file that handles the type of object defined by that CLSID.
- *InprocServer32.* Indicates a 32-bit in-process server.
- *LocalServer.* Contains the path and file name of a server application, which is the EXE file that handles objects of the specified type.
- *ProgID.* Contains a human-readable identifier for the CLSID, generally the short name for the object type (such as "txtfile").
- *ShellEx.* Contains subkeys that define which DLLs and commands are used to call up the object's context menu or Properties dialog box.

Some of the preceding items have already been described in the context of previous discussions. The following sections describe the InprocServer32 and ProgID items.

InprocServer32 Subkey

InprocServer32 subkeys are created for 32-bit applications and are subkeys of a CLSID, such as those shown in Figure 6.20. (InprocServer subkeys are created for 16-bit applications.) InprocServer32 contains pointers to an object's in-process server, which is a dynamic link library that handles the object type. An example of this is the InprocServer32 subkey for the Windows Briefcase CLSID, which points to the XLREC.DLL file.

FIG. 6.20
InprocServer32 subkeys determine the server for an OLE object, as well as the server's threading model.

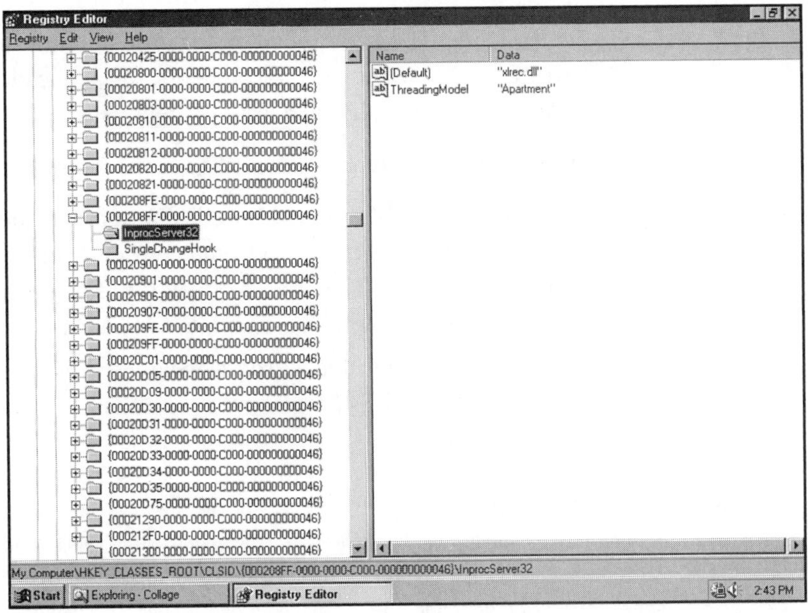

For in-process servers that are multithreaded, the InprocServer32 subkey also contains information about the server's multithreading model. The value entry for this setting is named ThreadingModel. The ThreadingModel value entry can contain the following values:

- *Apartment.* Specifies that the *apartment threading model* is used. This type of threading dictates that every object created by an OLE server can exist in only one thread, or apartment. Under this type of threading, multiple objects can be created, and each thread with an object has a unique message queue.

- *Both.* Specifies that the OLE server supports two types of threading models— apartment threading and free-threading. Free-threading is when a Common Object Model (COM) object can be accessed from multiple threads of a single process.

ProgID Subkey

ProgID subkeys in CLSIDs subkeys are an OLE component's programmatic identifier. These identifiers enable programs and other objects to refer to the object in an alternative way to CLSIDs. In most cases, the ProgID is much more human-readable than the long

Part

I

Ch

6

hexadecimal entries of class IDs. An example of a ProgID entry for the Microsoft Binder object, for example, is Office.Binder.8. Compare this to the CLSID for the same object, which is {59850400-6664-101B-B21C-00AA004BA90B}. Which one would you rather read?

ProgIDs are similar to identifiers located in the class-definition subkey for a file type. For file types that are both OLE servers and OLE clients, the application developer may even use the same names for the ProgIDs and class-definitions.

ProgIDs come in two flavors, which are described in the following list:

- *Version-independent.* Specifies that a ProgID does not include version identification. This makes it easier to port an object from one version of a macro language or application to a newer one. The basic syntax for version-independent ProgIDs is VendorName.ComponentName, such as MSMAPI.MAPIMessages.

- *Version-dependent.* Specifies that a ProgID includes version identification. The basic syntax for version-dependent ProgIDs is VendorName.ComponentName.Version, such as Office.Binder.8.

N O T E For situations in which both a version-dependent and version-independent ProgID are included, a subkey called CurVer is usually added to the version-independent subkey. The CurVer subkey denotes the mapping for a version-dependent ProgID. Also, the version-independent and version-dependent ProgIDs should have CLSID subkeys that list the CLSID of the OLE object application.

One use of the ProgID setting is when an application requires that a user selects an OLE object from a dialog box. In the case of Microsoft Office applications, for instance, a user can select a Microsoft WordArt 2.0 object as an object to embed in a document. When the user selects the Insert, Object command in Word, for instance, the Object dialog box appears (see Figure 6.21). Instead of the user seeing the ProgID for a WordArt object (MSWordArt.2), the user sees Microsoft WordArt 2.0, which is the value listed as the value entry in the CLSID subkey.

Common CLSIDs

When you install Windows and many of its components, several common CLSIDs are placed in the Registry. In addition, as you install applications under Windows that support OLE, those CLSIDs are added as well. A new installation of Windows NT Workstation 4.0, for instance, may have over 100 different CLSID Registry entries even before you start installing applications. To manually locate a specific CLSID for a specific application may take some time. In particular, in the Windows NT 4.0 Registry Editor, you do not have a search function that enables you to search on values or data, which you have with the Windows 95 Registry Editor.

FIG. 6.21
OLE objects that users can select from dialog boxes usually have ProgID settings in the Registry.

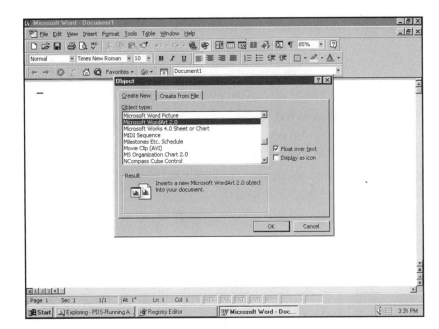

Table 6.2 lists several common CLSIDs that appear in the Registry.

Table 6.2 Common CLSIDs

Class ID	Object Name
{FC25B780-75BE-11CF-8B01-444553540000}	Internet Chart Object (ActiveX Control)
{FBF23B40-E3F0-101B-8488-00AA003E56F8}	Internet Shortcut
{08B0E5C0-4FCB-11CF-AAA5-00401C608501}	Java Control
{f414c260-6ac0-11cf-b6d1-00aa00bbbb58}	JavaScript Language
{11943940-36DE-11CF-953E-00C0A84029E9}	JPEG Image file
{f414c260-6ac0-11cf-b6d1-00aa00bbbb58}	LiveScript Language
{8CC49940-3146-11CF-97A1-00AA00424A9F}	Microsoft Access 97
{2B32FBC2-A8F1-11CF-93EE-00AA00C08FDF}	Microsoft ActiveX HotSpot Control 1.0
{06DD38D3-D187-11CF-A80D-00C04FD74AD8}	Microsoft ActiveX Plug-in
{00022602-0000-0000-C000-000000000046}	Microsoft AVI file
{85BBD920-42A0-1069-A2E4-08002B30309D}	Microsoft Briefcase
{166B1BCA-3F9C-11CF-8075-444553540000}	Macromedia Director Movie

Part
I

Ch
6

{00030035-0000-0000-C000-000000000046}	Micrografx Draw
{00024500-0000-0000-C000-000000000046}	Microsoft Excel 97
{00020820-0000-0000-C000-000000000046}	Microsoft Excel Add-In
{02B01C80-E03D-101A-B294-00DD010F2BF9}	Microsoft Fax Viewer
{5220cb21-c88d-11cf-b347-00aa00a28331}	Microsoft Licensed Class Manager 1.0
{00030027-0000-0000-C000-000000000046}	Microsoft Project
{0482E074-C5B7-101A-82E0-08002B36A333}	Microsoft Schedule+
{000209FF-0000-0000-C000-000000000046}	Microsoft Word
{00022601-0000-0000-C000-000000000046}	MPEG File
{0004A3C8-0000-0000-C000-000000000046}	Netscape Hypertext document
{00021401-0000-0000-C000-000000000046}	Shortcut Linkfile
{B54F3741-5B07-11cf-A4B0-00AA004A55E8}	VBScript
{73FDDC80-AEA9-101A-98A7-00AA00374959}	WordPad document

N O T E Another common way to amass CLSID entries is to hit World Wide Web sites that support ActiveX controls. Because ActiveX controls are just COM objects (with a lot of Microsoft marketing engineering behind them), they are registered each time you download one to your computer. ▨

Customizing and Troubleshooting with the Registry

Customizing Your Windows Desktop

by Jerry Honeycutt

The Windows 95 and NT Registries offer many different ways to customize and personalize your desktop. You can add actions to context menus, for example. You can make your Start menu pop up faster. You can change the names of all those desktop icons. You can change the icons that Explorer uses. You can even tell Explorer to use a BMP file's image as its Explorer icon. The list goes on and on.

Don't panic. The tips in this chapter are safe for you to try. You're not likely to break your computer if you follow the instructions closely. Regardless, don't forget to backup the Registry before you begin. Try one of the easy-to-use methods you learned about in Chapter 1, "Before You Begin." If nothing else, save the branch of the Registry on which you're working by exporting it to a REG file. You learned about this technique in Chapter 3, "Using REGEDIT with Windows 95 and NT 4.0." ■

Customize Windows using the Registry

This chapter shows you how to customize your Windows desktop just the way you want it—using the Registry, of course.

Experiment with the Registry

Don't find a tip you like in this chapter? Want to find your own customization tips? This chapter shows you tricks you can use to do just that.

Find more Registry tips online

You can find countless other Registry tips and tricks on the Internet. This chapter shows you where to look and how to search for them.

NOTE In most cases, the tips and tricks in this chapter work equally well for Windows 95 and NT. You will be informed of those instances where a tip is specific to one or the other. ■

Customizing Windows Using the Registry

Each of the sections that follow describes a single customization; in most cases, you'll find step-by-step instructions. The customizations in this section are also easy to do. The only thing you need is the Registry Editor and a bit of nerve. If you follow the instructions closely, however, you'll have no problems.

Most Windows NT users won't have any problem following the instructions in this chapter. That is, if you log on to a workstation with administrator privileges (most likely if you're using NT Workstation), you can change all of the settings described in this chapter. If you find that you can't change some Registry settings, however, see Chapter 12, "Securing the Windows Registry" to learn more about Registry security.

ON THE WEB

http://www.creativelement.com/win95ann/   The Windows 95 Annoyances Web page contains many of the customizations in this chapter. You'll also find tips that don't involve editing the Registry. Although the tips you find on this Web site are specific to Windows 95, many of them work equally well for Windows NT.

TIP You can use Microsoft PowerToy's Tweak UI (user interface) utility to change many of the settings described in this chapter. See Chapter 10, "Free and Shareware Software to Customize Windows," for more information.

Adding Actions to the Context Menus

If you have more than one program that accesses the same type of file, you'll want to add an action to the file extension's context menu that allows you to choose between both programs. This gives you two options for opening a file: open with program A and open with program B, for example.

Why? Take a look at DOC files. When you install Windows, it associates WordPad with DOC files. WordPad is a fast editor that is file-compatible with Microsoft Word. The trouble begins when you install Microsoft Word. It associates DOC files with itself—leaving you without a convenient way to open a DOC file in WordPad.

Fortunately, you can add a new action to the DOC file's context menu that allows you to open DOC files with WordPad, too. Just follow these steps:

1. Open the Registry Editor and find HKEY_CLASSES_ROOT\Word.Document.6\shell.

2. Add the subkey \Open with Wordpad, and add the subkey \command under \Open with Wordpad so that you've added the new branch \Open with Wordpad\command.

3. Set the default value entry for \Open with Wordpad\command to **C:\Program Files\Accessories\WordPad.exe "%1"**.

4. Close the Registry Editor.

N O T E The quotes around the %1 in the command line tell Windows 95 to put the file name inside of quotes. It's frequently called a *placeholder*. If you don't put "%1" in the command line and you select a long file name with spaces in it, WordPad won't be able to open the file. ▪

Now you can open DOC files with either Microsoft Word or WordPad. Double-click a DOC file to open it in Word. Right-click a DOC file and choose Open With WordPad to open it in WordPad (see Figure 7.1).

FIG. 7.1
Right-click a file to open its context menu, or, if you're mouse-phobic, highlight the file and press Shift+F10.

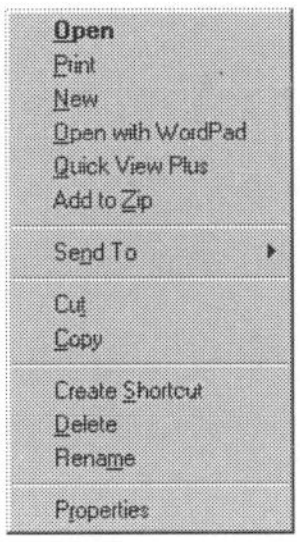

▶ **See** "Understanding Context Menu Registry Entries," **p. 113**

Add Environment Variables to the NT Registry

Environment variables let you specify settings for other programs to use. You're probably accustomed to using them in your AUTOEXEC.BAT file. The TEMP and TMP environment variables are pretty typical, for example. These contain paths that tell Windows and all other programs where to store temporary files.

In Windows NT (not Windows 95), you don't have to put your environment variables in AUTOEXEC.BAT. You can add them to the Windows NT Registry, too, in HKEY_CURRENT_USER\Environment. Each value entry corresponds to a single environment variable. The name of the value entry is the name of the environment variables and its string content represents the environment variable's value. You can add a subkey

Part II
Ch 7

called HKEY_CURRENT_USER\Environment\TEMP and set its value to **C:\TEMP** to have all Windows NT programs store their temporary files in c:\TEMP, for example.

T I P   You can also add environment variables using Windows NT's System icon in the Control Panel.

Adding Sounds for Application Events

In Windows 3.1, you can customize the sounds associated with different application events. In Windows 95 and NT, you can also add new events for different programs by doing the following:

1. Open the Registry Editor and find HKEY_CURRENT_USER\AppEvents\ Schemes\Apps.

2. Create a new subkey with the same name as the program.

3. Create new subkeys under the program's subkey for each event, such as Open and Close.

4. Close the Registry Editor.

 5. Double-click the Sounds icon in the Control Panel. Your new application shows up in the list. Change the sounds associated with each event.

Automatically Log on to NT Workstation

Do you ever tire of typing your user name and password every time you start Windows NT? You can tell Windows NT to automatically log you on. Here's how:

1. Open the Registry Editor, and find HKEY_LOCAL_MACHINE\SOFTWARE\ Microsoft\Windows NT\CurrentVersion\winLogon.

2. Add a new string value entry called AutoAdminLogon, and set its value to **1**.

3. Add a new string value entry called DefaultPassword, and set its value to the password of the user shown in DefaultUserName.

4. Close the Registry Editor.

> **CAUTION**
>
> Is your Windows NT 4.0 computer connected to a network? If so, think twice before customizing NT as described in this section. Customizing NT so that it automatically logs you on can cause a serious security hole in the network, which your network administrator will not like.

Changing Internet Explorer's Default Protocol

If you type a URL in Internet Explorer's toolbar, it automatically prefixes it with the appropriate protocol. If you type **www.microsoft.com**, for example, Internet Explorer changes it to **http://www.microsoft.com**. If you type **ftp.microsoft.com**, Internet Explorer changes it to **ftp://ftp.microsoft.com**. Notice that it chooses the protocol based upon how the URL begins.

But what happens when you type **rampages.onramp.net/~jerry**? By default, Internet Explorer is going to assume it's a Web page and add http:// to the beginning of it. If this isn't the behavior you want, you can specify a different prefix by following these steps:

1. Open the Registry Editor and find HKEY_LOCAL_MACHINE\SOFTWARE\ Microsoft\Windows\CurrentVersion\URL\DefaultPrefix.

2. Change the default value entry to the prefix you want Internet Explorer to use if it can't figure out what type of address you typed—for example, **ftp://**.

3. Close the Registry Editor.

Changing the Desktop Icons

You're not stuck with the icons or names that Windows 95 and NT uses for the special desktop icons (My Computer, Recycle Bin, and so on). You can change them all. Just do the following:

1. Open the Registry Editor and find HKEY_CLASSES_ROOT\CLSID.

2. Look up the icon you want to change in the following table. Then find the subkey for the icon under HKEY_CLASSES_ROOT\CLSID.

Icon Name	Subkey
Briefcase	{85BBD920-42A0-1069-A2E4-08002B30309D}
Control Panel	{21EC2020-3AEA-1069-A2DD-08002B30309D}
Dial-Up Networking	{992CFFA0-F557-101A-88EC-00DD010CCC48}
Inbox	{00020D75-0000-0000-C000-000000000046}
My Computer	{20D04FE0-3AEA-1069-A2D8-08002B30309D}
Network Neighborhood	{208D2C60-3AEA-1069-A2D7-08002B30309D}
Printers	{2227A280-3AEA-1069-A2DE-08002B30309D}
Recycle Bin	{645FF040-5081-101B-9F08-00AA002F954E}
The Internet	{FBF23B42-E3F0-101B-8488-00AA003E56F8}
The Microsoft Network	{00028B00-0000-0000-C000-000000000046}

Part

II

Ch

7

3. Change the default value entry to the name that you want displayed on the desktop. Change "Recycle Bin" to "Garbage," for example.

4. Open the DefaultIcon subkey, and change the default value entry to the path of the icon file and the index of the icon. If you want to use the fourth icon (0, 1, 2, 3) in SHELL32.DLL, for example, type **C:\Windows\System\Shell32.dll,3**. You can get icons from DLL, EXE, ICO, and other files.

5. Close the Registry Editor.

N O T E Most EXE and DLL files have icons in them. You'll find some DLLs that have a large number of useful icons—such as MORICONS.DLL, COOL.DLL, PIFMGR.DLL, PROGMAN.DLL, and SHELL32.DLL—in your \Windows or \Windows\System folder. Windows NT users should look in C:\WINNT, C:\WINNT\System, and C:\WINNT\System32 for these and other files that contain useful icons.

▶ **See** "How Default File Type Icons Are Registered," **p. 108** ◼

Changing the NT Logon Screen's Bitmap

The bitmap that Windows NT displays during the Ctrl+Alt+Del logon screen is sharp. I like it; you might not. You might want to display your company's logo or family portrait, instead. You can change this bitmap in the Registry by following these steps:

1. Open the Registry Editor, and find HKEY_LOCAL_MACHINE\.DEFAULT\Control Panel\Desktop.

2. Change the Wallpaper string value entry so that it contains the path and filename of the bitmap that you want to display on the logon screen.

3. Close the Registry Editor.

Changing the Location of System Folders

Have you ever tried to move the \ShellNew folder to a new location? How about Microsoft Word's \My Documents folder? You can't, unless you do it through the Registry. Try this: delete the \Recent folder from the Windows folder. Think it's gone? Nope. Windows will create it again. Windows keeps a list of shell folders in the Registry. This is how it knows where to find things such as your Start menu, desktop shortcuts, and recent documents.

You'll find these shell folders at HKEY_CURRENT_USER\SOFTWARE\Microsoft\ Windows\CurrentVersion\Explorer\Shell Folders. Table 7.1 shows you the value entries you'll find by default in Windows 95, and Table 7.2 shows you the value entries you'll find by default in Windows NT. Note that, in Windows NT, some entries point to C:\WINNT\Profiles. Each user that logs on to the workstation has their own folder under this path. My desktop would be stored in C:\WINNT\Profiles\Jerry, for example. In these cases, you'll notice that I've used a placeholder for the user's name that looks like *Username*. Substitute your own user name for *Username*. I've also included the entries that Microsoft Office adds.

Table 7.1 Default Shell Folders in Windows 95

Value Entry	Default
Desktop	C:\WINDOWS\Desktop
Favorites	C:\WINDOWS\Favorites
Fonts	C:\WINDOWS\Fonts
NetHood	C:\WINDOWS\NetHood
Personal	C:\My Documents
Programs	C:\WINDOWS\Start Menu\Programs
Recent	C:\WINDOWS\Recent
SendTo	C:\WINDOWS\SendTo
Start Menu	C:\WINDOWS\Start Menu
Startup	C:\WINDOWS\Start Menu\Programs\Startup
Templates	C:\WINDOWS\ShellNew

Table 7.2 Default Shell Folders in Windows NT

Value Entry	Default
AppData	C:\WINNT\Profiles*Username*\Application Data
Common Desktop	C:\WINNT\Profiles\All Users\Desktop
Common Programs	C:\WINNT\Profiles\All Users\Start Menu\Programs
Common Start Menu	C:\WINNT\Profiles\All Users\Start Menu
Desktop	C:\WINNT\Profiles*Username*\Desktop
Favorites	C:\WINNT\Profiles*Username*\Favorites
Fonts	C:\WINNT\Fonts
NetHood	C:\WINNT\Profiles*Username*\NetHood
Personal	C:\WINNT\Profiles*Username*\Personal
Programs	C:\WINNT\Profiles*Username*\Start Menu\Programs

Part

II

Ch

7

continues

Table 7.2 Continued	
Value Entry	**Default**
Recent	C:\WINNT\Profiles*Username*\Recent
SendTo	C:\WINNT\Profiles*Username*\Sendto
Start Menu	C:\WINNT\Profiles*Username*\Start Menu
Startup	C:\WINNT\Profiles*Username*\Start Menu\Programs\Startup
Templates	C:\WINNT\Profiles*Username*\ShellNew

Creating Your Own Tips

When you first installed Windows, it proudly presented the Welcome dialog box showing you a tip. You probably deselected Show This Welcome Screen Next Time You Start Windows right off the bat—didn't you?

Why don't you turn it on again and let Windows present tips of your own making? You can add the tips you find in this book, motivational tips from your favorite self-help book, or whatever by following these steps:

1. Open the Registry Editor and find HKEY_LOCAL_MACHINE\SOFTWARE\ Microsoft\Windows\CurrentVersion\Explorer\Tips. The tips are stored as string value entries with names ranging from 0 to 47.

2. Choose Edit, New, String Value from the main menu, and name the new value entry with the next number available in the key.

3. Double-click the entry, type the text you want to display as the tip, and click OK.

4. Close the Registry Editor.

Display a Custom Message During NT Logon

If your organization has certain policies that you want your users to know about, you can have Windows NT display those policies in a text box that they have to confirm when they log on to the workstation. You might want all your users to acknowledge an "acceptable usage policy," for example, that precludes them from visiting certain Web sites on the Internet. The user can't log on to the workstation without acknowledging that they read and understood the message. It's kind of like those shrink-wrapped software packages that have a notice which says "opening this package acknowledges that you don't have any rights at all."

Here's how to set both the caption for the text box and the message that Windows NT displays in the text box:

1. Open the Registry Editor, and find HKEY_LOCAL_MACHINE\SOFTWARE\ Microsoft\Windows NT\CurrentVersion\Winlogon.

2. Add a new string value entry called LegalNoticeCaption, and set its value to the string of characters you want Windows NT to display in the title bar of the text box.

3. Add a new string value entry called LegalNoticeText, and set its value to the string of characters you want Windows NT to display in the body of the text box.

4. Close the Registry Editor.

Expanding Your Icon Cache

The icons that Windows displays in the folder view, Start menu, and Explorer are stored in C:\Windows\ShellIconCache for Windows 95 user and C:\WINNT\ShellIconCache for Windows NT user. Doing so speeds up the process of displaying icons for files because they can be grabbed out of the cache, instead of loaded from the programs responsible for the icons.

The icon cache is limited to 512 icons. If you fill up the cache, it is destroyed and re-created from scratch. When this happens, you'll notice that your desktop clears and Windows 95 redraws each of the icons—really annoying.

Thankfully, you can raise the limit from 512 icons to a much larger number by doing the following:

1. Open the Registry Editor, and find HKEY_LOCAL_MACHINE\SOFTWARE\ Microsoft\Windows\CurrentVersion\Explorer.

2. Add a new string value entry called Max Cached Icons and set its value to **4000**.

3. Close the Registry Editor.

Ignoring Changes to Your Desktop

Each time you shut down Windows, it remembers the position of all the desktop icons, the taskbar, and any open Explorer windows. If you put Explorer in your StartUp program menu and forget to close Explorer before shutting down Windows, you'll have two copies of Explorer on your desktop when you restart Windows—the copy you loaded in the StartUp program menu and the copy that you left on your desktop when you shut down Windows.

Part

II

Ch

7

If you'd like Windows's memory to be a bit less permanent, follow these steps:

1. Arrange your desktop just the way you want it, and restart your computer.

2. Open the Registry Editor and find HKEY_CURRENT_USER\SOFTWARE\ Microsoft\Windows\CurrentVersion\Policies\Explorer.

3. Set the value of NoSaveSettings to **1**. If you don't see a value entry called NoSaveSettings, add it.

4. Close the Registry Editor.

Now your desktop will look the same every time you start Windows—even if you've messed around with it. Also, if you put Explorer in your Startup group and forget to close it before you restart Windows, you won't have two copies of Explorer running after Windows restarts.

Nuking the Annoying Windows Animation

When you minimize, maximize, or restore a window, Windows uses animation to show you where it's going. If you have a slower computer, the animation can rob you of that crisp feeling you get when a window pops open or disappears from the screen. Here's how you can turn off the window animation:

1. Open the Registry Editor and find HKEY_CURRENT_USER\Control Panel\ Desktop\WindowMetrics.

2. Change the value entry called MinAnimate to **0**.

3. Close the Registry Editor. This change won't take effect until restart your computer.

Launching Explorer from My Computer

There are many different ways to get to Explorer. You can launch it from the Start menu. You can right-click My Computer and choose <u>E</u>xplore. You can even double-click My Computer while you hold down the Shift key. So why can't you launch Explorer just by double-clicking My Computer? Well, you can. Here's how to set it up:

1. Open the Registry Editor and find HKEY_CLASSES_ROOT\CLSID\{20D04FE0-3AEA-1069-A2D8-08002B30309D}\shell.

2. Set the default value entry for this key to **explore**.

3. Add the subkey \explore, and add the subkey \command under \explore so that you've added the branch called \explore\command.

4. Set the default value entry for your new \explore\command to **explorer.exe**.

5. Close the Registry Editor.

Now when you double-click My Computer, Windows loads Explorer instead of opening the folder view.

> **N O T E** You'll have two entries in My Computer's context menu that say Explore, but this isn't harmful. The first entry is an action that Windows puts in My Computer's context menu—you won't find it in the Registry, and you can't get rid of it. The second entry is the one you added in the previous steps. ▨

Locating Windows NT's Registry Hives

Windows NT stores the location of each Registry hive in HKEY_LOCAL_MACHINE\ SYSTEM\CurrentControlSet\Control\hivelist. Here are the hives you'll find by default:

> \\REGISTRY\\MACHINE\HARDWARE
>
> \\REGISTRY\\MACHINE\SECURITY
>
> \\REGISTRY\\MACHINE\SOFTWARE
>
> \\REGISTRY\\MACHINE\SYSTEM
>
> \\REGISTRY\\USER\\.DEFAULT
>
> \\REGISTRY\\MACHINE\\SAM
>
> \\REGISTRY\\USER\SID_#

▶ **See** "What's in a Hive," **p. 49**

Making the Control Panel More Accessible

When you choose <u>S</u>ettings, <u>C</u>ontrol Panel from the Start menu, Windows opens a folder with all the Control Panel icons. But what if you don't want a folder? Wouldn't it be better if you could open a submenu on your Start menu that contains all the Control Panel icons? You can, and here's how:

1. Right-click the Start button, and choose <u>O</u>pen.
2. Create a new folder and rename it **Control Panel.{21EC2020-3AEA-1069-A2DD-08002B30309D}**.

Now when you choose Control Panel from the Start menu, it opens another submenu rather than opening a folder (see Figure 7.2).

> **N O T E** In reality, you can type anything you want before the period. Make sure that you type everything after the period exactly as shown in step 2, however. If you've typed the wrong number, you'll see a regular folder icon in the Start menu instead of the Control Panel icon. ▨

Part

II

Ch

7

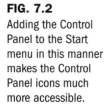

FIG. 7.2

Adding the Control Panel to the Start menu in this manner makes the Control Panel icons much more accessible.

You're not limited to the Control Panel. You can add any of the icons described in the following list (other icons, such as The Microsoft Network, are very useful). Replace the name in step 2 with one of the names from the list.

Folder name

Control Panel.{21EC2020-3AEA-1069-A2DD-08002B30309D}

Dial-Up Networking.{992CFFA0-F557-101A-88EC-00DD010CCC48}

Printers.{2227A280-3AEA-1069-A2DE-08002B30309D}

Recycle Bin.{645FF040-5081-101B-9F08-00AA002F954E}

Making the Start Menu Snappier

Have you ever noticed the slight delay when you choose a submenu on the Start menu? Many folks think this is annoying. You can eliminate the delay by performing these steps:

1. Open the Registry Editor and find HKEY_CURRENT_USER\Control Panel \Desktop.

2. Change the value of MenuShowDelay to a smaller number (the default is 400) to make the menus open faster. You can even set this value entry to 0. Note that you may have to add this string value entry to the subkey.

3. Close the Registry Editor. This change won't take effect until you restart Windows 95.

Slow Menu Speed?

One of the biggest complaints I've heard about Windows is how long it takes menus to pop up after you've clicked them. In fact, many people have posted this tip on the Internet as a "performance improvement" for Windows.

The delay is there for a purpose, however. It reduces the frustration level of folks who are far less proficient with the mouse than you and I. The delay makes sure that Windows doesn't change submenus if the user accidentally lets the mouse wander off the menu item for a second.

Imagine a new user without the delay. As they nervously take aim at a menu item, Windows pops up the submenu. If they briefly point to a different menu item, Windows closes the first submenu and opens the second. This user just might toss their computer out of the window after spending 15 minutes watching menus fluttering all over their screen.

Refreshing Your Desktop Automatically

When you add a new folder or file to an existing folder, you sometimes have to refresh Explorer to see the changes. To make Explorer and your desktop refresh themselves when there is a change, follow these steps:

1. Open the Registry Editor, and find HKEY_LOCAL_MACHINE\System\ CurrentControlSet\Control\Update.

2. Change the UpdateMode value entry to **00**.

3. Close the Registry Editor. This change won't take effect until you restart Windows.

Removing the Arrow from Shortcuts

Windows displays a little arrow in the bottom-left corner of shortcut icons. If you don't like this arrow, you can remove it entirely by doing the following (your shortcuts still work, though):

1. Open the Registry Editor, find HKEY_CLASSES_ROOT\lnkfile, and remove the IsShortcut value entry.

2. Find HKEY_CLASSES_ROOT\piffile, and remove the IsShortcut value entry.

3. Close the Registry Editor.

CAUTION

On some systems, removing the IsShortcut value entry causes Windows 95 to behave erratically.

Part

II

Ch

7

Removing the Special Icons from the Desktop

Just because you're using Dial-Up Networking to access the Internet doesn't mean you want the Network Neighborhood icon on your desktop. Likewise, you may care nothing about the Microsoft Network icon on your desktop. You can get rid of any of these icons by following these steps:

1. Open the Registry Editor and find HKEY_LOCAL_MACHINE\SOFTWARE\ Microsoft\Windows\CurrentVersion\Explorer\Desktop\NameSpace.

2. Delete the subkeys that represent the icons you want to remove from your desktop. Refer to the following table to see what each value represents.

Icon Name	Subkey
Briefcase	{85BBD920-42A0-1069-A2E4-08002B30309D}
Control Panel	{21EC2020-3AEA-1069-A2DD-08002B30309D}
Dial-Up Networking	{992CFFA0-F557-101A-88EC-00DD010CCC48}
Inbox	{00020D75-0000-0000-C000-000000000046}
My Computer Network	{20D04FE0-3AEA-1069-A2D8-08002B30309D}
Neighborhood	{208D2C60-3AEA-1069-A2D7-08002B30309D}
Printers	{2227A280-3AEA-1069-A2DE-08002B30309D}
Recycle Bin	{645FF040-5081-101B-9F08-00AA002F954E}
The Internet	{FBF23B42-E3F0-101B-8488-00AA003E56F8}
The Microsoft Network	{00028B00-0000-0000-C000-000000000046}
Inbox	{00020D75-0000-0000-C000-000000000046}
Recycle Bin	{645FF040-5081-101B-9F08-00AA002F954E}

3. Close the Registry Editor.

N O T E Windows insists that some icons appear on your desktop. You can't get rid of My Computer, for example, no matter how hard you try.

▶ **See** "Understanding Class Identifiers (CLSID)," **p. 117** ■

Using a Bitmap's Image for Its Icon

If you have a large collection of bitmaps, you may have to open a lot of pictures before you find the image you're looking for. Windows allows you to use the bitmap's actual image as its icon. To do so, follow these steps:

1. Open the Registry Editor and find HKEY_CLASSES_ROOT\
   Paint.Picture\DefaultIcon.
2. Change the default value entry to **%1**.
3. Close the Registry Editor.

T I P The icons are easier to see if you choose <u>V</u>iew, Lar<u>g</u>e Icons from Explorer's main menu.

It takes much longer to display a list of bitmaps in an Explorer window this way, because each bitmap has to be rendered into an icon. After the first time the bitmap is loaded, however, it'll go much faster because these icons are cached. If you find that Windows is redrawing all of your icons quite frequently, see "Expanding Your Icon Cache," earlier in this chapter, to learn how to stop it.

Using Different Icons for Folders

If you don't like the icon that Explorer uses for a folder, you can change it by following these steps:

1. Open the Registry Editor, and find HKEY_CLASSES_ROOT\Folder\DefaultIcon.
2. Change the default value entry to the path of the icon file and the index of the icon. If you want to use the fourth icon (0, 1, 2, 3) in SHELL32.DLL, for example, type **C:\Windows\System\Shell32.dll,3**. You can get icons from DLL, EXE, ICO, and other files.
3. Close the Registry Editor.

Using Better Short File Names

Windows keeps two different file names for every file on your computer. The long file name is the one you're accustomed to seeing in Explorer and File, Open dialog boxes. It also keeps an 8.3 file name for use by MS-DOS and Windows 3.1 programs that don't know how to handle long file names.

When Windows creates the 8.3 version of the file name, it removes the spaces from the file name. Then, it takes the first six characters of the long file name, adds a tilde (~), and attaches a number to the end to make the file unique. The extension is the same as before. A file called LONG DOCUMENT.DOC becomes LONGDO~1.DOC. Figure 7.3 shows an MS-DOS directory listing with both long and 8.3 file names.

Part
II

Ch

7

FIG. 7.3
You can sort files by name by typing **dir / on** at the MS-DOS prompt, and pressing Enter. Use **dir /oe** to sort files by type.

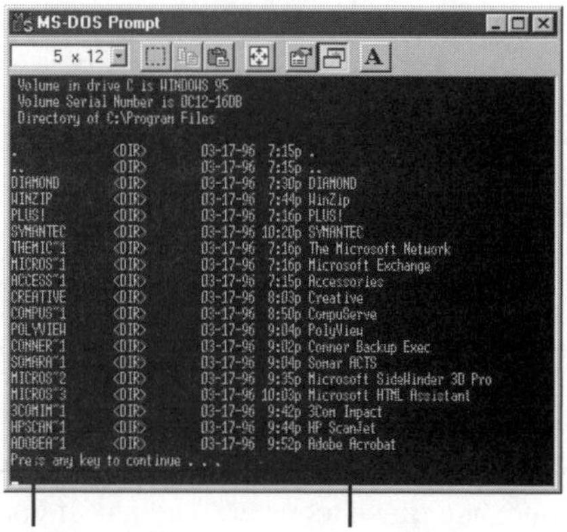

Short (8.3) file names   Long file names

If you don't like the tilde (~) that Windows 95 adds to the 8.3 version of long file names, you can show it a different way. Just do the following:

1. Open the Registry Editor, and find HKEY_LOCAL_MACHINE\System\ CurrentControlSet\Control\FileSystem.

2. Add a new binary value entry called NameNumericTail and set its value to **0**.

3. Close the Registry Editor.

If you create a file called A LONG FILE NAME.DOC, its 8.3 file name will be ALONGFIL.DOC instead of ALONGF~1.DOC. If you create another file in which the first eight characters are the same, however, Windows resorts to using the tilde for that file name.

> **CAUTION**
> Some programs may become confused if Windows isn't using the tilde for long filenames. If you're computer starts behaving erratically, remove the NameNumericTail value entry.

Using Your Own Backup Program

If you right-click a drive, choose Properties, and click the Tools tab of the drive's property sheet, you can launch the Windows backup program. If you're using a different backup program, you can launch it instead. Use the following steps to configure Windows for your backup program:

1. Open the Registry Editor, and find HKEY_LOCAL_MACHINE\SOFTWARE\ Microsoft\Windows\CurrentVersion\explorer\mycomputer\backuppath.

2. Change the default value entry to the path of your backup software.

3. Close the Registry Editor.

Viewing Unknown File Types

Have you ever right-clicked CONFIG.SYS hoping to open it in Notepad, only to find the Open With menu option? SYS files are registered as system files and have no commands associated with them. There are plenty of other files that would be useful to open in Notepad which have no commands associated with them. You can remedy this situation, however, by associating Notepad with all unknown file types. Then, the next time you right-click CONFIG.SYS (or any other unregistered file type), you'll see Notepad on the context menu. Just follow these steps:

1. Open the Registry Editor, and find HKEY_CLASSES_ROOT\Unknown\Shell.

2. Add the subkey \Notepad, and add the subkey \command under \Notepad so that you've added the new branch \Notepad\command.

3. Set the default value entry for \Notepad\command to **C:\Windows\Notepad.exe "%1"**.

4. Close the Registry Editor.

Experimenting with the Registry

Where do you think all the customizations in this chapter come from? Divine intervention? Sometimes. Most of them come from hard-working folks who have perilously tinkered with their Registry until they discovered something cool (I've restored my backup Registry on more than one occasion). You can use some of the same techniques to discover your own customizations.

Before you begin, make sure you understand how the Registry is organized. That means, take a closer look at Chapter 2, "Inside the Windows Registry." A full understanding of this information can lead you to some of the best customizations.

Next, take a look at the sections that follow. You learn how to find changes that Windows and other programs make in the Registry. You also learn how to test settings safely to see what they do.

Part
II

Ch
7

TIP Chapter 9, "Using ConfigSafe to Track Down Settings," shows you how to use ConfigSafe to compare two snapshots of the Registry. You can use this to see how Windows or a program changes the Registry.

Finding Entries by Comparing Snapshots

The easiest way to find changes in the Registry is to compare a version of it before and after Windows 95 (or another program) makes a change. To do that, however, you need a program to compare two text files and point out the changes.

I haven't found such a program on the Internet, but you'll find one included with Norton Utilities for Windows 95, Norton Navigator, Microsoft Win32 SDK, and Premia's Codewright for Windows 95. Many other utilities also include a program that compares two text files. The example that follows uses WinDiff from the Win32 SDK.

To compare two text files using WinDiff, follow these steps:

1. Open the Registry Editor, and choose Registry, Export Registry File from the main menu.

2. Choose the path to where you want to save the Registry, type **Before** in File Name, and then click Save. The Registry Editor exports the entire Registry to Before.reg in the path that you specified.

3. Close the Registry Editor.

4. Run a program, such as Explorer, and change any settings that you believe will change the Registry. Then close the program.

5. Open the Registry Editor, and choose Registry, Export Registry File from the main menu.

6. Choose the same path as you used in step 2, type **After** in File Name, and click Save. The Registry Editor exports the entire Registry to After.reg in the path that you specified.

7. Use the comparison utility to compare the differences between Before.reg and After.reg. Figure 7.4 shows the results of this comparison after restoring Explorer from a maximized window to a minimized window. This suggests that this key controls whether or not the Explorer window is maximized or normal.

▶ **See** "Importing and Exporting Registry Entries," **p. 66**
▶ **See** "Sniffing Around the Registry," **p. 170**

Testing Changes to See What They Do

You won't always be able to figure out which program on your computer will change a particular value entry. For that matter, you may not be able to figure out what actions on your part will cause a value entry to be changed. In these cases, you may have to resort to tinkering with the value entry until you see a noticeable change.

FIG. 7.4

Only two bytes have changed in the Registry when the Explorer window was restored from a maximized window.

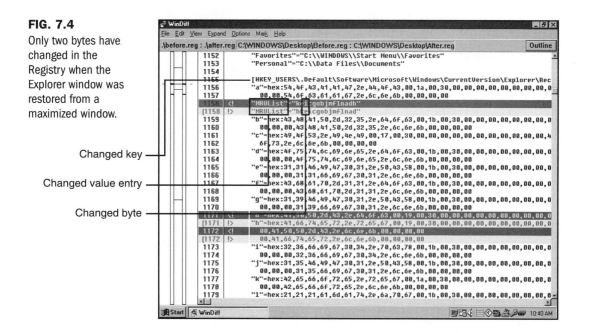

Changed key

Changed value entry

Changed byte

Modifying the value entry is generally safe to do as long as you can re-create the previous value when things go awry. It's easy to give yourself some insurance. Create a temporary value entry and copy the contents of the entry that you're changing into it. If anything goes wrong, you can copy the contents that you saved back into the original entry.

N O T E   If things go really wrong, you may not be able to start Windows. The StartUp disk that you created in Chapter 1, "Before You Begin," contains a real-mode version of the Registry Editor that you can use to repair your settings. ■

Finding More Registry Hints and Tips

Many of the customization tips in this chapter were found on the Internet. Several Web pages on the Internet are dedicated to Windows 95 hints and tips; Appendix B, "Internet Resources for Windows," contains some of the best. If you're not content with the list in Appendix B, you can use one of the search tools in Table 7.3 to find your own.

Part
II

Ch
7

Table 7.3 Internet Search Tools	
Search Tool	**Web Address**
AltaVista	**www.altavista.digital.com**
Deja News	**www.dejanews.com**
Excite	**www.excite.com**
Lycos	**www.lycos.com**
WebCrawler	**www.webcrawler.com**
Yahoo	**www.yahoo.com**

If you type the word **registry** in these search tools, you'll find everything from bridal registries to a registry that documents speed-traps across the nation (**www.nashville.net/speedtrap**). Limit your search a bit more by including the word **Windows.** Also, I suggest that you don't limit your search to Windows NT if you're a Windows NT user. Most of the Windows 95 hints-and-tips type of Web pages contain information that's equally useful to Windows NT. The following list shows you some of the keyword phrases that I've found to be useful for finding Windows Registry tips:

> windows registry
>
> windows registry tip
>
> windows hint
>
> windows custom
>
> windows q&a
>
> windows registry faq
>
> windows secret

If you're using a search tool that supports advanced searches with Boolean logic (Alta Vista), you'll have even better luck by combining search terms. Try this:

> (window and registry) and (hint or tip or secret)

This searches for all Web pages that contain the words **windows** and **registry** (it must find both); and that contain at least one of **hint**, **tip**, or **secret**. So, a Web page that contains **windows**, **registry**, and **tip** will match your search. A Web page that contains **windows** and **tip**, without the word **registry**, won't match your search.

▶ **See** "World Wide Web," **p. 424**

CAUTION

Many Web pages containing Registry tips also provide REG files that you can use to automatically make the changes for you. Before merging the REG file with your Registry, open it in Notepad. Make sure that you fully understand and agree to the changes that it will make. Well-meaning authors sometimes provide REG files that might break Windows 95.

CHAPTER 8

Troubleshooting Windows

by Jerry Honeycutt

You'll often encounter nagging problems in Windows. Many times, you'll just overlook those problems and press on. Other times, you're dead in your tracks until you get the problem fixed. Before you pull your hair out, take a look at this chapter. It describes some of the most common problems users encounter with Windows 95 and Windows NT 4.0.

In many cases, the shared experiences of other Internet users can help identify your dilemma. Open **http://www.dejanews.com** in your Web browser, and use it to search all of the UseNet postings for your problem (hopefully, a solution, too). You should also consult the Microsoft Knowledge Base. You'll learn much more about this wonderful resource in Appendix C, "Technical Resources for Windows." ∎

Fixing the most common problems in Windows 95

Whether Microsoft calls them bugs or not, you'll definitely encounter a variety of problems. This chapter shows you how to fix the most prevalent.

Fixing a variety of Windows NT 4.0 problems

Discover how to fix a handful of the most common problems with Windows NT 4.0 Workstation and Server.

Distributing fixes to all network users

Learn how to quickly and easily update the other computers on your network.

Windows 95

This section describes a variety of problems you might encounter with Windows 95. We've verified each one of these, so you can feel comfortable that, in most cases, they work as intended. Here's what you'll find:

Correcting Microsoft's File System Performance Profiles

Disabling NetBIOS Name Resolution on DNS

Displaying Domain Logon Confirmation in Windows 95

Fixing Internet Explorer's Browsing Problems

Preventing Internet Explorer from Opening EXE Files

Recovering Your TrueType Fonts

Repairing Internet Explorer's Cache and History Folder

Retaining MouseKeys' Custom Settings

Reinstalling Microsoft Plus!

Stopping the Repeated Detection of a PNP Printer

Toggling the NUMLOCK Key After Installing IntelliPoint

Correcting Microsoft's File System Performance Profiles

It's anyone's guess how this escaped Microsoft's attention before they shipped Windows 95, but the cache sizes for the different performance profiles are incorrect. These errors can cause your computer's file system performance to degrade if you change the performance profile. What are performance profiles? Right-click My Computer and choose P_roperties; click the Performance tab; click the F_ile System button; and you'll see a drop-down list called T_ypical Role of This Machine (Figure 8.1). This allows you to tune your computer's performance to its usage.

FIG. 8.1
If you use a UPS (uninterrupted power supply), consider changing T_ypical Role of This Machine to Server in order to better your machine's performance by using more memory for the cache.

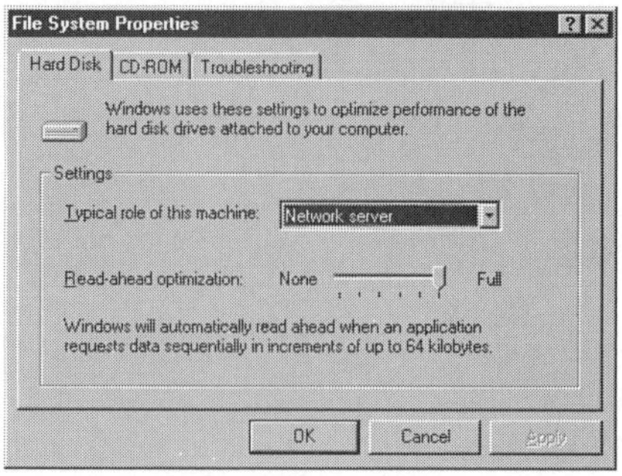

Here's how to fix the cache sizes that Microsoft sets for each profile:

1. Open the Registry Editor, and find HKEY_LOCAL_MACHINE\Software\ Microsoft\Windows\CurrentVersion\FS Templates\Mobile.

2. Change the NameCache value entry to **51 01 00 00** and the PathCache value entry to **10 00 00 00**.

3. Open the Registry Editor, and find HKEY_LOCAL_MACHINE\Software\ Microsoft\Windows\CurrentVersion\FS Templates\Server.

4. Change the NameCache value entry to **A9 0A 00 00** and the PathCache value entry to **40 00 00 00**.

5. Close the Registry Editor, and restart your computer.

Disabling NetBIOS Name Resolution on DNS

You can disable NetBIOS name resolution on the domain name service (DNS) so that it only shows the Windows Internet Name Service (WINS). This doesn't affect any of your other DNS settings. Here's how to do it:

1. Open the Registry Editor, and find HKEY_LOCAL_MACHINE\System\ CurrentControlSet\Services\VxD\MSTCP.

2. Change the string value entry called EnableDNS from **1** to **0**.

3. Close the Registry Editor.

Displaying Domain Logon Confirmation in Windows 95

You can make Windows 95 display a dialog box that shows you which NT domain is validating your login. This is particularly useful if you're an administrator trying to troubleshoot network problems. Note that your primary login must be set to Microsoft Networking for this to work. Here's how to do it:

1. Open the Registry Editor, and find HKEY_LOCAL_MACHINE\Network\Logon.

2. Change the value entry called DomainLogonMessage to **1**.

3. Close the Registry Editor, and restart your computer.

Disabling Routing

If you upgrade to Windows 95 from Windows for Workgroups, you might see a message that says Windows protection error. You need to restart your computer each time you start Windows 95. This can occur if you had IP routing enabled in Windows for

Workgroups. Windows 95 doesn't support IP routing, but it copies this setting to the Registry regardless. Here's how to fix the problem:

1. Open the Registry Editor, and remove HKEY_LOCAL_MACHINE\System\ currentControlSet\Services\VxD\MSTCP from the Registry.

2. Close the Registry Editor.

> **CAUTION**
>
> On some computers, enabling this setting will cause the computer to behave unpredictably. If you encounter problems after changing this setting, restore it.

Fixing Internet Explorer's Browsing Problems

Does Internet Explorer only occasionally work for you? Can you connect to Microsoft's Web site but not to anyone else's Web site? Do you use Novell's 32-bit networking client? Your problem might be simple to fix:

1. Open the Registry Editor, and find HKEY_CURRENT_USER\SOFTWARE\ Microsoft\Windows\Current Version\Internet Settings.

2. Add a new binary value entry called DontUseDNSLoadBalancing and set its value to **01 00 00 00**.

3. Close the Registry Editor.

Now, your downloads will be a bit smoother, and you'll have fewer problems connecting to Web sites.

Preventing Internet Explorer from Opening EXE Files

The first time you downloaded an EXE file using Internet Explorer, it displayed a dialog box with a check box that says Always Ask Before Opening This Type of File (Figure 8.2). If you cleared this check box, Internet Explorer will no longer prompt you when you download an EXE file; it'll just open the file. To prevent this, you have to change the EditFlags for the EXE file type:

1. Open the Registry Editor, and find HKEY_CLASSES_ROOT\exefile.

2. Change the EditFlags value entry from **D8 07 01 00** to **D8 07 00 00**.

3. Close the Registry Editor.

▶ **See** "Understanding Context Menu Registry Entries," **p. 113**

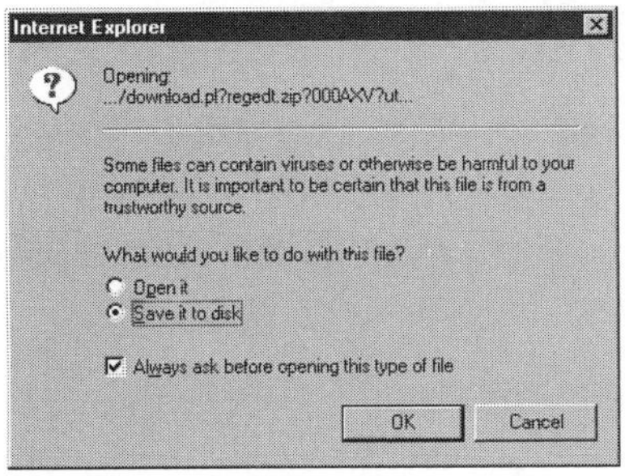

FIG. 8.2
Be careful running
EXE files on your
computer without first
checking them for
viruses.

Recovering Your TrueType Fonts

If you upgraded Windows 3.1 to Windows 95, your TrueType fonts may start acting up.
There are three symptoms to watch for:

- When you can successfully add a TrueType font, but you don't see it in the Fonts
  folder.

- Windows 95 reports that `The font TrueType font is already installed. To
  install a new version, first remove the old version.`

- Your TrueType fonts are missing from the Fonts folder.

This happens if the fonts key in the Registry is broken. Here's how to fix it:

1. Open the Registry Editor and find HKEY_LOCAL_MACHINE\SOFTWARE\
   Microsoft\Windows\CurrentVersion.

2. Do you see a fonts subkey? If not, add it.

3. Move all of the fonts from `C:\Windows\Fonts` to a temporary folder.

4. Open C:\Windows\Fonts in Explorer, and choose File, Install New Font. You'll see
   the dialog box shown in Figure 8.3. Select all of the fonts in the temporary folder
   you created in step 3, and click OK.

5. Close the Registry Editor.

FIG. 8.3
After you copy the
fonts from the
temporary folder, you
can remove the
temporary folder.

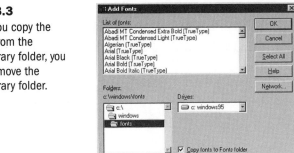

Repairing Internet Explorer's Cache and History Folder

If Internet Explorer can't find its cache or history folder, it displays an error message that says `Unable to Create Folder. Some features may not work properly`. This is either because Internet Explorer is looking in the wrong places for the folders, or the folders themselves are missing. Here's how to fix the problem:

1. Open the Registry Editor, and find HKEY_LOCAL_MACHINE\SOFTWARE\ Microsoft\Internet Explorer\Main.

2. Note the path contained in the Cache_Directory value entry. Does it exist? If not, create the folder. If the value entry doesn't contain a path, set it to the path of Internet Explorer's cache folder.

3. Note the path contained in the History_Directory value entry. Does it exist? If not, create the folder. If the value entry doesn't contain a path, set it to the path of Internet Explorer's history folder.

4. Close the Registry Editor. You don't need to restart your computer for this change to take effect.

Retaining MouseKeys' Custom Settings

IntelliPoint and IntelliType 1.1 have a nasty habit of causing the MouseKeys accessibility feature to forget its custom settings. Here's how you can fix this problem:

1. Open the Registry Editor, and find HKEY_CURRENT_USER\Control Panel\Microsoft Input Devices\WindowsPointer.

2. Remove the WindowsPointer subkey from the Registry.

3. Close the Registry Editor, and restart your computer.

Reinstalling Microsoft Plus!

When you try to reinstall Microsoft Plus!, the setup program may display `Microsoft Windows 95 Plus! Setup was not Completed Successfully`. This occurs when some of the Plus! files on your computer are damaged. Here's how to fix this problem:

1. Open the Registry Editor, and remove the HKEY_LOCAL_MACHINE\SOFTWARE\ Microsoft\Plus! key.

2. Remove the HKEY_LOCAL_MACHINE\SOFTWARE\Microsoft\MS Setup(ACME)\Table Files key.

3. Close the Registry Editor.

4. Remove C:\~Mssetup.t from your computer. If this folder is hidden, you'll need to show hidden files in Explorer: choose View, Options; and Show All Files.

5. Remove C:\Program Files\Plus! from your computer.

6. Try reinstalling Microsoft Plus!.

Stopping the Repeated Detection of a PNP Printer

With some printers, Windows 95 will redetect them each time it starts. You'll see a message each time Windows 95 starts that says Windows has Found New Hardware and is Installing the Software for It. In particular, this occurs with these printers:

Hewlett-Packard 4L

Hewlett-Packard DeskJet 660C

This problem is the result of a damaged Registry key. Here's how to fix it:

1. Open the Registry Editor and remove HKEY_LOCAL_MACHINE\Enum\Lptenum.

2. Close the Registry Editor.

3. Restart your computer. Windows 95 will redetect your printer and correctly replace the Registry key in step 1.

Toggling the NUMLOCK Key After Installing IntelliPoint

IntelliPoint 1.1 has a bug that disables your ability to toggle the NUMLOCK key. Here's how to fix it:

1. Open the Registry Editor and find HKEY_CURRENT_USER\Control Panel\Microsoft Input Devices.

2. Add a new value entry called NumLock to this key and set its string value to **ON**.

3. Close the Registry Editor, and restart your computer.

Windows NT 4.0

The remainder of this section describes a variety of problems you might encounter with Windows NT 4.0 Workstation and Server. Thanks to almost identical operating systems, these fixes work equally well with both. As with the fixes in the previous section, we've verified each one of these. Here's what you'll find.

Changing the Thread Priority for Background Print Jobs

Forcing Windows NT 4.0 to Logon Quickly

Restricting Remote Access to the Registry

Running the AT Scheduler in Non-administrative Accounts

Stopping Windows NT 4.0 from Parsing AUTOEXEC.BAT

Changing the Thread Priority for Background Print Jobs

Windows NT 4.0 doesn't use hardware interrupts to print: it uses threads to poll the port in the background. If you have very large print jobs, however, the performance of other applications may suffer. You can fix this by reducing the priority of background print jobs, like this:

1. Open the Registry Editor, and find HKEY_LOCAL_MACHINE\System\ CurrentControlSet\Control\ Print.

2. Add a value entry to this key called PortThreadPriority and set its REG_SZ value to **Thread_Priority_Below_normal**.

3. Close the Registry Editor.

Forcing Windows NT 4.0 to Logon Quickly

In Windows 95, you can configure the Microsoft Networking client to log on quickly by not automatically restoring networking connections. Windows 95 will only restore the network connection when you actually try to use it. You can do the same thing in Windows NT:

1. Open the Registry Editor, and find HKEY_LOCAL_MACHINE\System\ CurrentControlSet\Control\NetworkProvider.

2. Add a value entry to this key called RestoreConnection and set its REG_DWORD value to 0.

3. Close the Registry Editor.

Restricting Remote Access to the Registry

By default, access to the Windows NT 4.0 Server's Registry is restricted to administrators, and access to the Windows NT 4.0 Workstation's Registry is left completely open. You can change who can access the Registry, however.

NT looks for a Registry key called HKEY_LOCAL_MACHINE\System\ CurrentControlSet\Control\SecurePipServers\winreg each time a user tries to remotely connect to the Registry. If NT finds this key, the access control list (ACL) for this key determines who can remotely connect to the computer's Registry. If NT doesn't find this key, NT lets all users remotely connect to the computer's Registry. Use these steps to change it:

1. Open the Registry Editor, and find HKEY_LOCAL_MACHINE\System\ CurrentControlSet\control\SecurePipServers.

2. Add a new Subkey called winreg to this key if it doesn't exist.

3. Under that winreg, create a new REG_SZ value entry called Description, and set its value to **Registry Server**.

4. Change the security permissions for this subkey to reflect the users and groups that you want to be able to remotely access the computer's Registry. See Figure 8.4.

FIG. 8.4
Chapter 12, "Securing the Windows Registry," describes how to work with a Registry entry's ACL in detail.

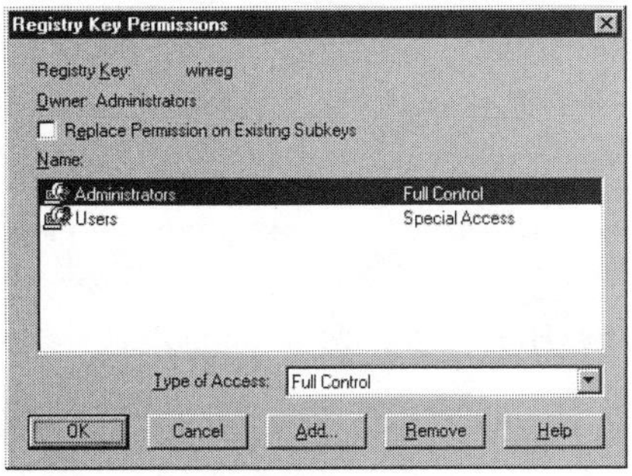

5. Close the Registry Editor.

Running the AT Scheduler in Non-Administrative Accounts

By default, Windows NT 4.0 requires that the account running the scheduler service has administrative privileges. You can change the account that starts the AT scheduler in the Services Control Panel applet, however. You can also allow a non-administrative account to start the AT scheduler by changing the Registry key's access control list. Here's how:

1. Open the Registry Editor, and find HKEY_LOCAL_MACHINE\ System\CurrentControlSet\Services\Schedule.

2. Change the ACL for this Registry key. The ACL for this key determines who can run the AT scheduler.

3. Close the Registry Editor. Then, stop and restart the Schedule service.

▶ **See** "Controlling Remote Access to the Registry," **p. 233**

Stopping Windows NT 4.0 from Parsing AUTOEXEC.BAT

Windows NT 4.0 doesn't do much with AUTOEXEC.BAT. It does parse out the `Set` and `Path` statements, however. If you don't want NT to set environment variables based upon your AUTOEXEC.BAT file, you can prevent NT from parsing it:

1. Open the Registry Editor, and find HKEY_CURRENT_USER\Software\ Microsoft\Windows NT\CurrentVersion\Winlogon.

2. Add a REG_SZ value entry called ParseAutoexec, and set its value to 0.

3. Close the Registry Editor.

Distributing Fixes to Users on a Network

Finding a fix to a problem is one thing. If you need to get that fix out to all the users on a network it's a whole different story. Chapter 14, "Working with REG and INF Files," shows you how to package fixes that involve the Registry in REG and INF files.

Use the information in Chapter 14 to insert one of the fixes you learn from this chapter, or any other resource, into a file that you can distribute to the users on the network. Then, the users can easily apply the fix. Here are some suggestions for distributing those files:

- If you have an intranet, put a link to a REG file on a Web page that everyone can access. Provide a brief description of the problem that it fixes. Then, the users on the network can simply click the link and Windows will automatically apply the fix to their Registry.

- E-mail the fix to the users on your network. In your mail message, instruct the users on how to execute the attachment (whether they double-click an icon in the message or in a special directory on their computer). Their mail client will execute the REG file, causing Windows to automatically apply the fix.

- Put a command that executes a REG file in the users' login script. Then, the next time they log onto the network, the login script will automatically apply the fix to the user's Registry. They won't even know it happened.

TIP Service Pack 1 is now available for Windows NT. You can get more information at **http:// www.microsoft.com/ntserver/default.asp**.

CHAPTER 9

Using ConfigSafe to Track Down Settings

by Jerry Honeycutt

ConfigSafe was originally designed to help hardware manufacturers better support their customers and computers. ConfigSafe records the configuration of a computer when the manufacturer ships it. Then, when a customer calls in with a problem, the support person uses ConfigSafe to determine what the user has changed on the computer. No more guessing.

It's available for you to use, too, and it's just as valuable. You can use it to take *snapshots* of your computer's configuration. Then, you can see what changed on your computer from time to time (snapshot to snapshot). Installed a program that changed your AUTOEXEC.BAT without asking? You can see exactly what the program changed. Did a program break your Registry? Use ConfigSafe to see exactly what it did.

ConfigSafe doesn't look like other Windows 95 programs that you've used. Thus, it might take some getting used to. Don't let that throw you, however, because you'll be well rewarded. ▪

Get an evaluation ConfigSafe

You can get a free evaluation copy of this hot, new product; then you can buy it if you like it.

ConfigSafe looks after your mental health

Learn how to use ConfigSafe to keep track of and fix your computer's configuration.

Use ConfigSafe's more advanced features

ConfigSafe gives you advanced features that you can use to manage the changes to your computer.

Track down Registry changes

Use ConfigSafe to snoop around the Registry and discover what entries Windows changes.

NOTE ConfigSafe provides similar functionality to that found in Windows 95's Emergency Repair Utility (see Chapter 1, "Before You Begin")—only it's much more advanced. ERU is just for recovering your configuration files; however, it doesn't let you browse changes to your configuration like ConfigSafe. You also can't use ERU to snoop around the Registry and uncover all those neat Registry hacks. ▪

Getting Started

Before you can do much with ConfigSafe, you need to get your own copy. The easiest—and fastest—way is to download an evaluation copy.

ON THE WEB

Open **http://www.imagine-lan.com** and follow the instructions you see on the Web page to download either ConfigSafe 95 or ConfigSafe NT.

You can also order it directly from the makers of ConfigSafe:

> imagine LAN, Inc.
> 76 Northeastern Blvd.
> Suite 34B
> Nashua, NH 03062-3174
> (603) 889-3883

Install ConfigSafe on Your Computer

If you downloaded the evaluation version of ConfigSafe, double-click the file you downloaded to start the installer. If you purchased the retail version of ConfigSafe, put the disk in the disk drive and run INSTALL.EXE. Then use these steps to complete the process:

1. Type the path in which you want to install ConfigSafe in the space provided.

2. Click OK to continue, and Install copies the files to your hard drive.

3. Select Add Shortcut to the Start Menu to add the ConfigSafe shortcut to the Windows Start menu and select Add Shortcut to the Desktop to add a ConfigSafe shortcut to the desktop. Click OK to continue.

4. Verify that Install has correctly identified the location of your configuration files. If the path of any files in the list is incorrect, select the file and click New Path to correct the path. When you're satisfied with all the configuration files, click OK to finish.

After you finish installing ConfigSafe, ConfigSafe starts so that it can take your first snapshot. This can take several minutes on a slow computer. The process can take even longer if you have massive hard drives or a huge Registry. ConfigSafe calls this snapshot Initial Configuration. ConfigSafe also identifies each snapshot by the date and time ConfigSafe took it. Consider this a baseline that you can use to compare all subsequent configuration snapshots.

Sit Back and Let ConfigSafe Protect Your Configuration

After ConfigSafe has taken a snapshot of the initial configuration, you don't really have to do much. Just sit back and let ConfigSafe do its job. ConfigSafe, by default, takes a new snapshot of your configuration once a week. This is more than enough to protect you and your computer against most problems. It also covers most of the bases by default. Here's a look at the information that ConfigSafe captures in each configuration snapshot.

Configuration Files	PROTOCOL.INI, SYSTEM.INI, WIN.INI, AUTOEXEC.BAT, and CONFIG.SYS
System Information	Processor, coprocessor, memory, and Windows version
Drive Information	Free space on each drive
Directory Information	Files in C:\WINDOWS and all its subdirectories
Registry Information	All value entries for all keys in the Registry

```
HKEY_LOCAL_MACHINE\SOFTWARE\Microsoft\Windows\CurrentVersion\Run contains a
value entry for ConfigSafe that automatically launches AUTOCHK.EXE each time
Windows starts.
```

Tracking Changes to Your Configuration

Yes, you can let ConfigSafe do its own thing, but you can get interactive with it, too. For example, you can visually inspect every change made to your configuration for just about any span of time you like. To run ConfigSafe, choose Programs, CfgSafe from the Start menu (see Figure 9.1). You'll note that ConfigSafe doesn't put an icon on the taskbar; thus, you have to use Alt+Tab to switch back and forth between it and other applications.

ConfigSafe indicates changes to your configuration in the same manner no matter which type of information it's reporting on. Table 9.1 shows how ConfigSafe represents changes to configuration file, system, drive, directory, and Registry information.

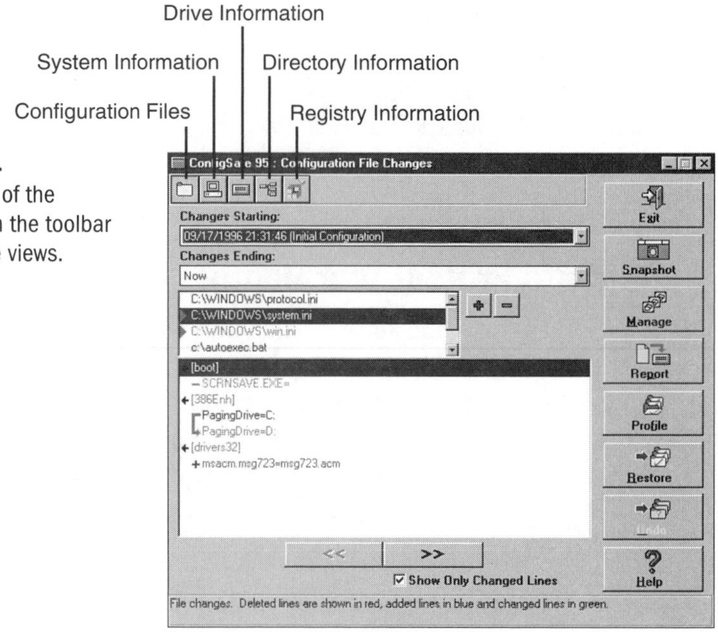

Drive Information

System Information | Directory Information

Configuration Files | Registry Information

FIG. 9.1
Click one of the
buttons in the toolbar
to change views.

Table 9.1   How ConfigSafe Indicates Changes

Type	Color	Icon
Add	Blue	+
Delete	Red	—
Change	Green	⌐

Configuration Files

ConfigSafe monitors the changes to each configuration file that you tell it to watch. By default, ConfigSafe monitors PROTOCOL.INI, SYSTEM.INI, WIN.INI, AUTOEXEC.BAT, and CONFIG.SYS. You can add any text file you want, however, such as a text file or another INI file. To see the configuration files that ConfigSafe is tracking and the changes to each file, click the Configuration Files button on the toolbar. You see a view that looks like Figure 9.2.

FIG. 9.2

The status line displays help for each object over which you move the mouse pointer.

Compare these two snapshots

Files included in snapshot

Changes to selected file

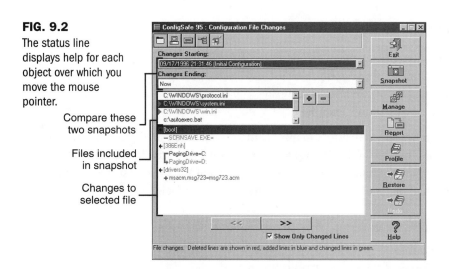

You have to tell ConfigSafe which snapshots you want to compare when building the list of changes. You can compare any two snapshots as well as the current configuration. For example, you can compare a snapshot you took two weeks ago to the current configuration (represented by the word "Now," instead of a date and time). You can also compare a snapshot you took four weeks ago to a snapshot you took two weeks ago. Choose the beginning snapshot from Changes Starting. Choose the ending snapshot from Changes Ending.

To see the changes in a particular file, select that file in the file list. ConfigSafe will go away for a moment to calculate the differences. ConfigSafe displays with the color green the files that have been changed between the two snapshots you selected. It displays with the color black the files that haven't changed. Look below the file list to see the actual lines changed in that file. You see the minus sign by each removed line; you see a plus sign by each added line. ConfigSafe displays before and after versions of changed lines with an arrow pointing from the old version of the line to the new version.

Adding a file to the snapshot is easy. Click the plus sign next to the file list and choose a text file on your hard drive. Removing a file from the list is just as easy. Select the configuration file you want to remove from the list and click the minus sign.

T I P Try adding the Windows 95 log files to the snapshot so that you know when something peculiar occurs. For example, you can monitor C:\BOOTLOG.TXT so that you know if something changes in the boot process.

Part
II

Ch
9

System Information

ConfigSafe also monitors changes to your system's hardware configuration. imagine LAN provided this feature for those companies that had to support hardware. If you're responsible for supporting hardware in your company, you'll find this feature useful. If you're a power user, you won't find this feature very helpful.

 Click the System Information button to display the view you see in Figure 9.3. Currently, ConfigSafe tracks the type of processor and coprocessor. It also tracks the amount of memory installed in the computer as well as the version of Windows installed on the computer. I expect that imagine LAN will include other, more useful information in the future.

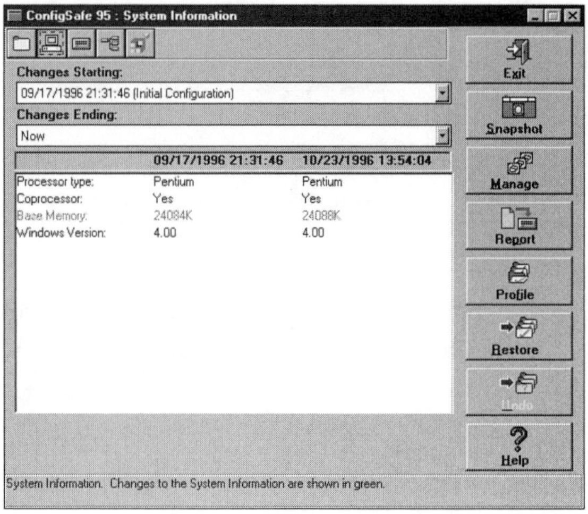

FIG. 9.3
System information isn't very useful for an individual power user, but it's handy for a support person.

Drive Information

Another feature that's useful to support professionals is the capability to track changes to the free space on a computer's hard drive and mapped network drives. Again, this isn't as useful to power users.

Click the Drive Information button, and you see a view similar to Figure 9.4. This view provides two useful bits of information. First, it lets you know whether the user has added or removed any drives. Second, it lets you look at the amount of free space available during both snapshots. It doesn't report the free space available for removable disks, however, because that would be senseless.

FIG. 9.4
Drive information
reports the free space
on fixed disks but only
the availability for
removable disks.

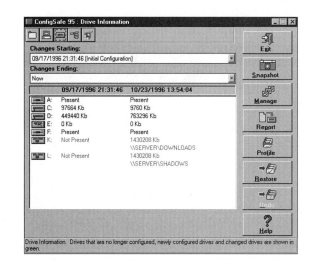

Directory Information

The capability to track directory information is the second most useful feature in
ConfigSafe (you learn about number one a bit later). It keeps track of the contents in each
directory that you tell ConfigSafe to watch, including every subdirectory. For example, if
you configure ConfigSafe to monitor C:\PROGRAM FILES, it tracks all the files in that
path and in all the subdirectories under that path. To see the directories that ConfigSafe is
tracking and the files that have changed in each directory, click the Directory Information
button on the toolbar. You see a view similar to Figure 9.5.

FIG. 9.5
Directory information
works similarly to
configuration files.

Compare these
two snapshots

Directories included
in snapshot

Changes to
selected directory

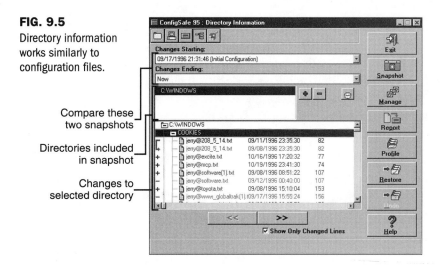

N O T E You can get a quick glimpse of the files that have changed during the previous day by using Windows 95's Find feature. Choose Find, Files or Folders from the Start menu. Then select a path in Look In, click the Date Modified tab, click During the Previous 1 Day(s), and click Find Now. Click the Modified heading to sort the most recently changed files to the top of the list. ▪

You have to tell ConfigSafe which snapshots you want to compare when building the list of changes, just like the configure files view. Choose the beginning and ending snapshots from the lists provided.

To see the changes in a particular directory, select that directory in the list. Then check out the list below that to see the actual files added, deleted, or changed in each sub-directory. You see the minus sign by a deleted file or a plus sign by a new file. For changed files, you see an arrow pointing from the old file to the new file, which tells you the date, time, and file size of the file at each snapshot.

By default, ConfigSafe monitors C:\WINDOWS and C:\DOS (if it exists). You'll probably want to monitor other paths. To do so, click the plus sign next to the directory list and choose a directory. To remove a directory from the list, select a directory you want to remove and click the minus sign.

T I P Just add the root directory of each drive to monitor every directory and file on your computer.

Registry Information

The best feature in ConfigSafe is the Registry (isn't that what this book is about?). ConfigSafe monitors the changes to each and every value entry in the Registry. Considering how big the Registry is, you need something on your side. ConfigSafe, by default, monitors HKEY_LOCAL_MACHINE and HKEY_USERS. It doesn't need to monitor any other root keys because they're all aliases for these two keys. To see Registry keys that ConfigSafe is tracking and the changes to each value entry, click the Registry Information button on the toolbar. You see a view similar to Figure 9.6.

▶ **See** "Aliases," **p. 47**

Just like the other views, you have to tell ConfigSafe which snapshots you want to compare. Choose the beginning and ending snapshots as described in "Configuration Files," earlier in this chapter.

To see the changes to a particular Registry key and all its subkeys, select a key from the list. ConfigSafe will go away again, possibly for a very long time, so keep your fingers off Ctrl+Alt+Del. Look under the list of Registry keys to see the actual value entries that have changed. You see a plus sign by each new Registry key and a minus sign beside each nuked Registry key. ConfigSafe displays before and after versions of changed keys with a green arrow pointing from the older value data to the newer value data.

FIG. 9.6
See "Sniffing Around the Registry" later in this chapter to learn how to use this view to track down changes in the Registry.

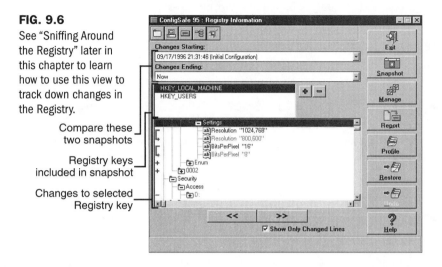

Compare these two snapshots

Registry keys included in snapshot

Changes to selected Registry key

You don't really need to add any other Registry keys to the snapshot because ConfigSafe monitors all the subkeys under HKEY_LOCAL_MACHINE and HKEY_USERS—that's all of them. You can remove those keys, however, by selecting one of the keys in the list and clicking the minus sign. Then you can add more specific keys, such as HKEY_LOCAL_MACHINE\SOFTWARE\Microsoft, by clicking the plus sign and choosing a Registry key.

T I P Double-click a value entry that doesn't fit neatly in the list to view it in its own window.

Recovering When Something Goes Wrong

Eventually, you will run into a problem that you wish you could find an easy way out of. I recently installed a program that completely trashed my Registry, for example. I had to manually remove all of its rubbish from the Registry by hand. How about those programs that change your AUTOEXEC.BAT or CONFIG.SYS without asking first? You could fix these problems, without a lot of work, if you could identify all the changes you need to make.

ConfigSafe to the rescue. You can use ConfigSafe to automatically restore the configuration files in a snapshot. For example, if you take a snapshot prior to installing a new product and regret the changes it made to the Registry, you can use ConfigSafe to restore the Registry to the state it was in when you took the snapshot. That, in conjunction with ConfigSafe's capability to track configuration files and directory contents, gives you the capability to completely and accurately uninstall programs after you install them.

Restoring a Previous Configuration

> **CAUTION**
>
> The capability to restore a snapshot is one of ConfigSafe's most powerful features. You need to respect it, however. Follow the instructions in this section closely. That is, make sure that you close down all programs running on your desktop before you restore a snapshot. Also, make sure that you restart your computer after restoring a snapshot.

Restoring a previous configuration snapshot is incredibly easy. Before restoring a snapshot, though, close any programs running on your desktop. Do this to prevent them from becoming confused by their configuration data changing behind their backs. Here's how:

1. On ConfigSafe's main window, click the Restore button, and a dialog box similar to Figure 9.7 appears.

FIG. 9.7
You don't have to restore your entire configuration; you can pick and choose from both lists.

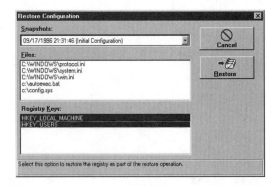

2. Choose the snapshot you want to restore from Snapshots.

3. Pick the configuration files and Registry keys you want to restore.

4. Click Restore, and ConfigSafe restores that configuration. I very strongly recommend that you restart your computer at this point to make sure that the new configuration takes effect.

> **CAUTION**
>
> Don't restore a snapshot that's too old (age is up to your best judgment). You might lose some settings that could cause some of your programs or even Windows itself to stop working properly.

Restoring Your Configuration When Windows Won't Start

Sometimes you won't even be able to start Windows because your configuration is so completely messed up. If you've let ConfigSafe do its job and create regular configuration snapshots, you can easily recover a working configuration using ConfigSafe's DOS program, called SOS.

Start your computer in MS-DOS. Then change to your ConfigSafe folder and run SOS.EXE. Follow the instructions you see on the screen. If SOS doesn't help you get your computer up and running again, take a look at Chapter 5, "Fixing a Broken Registry."

Managing Configuration Snapshots

ConfigSafe provides many more advanced features that you can use to manage configuration snapshots. For example, you don't have to wait for ConfigSafe to take a snapshot on schedule; you can do it at any time. If you don't like the schedule, you can change it. You can also rename and delete snapshots.

Create a New Snapshot

Creating a new snapshot is easy. Click the <u>S</u>napshot button. Then type in a name for the snapshot, as shown in Figure 9.8, and click OK.

FIG. 9.8
Type a description of
why you're taking the
snapshot, such as
**Before Internet
Explorer 3.0**.

Rename a Snapshot

If you're not completely happy with the name of a snapshot, you can rename it.

Here's how to rename a snapshot:

1. Click <u>M</u>anage to display the Manage Configuration Snapshots dialog box.

2. Select a snapshot from the list, and click <u>R</u>ename to display the dialog box in Figure 9.9.

FIG. 9.9

Changing a snapshot's name won't change the sort order of the list.

3. Type the new name of the snapshot in the space provided and then click OK to save your change.

4. Click OK to close the Manage Configuration Snapshots dialog box.

Delete a Snapshot

From time to time, you'll want to delete a snapshot. For example, if you created a snapshot prior to installing a new product or testing out a Registry hack, you can get rid of the snapshot after you're satisfied that everything is okay. Here's how:

1. Click <u>M</u>anage to display the Manage Configuration Snapshots dialog box.

2. Select a snapshot from the list and click <u>D</u>elete to delete the snapshot. ConfigSafe displays the dialog box shown in Figure 9.10.

FIG. 9.10

Delete older snapshots to save space on your hard drive.

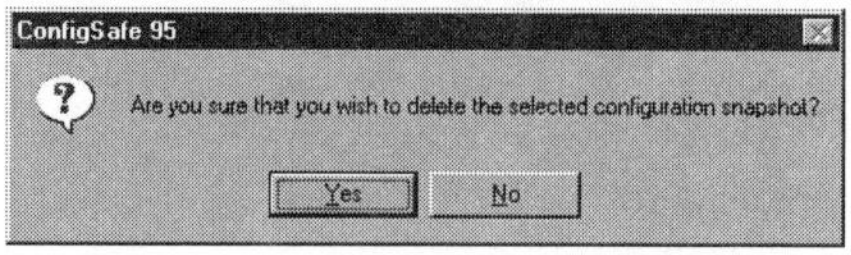

3. Click <u>Y</u>es to delete the snapshot, or click <u>N</u>o if you're not sure about it.

4. Click OK to close the Manage Configuration Snapshots dialog box.

Schedule Snapshots

By default, ConfigSafe takes a configuration snapshot once every week. You can change this schedule to suit your own needs. A monthly snapshot may be more suitable for folks who don't use their computer much. A daily snapshot is more appropriate for someone like me who tinkers around with his configuration day in and day out. Follow these steps to change the schedule:

1. Click <u>M</u>anage to display the Manage Configuration Snapshots dialog box, as shown in Figure 9.11.

FIG. 9.11
I don't recommend that you choose At Windows Startup because it makes Windows startup slower.

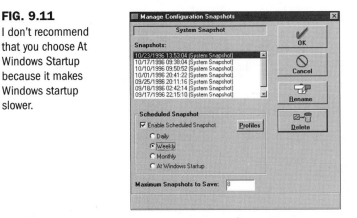

2. Make sure that Enable Scheduled Snapshot is checked.
3. Select Daily, Weekly, Monthly, or At Windows Startup.
4. Click OK to save your changes.

TROUBLESHOOTING

I've set Maximum Snapshots to Save to 5. Regardless, ConfigSafe takes many more snapshots than that. Maximum Snapshots to Save determines the number of snapshots that ConfigSafe will save in a profile. This value applies to only those snapshots that ConfigSafe takes automatically, though. Thus, you have to manually remove snapshots that you take by clicking the <u>S</u>napshot button. See "Delete a Snapshot," earlier in the chapter.

I clicked <u>P</u>rofiles to choose multiple profiles (see "Backing Up the Registry for Safe Tinkering," later in the chapter) for my scheduled snapshot, but I can only select one snapshot. Although the prompts suggest that you can select more than one profile for the scheduled snapshot, you can actually only select one. Select the one profile that you want for the scheduled snapshot.

Sniffing Around the Registry

Now we're getting to the meat of the matter: using ConfigSafe to figure out the Windows Registry. You can use it to see exactly how Windows and other programs use the Registry. You can sometimes discover great Registry hacks by observing how the Registry reflects different behaviors in Windows.

As important, you can use ConfigSafe to track down what went wrong with that great new program you installed. Have you ever downloaded a shareware program from the Internet and then had to figure out how to manually remove its Registry entries? You've got them beat because ConfigSafe tells you automatically.

Backing Up the Registry for Safe Tinkering

Tinkering with the Registry? Trying out those customization tips in Chapters 7 and 8? Why don't you protect yourself with ConfigSafe, first. In fact, you can take a snapshot with ConfigSafe, mess up your Registry as much as you want, and restore it to just the way it was before you went berserk. Use the following steps:

1. Create a new profile so that you can easily clean up your message when you're finished. Profiles are nothing more than individually named collections of snapshots. Click the Profile button, name the profile as shown in Figure 9.12, and click OK.

View Directory Information

View Configuration Files   View Registry Information

FIG. 9.12
For tinkering around with the Registry, you don't need to take a snapshot of the configuration files or directories.

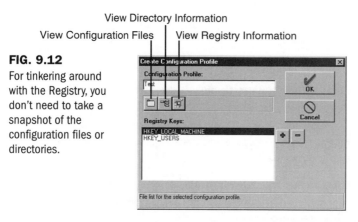

2. Take a snapshot of your configuration as described in "Create a New Snapshot," earlier in the chapter. This saves your configuration as it currently stands.

3. Tinker around with the Registry all you like. Delete keys. Change value entries. Test out your wildest ideas.

4. After you've had enough, and become quite nervous, restore the snapshot you took in Step 2 as described in "Restoring a Previous Configuration," earlier in the chapter. Take a look at Figure 9.13.

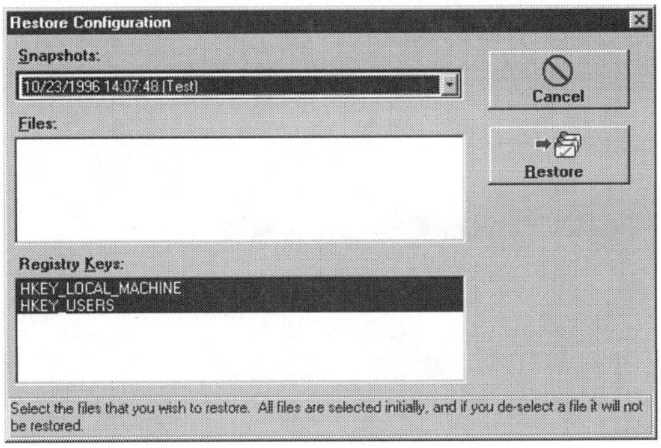

FIG. 9.13
The list of configuration files will be empty if you didn't add any to the configuration profile.

Finding Registry Changes a Program Makes

You can track down the Registry settings that a program changes using ConfigSafe. The steps are very similar to those in "Backing Up the Registry for Safe Tinkering." The difference is that instead of restoring the beginning snapshot, you're going to compare your configuration after the program makes its changes to the snapshot you took beforehand.

1. Create a new profile so that you can easily clean up your message when you're done. Profiles are nothing more than individually named collections of snapshots. Click the Profile button, name the profile, and click OK.

2. Take a snapshot of your configuration as described in "Create a New Snapshot." This saves your configuration as it currently stands. Close ConfigSafe.

3. Run the program and cause it to make the changes to the Registry that you want to uncover. You may have to execute menu commands or move the window. It depends on what you're trying to discover.

4. After you're sure that the program has changed the Registry, close it. Then run ConfigSafe again and compare the previous snapshot to the current configuration, as shown in Figure 9.14.

TIP Press F5 to refresh the comparison between two snapshots.

FIG. 9.14

This list works very much like the REGEDIT.

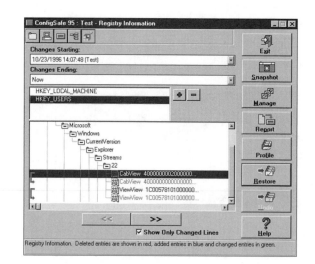

CHAPTER 10

Free and Shareware Software to Customize Windows

by Jerry Honeycutt

The Registry tools that come with Windows will suit most of your needs. The tools provided in this chapter make your life easier by providing a user interface to the Registry. For example, Microsoft's Tweak UI utility lets you change many of the most interesting Registry settings to customize your desktop.

This chapter describes Microsoft's Tweak UI in detail. It also describes a handful of shareware Registry utilities, including those you'll find on the Windows NT 4.0 Resource Kit.

If you're a programmer, you can learn to build Registry utilities in Chapter 19, "Programming the Registry Using C++," and Chapter 20, "Programming the Registry Using Visual Basic." If you don't have the exact Registry utility you want, the information in these chapters helps you construct your own. ■

Using Tweak UI to customize your Windows desktop

Learn how to use Tweak UI (User Interface)—a free program from Microsoft—to change the most interesting Registry settings in Windows.

Downloading shareware Registry utilities

Discover some of the best shareware Registry utilities on the Internet.

The Windows NT Resource Kit

Learn about the various Registry utilities available in the Windows NT 4.0 Resource Kit.

Customizing Windows with Tweak UI

If you're not comfortable with using the Registry Editor to customize Windows (see Chapter 7, "Customizing Your Windows Desktop"), Tweak UI will do it for you. Tweak UI is a freeware program from Microsoft that contains options for some of the most popular Windows customizations.

Tweak UI is part of Microsoft PowerToys—a collection of useful freeware utilities for Windows.

ON THE WEB

You can get your own copy of PowerToys from Microsoft's Web site at

www.microsoft.com/windows/software/powertoy.htm

Click the `PowerToys Set` link to download the entire collection of utilities, or click the `Tweak UI 1.1` link to download just the Tweak UI utility.

What Else Is in PowerToys?

PowerToys contains a lot more than just Tweak UI. It contains a wealth of desktop enhancements for the power user, too. Here are some of the highlights (this is not a complete list):

- *Desktop Menu.* A much needed utility on the taskbar. It makes all of your desktop icons available when they're obscured by windows.
- *DOS Prompt Here 1.0.* Opens an MS-DOS window; the folder you're pointing at is set as the current working directory.
- *CabView.* Makes accessible all those pesky CAB files you see on the Windows 95 CD-ROM, so that you can extract individual files from them.
- *Contents menu.* Places the contents of a folder on the folder's context menu so that you don't have to actually open the folder to see what's inside it.
- *Explore from Here.* Allows you to browse a target folder at the root of the Explorer Window.
- *Flexi CD.* A replacement for a CD Player that takes up no desktop real estate.
- *Quickres.* Allows you to change the screen and color resolution without restarting Windows 95.
- *Sent To X 1.4.* Extends the Send To menu so that you can send files to any folder you choose. You can also send files as mail attachments or send a file's long or short file name to the Clipboard.

Installing Tweak UI

Installing Tweak UI is easy. After you download Tweak UI as described earlier, follow these steps:

1. Make a temporary folder, and copy the file you downloaded into the folder.

2. Double-click the self-extracting, compressed file (its filename is `powertoy.exe`) to expand its contents into the temporary folder.

Tweakui

3. Right-click TWEAKUI.INF and choose Install. Windows copies the files it needs from the temporary folder and displays Tweak UI's help file.

4. Delete the temporary folder after you're finished installing all the PowerToys. Neither PowerToys nor Tweak UI needs these files anymore.

NOTE Tweak UI works equally well in Windows 95 and Windows NT 4.0. Some of Tweak UI's tabs are disabled, however, because those features are not available in NT or you don't have permission to change those settings.

Part

II

Ch

10

Using Tweak UI

To run Tweak UI, choose Settings, Control Panel from the Start menu. Double-click the Tweak UI applet to open it, and you see a property sheet with ten tabs: Mouse, General, Explorer, Desktop, My Computer, New, Add/Remove, Boot, Repair, and Paranoia.

The sections that follow describe the settings on each of these tabs. Click each tab and change the settings that you want. When you finish, click OK to save your changes.

Tweak UI

NOTE If you've previously installed and used Tweak UI, consider downloading the latest version. As you will notice in this chapter, Tweak UI has undergone a major renovation in the last few months.

Mouse Click the Mouse tab, and you see the Tweak UI dialog box shown in Figure 10.1. This tab lets you change settings that affect the mouse, such as the speed with which Windows 95 displays menus and the sensitivity of the mouse.

FIG. 10.1
Double-click, right-click, or drag the test icon to test your settings.

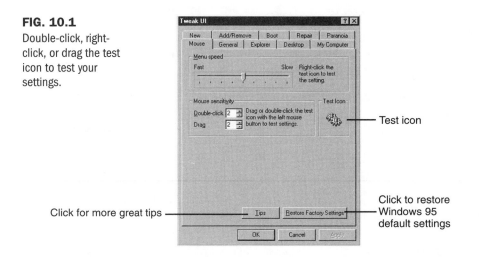

Test icon

Click for more great tips

Click to restore Windows 95 default settings

Table 10.1 describes the various options on the Tweak UI Mouse tab.

Table 10.1   Tweak UI's Mouse Tab

Option	Description
Menu Speed	Controls how long Windows 95 waits before popping up a menu after you click it. Drag the slider to the left to make menus pop up faster or to the right to make menus pop up slower.
Double-click	Determines how many pixels are allowed between two mouse clicks in order for them to be considered a double-click. Make this number larger to increase sensitivity or smaller to decrease sensitivity.
Drag	Determines how many pixels the mouse must move with the button clicked before it's considered a drag. Make this number larger to increase sensitivity or smaller to decrease sensitivity.

General   Click the General tab, and you see the dialog box shown in Figure 10.2. This tab lets you change miscellaneous settings—ones that don't fit any other particular tab category. You can turn off window animation and the location of each system folder, for example.

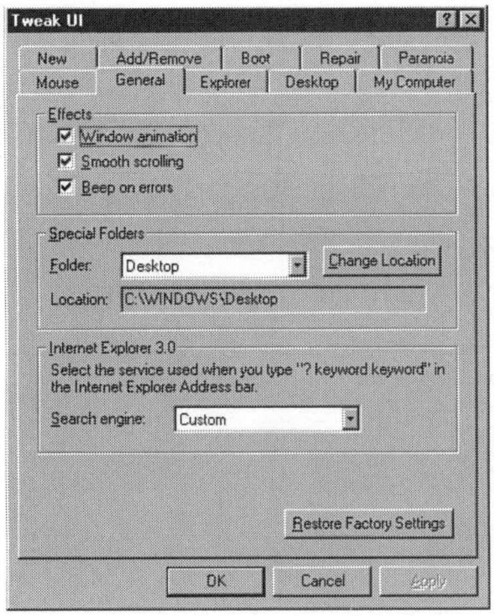

FIG. 10.2

If you're annoyed with the smooth scrolling that Internet Explorer 3.0 installed on your computer, you can disable it by deselecting Smooth Scrolling.

Table 10.2 describes the various options on the Tweak UI General tab.

Table 10.2   Tweak UI's General Tab

Option	Description
Window Animation	Controls whether or not windows are animated when you minimize, maximize, or restore them. Select this check box to turn on animation or deselect it to turn off animation.
Smooth Scrolling	Controls whether Windows smoothly scrolls an Explorer view or whether it crisply jumps to the next page. Select this check box to turn on smooth scrolling, or deselect it to turn off smooth scrolling.
Beep on Errors	Controls whether or not Windows 95 beeps when an error occurs. Select this check box to turn on sounds, or deselect it to turn off sounds.
Special Folders	Controls where the special system folders, such as Desktop, Startup menu, and so on, reside on your computer. Select a type of system folder from Folder, and click on Change Location to change it to a different location.
Internet Explorer	Controls which search engine Internet Explorer uses when you preface a keyword with a question mark (?) in the address bar. Select a search engine from Search Engine.

Explorer   Click the Explorer tab. The dialog box shown in Figure 10.3 appears. This tab lets you change settings, such as the overlay used for shortcuts and whether or not the words Shortcut to are prefixed to new shortcuts.

FIG. 10.3
Click Custom to choose your own icon overlay from a DLL, EXE, or ICO file.

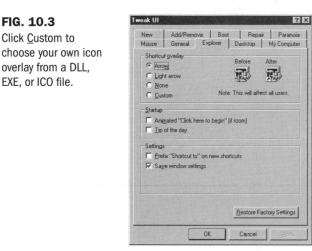

Table 10.3 describes the options you see in Tweak UI's Explorer tab.

Table 10.3   Tweak UI's Explorer Tab

Option	Description
Shortcut Overlay	Determines the overlay used for shortcuts. The overlay is usually a small arrow that Windows 95 displays in the lower-left corner of the shortcut's icon. Choose either Arrow, Light Arrow, None, or Custom.
Animated "Click Here to Begin"	Controls whether or not Windows 95 displays "Click here to begin" in the taskbar (If Room) after you log on.
Tip of the Day	Controls whether or not Windows 95 displays the Tip of the Day when you first log on.
Prefix "Shortcut to" on New Shortcuts	Controls whether or not the words Shortcut to are prefixed to new shortcuts.
Save Window Settings	Controls whether or not Windows 95 saves the location of any open windows and icons on the desktop when you shut down.

CAUTION
On some systems, setting the shortcut overlay to None causes Windows 95 to behave erratically.

Desktop   Click the Desktop tab and you see the dialog box shown in Figure 10.4. This tab allows you to add or remove each special desktop icon (Internet News and Network Neighborhood, for example) to or from the desktop. It also lets you create these special icons as files that you can put anywhere on your computer.

FIG. 10.4

The Printers and Control Panel icons can't be created directly on the desktop—you must create them as files.

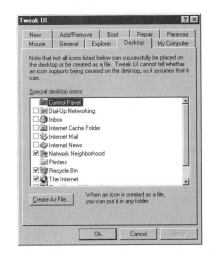

To add a special icon to your desktop, click the box next to the icon in the Special Desktop Icons list until you see a check mark inside it. To remove a special icon from your desktop, click the box next to the icon until the check mark disappears.

You can also create these special icons as files. Select one of the special icons, and click Create as File. Choose the folder in which you want to save the file, and click Save.

My Computer   Click the My Computer tab, and you see a dialog box similar to Figure 10.5. This is a list of all the possible drive letters for your computer. You use this dialog box to choose which drives show up in My Computer. You can remove the floppy drives from My Computer, for example. To remove a drive from My Computer, click the box next to the drive until you don't see a check mark inside it. To again display a drive in My Computer, click the box next to the icon until you see the check mark again.

FIG. 10.5

The icon next to the drive indicates the type of drive.

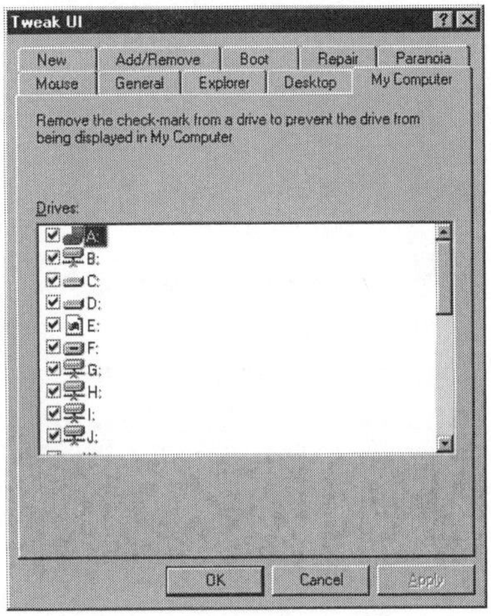

Part
II

Ch
10

N O T E In Windows NT 4.0, you won't see this tab if you don't have permission to alter the list of
drives that NT displays in My Computer. ▪

New If you right-click the desktop and choose New, you see a list of file types that
Windows 95 can create for you. Choose one of the file types, such as Text Document, and
Windows 95 creates a new icon on the desktop that is called something like "New Text
Document." Then, double-click the document to open it in Notepad.

You can also add your own file types to this list. You can even use a template. For example,
you might want to create HTML files that have the exact same contents every time. Just
follow these steps:

1. Create a file whose contents you want to use as a template. All new files of this type
   will have the same contents.

2. Click the New tab in Tweak UI, and you see the dialog box shown in Figure 10.6.
   This tab lets you add your own templates to the list.

3. Drag the file you created in step 1 to the drop area of the New tab. You can safely
   delete the original file.

FIG. 10.6
With Tweak UI 1.1,
you can now delete
templates: select the
template you want to
delete and click
Remove.

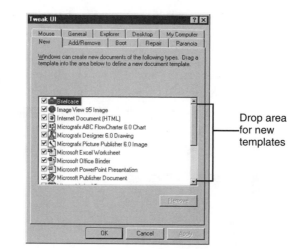

Add/Remove Have you ever removed a program from your hard drive and then
wondered how to remove it from the list of applications? The Windows Add/Remove
Programs Control Panel application can automatically do just that. The Add/Remove tab
lets you remove or add programs to the list in Add/Remove Programs; it even lets you
edit existing programs.

Click the Add/Remove tab to see a list of programs which Windows can automatically remove, as shown in Figure 10.7. This list contains an entry for programs you see in the Add/Remove Programs Control Panel application. Here's what you can do with it:

- Click Remove to remove a program from the list of applications that Windows can automatically remove.

- Click New to add a program to the list; then type the name of the program and the path to the uninstall program in the spaces provided. Click OK to save your changes.

- Click Edit to change a program that Windows 95 can automatically remove; then change the name of the application and path to the uninstall program. Click OK to save your changes.

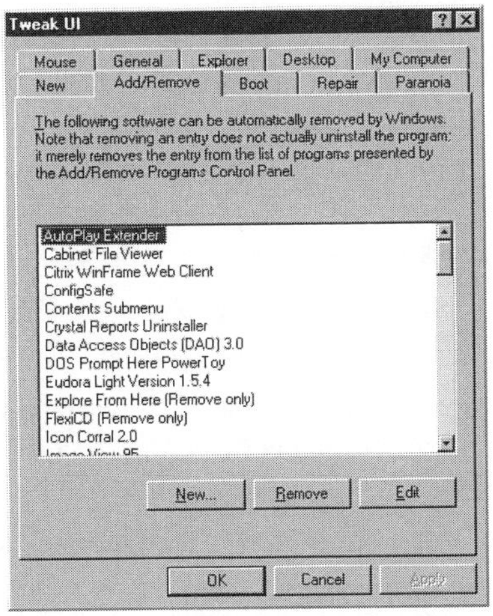

FIG. 10.7
The command lines for many entries in this list are frequently unintelligible—they use DLL and INF files.

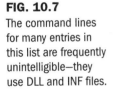

Boot Click the Boot tab. The dialog box shown in Figure 10.8 appears. This tab lets you customize how Windows 95 starts. You can disable the animated start-up screen, for example. You can also cause Windows 95 to start DOS 7.0 by default, instead of the graphical user interface.

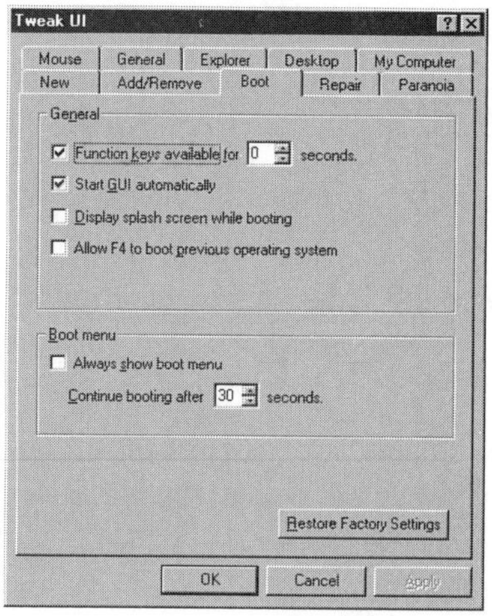

FIG. 10.8

The boot options are stored in a hidden file called C:\MSDOS.SYS.

Table 10.4 describes the options on the Boot tab of the Tweak UI dialog box.

Table 10.4   Tweak UI's Boot Tab

Option	Description
Function Keys Available For # Seconds	Determines how long Windows 95 will wait for you to press one of the function keys before it continues booting.
Start GUI Automatically	Controls whether or not Windows 95 starts the graphical user interface. Select this check box to start the GUI, or deselect it to start DOS 7.0.
Display Splash Screen While Booting	Controls whether or not Windows 95 displays the animated splash screen while it starts. Select this check box to allow the splash screen, or deselect it to disallow the splash screen.
Allow F4 to Boot Previous Operating System	Controls whether or not Windows 95 allows you to start the previous operating system by pressing F4. Select this check box to allow it, or deselect it to disallow it.
Always Show Boot Menu	Determines if Windows 95 will always display the boot menu. Select this check box to always display the boot menu, or deselect it to require you to press F8 before displaying it.
Continue Booting After # Seconds	Determines how long Windows 95 will wait for you to choose a boot option if the boot menu is displayed.

N O T E This tab isn't available in Windows NT 4.0 because NT doesn't support the boot options defined in MSDOS.SYS. ▪

Repair   You can solve a variety of problems using Tweak UI's Repair tab. You can rebuild Explorer's icons, for example, or repair the file associations in the Registry. Click on the Repair tab, and you'll see the dialog box shown in Figure 10.9. Table 10.5 shows you what each button does.

Table 10.5   Tweak UI's Repair Tab

Button	Description
Rebuild Icons	Rebuilds all of Explorer's icons. Click this button if Explorer is displaying the incorrect icons.
Repair Font Folder	Restores the special functionality of the Fonts folder so that you can preview fonts and find similar fonts.
Repair System Files	Restores files that are frequently overwritten by errant installation programs. Restores the backup files you find in \Windows\SysBckup folder.
Repair Regedit	Repairs REGEDIT's view information so that you can once again see all of its columns. Click this button if some of REGEDIT's columns are hidden.
Repair Associations	Restores all the icons and programs associated with the standard file types. Click this button if the icons and context menus for the standard Windows 95 file types don't work as expected.

Paranoia   You use the Paranoia tab—aptly named—to clear your tracks so that people don't know what you've been doing. For example, you can cause Windows 95 to automatically clear out the document history each time you start your computer. Click the Paranoia tab, and you'll see a dialog box that looks like Figure 10.10. Table 10.6 shows you what each of the options on this dialog box does.

Part

II

Ch

10

FIG. 10.9
Repair Regedit and
Repair Associations
don't work in Windows
NT 4.0.

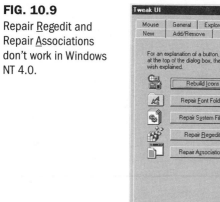

Table 10.6   Tweak UI's Paranoia Tab

Option	Description
Clear Run History at Logon	The run history is the list of programs you've run when you choose Run from the Start menu. Select this check box to clear this list each time you log on.
Clear Document History at Logon	The document history is the list of documents that you've opened. You see this list in the Start menu under Documents. Select this check box to clear this list each time you log on.
Clear Find Files History at Logon	The find files history is the list of file specifications for which you've searched using the Find utility (choose Find, Files or Folders from the Start menu). Select this check box to clear this list each time you log on.
Clear Find Computer History at Logon	The find computer history is the list of computers for which you've searched using the Find Computer utility (choose Find, Computer from the Start menu). Select this check box to clear this list each time you log on.
Play Audio CDs Automatically	Deselect this check box to prevent Windows from automatically playing audio CDs when you insert them into the drive.
Play Data CDs Automatically	Deselect this check box to prevent Windows from automatically playing data CDs when you insert them into the drive.
Log Application Errors to FAULTLOG.TXT	Select this check box to log all application errors in \Windows\FAULTLOG.TXT.

FIG. 10.10
Disabling Play Audio
CDs Automatically is
useful if you're tired of
holding down the Shift
key to stop CD-ROMs
from automatically
starting when you
insert them.

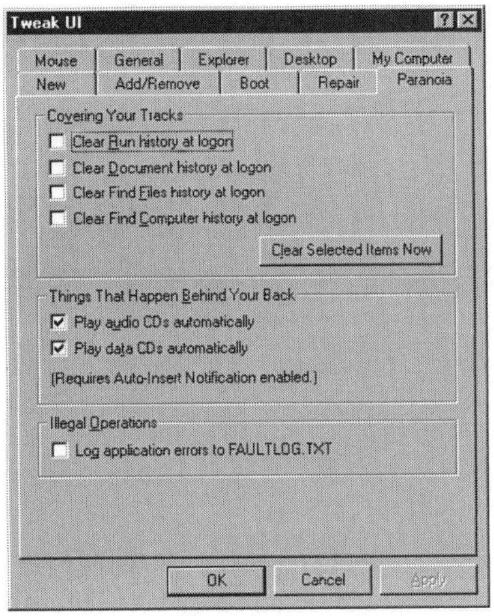

Part

II

Ch

10

Finding Other Freeware and Shareware Programs

You can find a handful of decent Registry utilities on the Internet. Most of them duplicate the functionality that either comes with Windows 95 (see Chapter 1, "Before You Begin") or Microsoft's Tweak UI, described earlier in this chapter. Here, you learn about three noteworthy Registry utilities that enhance or extend what Microsoft already provides:

- Registry Editor Extensions
- Registry Search & Replace
- WinHacker

ON THE WEB

The best place to find freeware and shareware Registry utilities is at the ZD Net Software Library Web site:

http://206.66.184.152/index.html

Search the library using the keyword **registry**. You'll find every Registry utility that this site catalogs.

Registry Editor Extensions

Registry Editor Extensions is a small, freeware program that adds a drop-down list to the Registry edit that you can use to quickly jump back to a previously edited Registry key.

Open the drop-down list, as shown in Figure 10.11, and click one of the Registry keys to open that key in the Registry Editor.

FIG. 10.11

The drop-down list that the Registry Editor Extensions adds to the Registry Editor works just like the history list in your favorite Web browser.

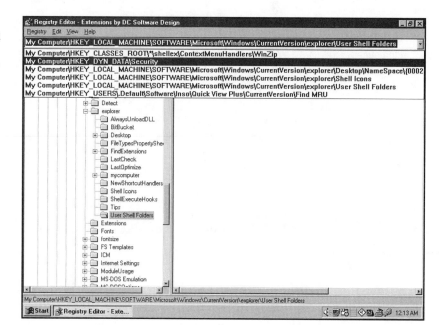

ON THE WEB

You can download the Registry Editor Extensions from the Internet at

http://www.dcsoft.com

Click RegEditX.zip, and follow your browser's instructions to download the file to your computer. Then, decompress REGEDITX.ZIP to a temporary folder, and run SETUP.EXE. Follow the instructions you see on the screen.

Running REGEDIT.EXE launches the Windows 95 Registry Editor, but it won't load the Registry Editor Extensions. Instead, choose Programs, RegEdit Extensions, RegEdit Extensions from the Start menu.

Registry Search & Replace

Registry Search & Replace (see Figure 10.12) is a familiar utility that you can use to automatically locate and change entries in the Registry. Windows Notepad has a search and replace feature, as does WordPad and Microsoft Word. Registry Search & Replace is a bit more complicated, however, because it works with the Windows Registry. Here's an overview of its features:

- You can search for any string of characters you like. You can restrict the search to values or data, as well as certain types of data and certain root keys.

- You can use Registry Search & Replace with remote computers. Both computers have to be configured to use the Remote Registry Search as described in Chapter 13, "Remotely Editing a User's Registry," however.

- For each match Registry Search & Replace finds, you can have it prompt you for a replacement, have it automatically replace the matching string with another string, or just display the matching entry.

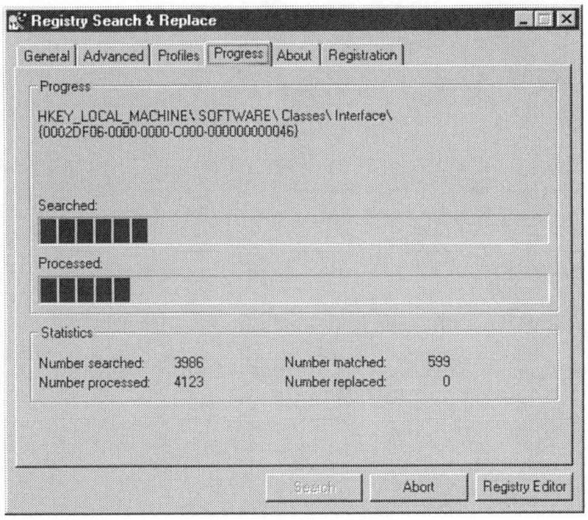

FIG. 10.12

Registry Search & Replace is shareware. You can use it 25 times before you're forced to register it.

Part
II

Ch
10

ON THE WEB

You can download Registry Search & Replace from the Internet at

http://ourworld.compuserve.com/homepages/shoek/REGSRCH.HTM

Select `Click here to download the latest version (~ 635K ZIP file)`, and follow your browser's instructions to download it to your computer. Decompress REGSRCH2.ZIP into a temporary folder and run SETUP.EXE. Follow the instructions you see on the screen.

WinHacker 95

WinHacker is a shareware utility that's very similar to Microsoft's Tweak UI. It provides many of the same options. Figure 10.13 shows you what WinHacker 1.1 looks like. The developer, however, is currently working on some unique features for WinHacker 2.0. With a look and feel very similar to the Windows 95 Policy Editor, WinHacker 2.0 also adds many more Registry settings that you can change. It is definitely worth the wait.

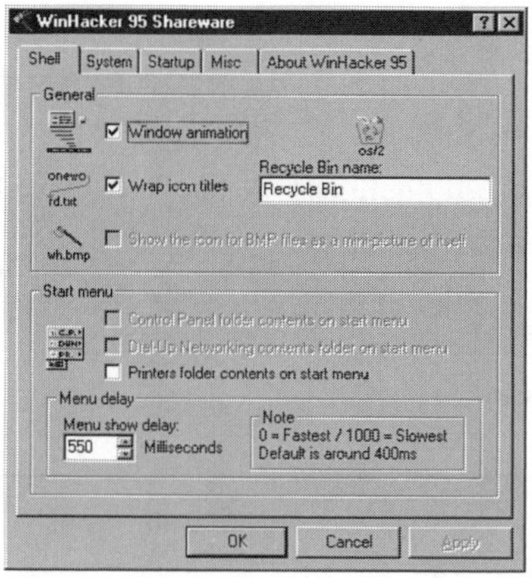

FIG. 10.13

WinHacker 1.1 doesn't stack up well to Microsoft's Tweak UI. WinHacker 2.0, soon to be released, promises to be the mother of all customization tools, however.

ON THE WEB

You can download WinHacker from the Internet at

http://home.wojo.com/wedge

Click wh95-11s.zip, and follow your browser's instructions to download it to your computer. Decompress wh95-11s.zip into its own folder. WinHacker 95 doesn't have a setup program, so you just run WinHack.exe.

TIP You can create a Start menu shortcut to WinHacker 95 by dragging WinHack.exe and dropping it on the Start menu.

The Windows NT Resource Kit Is Loaded

Most Windows NT 4.0 users already know about the Windows NT Workstation Resource Kit. Besides containing a wealth of information about Windows NT, it also has a CD-ROM that contains a large number of Registry tools. Most of these utilities provide functionality that you can use from the command line or in a batch file. For example, you can write a batch file that uses REGCHG.EXE to modify a Registry key. Here's a taste:

File	Description
COMPREG.EXE	Compares two Registry keys.
REGBACK.EXE	Backs up the Registry to a file.
REGCHG.EXE	Changes keys using the command line.
REGDEL.EXE	Removes keys using the command line.
REGINI.EXE	Adds keys using a batch file.
REGREAD.EXE	Displays keys using the command line.

File	Description
REGRTEST.EXE	Restores a backup of the Registry.
REGSEC.EXE	Removes the Everyone group from a key.
RREGCHG.EXE	Changes Registry keys over a network.
SAVEKEY.EXE	Saves a Registry key to a text file.
SCANREG.EXE	Scans the Registry for a string.
SECADD.EXE	Adds permissions to a Registry key.

Part
II

Ch
10

CHAPTER 11

Getting Your Windows 95 Configuration Just Right

by Jerry Honeycutt

Getting your configuration right the first time is a pain in the neck. You need to make sure your computer starts the way you want it to. You want to make sure that you're loading the appropriate files in your CONFIG.SYS and AUTOEXEC.BAT files. You also want to optimize Windows 95 so that it performs as well as possible on your computer. This is a lot to expect.

Fortunately, it's one of those things that you do once and forget about. Once you've configured your startup files, for example, you don't have to tinker with them anymore (unless an errant program messes with them). Likewise, once you've optimized your computer, you can forget about it. This chapter shows you how to get your configuration right the first time, so that you can move on to better things—like that game of solitaire you've had a hankering for. ■

Change how Windows 95 starts

You can easily change how Windows 95 starts. For example, you can skip the animated logo, or you can boot directly into MS-DOS 7.0.

Learn all about CONFIG.SYS and AUTOEXEC.BAT

These files are shrouded in mystery for a lot of folks. This chapter shows you when you do and don't need to worry about the contents of these files.

Optimize your Windows 95 system

Windows 95 doesn't have many ways for you to optimize it. Regardless, this section shows you how to optimize things such as your swap file.

> **N O T E**   Windows NT doesn't have as many settings as Windows 95 that you can tinker with in
> order to customize how it starts or to optimize it. For example, NT does parse the
> AUTOEXEC.BAT file, but only for Path, Prompt, and Set commands. It doesn't do anything at all
> with the CONFIG.SYS file. Thus, this chapter doesn't contain much useful information for Windows
> NT users. ▓

Changing How Windows 95 Starts

Windows 95 gives you a lot of control over how it starts. You can dual-boot with your previous version of MS-DOS, you can start in MS-DOS 7.0 instead of Windows 95, and you
can replace the animated startup screen with your own.

In this section, you learn about all of these things and more, including:

- What files in your root folder affect your startup.
- Configuring your Windows 95 boot options.
- Restarting Windows 95 without rebooting.
- Dual-booting Windows 95, Windows 3.1, and NT.
- What to do if you installed Windows 95 over Windows 3.1 and you want to be able to
  dual-boot.

Exploring the Files in Your Root Folder

You'll find a handful of files in your root folder that impact how your computer starts. For
example, you'll find the typical AUTOEXEC.BAT and CONFIG.SYS. Table 11.1 describes
the files you'll find in a dual-boot configuration. Since the files are renamed, depending on
whether you started Windows 95 or chose to start your previous version of MS-DOS, this
table has two columns, one for each choice. That is, Windows 95 explicitly changes the
names of the files in Table 11.1 so that it uses the appropriate startup files, depending on
which operating system you chose to start.

Table 11.1   Startup Files in Your Root Folder

Windows 95	Previous MS-DOS	Description
AUTOEXEC.BAT	AUTOEXEC.W40	Windows 95 AUTOEXEC.BAT
CONFIG.SYS	CONFIG.W40	Windows 95 CONFIG.SYS
COMMAND.COM	COMMAND.W40	Windows 95 command processor
IO.SYS	WINBOOT.SYS	Windows 95 real-mode code

Windows 95	Previous MS-DOS	Description
MSDOS.SYS	MSDOS.W40	Windows 95 boot options
AUTOEXEC.DOS	AUTOEXEC.BAT	MS-DOS's AUTOEXEC.BAT
COMMAND.DOS	COMMAND.COM	MS-DOS's command processor
CONFIG.DOS	CONFIG.SYS	MS-DOS's CONFIG.SYS
IO.DOS	IO.SYS	MS-DOS's operating system code
MSDOS.DOS	MSDOS.SYS	MS-DOS's operating system code

N O T E IO.SYS contains the real-mode DOS code for Windows 95. It executes a handful of commands and loads some device drivers that you'd normally load in CONFIG.SYS. Then it processes the CONFIG.SYS and AUTOEXEC.BAT files. See "The Truth About CONFIG.SYS..." later in this chapter, to learn more about what IO.SYS does. ▓

Configuring Your Boot Options

Part
II
Ch
11

In Windows 95, MSDOS.SYS is a hidden, read-only file in the root folder of your boot drive. It's a text file that looks very similar to an INI file. It's not like the old MS-DOS file by the same name—it doesn't contain any code. Instead, it contains a number of options that affect how your computer starts. For example, by editing this file, you can control whether or not Windows 95 displays its animated logo, or how long you have to press F8 in order to display the Start menu.

T I P Choose View, Options from Explorer's main menu, select Show All Files, and click OK to see the hidden files on your computer.

There are two sections in the file: [Options] and [Paths]. [Options] is where you change how Windows 95 starts, and [Paths] contains entries that tell the system where it'll find its files. Here's what a typical MSDOS.SYS looks like:

```
[Paths]
WinDir=C:\WINDOWS
WinBootDir=C:\WINDOWS
HostWinBootDrv=C

[Options]
BootMulti=1
BootGUI=1
Network=1
```

N O T E   The last part of MSDOS.SYS contains a number of lines filled with x's. These are there to make sure that MSDOS.SYS is compatible with other programs that think it has to be greater than 1024 bytes in length. ▪

Table 11.2 describes each of the options that you can use in the [Options] part of MSDOS.SYS. It describes the name of the option, the default value, and what the option is used for. When an option can have a value of 1 or 0, the 1 means yes or true; the 0 means no or false. You'll find more details about some of these options later in this section.

Table 11.2   Options in MSDOS.SYS

Option	Default	Description
BootDelay=x	2	Delay x seconds at startup
BootFailSafe=1 or 0	0	Start in Safe mode
BootGUI=1 or 0	1	Start Windows 95 GUI
BootKeys=1 or 0	1	Enable F4, F5, F6, F8
BootMenu=1 or 0	0	Display boot menu
BootMenuDefault=x	3	Default boot menu option
BootMulti=1 or 0	0	Allow dual-booting
BootWarn=1 or 0	1	Warn if starting Safe mode
BootWin=1 or 0	1	Start Windows 95 by default
DblSpace=1 or 0	1	Load DBLSPACE.BIN
DoubleBuffer=1 or 0	1	DoubleBuffer SCSI devices
DrvSpace=1 or 0	1	Load DRVSPACE.BIN
LoadTop=1 or 0	1	Load COMMAND.COM high
Logo=1 or 0	1	Display animated logo
Network=1 or 0	1	Safe mode with networking

N O T E   Safe mode is a special boot option that causes Windows 95 to load without most of its device driver support loaded. It uses the standard VGA, mouse, and keyboard drivers only. If you're experiencing a problem starting Windows 95, you can start in Safe mode to fix it. ▪

Allowing Yourself Enough Time to Press F8   Windows 95 displays "Starting Windows 95" as it starts. While this is on the screen, you can press one of the boot keys, such as F8, to do things like bring up the boot menu or step through the commands in CONFIG.SYS and AUTOEXEC.BAT line by line.

The problem is that you may not be quick enough on the draw, especially if you have a fast processor. You can change how long Windows 95 gives you the opportunity to press a boot key. Set BootDelay to a value such as five seconds by putting **BootDelay=5** in MSDOS.SYS. Don't make it much more than a few seconds, however, if you don't want to wait every time you start your computer.

Boot Keys Supported by Windows 95

Windows 95 supports a handful of keystrokes that let you change how it starts. Here are the keystrokes that are available:

Keystroke	Description
F4	Starts the previous version of MS-DOS (if installed) if you put **BootWin=1** in your MSDOS.SYS
F5	Starts Windows 95 in Safe mode
Shift+F5	Starts MS-DOS 7.0 in Safe mode without loading CONFIG.SYS and AUTOEXEC.BAT
Ctrl+F5	Starts MS-DOS 7.0 without loading any compressed drives
F6	Starts Windows 95 in Safe mode with networking
F8	Displays the Windows 95 Start menu
Shift+F8	Lets you confirm each line that IO.SYS, CONFIG.SYS, and AUTOEXEC.BAT execute

---

Part
II

Ch
11

Starting MS-DOS 7.0 Instead of the Graphical Interface   If you like your computer to start the old-fashioned way, you can start it with MS-DOS 7.0, and then run Windows when you're ready by typing **win** at the command line prompt and pressing Enter. Put **BootGUI=0** in MSDOS.SYS.

Disabling or Replacing the Windows 95 Logo   If you're having trouble starting Windows 95 or you want to see the messages that are displayed while Windows 95 starts, you'll want to disable the animated logo. Put **Logo=0** in MSDOS.SYS and Windows 95 won't display it.

You can use your own logo, too. The Windows 95 logo is stored in a file named LOGO.SYS. You'll find it the root directory of your boot drive. Don't let the name throw you—it's really just a BMP file. Create your own bitmap image that is the same size as LOGO.SYS, rename LOGO.SYS to LOGO.SAV, and name your bitmap image LOGO.SYS.

> **TIP** LOGOS.SYS and LOGOW.SYS are the bitmaps that Windows 95 uses when shutting down. You'll find both files in C:\Windows.

Restarting Windows 95 Without Rebooting

It's easy to restart Windows 95 without having to reboot your computer. Why do you want to do this, though? Maybe a program crashed and your computer has become unstable. You may have run a program that didn't let go of its memory. You might even be one of those individuals who just likes to compulsively restart his computer every once in a while. Just follow these steps:

1. Choose Shut Down from the Start menu.
2. Select Restart the Computer in the Shut Down Windows dialog box.
3. Hold down the Shift key while you click Yes.

While Windows 95 restarts, it displays a message that says Restarting Windows 95. This is definitely much faster than rebooting the whole system. Unfortunately, this doesn't work with Windows NT.

Setting Up Multi-Boot Windows 95, MS-DOS, and NT

If you're one of those individuals who needs to dual-boot both Windows 95 and Windows 3.1, you're in luck. It's easy to set up. You can even triple-boot Windows 95, Windows 3.1, and Windows NT, if you like. Note that although it's easy to configure your system to triple-boot, you may experience a few problems.

> **CAUTION**
> Don't use Windows NT's NTFS (NT File System) if you want to dual-boot NT and Windows 95, because Windows 95 can't read an NTFS volume.

If you haven't installed Windows 95 yet, setting up your computer to dual-boot is simply a matter of choosing the appropriate folder in which to install Windows 95. If you've already wiped out your previous system, however, it's not too late. You can put the appropriate files back onto your computer that allow you to dual-boot to your previous version of MS-DOS.

Setting Up to Multi-Boot When Installing Windows 95   The work begins before you install Windows 95. If you want to dual-boot with your previous version of MS-DOS and Windows 3.x, make sure both are set up and working correctly. Then install Windows 95 into a folder other than the folder in which Windows 3.x is installed.

Dual-booting only works if you don't install Windows 95 into the same directory as Windows 3.x. Windows 95 automatically configures your computer to dual-boot, making the necessary changes to MSDOS.SYS and creating the appropriate *.DOS files in your root folder.

If you want to dual-boot with Windows NT as well, set up your computer to dual-boot Windows 95 and MS-DOS before you install Windows NT. In this case, you'll choose your boot option in Windows NT before you choose it in Windows 95. You can install Windows 95 after installing Windows NT, because Windows 95 is aware of Windows NT; it won't over- write the Windows NT boot loader.

T I P Make a copy of your old MS-DOS files (in your DOS folder) before installing Windows 95 if you want to preserve them, because Setup removes some of them.

N O T E If you install Windows 95 in a different folder than your old version of Windows, you have to reinstall the programs you want to use in Windows 95. Most programs put files in the Windows folder and update settings in various INI files. Reinstalling these programs makes sure that your Windows 95 folder has the files and settings it needs. Note that when you change settings in a program running in Windows 95, your new settings may not be reflected when you run the same program under Windows 3.x. ■

Part
II

Ch
11

Setting Up to Dual-Boot After Windows 95 Is Installed   If you've already installed Windows 95 over your previous version of Windows, or if you installed Windows 95 on a newly formatted hard drive, you can still configure your computer to dual-boot. Grab a copy of your MS-DOS disk for the previous version of MS-DOS and follow these steps:

1. Show the hidden files on the disk by typing **attrib -h -r -s a:*.sys** at the MS-DOS command line prompt.
2. Rename IO.SYS to IO.DOS and MSDOS.SYS to MSDOS.DOS on the floppy disk. Copy these files to the root folder of your boot drive.

CAUTION
You won't be able to start Windows 95 if you copy IO.SYS and MSDOS.SYS from your DOS disk to your boot drive before renaming them. Also make sure you're using a copy of your MS-DOS disk so that you don't accidentally ruin your only MS-DOS disk.

3. Hide these files again by typing **attrib +h +r +s c:*.dos** at the MS-DOS command line prompt.

4. Rename COMMAND.COM to COMMAND.DOS on the disk and copy it to the root folder of your boot drive.

5. Create a CONFIG.DOS and an AUTOEXEC.DOS on the root folder of your boot drive that contains the commands and drivers required to start your previous version of MS-DOS. The contents of these files will probably be similar to your original CONFIG.SYS and AUTOEXEC.BAT.

6. Restart your computer.

Choosing Which System to Start　When Windows 95 displays Starting Windows 95, press F4 to automatically start the previous version of MS-DOS. You can also press F8 to display the Start menu, and choose menu option 8 to load the previous version of MS-DOS.

◆

TROUBLESHOOTING

I try to start Windows 3.1 and I get a message that says the swap file is corrupt. Windows 95 has changed your swap file (386SPART.PAR) and Windows 3.1 isn't sure what to do with it now. Delete the swap file and create a new one in Windows 3.1.

Can I start Windows 3.1 from within Windows 95? Yes, oddly enough. You can create a shortcut to Windows 3.1 that uses MS-DOS mode. This will shut down Windows 95, configure the devices in your computer, and start Windows 3.1.

The Truth About CONFIG.SYS...

You've probably heard both sides of the story. You've heard that your old configuration files, such as AUTOEXEC.BAT and CONFIG.SYS, are no longer necessary and you can delete them. You've also heard that these files aren't completely gone yet, and Windows 95 still needs them.

Which side of the story is correct? Both. AUTOEXEC.BAT, CONFIG.SYS, SYSTEM.INI, and WIN.INI didn't go away when you installed Windows 95. It still uses them, and it's a good thing, too—otherwise many of your Windows 3.1 and MS-DOS programs wouldn't work in Windows 95. These files are required for compatibility purposes.

In this section, you'll learn about these configuration files, including topics such as:

■ What Windows 95 Setup does to your configuration files when you install it.

■ How to tell if you really need the AUTOEXEC.BAT and CONFIG.SYS, and what you should put in them.

■ What parts of SYSTEM.INI and WIN.INI you'll find in the Registry now.

ON THE WEB

http://www.microsoft.com/kb   Microsoft's Knowledge Base is a huge database of the bugs, problems, incompatibilities, and other issues that Microsoft has recorded for all of their products. If you're having problems with your AUTOEXEC.BAT or CONFIG.SYS, or problems starting Windows 95, search this database to find answers. See Appendix C, "Technical Resources for Windows," for more information.

The Real Work Starts with Installation

A lot of the AUTOEXEC.BAT and CONFIG.SYS anxiety can be remedied by making sure Windows 95 has every chance to eliminate your need for these files when you install it. There are two different ways you can do this. You can eliminate AUTOEXEC.BAT and CONFIG.SYS altogether and let Windows 95 figure out what hardware is installed in your computer. You can also selectively eliminate certain device drivers and other programs from your configuration files that you're certain Windows 95 can replace with its own. You'll learn about both approaches in this section.

> **CAUTION**
>
> If you want to dual-boot Windows 95 and Windows 3.1, see "Changing How Windows 95 Starts," earlier in this chapter, before you use the suggestions in this section. You don't want to tamper with your configuration files before installing Windows 95, because you'll need these files to boot into Windows 3.1.

Real-Mode versus Protected-Mode Device Drivers   The older device drivers that you load in your CONFIG.SYS are known as *real-mode*, or 16-bit device drivers. The CD-ROM device driver that you used before Windows 95 is a real-mode device driver. The new device drivers that Windows 95 loads are known as *protected-mode*, or 32-bit device drivers. The distinction between the two types of device drivers is important for three reasons:

■ *Performance.* Protected-mode device drivers are much faster than their real-mode counterparts.

■ *Conventional Memory.* Protected-mode device drivers don't use up conventional memory like real-mode device drivers.

■ *Availability.* Windows 95 has protected-mode device drivers for most of the devices that you'll install in your computer, including CD-ROM drives, sound cards, and more.

Part

II

Ch

11

Clean up CONFIG.SYS and AUTOEXEC.BAT   When you install Windows 95, it tries to find all the real-mode drivers and other useless programs that you've installed in your configuration files, and then it disables them by putting "REM" in front of the command. Windows 95 uses protected-mode drivers for those devices. Table 11.3 shows the drivers and other commands that Windows 95 disables in CONFIG.SYS. Table 11.4 shows the programs and other commands that it disables in AUTOEXEC.BAT. Aside from these, Windows 95 also disables any disk cache, such as SMARTDRV.EXE, that it finds in either the CONFIG.SYS or AUTOEXEC.BAT. It also disables any mouse drivers you've loaded.

Table 11.3   Drivers/Commands Removed from CONFIG.SYS

biling	country	cpqcm	display	dos-up
cmd640x	ifshlp	fastopen	fastopen	rambios
dosdata	doshost	driver	dwcfgmg	ega
extrados	isl850	isl861	island	jdisp
jfont	jkeyb	kkcfunc	kkfunc	memdrv
mirror	msime	msimek	nav	navtsr
nemm	nfs-ndis	pcnfs	pcshel	pcshell
protman	rambios	redirect	sockdrv	st-dbl
share	share	share	smartdrv	smartdrv
st-dspc	tcpdrv	ubxps	undelete	vaccine
vdefend	vdefend	virstop	vsafe	vsafe
vwatch	wbide	workgrp		

Table 11.4   Programs/Commands Removed from AUTOEXEC.BAT

3C503ban	3C507ban	3C523ban	3C603ban	6510ban
8023ban	acinfo	arcban	arcmcban	asyncban
attstban	call	csiban	dblspace	dellmenu
diag5210	diag9210	diagarc	diage503	diage523
diage603	diagethr	diagintr	diagipa	diagiso
diagomni	diagpcnt	diagpro4	diagtokn	diagungr
diagvlan	diagwd	dnr	doshost	drvspace

emsbfr	etherban	expban	hughsban	i92ban
intelban	interban	intr2ban	ipaban	irmban
isoban	mirror	navtsr	ndarcban	nddgban
neban	net	netbind	netbind	nicmcban
nmtsr	oliban	omniban	pcnetban	pcshell
pro16ban	pro4ban	proban	probanmc	redirect
rin	rinAsync	script	snban	sockets
tcptsr	tinyrfc	tokbanmc	toknban	tokuiban
trban	ubniuban	umb	undelete	ungerban
vaccine	vdefend	virstop	vlanban	vsafe
vwatch	wbide	wdban	dosshell	setcfg
UnSet	=ascsi	fastopen	share	win

> **TIP** You can use SYSEDIT.EXE to edit all of your configuration files at once.

You can help the process along by removing all the real-mode drivers that you won't need from your configuration files. If you're installing from a CD-ROM or from a network, however, you do need to leave these drivers in your CONFIG.SYS and AUTOEXEC.BAT files. Otherwise, Windows 95 may not be able to access the installation files after it restarts the first time. If Windows 95 finds protected-mode drivers for these later, it will prevent the old drivers from loading, and replace them with the protected-mode drivers.

> **N O T E** Check the AUTOEXEC.BAT and CONFIG.SYS files after installing older Windows 3.1 and MS-DOS programs. They may try to add unnecessary files such as SHARE or SMARTDRV to your configuration. ■

Hide CONFIG.SYS and AUTOEXEC.BAT from Setup   Many people (myself included) have gone so far as to rename or remove CONFIG.SYS and AUTOEXEC.BAT before starting the setup program. That way, Windows 95 has to find protected-mode drivers for all the hardware in the computer. Afterwards, you can look in the System Properties' Device Manager tab to find any devices that didn't load properly. For example, Figure 11.1 shows what a device looks like in this dialog box when it doesn't load properly. If Windows 95 doesn't provide a protected-mode driver, add the real-mode driver for that device back into your CONFIG.SYS or AUTOEXEC.BAT files.

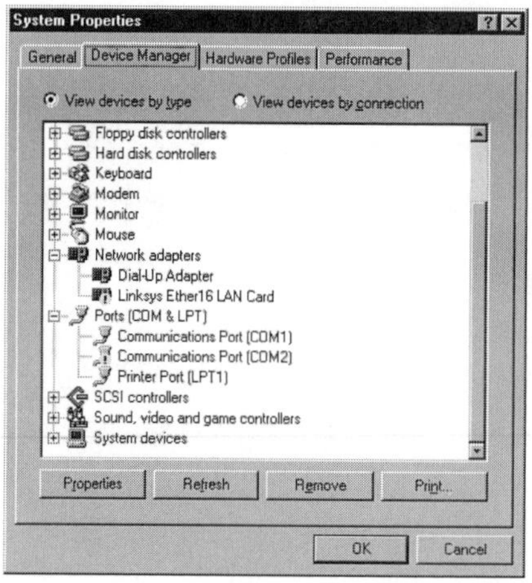

FIG. 11.1
Right-click My
Computer, choose
Properties, and click
the Device Manager
tab to see a list of
devices installed in
your computer.

N O T E   If you're removing your AUTOEXEC.BAT and CONFIG.SYS, copy the Windows 95
installation files to your hard drive before you begin. That way, if Windows 95 doesn't
recognize your CD-ROM immediately, you won't be left without the device drivers necessary to
support it. ■

Working with AUTOEXEC.BAT and CONFIG.SYS after Install

If your AUTOEXEC.BAT and CONFIG.SYS files are still loading real-mode device drivers
and running various commands after you've installed Windows 95, you should decide if
you need these commands. There's only one good reason to continue to load these device
drivers in your CONFIG.SYS—Windows 95 doesn't have a protected-mode driver for the
device.

If you don't have to load any real-mode device drivers in your CONFIG.SYS, you can eliminate these configuration files. Otherwise, you can minimize them to the point where they
contain only the most essential real-mode device drivers and commands required to access all of your devices. You will probably have to continue using a real-mode device
driver for your scanner, for example.

Introducing IO.SYS   IO.SYS and MSDOS.SYS were the two major files in MS-DOS.
These files contained the operating system. In Windows 95, they don't exist anymore, as such. However, there is another file called IO.SYS that contains a small
portion of a real-mode operating system. Windows 95 uses IO.SYS to start your
computer. It automatically handles a lot of the configuration chores that you handled
in CONFIG.SYS and AUTOEXEC.BAT. Table 11.5 shows the drivers that IO.SYS
installs for you, and the commands it executes.

Table 11.5   Commands Automatically Performed by IO.SYS

Command	Description
prompt pg	MS-DOS prompt set to "C:\>"
path=c:\windows;	Set path to Windows directory c:\windows\command
dos=high	Load DOS into upper-memory area
himem.sys	Load the memory manager
ifshlp.sys	Installable Files System helper
setver.exe	Set Windows version for older programs
files=60	Set number of files that can be open
fcbs=4	Set number of file control blocks
lastdrive=z	Set the drive letter of the last drive
buffers=30	Set number of buffers used for files
stacks=9,256	Set number of hardware stacks
shell=command.com	Specific location of interpreter

Because IO.SYS is doing all this work for you, you don't have to do it in your configuration files. If you don't like the settings that IO.SYS is using for these commands, however, you can override them by putting the command in your own CONFIG.SYS or AUTOEXEC.BAT.

Do You Need These Files?   Here's the ultimate test to see if you can safely eliminate AUTOEXEC.BAT and CONFIG.SYS:

1. Rename AUTOEXEC.BAT to AUTOEXEC.OLD and CONFIG.SYS to CONFIG.OLD.

2. Restart your computer.

 3. Let Windows 95 detect your hardware again by double-clicking Add New Hardware in the Control Panel. Follow the instructions.

TIP Print a device summary so that you have documentation of your original configuration. Right-click My Computer, choose Properties, click the Device Manager tab, and click Print. Select All Devices and System Summary, and click OK to print the device summary.

After Windows 95 has updated your system as necessary, look at the System Properties' Device Manager tab. Is all your hardware represented in this list, and does the Device Manager report that all your hardware is working correctly? If it does, you don't need your AUTOEXEC.BAT and CONFIG.SYS.

> **N O T E**   If you decide that you don't need AUTOEXEC.BAT or CONFIG.SYS, don't just delete
> them. Create an empty AUTOEXEC.BAT and CONFIG.SYS, so that your Windows 3.1 and
> MS-DOS programs don't get confused when they look for these two files. ■

If Windows 95 didn't recognize all your hardware, you have two options available:

- ■ Don't replace your configuration files with the old copies. Create new files that contain the real-mode drivers for the devices that Windows 95 didn't recognize.

- ■ Contact the device's manufacturer to get a protected-mode device driver. Alternatively, you can frequently find protected-mode drivers for many devices on the Internet or an online service.

Here's When You Do Need These Files   Even if Windows 95 does recognize all the devices in your computer, you may still need to install programs in your CONFIG.SYS or AUTOEXEC.BAT. If you boot to MS-DOS by pressing F8 when you see Starting Windows 95, or if you choose Shut Down from the Start menu, and select Restart the Computer In MS-DOS Mode, you may need to put real-mode drivers in your CONFIG.SYS so that you can access all your hardware from MS-DOS.

Here's the golden rule: If you want to use a device or a TSR (Terminate and Stay Resident) program in MS-DOS, you have to load it in your CONFIG.SYS. Don't confuse this situation with the MS-DOS window that you run inside of Windows 95. Since Windows 95 has already loaded the protected-mode drivers, all your devices are available to those MS-DOS windows. The only exception is that if you want a TSR program such as DOSKEY to be available in an MS-DOS window, you need to load that in AUTOEXEC.BAT. Note that if you're running a program in AUTOEXEC.BAT that you only need when you start up in DOS mode, put that program in your DOSSTART.BAT file, instead, so that it only loads when you start in DOS mode and not while Windows 95 is running.

> **N O T E**   If you're loading real-mode drivers for use in MS-DOS, you'll want to use a memory
> manager to load them into high memory so that you have more memory available for
> your MS-DOS programs. Add this line to your CONFIG.SYS:
>
>   DEVICE=C:\WINDOWS\EMM386.EXE NOEMS
>
> Then use the DEVICEHIGH statement in your CONFIG.SYS to load your real-mode drivers into
> upper memory, or use the LH command in your AUTOEXEC.BAT to load TSR programs into upper
> memory. ■

What Happened to SYSTEM.INI and WIN.INI?

Those two dreaded INI files, SYSTEM.INI and WIN.INI, aren't gone from Windows 95. Microsoft left them behind for compatibility with Windows 3.1 programs that expect to find certain entries in them. Other programs not only expect to find certain entries, they expect to be able to update these files and have Windows take notice. Thus, it's not really possible to eliminate them from your system.

Entries Moved into the Registry   While the files aren't gone, many entries have disappeared from them. Where did they go? Windows 95 moved many of them to the Registry. This is a logical place for them, since the Registry stores all of your hardware configurations. Tables 11.6 and 11.7 show the entries that were moved from SYSTEM.INI and WIN.INI into the Registry.

Table 11.6   SYSTEM.INI Entries Moved to the Registry

[386Enh]	[Network]
Network	AuditEnabled
Network3	AuditEvents
SecondNet	AuditLogSize
Transport	AutoLogon
V86ModeLANAs	Comment
	ComputerName
	DirectHost
	EnableSharing
	FileSharing
	LANAs
	LMAnnounce
	LMLogon
	LogonDisconnected
	LogonDomain
	LogonValidated
	Multinet
	PasswordCaching
	PrintSharing

Part

II

Ch

11

continues

Table 11.6   Continued

[386Enh]	[Network]
	Reshare
	SlowLanas
	Winnet
	Workgroup

Table 11.7   WIN.INI Entries Moved to the Registry

[Windows]	[WindowsMetrics]
Beep	BorderWidth
BorderWidth	CaptionHeight
CursorBlinkRate	CaptionWidth
DoubleClickSpeed	MenuHeight
KeyboardDelay	MenuWidth
KeyboardSpeed	MinArrange
MouseThreshold1	MinHorzGap
MouseThreshold2	MinVertGap
MouseSpeed	MinWidth
ScreenSaveActive	ScrollHeight
ScreenSaveTimeOut	ScrollWidth
SwapMouseButtons	SmCaptionHeight
	SmCaptionWidth

Entries Removed from SYSTEM.INI   Other entries in these files have been removed entirely, because they weren't typically used by other programs, and they certainly weren't required by Windows 95. Table 11.8 shows the entries that were removed from SYSTEM.INI. No entries are reported as being completely removed from WIN.INI.

Table 11.8 Entries Deleted from SYSTEM.INI

[386Enh]

device=*vfd

device=*configmg

device=serial.386

device=lpt.386

device=pagefile.386

device=isapnp.386

device=wshell.386

maxbps

timercriticalsection

Entries Kept for Compatibility A large number of entries were kept in both SYSTEM.INI and WIN.INI for compatibility with Windows 3.1 programs running in Windows 95. The values of these entries are always reflected in the Registry, and many of these entries aren't even used by Windows 95 at all. Tables 11.9 and 11.10 show the entries in SYSTEM.INI and WIN.INI that Windows 95 keeps around for compatibility.

Table 11.9 Entries in SYSTEM.INI Kept for Compatibility

[386Enh]	[Boot]	[NonWindowsApps]
AllEMSLocked	display.drv	CommandEnvSize
AllXMSLocked	keyboard.drv	
AltKeyDelay	mouse.drv	
AltKeyDelay	network.drv	
DMABufferSize	sound.drv	
Display	386grabber	
DOSPromptExitInstructions	comm.drv	
Keyboard	drivers	
KeyPasteCRSkipCount	fixedfon.fon	
KeyPasteKeyDelay	fonts.fon	
PasteSkipCount	language.dll	

continues

Table 11.9   Continued

[386Enh]	[Boot]	[NonWindowsApps]
KeyPasteTimeout	oemfonts.font	
MaxDMAPGAddress	shell	
MaxPagingFileSize	system.drv	
MinUserDiskSpace	TaskMan.Exe	
Mouse	alias	
Paging		
PagingDrive		
ScrollFrequency		
Device		
KeybdPasswd		
Local		
Local Reboot		
MessageBackColor		
MessageTextColor		
NetAsyncTimeout		
NetAsynchFallback		
NetDMASize		

Table 11.10   Entries in WIN.INI Kept for Compatibility

[Windows]	[Intl]
CursorBlinkRate	iCountry
Device	iCurrDigits
DoubleClickHeight	iCurrency
DoubleClickWidth	iDate
DoubleClickSpeed	iDigits
KeyboardDelay	iLZero
KeyboardSpeed	iMeasure
MouseSpeed	iNegcurr
MouseTrails	iTime

[Windows]	[Intl]
SwapMouseButtons	iTLZero
	s1159
	s2359
	sCountry
	sCurrency
	sLanguage
	sList
	sShortDate
	sLongDate
	sThousand
	sTime

Optimization Tips for Windows 95

Part
II

Ch
11

Everyone wants their computer to work faster, and they'd rather make it happen without buying any new hardware. They're always on the lookout for a new tweak they haven't tried, or a magical program that gives them faster disk access, blazing video speed, and more memory.

Fortunately, Windows 95 removes much of your need to hand-tweak its performance, because Windows 95 is somewhat self-tuning. Here are some examples:

- The swap file dynamically shrinks and grows, depending on your immediate need. The disk cache dynamically resizes, too. Thus, under normal circumstances, you don't need to mess with these settings.

- Windows 95 has 32-bit disk and file access built right in. It can access the disk directly, for example, instead of going through your computer's BIOS.

- Windows 95 automatically adjusts its configuration, depending on how much memory you have and how large your hard disk is. You don't have to tweak these settings yourself.

Even though Windows 95 is largely self-tuning, you'll still find plenty of ways to tweak its performance. That's what this section is all about. Here's what you'll learn:

- Adjusting disk performance to get the fastest access.

- Configuring Windows 95 to get the most free memory possible.
- Making your display as fast as possible.

Optimizing Disk Access

Windows 95 removes a lot of the guessing games from optimizing disk access. It provides 32-bit protected-mode drivers that access the files on your disk faster. It also dynamically optimizes the size of your cache, depending on how much memory and disk space you have. There remain a few tricks for those who like to tweak their computer's performance, however.

◆ TROUBLESHOOTING

What is 32-bit file access? 32-bit protected-mode file access allows Windows 95 to access your computer's files directly—without going through MS-DOS or the BIOS. Without it, Windows 95 would have to go through MS-DOS and the BIOS for every disk access. This would require your CPU to change to 16-bit real-mode each time—wasting valuable time.

Configuring Your Hard Disk   Windows 95's disk cache automatically configures itself, but there are a few things you can do to give it a few hints. Right-click My Computer, choose Properties, and click the Performance tab. Click the File System button, and Windows 95 displays the dialog box shown in Figure 11.2.

FIG. 11.2
There isn't much
to optimizing your
file system in
Windows 95.

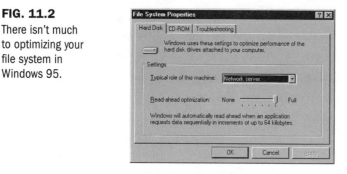

TIP   Make sure you don't have SMARTDRV in your startup files—you don't need it.

Choose the role that your computer plays from Typical Role of This Machine. You can choose Desktop Computer, Mobile or Docking System, or Network Server. Table 11.11 describes the differences between these options. Click OK to save your changes.

Table 11.11 Description of Machine Roles

Role	Description
Desktop Computer	Creates a smaller disk cache, leaving plenty of RAM available for applications
Mobile or Docking System	Creates a larger disk cache, so that continuous disk access doesn't drain your battery
Network Server	Creates a large disk cache, leaving little RAM available for applications

TROUBLESHOOTING

I changed the machine role, but I didn't notice a difference in performance, or I noticed a decrease in performance. Microsoft goofed. They set the registry entries for Mobile or Docking System and Network Server machine roles incorrectly. To fix this problem, open HKEY_LOCAL_MACHINE\Software\Microsoft\Windows\CurrentVersion\FS Templates\Mobile in the Registry Editor; and change the NameCache value entry to **51 01 00 00** and the PathCache value entry to **10 00 00 00**. Then, open HKEY_LOCAL_MACHINE\Software\Microsoft\Windows\CurrentVersion\FS Templates\Server in the Registry Editor, and change the NameCache value entry to **A9 0A 00 00** and the PathCache value entry to **40 00 00 00**.

Part
II
Ch
11

You can also configure how much memory Windows 95 will use for Read-Ahead Optimization. (That is, when a program requests data sequentially, how much ahead of the program will Windows 95 read into the cache so that it doesn't have to hit the disk again?) Since much of your disk access is probably sequential reading, you should leave this value set to 64K—the highest possible.

You can also set the minimum and maximum disk cache in SYSTEM.INI. If you feel like too much memory is going to the disk cache, or that a larger disk cache would make disk access faster, you can add the following lines to the [vcache] section of SYSTEM.INI:

> MinFileCache=0
>
> MaxFileCache=X

X is the maximum amount of memory that you want Windows 95 to use for the disk cache.

N O T E If your drive is using MS-DOS compatibility mode, the biggest improvement you can make to your computer's performance is to make sure you're using 32-bit protected-mode disk drivers. See "The Dreaded MS-DOS Compatibility Mode," later in this chapter, to learn more about getting out of MS-DOS compatibility mode. ■

Configuring Your CD-ROM Drive Your CD-ROM has a cache that is separate from your hard disk's cache. This is because the characteristics of the two devices are different. The CD-ROM's cache can be swapped out to the hard disk, but it's useless to do this for the hard disk's cache. Reading data from the hard disk is still many times faster than reading it from the CD-ROM.

Like the Windows 95 file system, there isn't much you can do to optimize your CD-ROM except give Windows 95 a few hints. Here's how:

1. Right-click My Computer, choose Properties, and click the Performance tab. Click the File System button and then click the CD-ROM tab, and Windows 95 displays the dialog box shown in Figure 11.3.

FIG. 11.3
Windows 95 reports how much memory it'll use for the cache at the bottom of this dialog box.

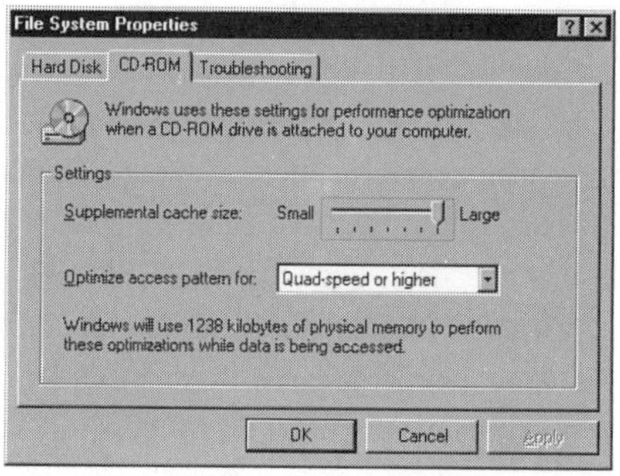

2. Set the size of the cache in Supplemental Cache Size. Notice that the size of the cache is different for each setting, depending on which type of CD-ROM you select in Optimize Access Pattern For.

T I P A large cache probably won't help your computer's performance much at all. Keep it small.

3. Select which type of CD-ROM is installed in your computer in Optimize Access Pattern For.
4. Click OK to return to System Properties. Click OK again to save your changes.

Defragmenting Your Hard Disk If you've been using your computer for a long time, your files have probably become quite fragmented. *Fragmentation* is when parts of a file are not stored contiguously on your hard disk. This occurs when Windows 95 can't find enough contiguous free hard disk space to store a file.

Reading unfragmented files is much faster than reading fragmented files, because Windows 95 doesn't have to look for the file on different parts of your hard disk. Here's how to defragment your hard disk:

1. Right-click the drive you want to defragment in My Computer, choose Properties, and click the Tools tab. You'll see a dialog box similar to Figure 11.4.

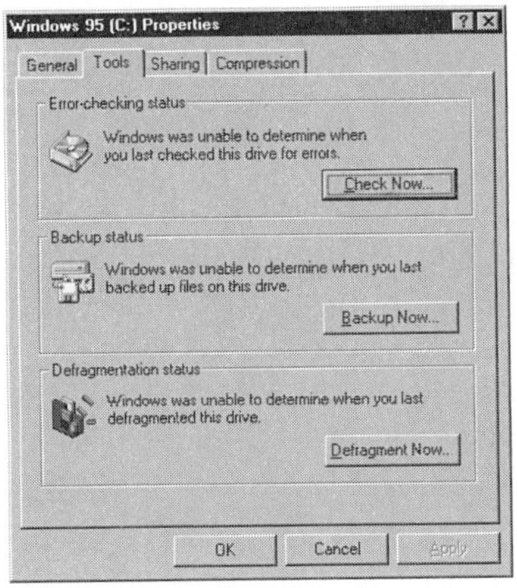

FIG. 11.4
This tab lets you conveniently maintain your hard disk.

2. Click Defragment Now.
3. Click Start, and Windows 95 starts defragmenting your drive. If you click Show Details, you'll see a window that shows the status of the operation (see Figure 11.5).

Part
II

Ch
11

FIG. 11.5
Click Legend to see what each colored block represents.

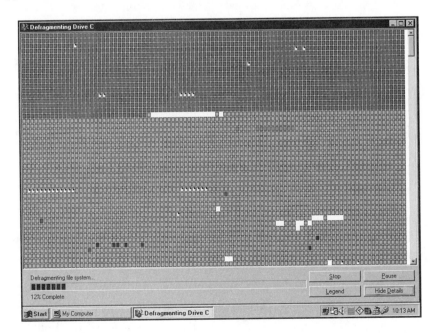

4. Click Yes to finish.

N O T E   Windows 95 tries to find at least 500K of contiguous drive space to allocate to a file. If it can't, or if the file is larger than 500K, it fragments the file. You can prevent fragmentation by adding the binary value entry ConfigFileAllocSize to HKEY_Local_Machine\System\CurrentControlSet\Control\FileSystem in the Registry and setting it to something larger than 500K. ■

Optimizing Your Display

There isn't a magical software setting that'll make your video faster, but there are some other things you can do. Here are some suggestions:

- Get updated video drivers from the manufacturer of your video card. This can have a dramatic improvement in its performance. You can also find updated video drivers online.

- Set your color depth to 256 colors in your Display Properties' Settings tab. This can have a dramatic impact on the crispness of your display, and most people don't need 16-bit color anyway.

- Don't use background wallpaper. If Windows 95 swaps the wallpaper to disk, the screen repaints very slowly when you minimize or close a window.

- Turn off mouse animation. On slower computers, you can waste a lot of CPU time for that waving flag.

- Turn off window animation using Tweak UI. Deselect Window Animation in Tweak UI's General tab. This makes Windows appear to draw more quickly.

Optimizing Memory

Windows 95 has done a lot to give you more free conventional memory. You don't even have to lift a finger. Windows 95 replaced all those real-mode device drivers with 32-bit protected-mode device drivers that don't load in conventional memory. CD-ROM drivers, disk caches, mouse drivers, and those pesky network drives are all gone. It's not uncommon for you to have over 600K of free conventional memory now.

T I P   You can use MEMMAKER, from the previous version of DOS, to optimize your conventional memory if you set BootGUI to **0** in MSDOS.SYS.

You may still need to load a few real-mode drivers, however. Optimizing conventional memory in those cases is much the same as optimizing it in MS-DOS. You still use HIMEM.SYS and EMM386.EXE. You also use DEVICEHIGH and LOADHIGH to load 16-bit device drivers into the upper-memory area.

If you need to load some resident programs that you'll only need in DOS mode, put them in DOSSTART.BAT. Windows 95 runs this batch file each time you shut down to MS-DOS or run an MS-DOS program in DOS mode. You set up a temporary CONFIG.SYS and AUTOEXEC.BAT for a specific DOS mode program in its property sheet.

Optimizing the Swap File   Most of your programs and data are kept in memory. If you run out of memory, Windows 95 swaps some of this information to a special file on your hard disk called a *swap file*. Windows 95 only swaps the parts of programs and data that it hasn't used in a while and that it doesn't foresee needing immediately. Then, it loads the information back into memory when a program needs access to it. This makes more memory available to your programs.

The swap file is a hidden file called WIN386.SWP. It is a temporary file in your Windows 95 folder, as opposed to Windows 3.1's permanent swap file. If you've set a specific size for your swap file, you may find it in the root folder of your boot drive (shared with Windows 3.1).

> **N O T E**   If you notice a lot of disk activity while using Explorer, this doesn't mean that there's a lot of swap file activity. Explorer keeps a cache of the recent icons that it's displayed in your Windows folder. It's merely keeping this updated. ■

You may perceive that your hard disk is thrashing much more than it did in Windows 3.1, particularly while your computer is idle. Windows 95 is busily updating your swap file while you're not using your computer, so that it doesn't have to swap as much while you are using it. Also, more of the Windows 95 code can be swapped to the swap file than was possible in Windows 3.1, giving you more free memory.

Windows 95 doesn't leave much for the power user to optimize, but here are some suggestions for tweaking your swap file:

- Move your swap file onto a hard drive that you don't use much. This won't do any good if you're just moving it to another partition on the same drive; it must be a different physical drive. Click Virtual Memory on the System Properties' Performance tab. Select Let Me Specify My Own Virtual Memory Settings, and type a path for your swap file in Hard Disk. Click OK to save your changes.

- If your drive seems to thrash around a lot when you close a program, try setting your swap file to a specific size. Click Virtual Memory on the System Properties' Performance tab. Select Let Me Specify My Own Virtual Memory Settings, and fill Minimum and Maximum with values that are about two to three times the amount of memory installed in your computer. Then click OK to save your changes. You can safely ignore Microsoft's warning.

The Dreaded MS-DOS Compatibility Mode

I've seen the plea for help many times. "I'm stuck in MS-DOS compatibility mode, and I can't get out!" The first indication that you have this problem is that the performance of your computer suddenly slows to a crawl, or it just doesn't perform as well as you think it should. It takes most people awhile to diagnose their problem as the MS-DOS compatibility mode, so they suffer until they've finally had enough, and start poking around as a result.

Getting out of MS-DOS compatibility mode can be difficult if you don't understand why it occurred. This section addresses compatibility, along with the following topics:

- What MS-DOS compatibility mode is and what causes Windows 95 to use it.
- Finding out if you're in MS-DOS compatibility mode.
- Getting out of MS-DOS compatibility mode with step-by-step suggestions for diagnosing and fixing it.

CAUTION

If everything has worked quite well, and you suddenly come down with MS-DOS compatibility mode, you should suspect a boot virus. Use a virus scanner such as Norton Antivirus to remove it from your computer.

Understanding MS-DOS Compatibility Mode

The most common cause of MS-DOS compatibility mode is real-mode drivers that Windows 95 considers unsafe. Under normal circumstances, Windows 95 replaces any real-mode drivers that you've loaded in your CONFIG.SYS with 32-bit protected-mode drivers of its own liking. If Windows 95 finds a real-mode driver that it can't replace, however, it'll start in MS-DOS compatibility mode to keep things safe and tidy.

 Windows 95 keeps a list of known safe real-mode drivers in IOS.INI, which you'll find in your Windows 95 folder.

A real-mode driver is safe if it doesn't do anything that the protected-mode driver can't do by itself. In this case, the protected-mode driver can take over all operations for the device. If the real-mode driver is unsafe, it has functionality that isn't built into the protected-mode drivers, so that the protected-mode driver can't take over the operations for that device. Examples of unsafe drivers include those that provide geometry translation, data compression, and data encryption.

N O T E OnTrack Disk Manager is a geometry conversion utility that allows you to install a larger hard disk in your computer than your BIOS supports. Windows 95 isn't compatible with OnTrack Disk Manager version 6.02 or earlier. The current version is 7.0 and is available from OnTrack. You can find more information about OnTrack Disk Manager version 7.0 at **www.ontrack.com**. ■

There are a handful of other reasons why Windows 95 would use MS-DOS compatibility mode:

- Windows 95 found a device driver or memory resident program that hooked into the system before Windows 95 loaded. This could also be a boot virus.

- Windows 95 couldn't detect what type of hard disk controller is installed in your computer, or you removed the hard disk controller from the current configuration in the Device Manager.

- There is a resource conflict between your hard disk controller and another device in your system.

- The Windows 95 32-bit protected-mode driver is missing from your computer, or it's corrupted.

- Your hardware is not compatible with Windows 95.

Checking for MS-DOS Compatibility Mode

Windows 95 reports information about its performance in the System Properties' Performance tab. Right-click My Computer and choose Properties. Click the Performance tab, and Windows 95 displays the dialog box shown in Figure 11.6. You learned about this tab in "Optimization Tips for Windows 95," earlier in this chapter. If the middle portion of this tab reports Your system is configured for optimal performance, you don't have anything to worry about—you're not using MS-DOS compatibility mode.

T I P If your animated cursors aren't working, you're probably in MS-DOS compatibility mode.

For more information about the problem, select one of the lines in the list and click Details. This rarely produces satisfactory information to help you fix the problem, however. The next section provides much more help.

Part

II

Ch

11

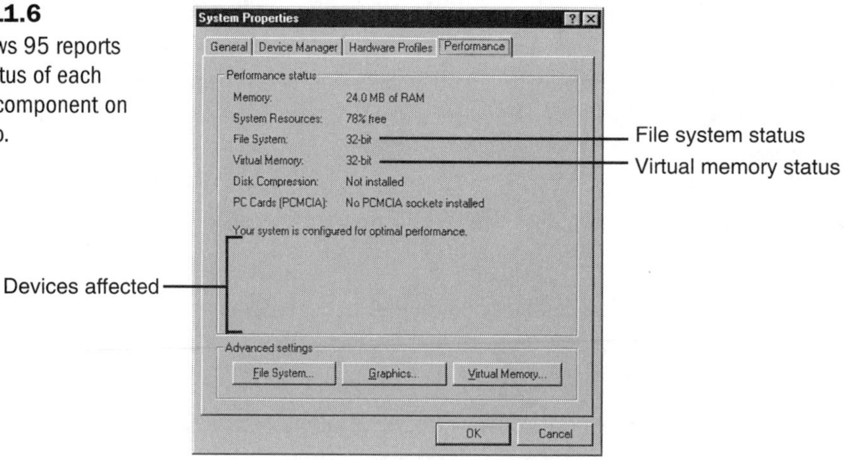

FIG. 11.6
Windows 95 reports the status of each major component on this tab.

File system status
Virtual memory status

Devices affected

Getting Out of MS-DOS Compatibility Mode

Getting unstuck is a hit-and-miss process. Try one thing, and if that doesn't work, try another. You first need to identify which drive is causing the problem by looking in the System Properties' Performance tab as described earlier. If it reports Some drives using MS-DOS compatibility mode file system, the culprit could be any one of your hard disks, floppy drives, CD-ROM, or even your ZIP drive.

> **T I P** Starting a computer that has a Syquest EZ-Drive without a cartridge in the drive causes Windows 95 to start in MS-DOS compatibility mode.

> **N O T E** Don't use GUEST.EXE for your ZIP drive. This causes Windows 95 to start in MS-DOS compatibility mode. Install the drivers you'll find on your Windows 95 CD-ROM in \Drivers\Storage\Iomega or that come with the Iomega ZIP drive. Use the Add New Hardware wizard in the Control Panel. ▇

The following list shows you the things you should check. Start with the first item, and if that doesn't work, move on to the next. If you exhaust these suggestions and are still stuck, your problem is more specific to your configuration. You need to seek online help or contact the Microsoft Product Support Services.

> **T I P** Often, a BIOS upgrade is all you need to fix a geometry problem. Call your hardware manufacturer for details.

▇ If the Performance tab reports that a device driver called MBRITN13.SYS is the culprit, your computer may be infected by a virus, or you may be using geometry translation software such as OnTrack that makes your computer recognize larger hard drives than your BIOS supports.

■ If the Performance tab reports that a device driver that you've installed in your CONFIG.SYS is the culprit, you need to find a replacement that is compatible with Windows 95. You can contact the manufacturer, or look online for a replacement. If the driver is not essential, remove it from your CONFIG.SYS.

■ If the Device Manager doesn't show a hard disk controller for your computer, use the Add New Hardware wizard to install one. You may have to manually configure your hard disk controller if the wizard doesn't auto-detect yours. If you're using hardware profiles, make sure that your hard disk controller has been enabled for the current configuration. If it's disabled, you'll see a red x over it in the Device Manager, as shown in Figure 11.7.

FIG. 11.7
The Device Manager shows you at a glance which hardware is working and which is not.

Part
II

Ch
11

N O T E Many computers, especially older models, use proprietary disk controllers that aren't compatible with Windows 95. The only thing you can do is install a third-party disk controller that does work with Windows 95 and disable the on-board controller. ■

■ If the hard disk controller listed in the Device Manager has a yellow exclamation point over it, you have a resource conflict between the hard disk controller and another piece of hardware. The driver may also be damaged or missing, or you may have the Disable All 32-bit Protected-Mode Disk Drivers check box selected in the File System Properties' Troubleshooting tab.

■ Fix any resource conflicts such as IRQ, I/O, DMA, or RAM addresses.

■ Make sure the protected-mode driver is in the \Windows\System\Iosubsys folder. Look on the Driver tab in the Device Manager and note what drivers are associated with your hard disk controller. Then restart your computer and press F8 when you see `Starting Windows 95`. Select a Logged (/BOOTLOG.TXT) start. Look at the BOOTLOG.TXT file (an excerpt is shown in Figure 11.8) to see if the driver is loading correctly. If it says there is an `Init Failure` or `Load Failure` for the drive make, replace the ESDI_506.PDR, SCSIPORT.PDR, and SCSIPORT.MPD drivers in your IOSUBSYS folder. You can also run Setup, and choose the Verify option.

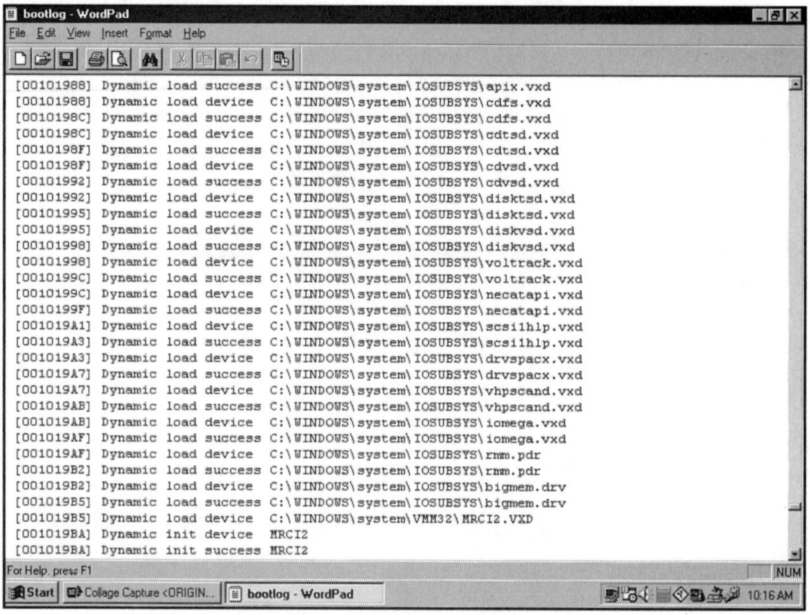

```
[00101988] Dynamic load success C:\WINDOWS\system\IOSUBSYS\apix.vxd
[00101988] Dynamic load device  C:\WINDOWS\system\IOSUBSYS\cdfs.vxd
[0010198C] Dynamic load success C:\WINDOWS\system\IOSUBSYS\cdfs.vxd
[0010198C] Dynamic load device  C:\WINDOWS\system\IOSUBSYS\cdtsd.vxd
[0010198F] Dynamic load success C:\WINDOWS\system\IOSUBSYS\cdtsd.vxd
[0010198F] Dynamic load device  C:\WINDOWS\system\IOSUBSYS\cdvsd.vxd
[00101992] Dynamic load success C:\WINDOWS\system\IOSUBSYS\cdvsd.vxd
[00101992] Dynamic load device  C:\WINDOWS\system\IOSUBSYS\disktsd.vxd
[00101995] Dynamic load success C:\WINDOWS\system\IOSUBSYS\disktsd.vxd
[00101995] Dynamic load device  C:\WINDOWS\system\IOSUBSYS\diskvsd.vxd
[00101998] Dynamic load success C:\WINDOWS\system\IOSUBSYS\diskvsd.vxd
[00101998] Dynamic load device  C:\WINDOWS\system\IOSUBSYS\voltrack.vxd
[0010199C] Dynamic load success C:\WINDOWS\system\IOSUBSYS\voltrack.vxd
[0010199C] Dynamic load device  C:\WINDOWS\system\IOSUBSYS\necatapi.vxd
[0010199F] Dynamic load success C:\WINDOWS\system\IOSUBSYS\necatapi.vxd
[001019A1] Dynamic load device  C:\WINDOWS\system\IOSUBSYS\scsi1hlp.vxd
[001019A3] Dynamic load success C:\WINDOWS\system\IOSUBSYS\scsi1hlp.vxd
[001019A3] Dynamic load device  C:\WINDOWS\system\IOSUBSYS\drvspacx.vxd
[001019A7] Dynamic load success C:\WINDOWS\system\IOSUBSYS\drvspacx.vxd
[001019A7] Dynamic load device  C:\WINDOWS\system\IOSUBSYS\vhpscand.vxd
[001019AB] Dynamic load success C:\WINDOWS\system\IOSUBSYS\vhpscand.vxd
[001019AB] Dynamic load device  C:\WINDOWS\system\IOSUBSYS\iomega.vxd
[001019AF] Dynamic load success C:\WINDOWS\system\IOSUBSYS\iomega.vxd
[001019AF] Dynamic load device  C:\WINDOWS\system\IOSUBSYS\rmm.pdr
[001019B2] Dynamic load success C:\WINDOWS\system\IOSUBSYS\rmm.pdr
[001019B2] Dynamic load device  C:\WINDOWS\system\IOSUBSYS\bigmem.drv
[001019B5] Dynamic load success C:\WINDOWS\system\IOSUBSYS\bigmem.drv
[001019B5] Dynamic load device  C:\WINDOWS\system\VMM32\MRCI2.VXD
[001019BA] Dynamic init device  MRCI2
[001019BA] Dynamic init success MRCI2
```

FIG. 11.8
BOOTLOG.TXT tells you which drivers successfully loaded and which didn't.

NOTE Some programs are obnoxious enough to tamper with the protected-mode disk drivers (*.PDR) in the \Windows\System\Iosubsys. This sometimes causes Windows 95 to start in MS-DOS compatibility mode. Fortunately, these programs usually save a backup copy of the old driver that you can restore if you like.

On the other hand, some computer manufacturers require that you install their special versions of these drivers in order to get out of MS-DOS compatibility mode. The only way to know for sure is to check online or call the manufacturer.

- Look at the IOS.LOG file in the Windows folder to see if it offers an explanation. Figure 11.9 shows an excerpt from this file.

FIG. 11.9
IOS.LOG helps you nail
down which device is
causing problems.

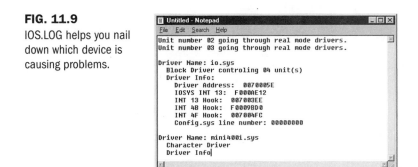

Your last resort is to contact the hardware manufacturer for more information about compatibility with Windows 95 or updated drivers. ●

III

Adminstering the Windows Registry

CHAPTER 12

Securing the Windows Registry

by Jerry Honeycutt

Windows 95 isn't a secure operating system? No, it's not. You can't restrict access to any of its resources. Considering how Microsoft positions Windows 95 (a personal, non-mission critical operating system), however, this isn't much of a problem. The problem here is that you can't secure the Windows 95 Registry as a result. On the other hand, Windows NT 4.0 is a very secure operating system. In fact, security is a cornerstone of the operating system—so much so that Microsoft positions Windows NT that way.

In Windows NT 4.0, securing obvious resources is easy. You know exactly which folders and files you want people to access. You know exactly which printers you want to provide access to as well. Securing the NT Registry is a bit less obvious, however, because it's usually hiding behind the scenes. But you can take advantage of NT's security to secure the NT Registry. This chapter shows you how. ■

Learn why Windows 95 can't secure the Registry

There is no way to secure the Windows 95 Registry. This chapter explains why.

Secure individual Registry keys in Windows NT 4.0

In Windows NT 4.0, you can secure specific branches and Registry keys.

Audit Registry keys in the Windows NT 4.0 Registry

This chapter shows you how to audit changes to the Registry for an entire branch or a specific key.

Securing the Windows 95 Registry—
Not Possible

Windows 95 doesn't provide any security for the Registry whatsoever. In fact, any user can log on to a Windows 95 computer without providing a name or password; all they have to do is press Esc at the logon window. Likewise, any user can move or delete the Registry files (SYSTEM.DAT and USER.DAT) without Windows 95 moaning much at all. A user can add, remove, or change any Registry key they like. Again, all they'll get when they try to remove an entire branch of the Registry is a simple confirmation dialog box to which they can click <u>Y</u>es and, poof, everything's gone.

There doesn't seem to be much hope, does there? Well, you can't secure the Registry itself, but you can protect the user from most mistakes or tampering. Here's how:

■ If you've configured a Windows 95 computer for remote administration, make sure you know who has permission to remotely administer the computer's Registry. Chapter 13, "Remotely Editing a User's Registry," shows you how to set up remote administration. It also shows you how to limit remote access to a user's Registry.

■ Use one of the techniques you learned about in Chapter 1, "Before You Begin," to back up the user's Registry. You can set up many of these methods so that they occur automatically. Then, if the user makes a mistake, you can easily fix it. Also, you can install ConfigSafe 95 on the user's computer so that you can restore a previous configuration if something goes wrong. See Chapter 9, "Using ConfigSafe to Track Down Settings," for more information.

   ▶ **See** "Backing Up the Windows 95 Registry," **p. 17**
   ▶ **See** "Windows 95," **p. 244**

Sad Attempts at Securing Windows 95

Okay, so Windows 95 isn't a secure operating system. There are a few things you can do to limit your risk, however. Some are more extreme than others. Pick and choose from the following list the items that best fit your organization:

● Remove the floppy drive from the computer after you've installed Windows 95. In particular, you may want to remove the floppy drive if you have a guest computer connected to your network to keep folks from sneaking off with valuable data. This also prevents the user from booting to a DOS disk and can prevent a number of viruses that are caught from floppy disks.

● Disable the Registry Editor using the Policy Editor as described in Chapter 15, "Using the Policy Editor to Administer the Registry," or remove REGEDIT.EXE from the user's computer altogether.

- Prevent the user from starting their computer to the command-line prompt by changing MSDOS.SYS as described in Chapter 11, "Getting Your Windows 95 Configuration Just Right."

- Use the Policy Editor to hide various components from the user, such as the Network and System icons in the Control Panel. You can also prevent the user from running certain programs or accessing certain drivers.

Securing the Windows NT 4.0 Registry

Windows NT 4.0 makes it very easy to manage the security of the Registry. You can do things as simple as blocking a user's access to the Registry Editor. You can also manage the security of individual branches and Registry keys. That's what the remainder of this section is about. Here's what you'll learn:

- If your only concern is preventing a user from tampering with their Registry, use Windows NT 4.0's file permissions to prevent them from even getting at the Registry Editor.

- Windows NT 4.0 creates an Access Control List (ACL) for each and every Registry branch and key. This list determines who can and can't access each key. You can modify these permissions for an entire branch or just a specific Registry key.

- Windows NT 4.0 allows you to audit what a user does in the Registry. You can audit both successes and failures for a variety of event types.

- Windows NT 4.0 also provides a mechanism to control who can access the Registry remotely. This mechanism is a completely cryptic way to control remote access to the Registry. This section shows you how to do it, nonetheless.

Part
III

Ch
12

Blocking a User's Access to the Registry

The easiest way to prevent a clumsy user from messing up their Registry is to prevent them from getting at the Registry Editor. You don't have to worry with the permissions of individual Registry keys at all. If the user has no access to the Registry Editor, it doesn't matter. Here are some pretty obvious methods you can use to completely prevent access to the Registry through the Registry Editor:

- Maintain complete control of who can log on to an NT computer with administrative privileges. I've worked in many shops where just about every programmer had some sort of administrative privilege to the server. You should maintain more control than this if you want to secure your server.

■ Don't install REGEDT32.EXE or REGEDIT.EXE on each user's individual workstation. If they don't have access to the Registry Editor, they can't tamper with their Registry. They could locate a copy of the Registry Editor if they wanted, but, for most folks, this is entirely too much trouble. As well, if you need access to a user's computer as the administrator, you can access it remotely.

■ Short of actually removing REGEDT32.EXE and REGEDIT.EXE from an NT workstation or server, you can place restrictions on which groups and users can actually run the Registry Editor. Locate REGEDT32.EXE in C:\WINNT\System32, right-click it, and click the Security tab. Do the same for REGEDIT.EXE in C:\WINNT. You'll see a dialog box that looks like Figure 12.1. Change the permissions for REGEDT32.EXE as necessary, and click OK.

FIG. 12.1

I recommend that you remove permission to REGEDT32.EXE and REGEDIT.EXE for everyone but the Administrators group.

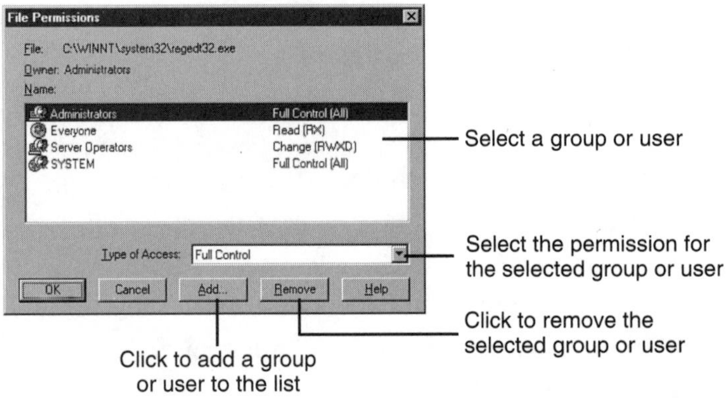

Select a group or user

Select the permission for the selected group or user

Click to remove the selected group or user

Click to add a group or user to the list

■ Control access to each user's profile by changing the permissions on the hive's file in Windows NT Explorer. Locate the user's profile in C:\WINNT\Profiles, and change the permissions for it just as you did in the previous bullet for REGEDT32.EXE.

CAUTION

Don't try changing permissions for the other hives you find in C:\WINNT\System32\Config. Windows NT 4.0 automatically manages the permissions on these files. You can cripple your NT system if you tinker with these.

▶ **See** "What's in a Hive," **p. 49**

Changing the Access Control List (ACL) for a Key

You can control who has access to a particular branch or Registry key. For example, you can prohibit users from removing any subkeys under HKEY_CLASSES_ROOT or you can allow only administrators to change a custom key you've added to the Registry.

In general, however, you should only change the ACL for Registry keys that you've specifically added to support your own needs. In other words, I don't recommend that you tinker with the ACL for the Registry keys that Windows NT 4.0 or other programs install in your Registry. NT automatically manages those for you. Why? Changing an ACL to No Access for a key that the system must have access to in order to start can prevent NT from starting.

> **T I P** You can change the ACL for a Registry key whether you're using NTFS or FAT.

If you really must change the ACL for a Registry key, use the Registry Editor. Just do the following:

1. In REGEDT32, select the branch or Registry key for which you want to change the ACL.

2. Choose Security, Permissions from the main menu. You'll see the Registry Key Permissions dialog box shown in Figure 12.2.

FIG. 12.2

Look familiar? The Registry Key Permissions dialog box is very similar to the File Permissions dialog box.

Select a group or user

Select the permission for the selected group or user

Click to remove the selected group or user

Click to add a group or user to the list

3. Select Replace Permission on Existing Subkeys if you want to update the permissions for all subkeys under the selected key.

4. Click Add to add names to the list of users and groups that you want to be able to access this Registry key. Select a name and click Remove to remove a name from the list of users and groups that you don't want to be able to access this Registry key.

5. For each name in the list, change its permissions by selecting the name, and selecting a type of permission in Type of Access. Table 12.1 describes each type of access. Full Control is the default value.

Table 12.1   Access Types for Registry Keys

Access Type	Description
Read	The selected group or user can read the key's contents but not change the key.
Full Control	The selected group or user can read, change, or delete the Registry key.
Special Access	The selected group or user has the permissions set in the Special Access dialog box, which pops up right after selecting this option. See "Auditing Registry Access," later in this chapter, for more information.

4. Click OK to save your changes.

N O T E If you've changed the ACL for a Registry key, turn on auditing for failures (see "Auditing Registry Access," later in this chapter) and test the system thoroughly to make sure it still works as expected. If you encounter errors, check the event log to find out why. After you're satisfied that the change didn't prevent Windows NT 4.0 from working properly, turn off auditing. Otherwise, restore the ACL for the Registry key and try again. ■

Auditing Registry Access

Setting up permissions for branches and individual Registry keys is only the first front. The second front is to audit what goes on in the Registry. Windows NT 4.0 will log when a user unsuccessfully attempts to do something with a Registry key. You can also have NT log all access to the Registry, but that's a bit of a grind on NT's resources.

 TIP You can use auditing to determine what Registry keys an application adds or changes.

Auditing changes in the Registry is a two-step process. First, you have to turn on auditing in the User Manager by following these steps:

1. Open the User Manager or User Manager for Domains.

2. Choose Policies, Audit from the main menu. You'll see the Audit Policy dialog box shown in Figure 12.3

FIG. 12.3

File and Object Access events include events that occur in the Registry.

Enable logging for each of these events

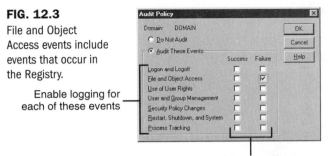

Select Success and/or Failure for each event

3. Select Audit Permission on Existing Subkeys if you want to audit all subkeys under the selected Registry key. If you're not careful about the size of the branch you select, your system could grind to a halt.

4. Select Audit These Events and select Success and/or Failure for each type of event you want to audit. In particular, you should at the very least select Failure for File and Object Access.

5. Click OK to save your changes and close the User Manager. If you didn't select Audit Permission on Existing Subkeys, the Registry Editor asks you if you want to audit all subkeys under the selected key.

TIP Drag a shortcut to the Event Viewer into your Start menu's StartUp group so that you can check audit event frequently.

After you've enabled auditing in the User manager, you need to enable auditing in the Registry. You can enable auditing for a specific key or for an entire branch of the Registry. Just do the following:

1. Select the branch or Registry key that you want to audit. For example, if you've recently changed the ACL for a Registry key, select that key.

2. Choose Security, Auditing from the main menu. You'll see the Registry Key Auditing dialog box shown in Figure 12.4.

3. Click Add to add names to the list of groups and users who you want to audit. Select a name and click Remove to remove names from the list of groups and users who you want to audit.

4. Select a name in the list of groups and users, and change the Success or Failure for each type of event you want to audit. Table 12.2 describes each type of event.

Part
III

Ch
12

FIG. 12.4

The Registry Key
Auditing dialog box
works similarly to other
auditing dialog boxes
in Windows NT 4.0.

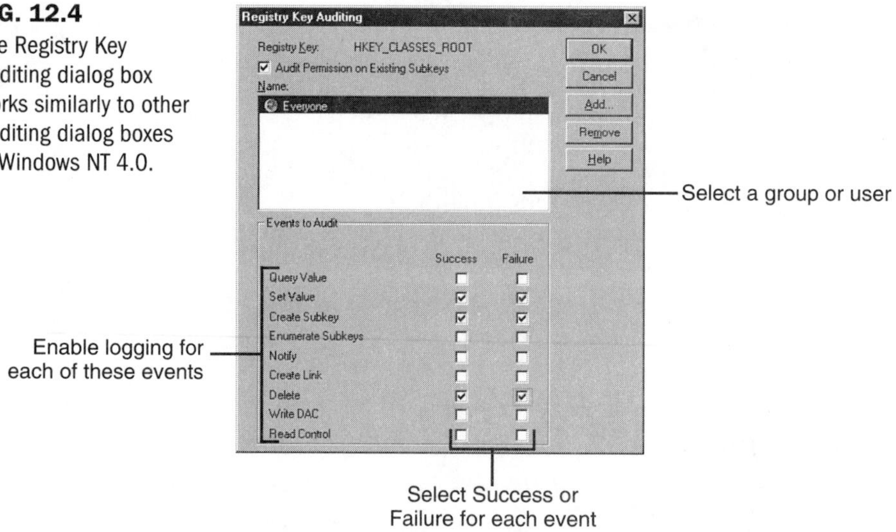

Select a group or user

Enable logging for
each of these events

Select Success or
Failure for each event

Table 12.2 Types of Audit Events

Audit Event	Description
Query Value	Log events that try to open the key with Query Value access
Set Value	Log events that try to open the key with Set Value access
Create Subkey	Log events that try to open the key with Create Subkey access
Enumerate Subkeys	Log events that try to enumerate subkeys under the selected key
Notify	Log events that try to open the key with Notify access
Create Link	Log events that try to open the key with Create Link access
Delete	Log events that try to delete the key from the Registry
Write DAC	Log events that try to determine who has access to the key
Read Control	Log events that try to determine the owner of the key

5. Click OK to save your changes.

After you've enabled auditing for the Registry, you can view the events you're auditing in
the Event Viewer. Open the Event Viewer, and choose Log, Security from the main menu.
You'll see a window similar to Figure 12.5.

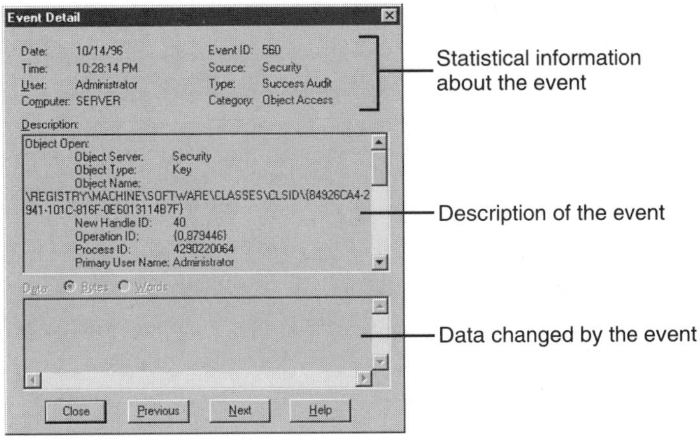

FIG. 12.5

If the event actually changed a value, you'd see it in the bottom part of this window.

Statistical information about the event

Description of the event

Data changed by the event

N O T E Consider limiting your audit to failures for the File and Object Access type of event. This limits the numbers of entries in the Event Viewer and reports failed attempts to access the Registry. This also prevents the heavy burden on the computer that comes from auditing too many types of events for too many Registry keys.

Controlling Remote Access to the Registry

In the previous sections, you learned how to control who can access each Registry key. You can also use this ACL for a special Registry key to determine who can access the Registry remotely. This method is a bit cryptic but it works.

When a user tries to remotely connect to the Windows NT 4.0 Registry, NT checks the ACL for this Registry key (I'll just call it winreg from now on):

```
HKEY_LOCAL_MACHINE\System\CurrentControlSet\Control\SecurePipeServers\winreg
```

One of two things can happen:

- If NT finds winreg in the Registry and the user has permission according to the ACL for winreg, the user is allowed to remotely connect to the Registry. In other words, the ACL for winreg determines which users can remotely access the Registry. Then, the ACL for each key the user tries to access defines what the remotely connected user can and can't do to it.

- If NT doesn't find winreg in the Registry, it allows all users to remotely connect to the Registry. The ACL for each key then defines what the remotely connected user can and can't do to it.

Part

III

Ch

12

N O T E   Windows NT 4.0 Workstation doesn't create winreg by default. Windows NT 4.0 Server
does. It gives administrators full control of the Registry when they remotely connect
to it. ■

To change the ACL for winreg, thus controlling who can remotely connect to the Registry,
do the following:

1. Open REGEDT32 (you can't use REGEDIT), and add HKEY_LOCAL_MACHINE\
   System\CurrentControlSet\Control\SecurePipeServers\winreg to the Registry.

2. Select the new key, and choose Security, Permissions from the main menu. You'll
   see the Registry Key Permissions dialog box shown in Figure 12.6. By default,
   Windows NT 4.0 gives full control to administrators and pretty much everything but
   delete permission to users.

FIG. 12.6

To restrict remote
access to the Registry
to administrators,
remove Users from
the list.

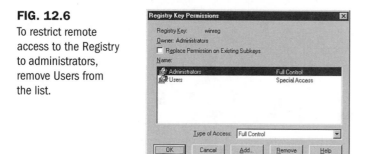

3. Add, remove, or change the permissions as you learned in "Changing the Access
   Control List (ACL) for a Key," earlier in this chapter.

4. Click OK to save your changes.

   ▶ **See** "Windows NT," **p. 250**

A Super-Duper Secure Registry

Microsoft makes some specific recommendations for creating a highly secure installation. They
recommend that you change the ACL for the following Registry keys so that the Everyone group
only has Query Value, Enumerate Subkeys, Notify, and Read Control access:

HKEY_LOCAL_MACHINE\Software\Microsoft\RPC and all of its subkeys

HKEY_LOCAL_MACHINE\Software\Microsoft\Windows NT\CurrentVersion

HKEY_LOCAL_MACHINE\Software\Microsoft\Windows NT\CurrentVersion\Profile List

HKEY_LOCAL_MACHINE\Software\Microsoft\Windows NT\CurrentVersion\AeDebug

HKEY_LOCAL_MACHINE\Software\Microsoft\Windows NT\CurrentVersion\Compatibility

HKEY_LOCAL_MACHINE\Software\Microsoft\Windows NT\CurrentVersion\Drivers

HKEY_LOCAL_MACHINE\Software\Microsoft\Windows NT\CurrentVersion\Embedding

HKEY_LOCAL_MACHINE\Software\Microsoft\Windows NT\CurrentVersion\Fonts

HKEY_LOCAL_MACHINE\Software\Microsoft\Windows NT\CurrentVersion\FontSubstitutes

HKEY_LOCAL_MACHINE\Software\Microsoft\Windows NT\CurrentVersion\GRE_Initialize

HKEY_LOCAL_MACHINE\Software\Microsoft\Windows NT\CurrentVersion\MCI

HKEY_LOCAL_MACHINE\Software\Microsoft\Windows NT\CurrentVersion\MCI Extensions

HKEY_LOCAL_MACHINE\Software\Microsoft\Windows NT\CurrentVersion\Port and all of its subkeys

- HKEY_LOCAL_MACHINE\Software\Microsoft\Windows NT\CurrentVersion\WOW and all of its subkeys

HKEY_LOCAL_MACHINE\Software\Microsoft\Windows NT\CurrentVersion\Windows3.1 MigrationStatus and all of its subkeys

HKEY_CLASSES_ROOT and all of its subkeys

CHAPTER 13

Remotely Editing a User's Registry

by Jerry Honeycutt

Did you read the introduction of this book? Because many folks skip right past it, I'm going to repeat an important tidbit of information that it contains. In a nutshell, most IT managers never witnessed a decrease in their support costs after deploying Windows 95 in their organization. Ironically, however, those same IT managers have yet to use the remote administration tools that Microsoft provides for Windows 95 and NT 4.0. Few administrators use policies to restrict a user's privileges, for example. Only a handful remotely edit a user's Registry to solve problems.

This is sad. Windows 95 and NT 4.0 provide a number of useful tools that you can use for everyday administrative tasks. You don't even have to get up from your desk, because you use them remotely over the network. Remote administration is so easy to set up, and, once it is set up, provides tools like those in Table 13.1. ■

Learn what remote administration encompasses

Remote administration is much more than just fiddling with the files on the user's computer. Learn here about the tools Windows provides.

Enable remote Administration on your network

This chapter shows you how to enable remote administration, including remote registry editing, on your network's workstations.

Windows 95 and NT 4.0 provide different tools

Windows 95 and NT 4.0 don't have the same administration tools. In this chapter, you learn what each flavor of Windows does provide.

Remotely edit a workstation's Registry

Finally, this chapter shows you how to set up the Remote Registry Service and how to remotely edit a workstation's Registry using REGEDIT or REGEDT32.

Understanding Remote Administration

So, what is remote administration? *Remote administration* lets you (the administrator) inspect settings on one computer from another computer on the network. You can even change many settings. For example, you can use remote administration to browse the other computer's file system or monitor the other computer's performance. You can also set policies that define what the user can and can't do on their computer. How many times have you been on the phone with an inexperienced user and wished that you could just leap through the phone line and take control of his keyboard? Remote administration sure beats walking such a user through the complex steps required to fix their computer when they don't have the foggiest idea what a DOS directory is or how to describe what's wrong with their computer.

Given that this book is about the Registry, this chapter focuses mostly on remotely editing the Registry. It does introduce you to the other tools you see in Table 13.1, however. For complete information about these tools and Windows 95 network administration, see *Platinum Edition Using Windows 95* by Que or *Special Edition Using Windows NT Workstation 4.0* by Que.

Table 13.1   Administrative Tools for Windows

Tool	Description
Windows 95	
Network Neighborhood	Administrate a workstation's files
Net Watcher	Manage shared resources on a network
Policy Editor	Control what a user can and can't do
Registry Editor	Remotely edit another user's Registry
System Monitor	Monitor a workstation's performance
Windows NT 4.0	
Diagnostics	View a workstation's configuration
Event Viewer	View the events on a workstation
Performance Monitor	Monitor a workstation's performance
Policy Editor	Control what a user can and can't do
Registry Editor	Remotely edit another user's Registry
Server Manager	Manage shared resources on a network

Setting Up Remote Administration

Enabling remote administration for Windows 95 is different from NT 4.0. If you work with Windows 95 computers, you have to do a couple of things to enable remote administration. First, you have to actually turn on remote administration in the Control Panel. Then, you need to install the Remote Registry Service so that you can remotely work with a workstation's Registry. Afterwards, you can administer a Windows 95 computer from any other Windows 95 computer. If you only work with Windows NT 4.0, however, you have it made. You can skip the rest of this section, because you don't have to do anything special to enable remote administration in NT. It's built-in and automatically enabled.

Before or After: That Is the Question

Did you deploy Windows 95 in the organization without enabling remote administration? Ouch. If so, you'll have to manually enable remote administration on each workstation in order to take advantage of the tools that this chapter describes. You learn how to do exactly that in this chapter.

There is a better way, however. If you haven't yet deployed Windows 95, you can use Windows 95's Server Based Setup. Here's how it works: you copy the Windows 95 source files onto the network; define how Windows 95 will install on each user's computer by creating an installation script; and either instruct the users to install from the network or add a command to their login script that automatically installs Windows 95 the next time they log on to the network. Using Server Based Setup, for example, you can create an installation script that enables system policies, user profiles, remote administration, and user-level security for every user on your network.

You do all this with the Server Based Setup utility you'll find on your Windows 95 CD-ROM. It's in the \Admin\Nettools\Netsetup folder. The file name is NETSETUP.EXE. You can also find extensive information about Server Based Setup in *Platinum Edition Using Windows 95* by Que or in the *Windows 95 Resource Kit*, which is also on your Windows 95 CD-ROM.

Enabling Remote Administration for Windows 95

Before you enable remote administration, you need to double-check the computer's configuration. Its configuration should match these requirements:

- Make sure that this computer is using File and Printer Sharing for Microsoft Networks or File and Printer sharing for NetWare Networks, whichever is appropriate. To do so, right-click Network Neighborhood and click File and Print Sharing. Select I want to be able to give others access to my files and select I want to be able to give others access to print to my printer(s). Click OK to save your changes, and then click OK again and restart your computer when asked.

■ Make sure that both computers are using the same security level. That is, both the computer from which you are administering and the computer you're administering must both use either user-level or share-level security. If you want to remotely edit the user's Registry, by the way, you have to use user-level security.

CAUTION

I strongly recommend that you use user-level security, particularly if you're enabling remote administration. User-level security allows you to specify exactly which users can remotely administer a computer. With share-level security, the only thing preventing access to all of the computer's resources by an unscrupulous intruder is a password (which is probably on a Post-it note next to your monitor).

In Windows 95, you have to physically enable remote administration on each computer that you want to administer remotely. It's easy. You check a box that turns on remote administration and select the users and groups which will have dominion over the computer. To enable remote administration on a computer, perform these steps on that computer:

 1. Double-click the Passwords icon in the Control Panel, and click the Remote Administration tab. You'll see a dialog box similar to Figure 13.1.

FIG. 13.1
You'll see a different dialog box if this computer is using share-level security.

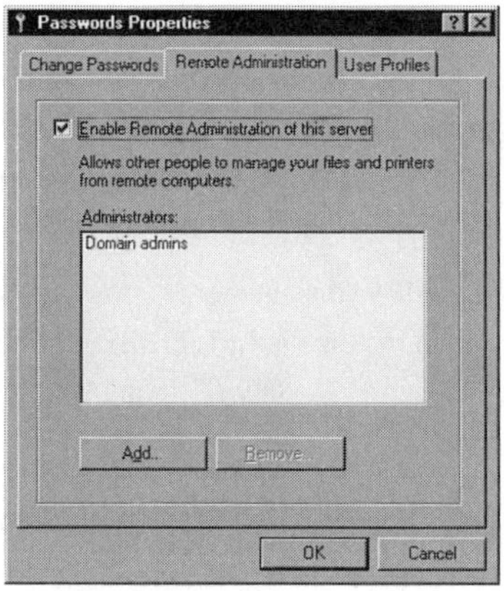

2. Select Enable Remote Administration Of This Server to enable remote administration. This also enables the password prompts or the list of administrators.

3. If this computer is using share-level security, type a password in the spaces provided, and click OK to save your changes. You're done; ignore the rest of the following steps.

4. If this computer is using user-level security, click Add, and you'll see a dialog box similar to Figure 13.2.

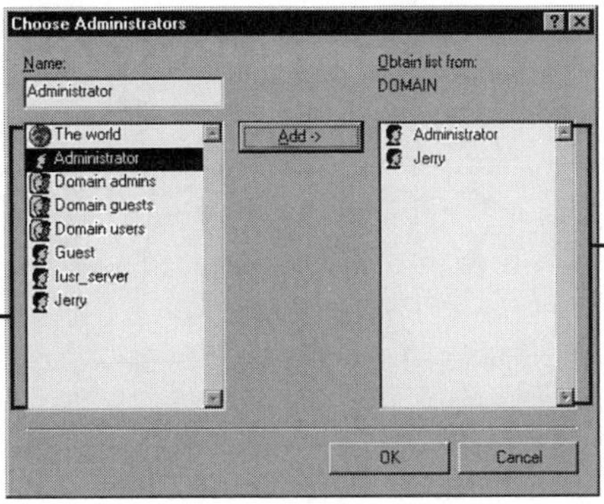

FIG. 13.2

You can add both individual users and groups to the list of administrators.

Select administrators ——

—— Click to add selected administrators

5. Select a name in the left-hand list and click Add to add it to the list of administrators for this computer. Repeat as necessary.

6. Click OK to save your changes. Click OK again to save your changes and enable remote administration for this computer.

N O T E When you enable user-level security, Windows 95 automatically enables remote administration and adds the Domain Admins group to the list of administrators. Thus, computers using user-level security probably already have remote administration enabled for the network's administrators. Note that user-level security requires either an NT or NetWare server to act as a security provider. ▪

You should restart the computer before trying to administer it remotely. Afterward, you'll notice a few new hidden shares on the computer:

C$, D$, and so on	Provides shares for each nonremovable drive on the workstation's computer. You can browse these with Explorer.
ADMIN$	Gives full access to the folder in which Windows 95 is installed. ADMIN$ remains hidden, but you can browse it by choosing Run from the Start menu; then, type **\\Computer\ADMIN$** and press Enter (*Computer* is the name of the computer you're administering).
IPC$	Provides a channel for interprocess communication between two computers. IPC$ remains hidden, and you can't browse it.

Part
III

Ch
13

T I P Shares whose names end with a dollar-sign ($) are invisible. That is, they don't show up in browse lists. You can create hidden shares, which other users can connect to only if they know the exact name, by appending a dollar-sign to the end of the name.

Enabling the Remote Registry Service for Windows 95

Enabling the Remote Registry Service, which you learn about in this section, is different from enabling remote administration. Remote administration is useful to inspect the files and shares on a remote computer, but it doesn't give you access to the other computer's Registry. Access to the Registry is required if you want to use tools such as the Registry Editor, System Monitor, or the System Policy Editor. You must enable Remote Administration before you can use the Remote Registry Service, however.

Just like remote administration, the Remote Registry Service has a few requirements. Check these configuration items before you try to enable it:

- The network must have a security provider: NT and NetWare servers are equally suitable.

- Both your computer and the computer you're administering must have remote administration enabled. The previous section, "Enabling Remote Administration for Windows 95," describes how to enable it on each workstation.

- Both computers must use user-level security. To configure the computer to use user-level security, right-click Network Neighborhood. Click the Access Control tab and select User-level Access Control. Type the name of the domain in the space provided (see Figure 13.3), and click OK to save your changes.

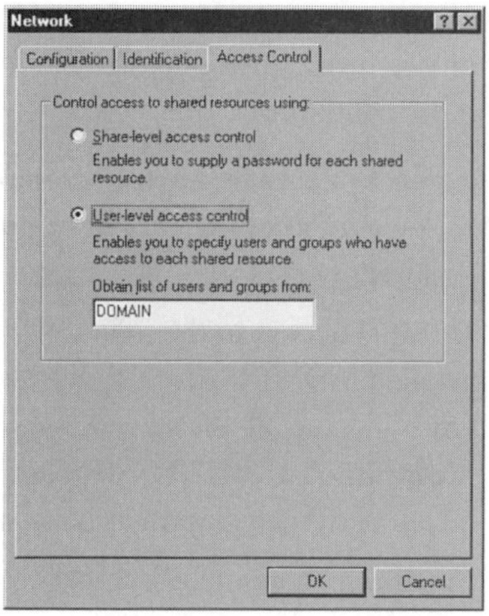

FIG. 13.3
Windows 95 will let you enable user-level security even though you don't have a security provider on the network.

Just like enabling remote administration, you have to physically install the Remote Registry Service on the computer you want to remotely administer. You'll need your Windows 95 CD-ROM to install the Remote Registry Service. Here's how:

1. Right-click Network Neighborhood, and choose Properties. You'll see the Network Properties dialog box.

2. Click Add to display the list of network components. Select Service from this list, and click Add. Windows 95 may pause a bit while it builds a driver information database. Then, you'll see the Select Network Service dialog box.

3. Click Have Disk to locate the Remote Registry Service on your Windows 95 CD-ROM. The Remote Registry Service isn't a part of the normal Windows 95 installation. Thus, you'll point Windows 95 to a different folder on the CD-ROM.

4. In the space provided in the Copy Manufacturer's Files From dialog box, type the path to **\Admin\Nettools\RemotReg** (note the missing "e" in RemotReg) on your Windows 95 CD-ROM. Click OK to continue. As a result, you'll see the Select Network Service dialog box.

5. Select Microsoft Remote Registry from the list, and click OK.

6. In Network properties, click OK, and Windows 95 copies the appropriate files to your computer. Restart your computer when asked.

◆ TROUBLESHOOTING

Windows 95 copied part of the files from the CD-ROM, and then asked me to insert my Windows 95 CD-ROM. Windows 95 isn't smart enough to know that you have already inserted your Windows 95 CD-ROM. You specified an exact path to the Remote Registry Service earlier in step 4. Now it needs files from the \Win95 path on your Windows 95 CD-ROM. Thus, when asked to insert the CD-ROM, type the path to \Win95 on your Windows 95 CD-ROM and click OK.

You have to install the Remote Registry Service on both computers in order to connect to a remote computer's Registry. That is, if you want to connect to a workstation from your computer, you have to enable the Remote Registry Service on the remote computer as well as your computer. With the Remote Registry Service installed, you can now administer the remote computer's Registry with tools such as the Registry Editor and Policy Editor. The sections that follow describe the types of things you can now do remotely with that computer.

Part
III

Ch
13

Administering a Remote Computer

Table 13.1, in this chapter's introduction, described the Windows 95 and NT 4.0 tools that you can use to remotely administer a computer on the network. Remotely administering a Windows 95 computer from another Windows 95 computer is straightforward. You use tools such as Network Neighborhood, Net Watcher, and System Monitor. Likewise, administering a Windows NT 4.0 computer from another Windows NT 4.0 computer is straightforward with tools such as Event Viewer, Performance Monitor, and Server Manager.

The trouble begins when you try to administer computers in a mixed environment. Most of the Windows NT 4.0 remote administration tools don't work with a Windows 95 workstation and vise-versa. Thus, you have to actually log on to a computer that is running the same platform as the computer you're administering. Not too tough if you have both platforms nearby. The one exception is that you can remotely edit a Windows 95 Registry from NT 4.0. You can't edit an NT 4.0 Registry from Windows 95, however.

Administer an NT 4.0 Server from Windows 95

Microsoft provides many of the Windows NT 4.0 Server administrative tools for use in Windows 95. You can add users to a domain or view the event log on the server, for example—all from your Windows 95 computer. You'll find these tools on your NT 4.0 Server CD-ROM. Look in `\Clients\Srvtools\Win95`. Here's how to install them in Windows 95:

1. Double-click the Add/Remove Programs icon in the Control Panel, and click the Windows Setup tab. Look familiar?

2. Click the Have Disk button. Type the path to the `\Clients\Srvtools\Win95` folder on your NT 4.0 Server CD-ROM in the space provided, and click OK.

4. Select Windows NT Server Tools from the list, and click Install. Windows 95 will copy the appropriate files to your computer.

5. Click OK to close the Add/Remove Programs dialog box. You don't need to restart your computer before using these tools.

Windows 95 installs shortcuts to the NT 4.0 Server Tools in your Start menu. You'll find them in Programs, Windows NT Server Tools. They include the Event Viewer, Server Manager, and User Manager for Domains. Note that you must log on to the Windows 95 computer using an account that has administrative privileges.

The following sections provide an overview of the administrative tools available for both Windows 95 and Windows NT 4.0. Note that because this is a book about the Registry, you'll find more coverage about remotely editing the Registry, and only a brief introduction of the other administrative tools available.

Windows 95

Windows 95 provides more remote administration tools than any other Microsoft operating system before it. Windows NT 3.51 certainly provided a lot of tools to administer servers, but it didn't compare to the tools Windows 95 provides to administer an individual user's computer. You can work with a user's file system, identify bottlenecks in his computer's performance, and more. Here's what you'll find in this section:

- An overview of the tools available in Network Neighborhood, including file system administration, Net Watcher, and System Monitor.

- An overview of the System Policy Editor, which you can use to establish rules for what a user can and can't do on their computer.

- Detailed information about remotely editing the Windows 95 Registry from another computer on the network.

Using Network Neighborhood to Administer a Workstation The property sheet for each Windows 95 computer in Network Neighborhood has a Tools tab that contains three useful administrative tools: Net Watcher, System Monitor, and file system administration. To see the Tools tab, however, you need to make sure that remote administration is enabled on both the remote computer and the computer from which you're working. Likewise, in order to use System Monitor, you need to make sure that the Remote Registry Service is installed. "Setting Up Remote Administration for Windows 95," earlier in this chapter, gives you all the dirty details of setting these up.

With remote administration properly set up, you can perform a lot of routine administrative tasks through Network Neighborhood. Go ahead. Double-click the Network Neighborhood icon you see on your desktop. Then, right-click one of the Windows 95 workstations, choose Properties, and click the Tools tab. You'll see a dialog box similar to Figure 13.4.

FIG. 13.4
You can also get to these tools by launching them directly from the Start menu. You find them in Programs, Accessories, System Tools.

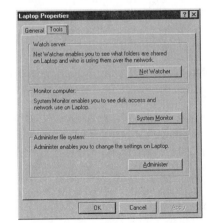

Part
III

Ch
13

Click Net Watcher to inspect the shares available on that computer. Figure 13.5 shows what Net Watcher looks like. The left-hand pane shows you each user that is using a resource on this computer. The right-hand pane shows you the shares to which the selected user is connected and the files the selected user has open. Besides inspecting the shares on a remote computer, you can also add shares or remove shares.

FIG. 13.5
Net Watcher is the only tool in which you can see the hidden shares IPC$ and ADMIN$.

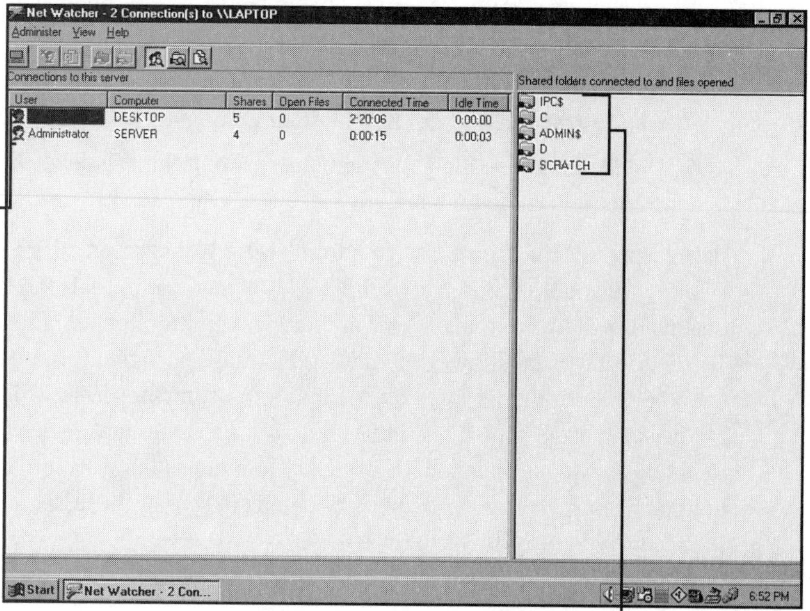

Users connected to this computer

Shares to which the selected user is connected

Back to the Tools tab, click System <u>M</u>onitor to monitor the target computer's performance. You can monitor dozens of variables, including file system, CPU, memory, and network performance variables. You can also watch as many variables as you like. Click the Add button in the toolbar to see additional variables for this computer. Figure 13.6 shows System <u>M</u>onitor while it's monitoring a remote computer. You can see the target computer's name in the System Monitor's title bar.

The last button on the Tools tab is the <u>A</u>dminister button. Click <u>A</u>dminister to browse all the folders and files on the remote computer as shown in Figure 13.7. You'll notice the computer's normal shares (c, d, and scratch in Figure 13.7). You'll also see special shares such as c$, which are administrative shares that give you full access to the nonremovable driver on that computer. Other than the administrative shares, this window works exactly like your normal Network Neighborhood folder.

FIG. 13.6
You can open multiple instances of System Monitor so that you can monitor more than one computer at a time.

Add button

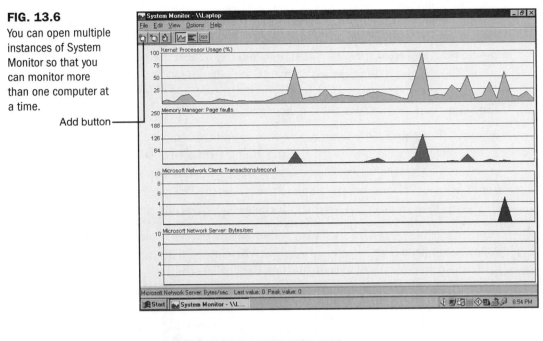

FIG. 13.7
You can just as easily double-click the computer's icon in Network Neighborhood to get this same list.

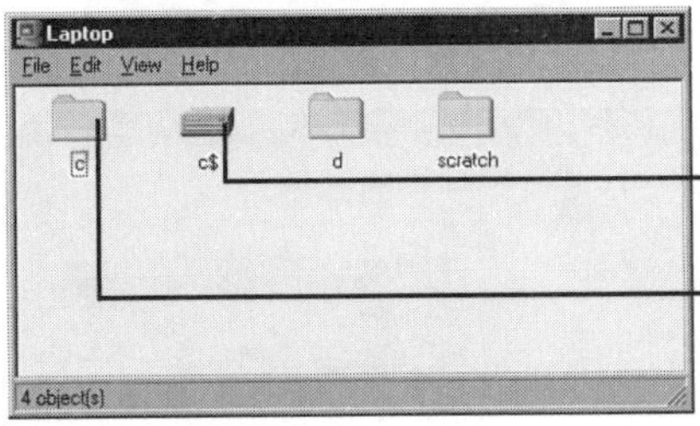

Administrative share

Normal shares

Part
III

Ch
13

TROUBLESHOOTING

I enabled remote administration and the Remote Registry Service on the other computer. Regardless, I can't connect to the other computer with System Monitor. You must enable remote administration and the Remote Registry Service on both computers. That is, you must enable the Remote Registry Service on the computer from which you're administering as well as the computer you're administering.

I've successfully administered this particular computer many times. However, I recently tried to administer it using Net Watcher, but it doesn't work. Remote administration only works if someone is logged on to the remote computer. Thus, make sure someone is logged on before administering the computer.

Setting Policies with the Policy Editor   The Windows 95 Policy Editor lets you define what a user can and can't do on their computer. I'll give you a few examples. You can block certain programs from running (Solitaire?). You can disable the Run option on the Start menu. You can also hide all of the floppy drives on the user's computer. The Policy Editor defines dozens of other settings that you can control remotely. Not only that, but you can also define your own settings using policy templates.

In reality, the Policy Editor is just a fancy way to edit the remote user's Registry. That's all it does. What separates it from the Registry Editor (REGEDIT) is that it provides a user interface that prompts for specific settings—in plain English. Once you choose a setting from a list or check box, or type text into a text box, the Policy Editor makes the appropriate change to the Registry. It's virtually a goof-proof way to edit the Registry.

Figure 13.8 shows you what the Policy Editor looks like. The background window is the Policy Editor itself. The foreground window, which pops up when you double-click one of the icons in the Policy Editor, contains the actual policies for the selected user or computer. Chapter 15, "Using the Policy Editor to Administer the Registry," describes how to use the Policy Editor in excruciating detail. As an added bonus, Chapter 16, "Creating Your Own Policies," shows you how to extend the Policy Editor with your own policies (policy templates).

FIG. 13.8

If the remote computer uses user profiles, you'll see an icon for each user that logs on to that computer.

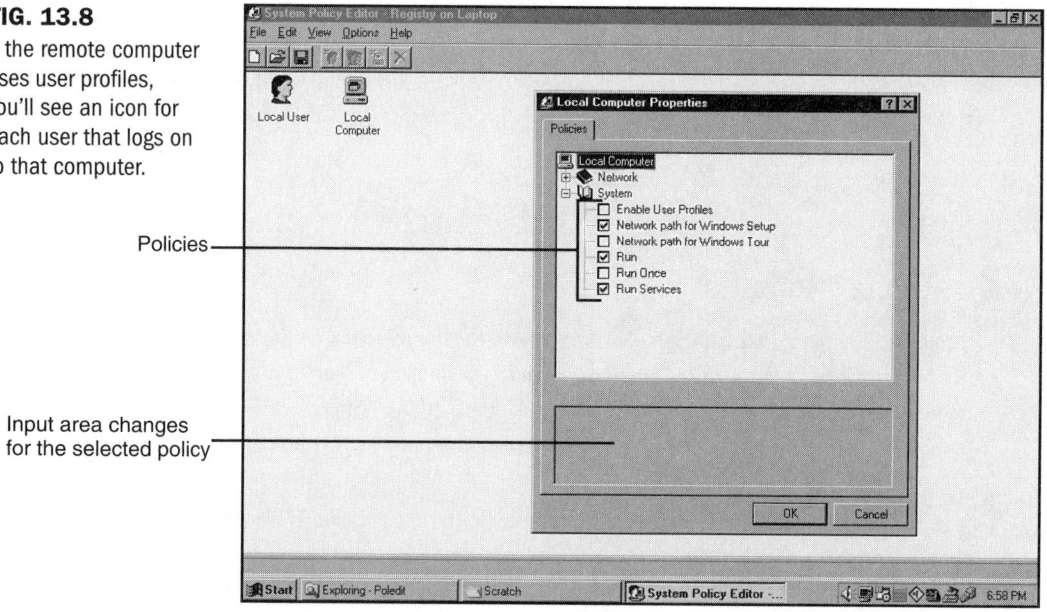

Policies

Input area changes for the selected policy

Editing a Remote Computer's Registry   If you're battling a problem on a user's computer, the Policy Editor probably won't do the trick. It limits you to a small subset of the Registry. You may need to tinker with their entire Registry—just as you would on your own computer if you were trying to fix a problem. Using the Registry Editor that you know and love, you can connect to another computer's Registry remotely. Then, you can change any settings you need.

In order to remotely edit a computer's Registry, you need to make sure that you've installed the Remote Registry Service as described in "Enabling the Remote Registry Service for Windows 95," earlier in this chapter.

> **CAUTION**
>
> Changing settings in a remote computer's Registry is no less dangerous than changing settings in your own Registry. Windows 95 implements no Registry security whatsoever. Thus, the remote user's entire Registry is at your disposal. Review the precautions you learned in Chapter 1, "Before You Begin," before making any changes to another user's Registry.

To connect to a remote computer's Registry, choose Registry, Connect Network Registry from the main menu. Then, type the name of the remote computer or click Browse to select a computer on the network. As a result, you'll see your computer and the remote computer in the Registry Editor as shown in Figure 13.9.

FIG. 13.9
You can connect to more than one Registry at a time.

Local computer

Remote computer

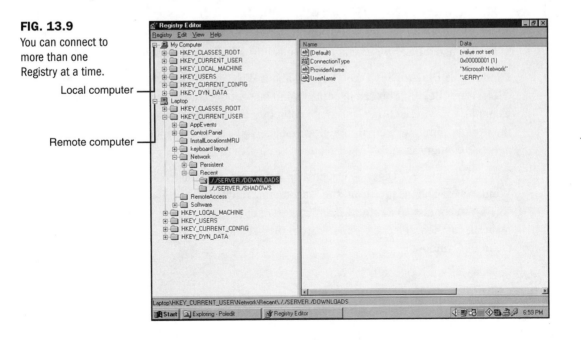

Part
III

Ch
13

After you've connected to the remote computer's Registry, everything works exactly the same as usual. For example, you can add and remove Registry keys. You can add, remove, and change value entries. Just make sure that you're selecting keys and value entries in the computer for which you intend. Otherwise, you just might change a Registry key on your own computer when you really intended to change a key on the remote computer.

Windows NT

Windows NT 4.0 provides many more remote administration tools than Windows 95. In fact, you can use most of the tools that you use on your own NT 4.0 computer with other computers on the network. For example, you probably are quite familiar with the Event Viewer. You can also use this tool to view the event log on other NT computers on the network. This section gives you a brief overview of each of these:

- You use the Windows NT Diagnostics to inspect the settings on a remote NT computer.

- You can view a remote NT computer's event log using the Event Viewer.

- You use the Performance Monitor to monitor the performance on a remote NT computer.

- The NT 4.0 Policy Editor works very similarly to the Windows 95 Policy Editor. You use it to set policies for a remote NT computer.

- The Windows NT 4.0 Registry Editor (REGEDT32) lets you remotely edit another NT 4.0 computer's Registry.

- You use the Server Manager to inspect the shares on a remote NT computer.

Windows NT Diagnostics   You learned about Windows NT Diagnostics in Chapter 1, "Before You Begin." You can use this tool to inspect the settings on another computer. For example, you can see how the remote computer is using its memory. You can check out the remote computer's environment variables. You can even inspect the other computer's network configuration.

To run Windows NT Diagnostics, choose Programs, Administrative Tools (Common), Windows NT Diagnostics from the Start menu. You'll see a window similar to Figure 13.10. You connect to a remote computer by choosing File, Select Computer from the main menu; then, select a computer from the list and click OK. Table 13.2 describes each tab in this window.

FIG. 13.10
You can't change any settings using Windows NT Diagnostics.

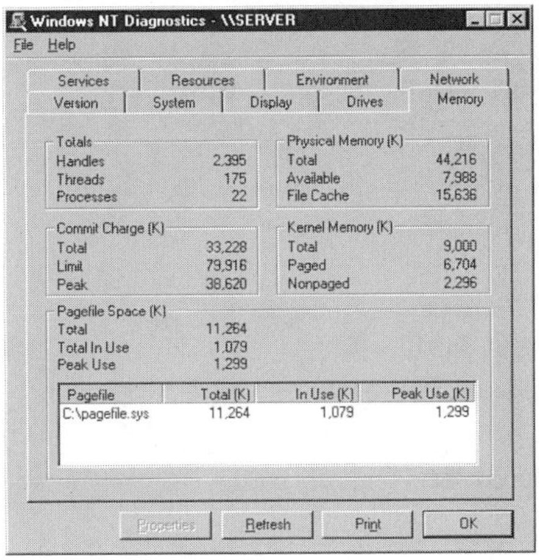

Table 13.2   Tabs in Windows NT Diagnostics

Tab Name	Description
Version	Version and registration information
System	The computer's BIOS and CPU information
Display	The computer's video adapter information
Drives	Drives installed on the computer
Memory	Physical memory, page file, and performance
Services	Services running on the computer
Resources	Device information: IRQ, I/O address, and so on.
Environment	Environment variables on the computer
Network	Access rights and share information

Event Viewer   I know that you've used the Event Viewer before. You use it to check the event log for errors, warnings, and other informative messages from Windows NT. Other programs and a variety of NT services also log messages in the event log.

To open the Event Viewer, choose Programs, Administrative Tools (Common), Event Viewer from the Start menu. You'll see a window similar to Figure 13.11. You connect to a remote computer by choosing Log, Select Computer from the main menu; then, select a computer from the list and click OK. Double-click one of the events to see more information.

Part
III

Ch
13

FIG. 13.11
Viewing the event log
is a useful way to see
why a computer is
failing, particularly as
it starts.

Date	Time	Source	Category	Event
ℹ 10/13/96	6:51:21 PM	Print	None	10
① 10/13/96	6:44:38 PM	Rdr	None	3012
❶ 10/13/96	6:44:29 PM	Print	None	10
❶ 10/13/96	5:07:00 PM	Print	None	10
❶ 10/13/96	4:50:04 PM	Print	None	10
❶ 10/13/96	4:20:06 PM	Print	None	10
① 10/13/96	3:35:27 PM	Rdr	None	3012
❶ 10/13/96	3:14:18 PM	Print	None	10
① 10/13/96	3:04:24 PM	Rdr	None	3012
① 10/13/96	3:04:19 PM	Rdr	None	3012
① 10/13/96	12:16:00 PM	Rdr	None	3012
① 10/13/96	9:52:22 AM	Rdr	None	3012
① 10/13/96	9:51:32 AM	Rdr	None	3012
❶ 10/13/96	9:46:49 AM	Print	None	10
❶ 10/10/96	3:25:09 PM	Print	None	10
❶ 10/10/96	3:18:18 PM	Print	None	10

T I P The Windows NT 4.0 Resource Kit contains complete documentation of the messages it logs in the event log.

Performance Monitor   As its name implies, you use the Performance Monitor to check up on a remote computer's performance. You can monitor the computer's disk and network performance, for example. You can also monitor the remote computer's memory and CPU—among other things.

To open the Performance Monitor, choose Programs, Administrative Tools (Common), Performance Monitor from the Start menu. You'll see a window similar to Figure 13.12. Each time you add a counter to the Performance Monitor, you specify which computer on the network you're monitoring. Thus, choose Edit, Add to Chart from the main menu to pick a computer and configure the counter.

Policy Editor   The Windows NT 4.0 Policy Editor lets you define what a user can and can't do on their computer—just like in Windows 95. Like Windows 95, the NT Policy Editor puts a user interface in front of the Registry. That is, it lets you change a computer's Registry settings by answering questions and picking options.

Figure 13.13 shows you what the NT 4.0 Policy Editor looks like. It has many more options than the Windows 95 Policy Editor. Chapter 15, "Using the Policy Editor to Administer the Registry," describes how to use the NT 4.0 Policy Editor. Also, Chapter 16, "Creating Your Own Policies," shows you how to extend the NT 4.0 Policy Editor with your own policies.

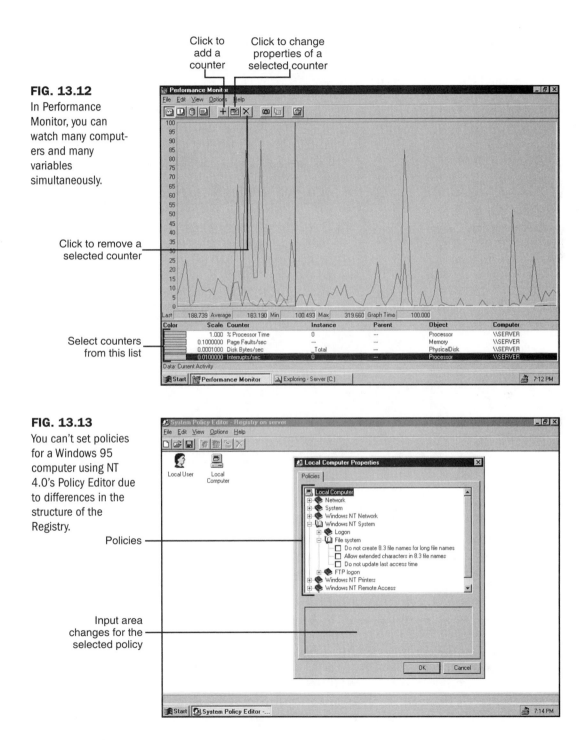

FIG. 13.12
In Performance Monitor, you can watch many computers and many variables simultaneously.

Click to add a counter

Click to change properties of a selected counter

Click to remove a selected counter

Select counters from this list

FIG. 13.13
You can't set policies for a Windows 95 computer using NT 4.0's Policy Editor due to differences in the structure of the Registry.

Policies

Input area changes for the selected policy

Part
III

Ch
13

Registry Editor   In Chapter 4, "Using REGEDT32 with Windows NT 4.0," you learned how to use Windows NT 4.0's Registry Editor. Remotely editing a Registry works very much the same way, except that you have to explicitly open that computer's Registry. Choose Registry, Select Computer from the main menu. Then, type the computer's name in the space provided or select the computer from the list. Click OK, and you'll see the remote computer's Registry as shown in Figure 13.14.

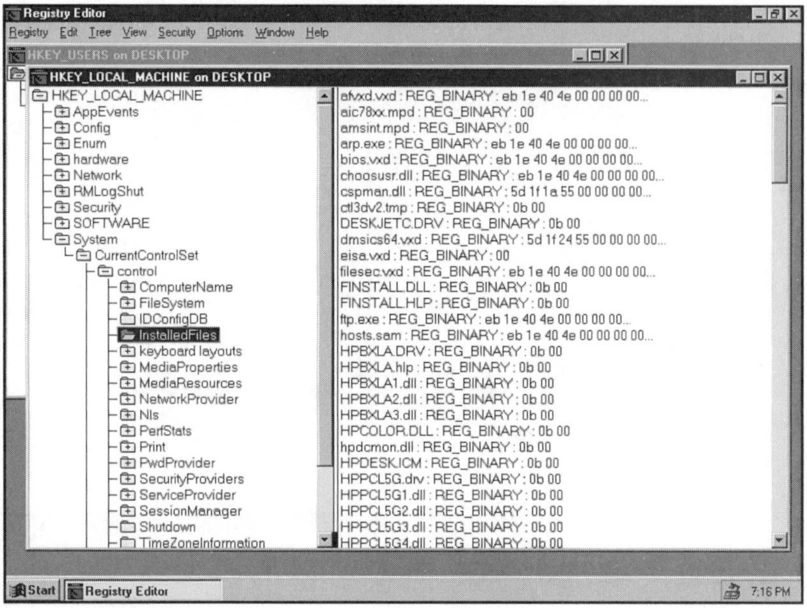

FIG. 13.14
REGEDT32 is easier to navigate if you only open one Registry at a time. Choose Registry, Close from the main menu before opening another computer's Registry.

TROUBLESHOOTING

When I try to connect to a remote NT computer's Registry, I get a message that says `Unable to connect to all of the roots of the computer's Registry. Disconnect from the remote registry and then reconnect before trying again.` **You're not using the correct Registry Editor. Use REGEDT32 instead of REGEDIT to edit a remote computer's Registry.

Restricting Access to Your Registry

By default, access to the Windows NT 4.0 Server's Registry is restricted to administrators and access to the Windows NT 4.0 Workstation's Registry is left completely open. You can change who can access the Registry, however. NT looks for a Registry key called

    HKEY_LOCAL_MACHINE\System\CurrentControlSet\Control\SecurePipServers\winreg

each time a user tries to remotely connect to the Registry. If NT finds this key, the access control list (ACL) for this key determines who can remotely connect to the computer's Registry. If NT doesn't find this key, NT lets all users remotely connect to the computer's Registry.

Here's how to set the ACL for a computer's Registry:

1. Add HKEY_LOCAL_MACHINE\SYSTEM\CurrentControlSet\Control
   \SecurePipeServers\winreg to the computer's Registry if it doesn't already exist.

2. Under that key, create a new REG_SZ value entry called Description. Then, set its value to
   Registry Server.

3. Change the security permissions for this subkey to reflect the users and groups that you
   want to be able to remotely access the computer's Registry.

Chapter 12, "Securing the Windows Registry," contains much more information about Registry security.

Server Manager   You use the Windows NT 4.0 Server Manager (not available in Windows NT Workstation) to manage the members of a domain. You can perform a variety of tasks, including managing the services running on remote computer, but one of the most useful is the ability to manage the shares on a remote computer. For example, you can change the permissions of a share on the remote computer or even add new shares to the remote computer (pretty sneaky).

To open the Server Manager, choose Programs, Administrative Tools (Common), Server Manager from the Start menu. Select an NT computer in the list, and choose Computer, Shared Directories from the main menu. You'll see a window similar to Figure 13.15.

FIG. 13.15
Click Properties to change permissions for the selected share.

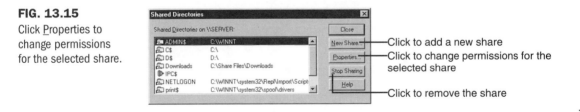

Click to add a new share
Click to change permissions for the selected share
Click to remove the share

Part
III

Ch
13

TIP   You can view a remote computer's shares using Windows NT Workstation 4.0. Double-click the Server icon in the Control Panel and click Shares.

CHAPTER 14

Working with REG and INF Files

by Jerry Honeycutt

You've learned many tips and tricks in this book that involve adding keys and value entries to the Registry. You'll find many more on the Internet and in places such as the Microsoft Knowledge Base.

Great for you; but what about all of the other users on the network? If you're responsible for more users than just yourself, you'll be happy to know that you can easily distribute those Registry changes to them through REG files. ■

Creating REG Files

Learn how to create REG files both by hand and with the Registry Editor.

Distributing REG Files to All Your Users

Discover how you can distribute REG files to users on a Web page, in a mail message, or in a login script.

Creating a REG File

REG files are text files that you can easily import into the Registry. In fact, when you double-click a REG file, Windows automatically imports it into the Registry by default. This fact makes it easy for you to distribute the REG file. When the user opens it, Windows 95 automatically makes the changes that the REG file contains.

> **CAUTION**
>
> Don't double-click a REG file unless you know for sure what it contains. Double-clicking a REG file merges its contents into the Registry without any confirmation.

REG files resemble INI files. Take a look at the following listing. The first line always contains REGEDIT4. This indicates that the file was created by REGEDIT. The remainder of the listing contains keys and value entries you'd normally find under HKEY_LOCAL_MACHINE\SOFTWARE\Microsoft\Windows\CurrentVersion\FS Templates.

```
REGEDIT4

[HKEY_LOCAL_MACHINE\SOFTWARE\Microsoft\Windows\CurrentVersion\FS Templates]
@="Server"

[HKEY_LOCAL_MACHINE\SOFTWARE\Microsoft\Windows\CurrentVersion\FS
   Templates\Desktop]
@="Desktop computer"

[HKEY_LOCAL_MACHINE\SOFTWARE\Microsoft\Windows\CurrentVersion\FS
   Templates\Mobile]
@="Mobile or docking system"
"PathCache"=hex:10,00,00,00
"NameCache"=hex:51,01,00,00

[HKEY_LOCAL_MACHINE\SOFTWARE\Microsoft\Windows\CurrentVersion\FS
   Templates\Server]
@="Network server"
"PathCache"=hex:40,00,00,00
"NameCache"=hex:a9,0a,00,00
```

▶ **See** "Correcting Microsoft's File System Performance Profiles," **p. 148**

The file is split into multiple sections, with each Registry key in its own section. The fully qualified name of the Registry file key is given—that is, you see the entire name of the path to that key, beginning with the name of the root key—between two brackets. Each value entry for a key is listed under that key's section. The value entry's name is quoted, except for default value entries, which REGEDIT represents with the at-sign (@). The value entry's data looks different depending on its type, as shown in Table 14.1.

Table 14.1   Formats for String, DWORD, and HEX Data

Type	Example
String	`"This is a string value"`
DWORD	`DWORD:00000001`
HEX	`HEX:FF,00,FF,00,FF,00,FF,00,FF,00,FF,00`

Creating REG Files by Hand

Creating a REG file by hand is easy enough. Create a new file with the REG extension, then follow these steps:

1. Put `REGEDIT4` at the top of the file. This must be the first line in the file. Also, make sure that you insert one blank line between `REGEDIT4` and the first section of the REG file, as shown in the earlier listing.

2. Add a section for each key that you want to add to or change in the Registry. Put each key name in square brackets, like this: `[Keyname]`. Make sure that you use the fully qualified path to the key, beginning with the root key.

3. Put an entry under each key for each value entry that you want to add or change. Each entry has the form `"Name"=Value`, where `Name` is the name of the value entry that you're adding or changing. If you're changing the default value entry, use the at-sign (@) for `Name`, without the quotes. `Value` is the value to which you want to set the value entry. Make sure it follows one of the forms shown in Table 14.1.

4. Save your changes to the REG file.

> **N O T E**   You can't use a REG file to remove a key from the Registry. If you need to create a script to do this, consider building an INF file. The Windows 95 Resource Kit contains complete information about building INF files. ▪

Creating REG Files Using REGEDIT

Creating REG files by hand seems easy enough, but it's not recommended. There are entirely too many chances for errors—especially if you're a bad typist. Thus, you should use REGEDIT if at all possible. Chapter 3, "Using REGEDIT with Windows 95 and NT 4.0," shows you how to export a branch of the Registry to a REG file. For your convenience, however, those instructions are repeated here:

1. Select the key that represents the branch you want to export in the left pane of the window.

Part
III

Ch
14

2. Choose Registry, Export Registry File from the main menu. REGEDIT displays the dialog box shown in Figure 14.1.

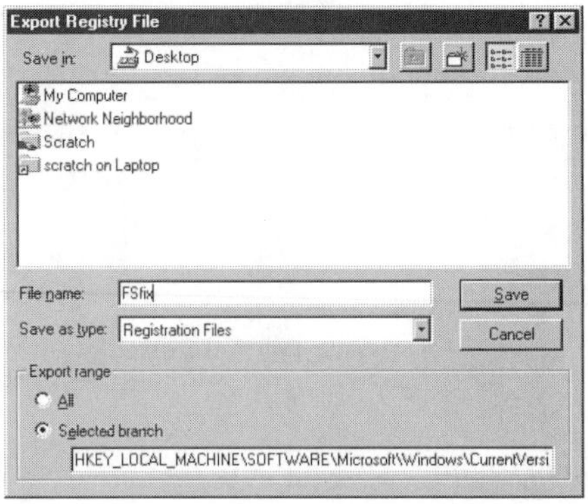

FIG. 14.1
If you don't type a file extension, REGEDIT uses the default file extension (REG).

3. Select Selected Branch. REGEDIT automatically fills in the key you selected in step 1.

4. Type the file name into which you want the Registry exported in File Name, and click Save.

There are a couple of issues you should be aware of when using this technique:

■ When you export a key using REGEDIT, you're exporting all of that key's subkeys and value entries. Thus, you'll need to open the file (right-click it, and choose Edit), and remove any keys and value entries that you don't want to distribute in the REG file.

■ You can change any of the values in the REG file; that is, if you're not satisfied with the settings that you exported from the Registry, you can alter those settings in the REG file before you distribute it.

▶ **See** "Importing and Exporting Registry Entries," **p. 66**

Working with INF Files

The INF file's file-type describes INF files as "Setup Information" files. This is a much more generic description than Microsoft usually uses for INF files, which is that INF files contain device driver information. In fact, you can put much more in an INF file than device driver information. You can put software setup information. More importantly, to this book anyway, you can put lines in an INF file that add, change, and remove Registry entries when the user installs the INF file.

INF files are pretty complex. Microsoft has created a whole language for INF files and has defined intricate rules that link various sections of the INF file together. Most of the statements and sections that programmers use in INF files are irrelevant to the topic at hand—you don't need to worry about all the complexity in order to use an INF file to script changes to the Registry.

The sections that follow describe how to create such an INF file from scratch. INF files look very similar to INI files. They're divided into sections and each section contains a number of assignments. Each of the following sections describes a single section within the INF file.

Version

The first section in all INF files is the [Version] section. For the purpose of editing the Registry, this section will always look like the following:

```
[Version]
signature="$CHICAGO$
```

Note that the Class item, which you normally see in INF files, isn't required in order to create a file to edit the Registry. $CHICAGO$ identifies that the INF file is for Windows 95 (Chicago was the beta name for Windows 95). It also works for Windows NT 4.0.

DefaultInstall

The [DefaultInstall] section contains the names of other sections, which specify the changes you're making to the Registry within the INF file. For example, you may have a section that contains Registry entries you're adding and another section that contains Registry entries you're removing. Here's what a typical [DefaultInstall] section looks like:

```
[DefaultInstall]
AddReg=MyAddReg
DelReg=MyDelReg
```

You must type the name of each item (on the left side of each equal sign) as shown here. You can name the section (on the right side) anything you like, however. The AddReg item identifies the section that contains new Registry entries. The DelReg item identifies the Registry entries that you're deleting.

Registry Sections

For each item you put in the [DefaultInstall] section, you have to create another section. The name of the section will be the value on the right side of each item. Thus, carrying on the example, you'd create two sections, called [MyAddReg] and [MyDelReg]. The items listed in [MyAddReg] are added to the Registry. The items listed in [MyDelReg] are removed from the Registry.

Each line within these sections has a similar format, shown in the following example. You use all of the parameters shown if you're adding a Registry entry. If you're removing a Registry entry, you only use the first three.

```
HKEY, Subkey, Name, Type, Value
```

Here's a description of each part of this line:

HKEY	One of the abbreviations for the root keys shown in Table 14.2.
Subkey	The subkey under the root key, not including the name of the root key itself.
Name	The name of the value entry that you're adding. Leaving this item blank implies you're working with the default value entry.
Type	The type of value entry (**0** for string or **1** for binary).
Value	The data for the value entry. Use the appropriate format for the *type* you specified; strings should be quoted, and binary should be in hexadecimal notation with each byte separated by a comma.

Table 14.2   Abbreviations for Root Keys

Abbreviation	Root Key
HKCR	HKEY_CLASSES_ROOT
HKCU	HKEY_CURRENT_USER
HKLM	HKEY_LOCAL_MACHINE
HKU	HKEY_USERS
HKCC	HKEY_CURRENT_CNOFIG
HKDD	HKEY_DYN_DATA

For example, the following lines would change the value of HKEY_LOCAL_MACHINE\Software\Microsoft\Windows\MyEntry to "Howdy":

```
[MyAddReg]
HKLM,Software\Microsoft\Windows\MyEntry,Howdy,0,"Hello World"
```

The next line removes KEY_LOCAL_MACHINE\Software\Microsoft\Windows\MyEntry from the Registry.

```
[MyDelReg]
HKLM,Software\Microsoft\Windows\MyEntry,Howdy
```

> **CAUTION**
>
> If you don't specify the name of a value entry when removing a value entry with an INF file, Windows removes the entry branch.

A Complete INF File

So far, you've seen each section of an INF file described, but you haven't seen a completed INF file. The following is a very simple example of an INF file that adds the value entry Howdy to HKEY_LOCAL_MACHINE\Software\Microsoft\Windows\MyEntry and sets its value to "Hello World." It also removes the entry branch starting with the subkey called TestEntry from HKEY_CURRENT_USER\Software and removes the value entry called TestValue from HKEY_LOCAL_MACHINE\Software\TestEntry.

```
[Version]
signature="$CHICAGO$"

[DefaultInstall]
AddReg=MyAddReg
DelReg=MyDelReg

[MyAddReg]
HKLM,Software\Microsoft\Windows\MyEntry,Howdy,0,"Hello World"

[MyDelReg]
HKCU,Software\TestEntry
HKLM,Software\TestEntry,TestValue
```

Here's how to test this example:

1. Create a new INF file and type in the contents as shown in the previous listing. Save the INF file to your disk.

2. Create a new subkey called HKEY_CURRENT_USER\Software\TestEntry. Add a few subkeys underneath this one.

3. Create a new subkey called HKEY_LOCAL_MACHINE\Software\TestEntry and add a value entry called TestValue. Set the value entry to anything you like.

4. Right-click the INF file, and choose Install. Open the Registry Editor to observe the changes.

Part
III

Ch
14

Distributing REG and INF Files

A good way to impress the users that you support is to distribute fixes to them without them asking. Better yet, make it as simple as possible and they'll really adore you.

If you have an intranet in your organization, you can make REG and INF files available on a Web page. Lacking an intranet, you can also distribute REG files in mail messages or in the user's login script. You'll learn about each in the remaining sections.

On a Web Page

Remember, the default Windows 95 action for a REG file is to import it. The default action for an INF file isn't to install it, however, so you won't be able to distribute an INF file on a Web page (you can use e-mail or other methods as shown later). You can put a link to a REG file on a Web page. Then, when a user clicks that link, the browser will download the file to the user's computer and automatically apply the change that it contains. This works fine for Internet Explorer users, but Netscape users will have to register a helper application for REG files. Figure 14.2 shows you an example of a Web page that contains a few REG files. When you build such a Web page, it's recommended that you follow these suggestions:

- Provide clear information about who needs to apply each particular REG file. For example, if you post a REG file that only affects Microsoft Mail users, say so on the Web page.

- Provide clear information about what the REG file does to the user's computer. Some people are control freaks—a bit nervous about doing something like this when they don't know exactly what's going to happen.

- Provide instructions that the user can use to download the REG file to their own computer without applying it. That way, if the user wants to, the user can inspect the file before applying it.

- Provide contact information for yourself. Provide your office number, phone number, pager number, and so on. If a user is about to get into a panic, they'll feel better knowing that they can quickly reach you.

FIG. 14.2
Some Web pages are
simple, containing
only a few REG files.
Make sure that yours
fits in with the overall
Web site, so users
don't feel they've
dropped into Dr.
Jekyll's laboratory.

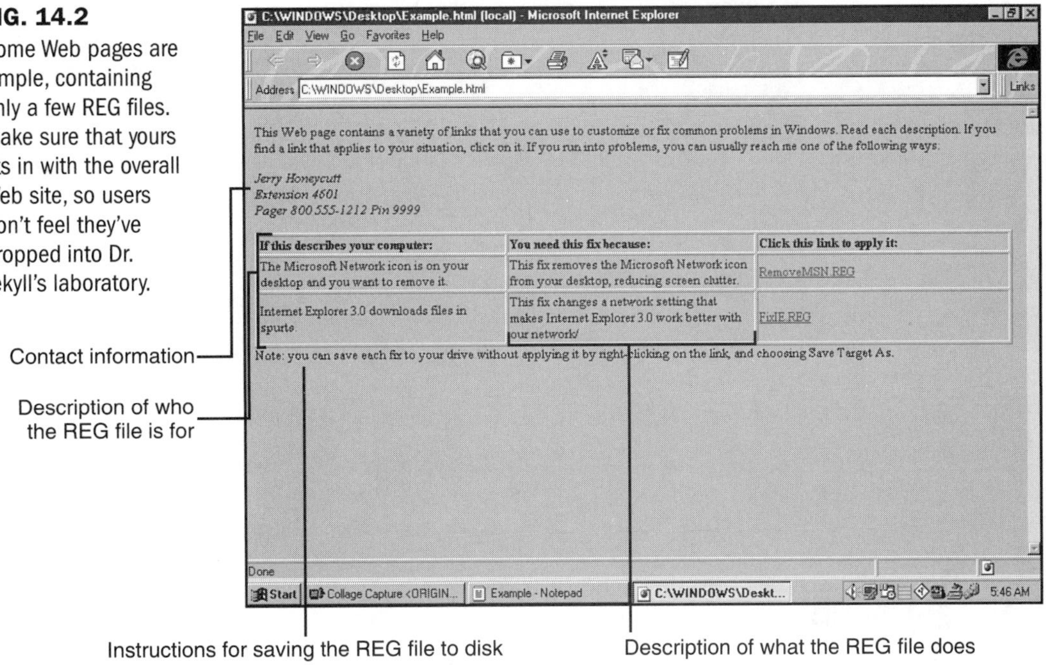

Contact information

Description of who
the REG file is for

Instructions for saving the REG file to disk

Description of what the REG file does

In an E-mail Message

If you don't have an intranet in your organization, the next best thing to do is distribute a
REG or INF file in an e-mail message. Attach the file to the message and instruct the user
on how to apply the file. In most e-mail programs, the user will just have to double-click
the attachment to apply the REG or right-click on an INF file and choose Install.

The same recommendations apply as for Web pages. Tell the recipients whether or not
they need to apply the REG file, tell them what it's going to do to their computer, tell them
how to view the file, and make sure they know how to reach you. Figure 14.3 shows you
an example of such an e-mail message.

Part
III

Ch

14

FIG. 14.3

You can also post a REG file on a Web page and e-mail a notice containing its description and URL.

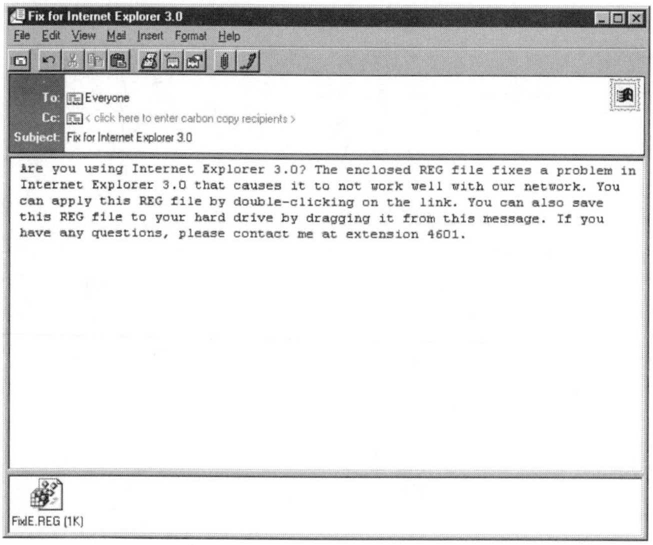

In a Login Script

It takes a bit of work, but you can also put a command in each user's login script that automatically applies the REG or INF file when the user logs onto the network. If you've set up a login script for multiple users, you can slip the command in that script, instead. All you have to do is put the following command in the script (*filename* is the name of the REG file):

```
start filename.reg
```

The one problem with this method is that every time the user logs onto the network, the login script will apply the REG file. You can avoid this problem by putting the previously listed command in a batch file. Then, the login script can check for the existence of this batch file on the user's computer. If it doesn't exist, the login script copies the batch file to the user's computer and executes it. Otherwise, it just ignores it.

The command line for INF files is a bit more convoluted. That's because the default action for an INF file isn't to install it. Thus, you'll actually specify the command line that Windows uses for the Install action of the INF file type, like this (*Filename* is the name of the INF file):

```
C:\WINDOWS\rundll.exe setupx.dll,InstallHinfSection DefaultInstall 132
    Filename.inf
```

Using the Policy Editor to Administer the Registry

by Kelly Millsaps

User profiles enable you to define numerous user-specific settings logged in the Registry. This can enable user information to "follow" mobile customers as they move from computer to computer in your network. Profiles can help you reduce support and administration overhead by limiting the access of users, groups of users, or machines to configuration settings. The System Policy Editor (POLEDIT) offers an efficient tool to create user profiles and administer related policy files and templates. In addition, POLEDIT is a terrific tool to make changes to Registry settings in a graphical, user-friendly manner, without the risks inherent in making modifications to the Registry directly.

If you're already familiar with these functions in Windows 95, the incorporation of 95's interface in the release of Windows NT 4.0 will make you feel right at home. In this chapter, you will examine each of these components in more detail.

Understanding the differences between the System Policy Editor in Windows 95 and NT

Learn how to make use of key differences in the Policy Editors for Windows 95 and NT.

Understanding User Profiles

Explore how controlling User Profiles offers key benefits in the maintenance of user-specific information contained in the Registry.

Understanding policies

Use System Policies to set, change, and maintain Registry entries on a per user, per machine, or per group basis.

Installing and using the Policy Editor

The System Policy Editor (POLEDIT) is the engine used to create and administer policy files. Learn how to install and use the Policy Editor to optimize Registry administration locally and throughout your network.

N O T E Throughout this chapter, the user-specific information stored in the USER.DAT and NTUSER.DAT files (of Windows 95 and NT, respectively) will be mutually referred to as the *user data file.* ■

Understanding the Differences Between the System Policy Editor in Windows 95 and NT

Registry-specific information is stored differently on Windows 95 and NT. In both cases, data from the HKEY_Current_User section of the Registry is stored in a user file. In Windows 95, this file is located in the Windows directory as USER.DAT. In Windows NT, the equivalent file—NTUSER.DAT—is also stored in the Windows directory. Though these files are similar, they are neither compatible nor interchangeable.

> **CAUTION**
>
> Use caution when importing registries. Loading a Windows NT Registry on a 95 machine, or vice versa, can cause serious problems and functionality loss. Lack of Registry compatibility necessitates network users (who operate machines running both Windows 95 and NT) to have both the USER.DAT and NTUSER.DAT files stored in their network directory.

> **CAUTION**
>
> Before using any tool to edit the Registry, it is always a good idea to make a quick backup of your current Registry settings. There are several options for backing up your registry. Be sure to make a backup copy of your Registry settings before using POLEDIT.EXE.

▶ **See** "Backing Up the Windows 95 Registry," **p. 17**

The System Policy Editor (POLEDIT.EXE) is functionally similar in Windows 95 and NT. The main distinction is that POLEDIT.EXE for Windows 95 is a convenient way to make Registry changes for individual users or computers. POLEDIT.EXE for Windows NT can be used for local Registry administration, but is mainly used for making changes to users, machines, or groups of users in networked environments throughout the domain.

The visual aspects of the POLEDIT.EXE GUI front end are nearly identical in Windows 95 and NT. This can be seen in Figures 15.1 and 15.2.

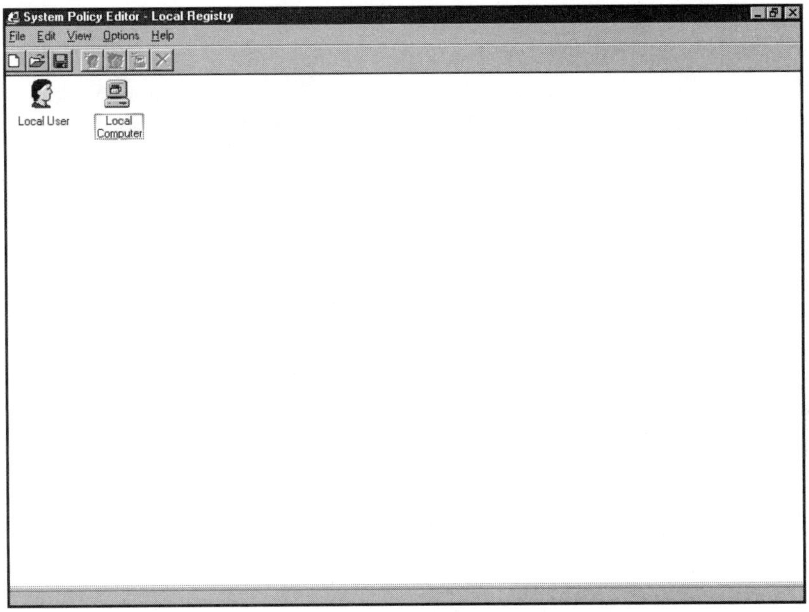

Part

III

Ch

15

FIG. 15.1

The interface for
System Policy Editor
is nearly identical in
Windows 95 and NT.

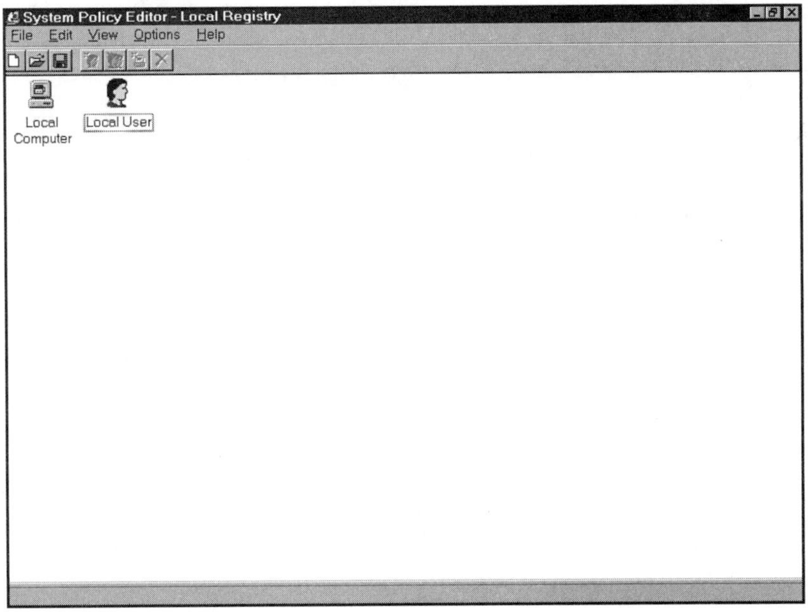

FIG. 15.2

The interface for
System Policy Editor
in Windows NT.

One other distinction in the System Policy Editor for Windows 95 versus NT is the actual installation. In Windows 95, you manually install the Policy Editor and supporting files from the source media. In Windows NT 4.0 (Server and Workstation), the Policy Editor is installed by default as one of the administrative tools. (See "Installing and Using the Policy Editor," later in this chapter.)

Once installed, the System Policy Editor can conveniently edit the Registry. Its GUI and intuitive nature help to minimize errors that can occur by other, more direct means of Registry editing in both Windows 95 and NT.

Understanding User Profiles

User Profiles offer MIS professionals a tool for dictating what settings in the Windows interface are configurable by the user versus what settings are predetermined at logon. Mandatory profiles and policies are the primary mechanism for administrating profiles across a broad user base.

N O T E   Consider the "big picture" ramifications of introducing restrictions on end users through management of profiles and policies. There can be a lot of political friction generated if users previously had the freedom to change anything they wanted. A well-communicated implementation strategy that is supported by upper management within your organization can save you a lot of headaches down the road. It is also a good idea to justify changes by explaining the value they add to the end user (better support, ease of use, consistent desktops, and so on). This creates a team approach in your IS structure, making users feel involved in making changes rather than victimized by oppressive corporate policy.

User-specific information contained in the user data file of the Windows 95 and NT registries is the major component of a user profile, as shown in Figure 15.3. A user profile will generally consist of the user data file itself and a backup of the user data file (User.da0), as well as a Desktop, Recent, and Start Menu folder. The Start Menu folder contains a Programs folder within it.

Profiles can be useful in a variety of circumstances. In situations where one computer is shared by multiple users, profiles enable each user to have an optimized profile for their activities. Conversely, when a single user operates multiple machines on the same network, a roving profile can maintain the same settings on each machine for that user. Perhaps the most powerful use of profiles is the capability to enforce common settings to a specific user, machine, or group of users. Establishing common settings can greatly decrease training, support, and administrative costs, as this use of profiles re-creates specified settings each time the user logs in.

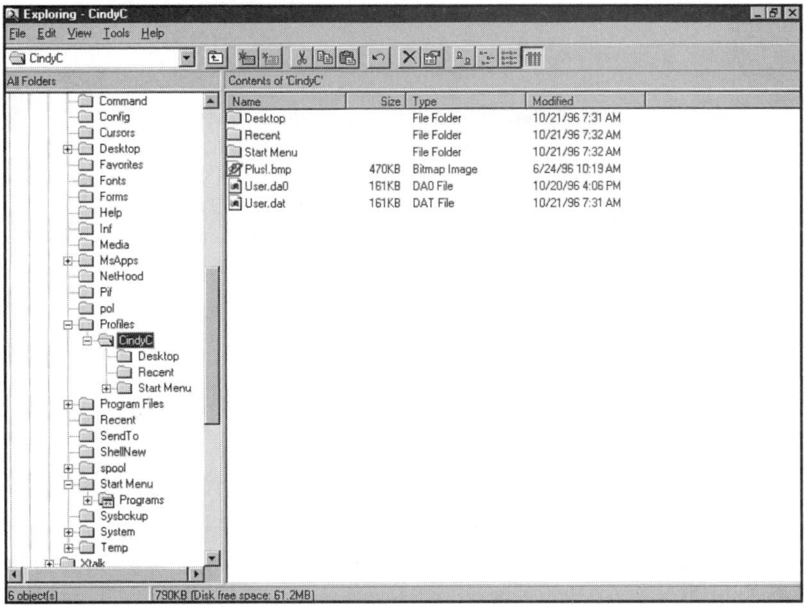

FIG. 15.3
Windows Explorer
view of a user profile
in Windows 95 and
typical contents.

User Profiles can contain the following user-specific information:

- Desktop settings for display layout, colors, background, sounds, screen saver, and so on

- User-definable settings for Explorer, Start menu, and taskbar

- Persistent printer and network connections

- Desktop shortcuts

- Recent documents

- User-defined application settings (Many applications like Microsoft Plus! save customized settings in the user's profile)

TROUBLESHOOTING

I see the Profiles directory in my Windows folder, but I can't change or save any of my personal settings. If you're using a computer in a networked environment, your systems administrator might have enforced a common profile onto your desktop. You'll have to request that your administrator grant access for you to customize your desktop settings.

Your profile settings may not be enabled. Enable custom profiles by choosing Start, Settings, Control Panel, Password, and configuring the settings as shown in Figure 15.4.

FIG. 15.4

Customization of
user profiles must
be set as indicated
in the Passwords
Properties dialog box
to be fully enabled.

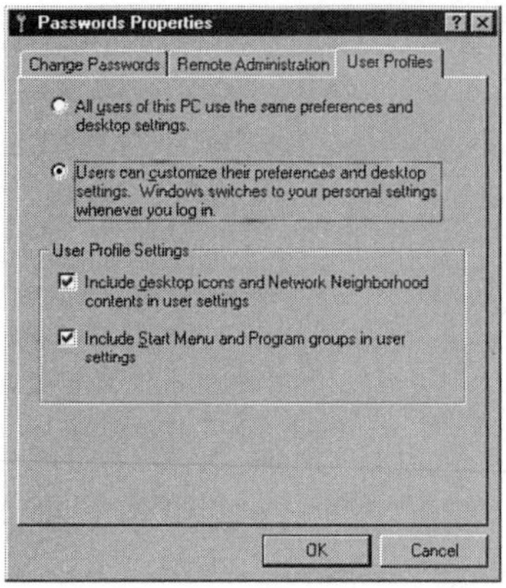

N O T E   Your system administrator may disable the User Profiles tab in a networked environment so that it does not appear in the Passwords control settings. ▨

In networked environments, roving profiles enable users to maintain their profile settings
as they move from machine to machine in your network. This can help optimize the user's
time because all settings are where the user expects on each computer at each location.
Conversely, "default" or mandatory profiles can be forced onto users as they log on. This
can help ensure that all desktop icons and general configuration parameters remain con-
stant on machines shared by multiple users, preventing both user frustration and use of
support resources as one user finds that the previous has moved icons, disabled drivers,
deleted files, changed printers, and so on. It can also help prevent accidental configuration
changes, again limiting contention for your already strained support resources.

T I P   User profiles are stored in different locations on different network operating systems. In a
Windows NT network, user profiles for Windows 95 clients are found in the user's home directory.
Profiles for Windows NT clients are located in the Profiles directory on a Windows NT server. In
Novell Netware networks, all Windows client profiles are stored in the user's mail directory.

Mandatory user profiles can be used when you want a specific profile applied to a given
user, machine, or group of users. To create a mandatory profile, simply rename the user's
User data file to USER.MAN in the appropriate local or network directory. When a mandatory profile is used, changes made by the user are not saved. This enables consistent
profile settings to be applied to a user (machine or group of users) at each logon. Mandatory profiles control all Registry values stored in the user data file. This tool does not
allow any flexiblity in what values the user may customize. Policies, described in the next
section, offer more flexibility than mandatory profiles in what restrictions you want to
enforce and on whom.

Understanding Policies

System policies allow administrators to manage and control Registry settings applied to users, machines, or groups of users across the network. Policies files affect the HKEY_Current_User and HKEY_Local_Machine keys in the Registry. These keys define the contents of the user data and SYSTEM.DAT files, respectively. Policy settings allow administrators the ability to:

- Configure desktop and network settings
- Restrict application functionality based on the user
- Specify access to Control Panel options
- Customize the control of nearly any Registry setting

System Policies are created using the Policy Editor (POLEDIT.EXE). Two file types are involved in the establishment of system policies:

- ADM extension files are administrative templates that dictate the scope of policies.
- POL extension files are the policy files themselves that actually specify the value of a variety of Registry settings.

In order to create any POL files, you must make reference to an ADM template file. The ADMIN.ADM file is distributed with Windows 95 and NT. It is possible to write your own ADM file that can be a subset of the ADMIN.ADM file or expand on the Registry values controlled in that file. It is possible to include control for nearly any registry function in an ADM file. A listing of user configurable information found in the ADMIN.ADM file is pictured in Figure 15.5.

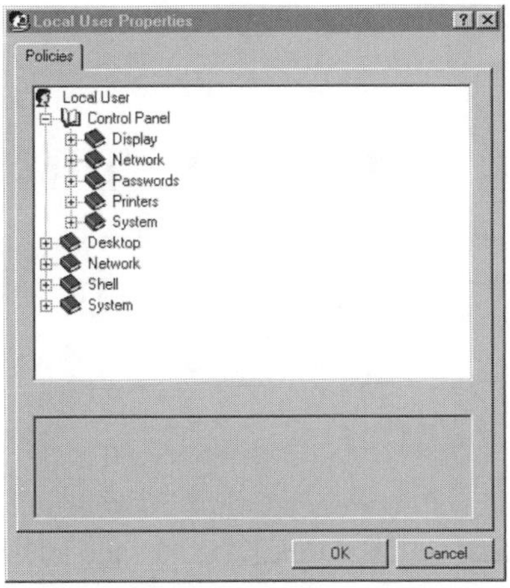

FIG. 15.5
Policies under Local User Properties in the System Policy Editor.

> **T I P** You should strongly consider setting a default of user and system related policies before initiating a rollout of Windows 95 or Windows NT to any networked user group.

Windows 95 and NT search for policy files (POL) during the boot process. By default, Windows will search the user's home directory on Microsoft NT networks—the user's mail directory on Novell Netware networks—and the Windows directory on share level security networks (peer to peer). If a policy file is found, it will be enforced at that time; otherwise, no policies will be loaded. This doesn't imply that profiles aren't enabled. Although policies administer profiles, user profiles can function independently of any policy. Thus, even if no policies are enforced in the boot cycle, it is still possible to activate mandatory or uncontrolled user profiles.

> **T I P** Because system policies are based on Registry entries, you cannot edit them with a text editor. You can, however, use a text editor to modify a template (ADM files).

It is important to determine your desired scope of control when you consider imposing restrictions on your network community. Policy files allow control for values in both the User data and SYSTEM.DAT portions of the Registry. They allow very flexible design of environment control and user enforcement options. Mandatory profiles, mentioned earlier in "Understanding User Profiles," are a second tool for managing desktops. Mandatory profiles allow no flexibility in environment control and are limited solely to values contained in the User data portion of the Registry. Mandatory profiles are either disabled or dictating 100 percent of user settings to your customer base.

Proper implementation of mandatory profiles and policies offer MIS professionals and LAN administrators a robust set of tools for managing the Windows environment. A detailed examination of policies can be found in the next section.

Installing and Using the Policy Editor

In this section, a step-by-step description of how to install the System Policy Editor is outlined. In addition, connecting to and managing registries remotely with POLEDIT.EXE is explored in detail.

Installing the System Policy Editor

In Windows 95, you must install System Policy Editor in order to use it. Installation can be accomplished by copying POLEDIT.EXE, POLEDIT.INF, and ADMIN.ADM from the Admin\Apptools\Poledit directory of your Windows 95 installation CD. The ADMIN.ADM file must be placed in the INF directory of the Windows folder. It's recommended that the two POLEDIT files be placed in the Windows directory, allowing them to be within the scope of a typical path statement. It is also convenient to make a shortcut pointing at the executable application.

In Windows NT, the System Policy Editor is loaded by default in a standard installation of both Workstation and Server. A shortcut to the policy editor executable can be found by choosing Start, Programs, Admin Tools, Policy Editor.

Now that you have the policy editor installed, you're ready to use it. To initiate the policy editor, simply choose Start, Run, type **Poledit**, and press Enter. This works for both Windows 95 and NT. If you are prompted for the location of your ADM file, browse to the INF folder in the Windows directory. Choose File, Open Registry. Figure 15.6 shows the differences between the user setting options in the ADMIN.ADM template of Windows 95 and Windows NT.

FIG. 15.6
POLEDIT.EXE should bring up this screen with Local User and Local Computer icons depending on the ADM file you use as your template. This figure includes the user properties in Windows 95 (top) and Windows NT (bottom) based on Admin.adm templates.

TIP

Create a shortcut on your desktop or in the desired program location. Right-click the desired location (Desktop for example), and choose New, Shortcut. Enter **Poledit.exe** in the command line, select Next, name the shortcut, and click Finish. These steps allow you quick access to the System Policy Editor.

TROUBLESHOOTING

Initiating the Policy Editor doesn't bring up the options illustrated in Figure 15.6. What could be wrong ? If you are on a networked environment, the policies enforced on you or your machine can restrict your options in Poledit view. This is done using a particular ADM file which is applied as a default each time you log on. You can manually change your policy settings using an appropriate template (ADM) file, but all changes will be overridden the next time you log on.

Connecting to a User's Computer Remotely

The System Policy Editor can be used to configure and restrict the rights of a user, group of users, or a machine. It can also be used to remotely manage a given user's Registry. You can remotely administrate users only after you're granted permission. You can configure this in a policy, which can then be applied across the network. You can also set permissions up manually.

Setting up remote permissions requires enabling remote permissions and selecting to whom you want to grant access. In networked environments you can select a user name validated by your network operating system. In share-level networks, a password is specified for access. Any user who knows this password can gain remote administration authority with share-level security.

Enabling remote administration merely requires placing a check mark in the Enable Remote Administration field of the Remote Administration tab, as shown in Figure 15.7. Just choose Start, Settings, Control Panel, Passwords.

Connecting to a remote computer requires several steps:

1. Find the target computer in Network Neighborhood.
2. By using the right mouse button, select the specified computer and bring up the Properties sheet.
3. Click the Tools tab and click the Administration button as shown in Figure 15.8.

FIG. 15.7
Enabling remote
administration
in a networked
environment.

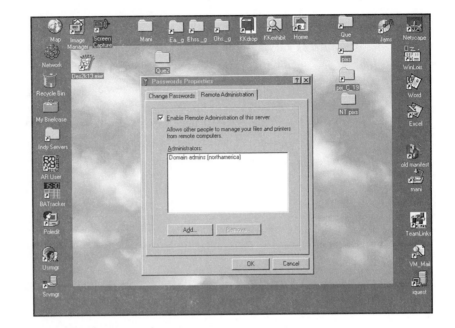

FIG. 15.8
Remote machine's
Properties menu as
seen from the
administrator's
machine.

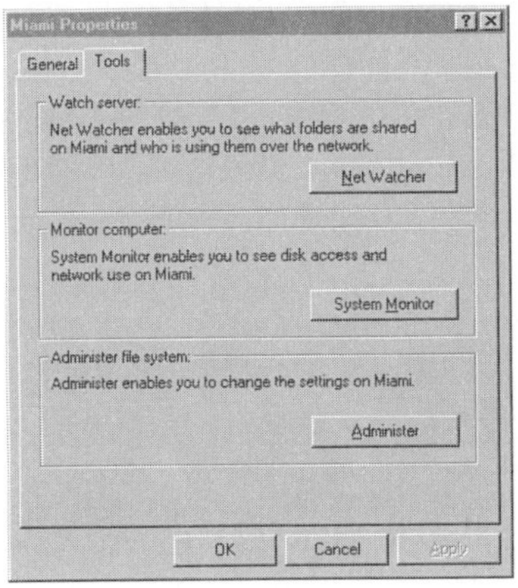

TROUBLESHOOTING

There is no Remote Administration Tab under Control Panel, Passwords. If you are on a
networked environment, the policies enforced on you or your machine can restrict your options
under Control Panel, Passwords. If you have no Remote Administration tab, you can either request
access from your LAN administrator, or use POLEDIT.EXE to manually give yourself access. Each
time you log on, you are again subject to administrative policies enforced on your network.

This brings the administrative tools window with three primary options:

- *Net Watcher.* Allows administrator to determine who is using what resources of the target computer across the network.

- *System Monitor.* Allows administrator to review allocation of a wide range of system resources in use on the remote machine. This includes RAM, hard drive space, free memory, network activity, and paging, among others. This tool must be loaded on the target computer in order to be used remotely.

- *Administrator.* Allows administrator to remotely configure, monitor, and manage a variety of resources, including the Registry when remote Registry administration is enabled.

Once connected, you can manage Registry settings based on the ADM template you are using, much like how you administer the same settings on a local machine.

Common Settings Managed Using System Policy Editor

The following gives a brief synopsis of what settings can be administered locally or remotely using the System Policy Editor. These configuration options are based on the Admin.adm template. Creation of custom templates is considered in Chapter 16.

User Configuration (Remote or Local)   The System Policy Editor allows you to change User Configuration information that directly affects the User data Registry file. Numerous configuration options are available within these settings and are described in the following sections.

Control Panel Policies affect or limit options of specific modules within the control panel. Some common configuration options are:

Option	Description
Display	Enables restrictions to display options as follows: Disable Display Control Panel, Hide Background Page, Hide Screen Saver Page, Hide Appearance Page, and Hide Setting Page.
Network	Enables restrictions to network options as follows: Disable Network Control Panel, Hide Identification Page, and Hide Access Control Page.
Passwords	Enables restrictions to password options as follows: Disable Passwords Control Panel, Hide Change Passwords Page, Hide Remote Administration Page, and Hide User Identification Page.

Option	Description
Printers	Enables restrictions to printer options as follows: Hide General and Details Pages, Disable Deletion of Printers, and Disable Addition of Printers.
System	Enables restrictions to system options as follows: Hide Device Manage Page, Hide Hardware Profile Page, Hide File System, and Hide Virtual Memory.

Desktop Settings   Desktop Policies affect or limit specific aspects of the user desktop. Some common configuration options are:

- *Wallpaper*. Enables wallpaper to be included with the User Profile.
- *Color Scheme*. Enables color scheme to be included with the User Profile.

Network Policies   Network Policies affect or limit sharing of files or printers in peer-to-peer (share-level security) networks:

- *File*. Enables File sharing.
- *Print*. Enables Printer sharing.

Shell Policies   Shell Policies affect or limit specific facets of the user interface:

- *Custom Folders*. Enables several customized aspects of the Windows interface to become part of the User Profile. Those included in the Admin.adm template are:

Custom Program Folder	Custom Startup Folder
Custom Desktop Icons	Custom Network Neighborhood
Hide Start Menu subfolders	Custom Start Menu

- *Restrictions*. Enables restrictions to the following:

Remove "Run" command	No "Entire Network" in Network Neighborhood
Remove folders from "Settings" on Start Menu	
Remove taskbar from "Settings" on Start Menu	No workgroup contents in Network Neighborhood
Remove "Find" command	Hide all items in Desktop
Hide drives on "My Computer"	Disable Shut Down command
Hide Network Neighborhood	Don't save settings on exit

System Policies System Policies restrict functional components of Windows 95 or NT. The following are restricted options in System Policies:

■ Disable Registry Editing Tools

■ Only run allowed Windows applications

■ Disable MS-DOS Prompt

■ Disable Single mode MS-DOS applications

Computer Configuration (Remote or Local) The System Policy Editor enables you to change Computer configuration information that directly affects the SYSTEM.DAT Registry file. Numerous configuration options, as shown in Figure 15.9, are available within these settings and are described as follows.

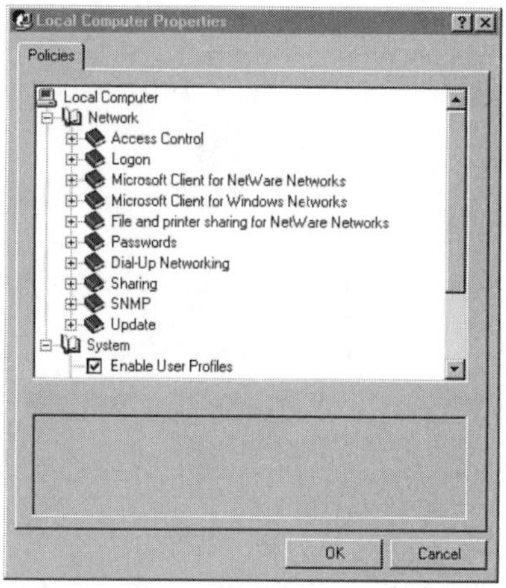

FIG. 15.9
You can change Computer configuration information in the System Policy Editor.

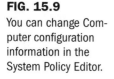

Network Policies Network Policies affect or limit network-related hardware functions as follows:

■ *Access Control.* Enables user-level access (User-Level Access Control).

■ *Logon.* Configures Windows access based on logon:

　　　Logon Banner

　　　Require Validation by Network for access to Windows

■ *Microsoft Client for Netware.* Provides Novell Netware network-specific configuration options:

　　　Preferred Server

　　　Support Long File Name

Search Mode

Disable automatic Netware Login

■ *Microsoft Client for Windows Networks.* Provides Microsoft Windows network-specific configuration options:

Logon to Windows NT

Workgroup

Alternate workgroup

■ *File and Print Sharing for Netware Networks.* Controls Netware-specific sharing options: Disable SAP advertising

■ *Passwords.* Provides Password configuration options:

Hide Share Passwords With Asterisks

Disable Password Caching

Require Alphanumeric Windows Password

Minimum Windows Password Length

■ *Dial-Up Networking.* Configures Dial-up Adapter (Disable Dial in).

■ *Sharing.* Configures Sharing options in peer-to-peer networks:

Disable File Sharing

Disable Print Sharing

■ *SNMP.* Provides Network packet protocol configuration:

Communities

Permitted Managers

Traps for "Public" Community

Internet MIB

■ *Update.* Control Remote updating (Remote Update).

System Policies System Policies configure defaults for the operation of the Windows interface:

Enable User Profiles

Network Path for Windows Setup

Network Path for Windows Tour

Run

Run Once

Run Services

CHAPTER 16

Creating Your Own Policies

by Kelly Millsaps

The System Policy Editor must use a policy template (ADM files) to determine which policies can be modified or enabled in the creation of policy files (POL files). Policy files based on different templates configure different values in the Registry.

System policies defined for applications will function properly only for those capable of reading the Registry.

The motivation for custom templates varies widely and is as numerous as the number of users. This chapter explores the process for creating custom system policy templates in detail. ∎

Creating policy templates

Policy templates (ADM files) determine what subset of policies you can enable or modify. Templates can be written to configure anything in the Registry. A detailed description of the design of policy templates is explored in this chapter.

Understanding template keywords

Specific keywords are used to describe and design policy templates. These keywords must follow a specific hierarchy. Learn the proper keyword format to create customized templates.

Creating Policy Templates

Microsoft includes a default template called ADMIN.ADM in the source media for Windows 95. This template doesn't cover every possible Registry setting or allow the configuration of unique corporate applications. Custom templates will be helpful in the configuration of Registry settings you would like to include in your system policies, but are not definable in the standard default template.

N O T E   Installation of the System Policy Editor can be accomplished as follows:

Windows 95: The source files are located in the Admin\Apptools\Poledit directory of your Windows 95 installations CD. The ADMIN.ADM file should be placed in the Windows\Inf subdirectory of your local PC. The POLEDIT.EXE and POLEDIT.INF files should be placed in the Windows directory.

Windows NT: The System Policy Editor is installed by default in Windows NT Server and can be found in the Start, Programs, Admin Tools pull-down menu. The System Policy Editor cannot be installed or run on Windows NT Workstation. ■

There are two distinct options for expanding on the policy options in the ADMIN.ADM template. First, you can try to find a template file, created by third-party programmers, that exactly meets your needs. Second, you can write your own templates. In the first option, you need to load the third-party template on which to base your policy files. To open the template, follow these steps:

1. Open the System Policy Editor and close any open policy files.
2. Choose Options, Template.
3. Choose Open Template and select the ADM file you want to use.
4. Choose Open, and then choose Close to return to the System Policy Editor.

Any policy files you now create will be based on the ADM file you selected. This procedure can be used to specify a particular template when working among several templates.

In the second option, you can create your own template. Template files are text files with the extension ADM, so you can create them with any text editor including Notepad and WordPad. I recommend starting with the default ADMIN.ADM file as the basis for the ADM files you create, simply adding and deleting keyword sequences associated with policies you would like to configure. Starting with the Admin.adm template can also help to increase your familiarity with the format of keywords as described in the next section.

Understanding Template Keywords

As you create custom templates, it is important to work within the basic template syntax, as follows:

```
CLASS     category_type
    CATEGORY    category_name
        [KEYNAME    key_name]
            [definition statements for the policy ...]
    END CATEGORY
    POLICY    policy_name
        [KEYNAME    key_name]
            [definition statements for the policy ...]
    END POLICY
    PART    part_name    part_type
        type dependent data ...
        [KEYNAME    key_name]
        VALUENAME    value_name
    END PART
```

Part III

Ch 16

Optional values are enclosed in brackets.

The four primary keywords are CLASS, CATEGORY, POLICY, and PART. These keywords, as well as the secondary keywords VALUEON, VALUEOFF, KEYNAME, VALUENAME, VALUE, and value types, are described in the following sections.

CLASS

The CLASS keyword defines the Registry key your template will modify. The value must be either USER or MACHINE. The USER setting indicates that your template will edit values in the HKEY_Current_User branch of the Registry. The MACHINE setting indicates that your template will edit values in the HKEY_Current_Machine branch of the Registry. The USER and MACHINE values correspond to the Local User and Local Machine icons in the System Policy Editor.

Example:

> CLASS   user

TIP Comments can be included in your templates. Comments should be preceded by a semicolon:

> CLASS   user ; edit values in the HKEY_Current_User branch of the Registry

---

CATEGORY

The CATEGORY keyword defines a category name in the System Policy Editor. Category statements can appear only once for each category name. Any category name that has spaces in it must be enclosed in quotation marks. String values should be preceded by two exclamation marks (!!).

END CATEGORY

The END CATEGORY keyword indicates the end of a category and all related policies.

Example:

```
CATEGORY  !!AccessControl
    ...
    ; Access control entries go between these headers
    ...
END CATEGORY
```

> **TIP**
>
> Strings are handled in a consistent manner in template design:
>
> | | |
> |---|---|
> | !! | This prefix indicates a string value. For example: !!AccessControl |
> | [strings] | This defines a section of string values. The values are defined by the following syntax:

var_name = string value

For example:

Strvar="String Name" |
> | Comments | Are preceded by a semicolon (;). Once a semicolon is used on a line of text, the remainder of the line will be treated as text. |

PART

The PART keyword defines one or more controls setting the value of a policy. PART names that include spaces must be enclosed in quotation marks. The controls can be PART types like text boxes and check boxes, and type dependent information like check box values, numeric values, and so on.

The PART controls and associated parameters are described here in detail.

CHECKBOX The CHECKBOX PART control indicator displays a check box. The value is nonzero when checked, and its value entry is deleted if unchecked.

The associated CHECKBOX values are described in the following table.

Part

III

Ch

16

CHECKBOX Value	Description
ACTIONLIST	Defines actions or events initiated when the user enters a response. The end of all ACTIONLIST functions is indicated by the END ACTIONLIST keyword.
ACTIONLISTON	Defines parameters that are set when the check box is ON. The ON value is generally synonymous with a checked setting. This can, for example, pass specific settings to a DLL file in the Registry. The end of all ACTIONLISTON actions is indicated by the END ACTIONLISTON keyword.
ACTIONLISTOFF	Defines parameters that are set when the check box is OFF. The OFF value is generally synonymous with an unchecked setting. This can, for example, pass specific settings to a DLL file in the Registry. The end of all ACTIONLISTOFF actions is indicated by the END ACTIONLISTOFF keyword.
DEFCHECKED	Defines the default value of the CHECKBOX PART control to be checked, or true.
VALUEON	Defines a Registry action to be taken when the ON value is selected, taking precedence over the default action of the ON value for CHECKBOX control.
VALUEOFF	Defines a Registry action to be taken when the OFF value is selected, taking precedence over the default action of the OFF value for CHECKBOX control.

COMBOBOX The COMBOBOX PART control indicator displays a combo box in the System Policy Editor. A combo box consists of an edit field and a drop-down menu that lists suggested values.

The associated COMBOBOX values are described in the following table:

COMBOBOX Value	Description
DEFAULT value	Defines the default string that is entered in the combo box when it is initially executed. No default value corresponds to the combo box being initially blank. The *value* parameter indicates the actual string for display.
MAXLEN value	Defines the maximum length of the related field. The *value* parameter must be an integer between 1 and 255.
REQUIRED	Prevents the user from adding a new value and forces the user to choose an option from the drop-down list to enable policy.
SUGGESTIONS	This is where you specify the options available in the drop-down list. Each entry is separated by spaces. Any values with spaces in them must be enclosed with quotation marks. The END SUGGESTIONS keyword defines the end of the list of data. For example:

```
SUGGESTIONS

    blue yellow "dark green" orange

END SUGGESTIONS
```

DROPDOWNLIST   The DROPDOWNLIST PART control indicator creates a drop-down list and defines the entries in the list. The user cannot enter a new value and must select a value from the list.

The associated DROPDOWNLIST values are described in the following table:

DROPDOWNLIST Value	Description
ITEMLIST	Defines the list of items included in the System Policy Editor drop-down list. The format for this keyword follows:

```
NAME    item_name    VALUE    item_value

ACTIONLIST    action_items
```

In the indicated syntax, `item_name` is the name you want to appear in the drop-down list. The `item_value` is the value set in the Registry when the item is selected. The default data type for the `item_value` field is String. Use VALUE NUMERIC rather than VALUE to designate numeric data on the list.

DROPDOWNLIST Value	Description
REQUIRED	Prevents the user from adding a new value and forces the user to choose an option from the drop-down list to enable policy.

EDITTEXT   The EDITTEXT PART control indicator creates a text field for entry of alphanumeric data. Examples of such prompts include logon banners, path values, and so forth.

The associated EDITTEXT values are described in the following table:

EDITTEXT Value	Description
DEFAULT value	Defines the default string that is entered in the combo box when it is initially executed. No default value corresponds to the combo box being initially blank. The value parameter indicates the actual string for display.
MAXLEN value	Defines the maximum length of the related field. The value parameter must be an integer between 1 and 255.
REQUIRED	Prevents the user from adding a new value and forces the user to choose an option from the drop-down list to enable policy.

LISTBOX   The LISTBOX PART control indicator displays a list box with Add and Remove buttons. This PART type can be used to manage multiple values under one Registry key at the same time.

N O T E   LISTBOX is the only PART type that can be used to manage multiple values under a single Registry key. ▪

The associated LISTBOX values are described in the following table:

LISTBOX Value	Description
ADDITIVE	By default, LISTBOX overrides Registry settings. The ADDITIVE modifier prevents LISTBOX from overriding existing Registry settings, but allows it to add to the Registry settings that are not yet specified.
EXPLICITVALUE	Requires the user to specify value name and value data. The associated list box displayed has two fields, one for value name and the other for value data.

continues

Part

III

Ch

16

continued

LISTBOX Value	Description
VALUENAME	Defines a name for the list box. A value name and value data field are created for each entry in the list box.
VALUEPREFIX prefix_name	Defines a prefix that is used in conjunction with a changing value to create the full value name. A suffix is created and automatically increments by one for each change in the value. For example, a prefix_name of "item" would progress as item1, item2, item3, and so on.

CAUTION

You cannot use the EXPLICITVALUE and VALUEPREFIX as modifiers in the same LISTBOX PART control indicator.

NUMERIC   The NUMERIC PART control indicator displays an edit field that accepts numeric data with optional spin control. The spin control increments the value as data is entered.

The associated NUMERIC values are described in the following table:

NUMERIC value	Description
DEFAULT value	Defines the default string that is entered in the combo box when it is initially executed. No default value corresponds to the combo box being initially blank. The value parameter indicates the actual string for display.
MAX value	Allows specification of a data length limit. The default value is 9999.
MIN value	Allows specification of a data length minimum. The default value is 0.
REQUIRED	The user must input a value in order to enable this part.
SPIN value	Allows you to specify the spin increment value. The default is SPIN1, which adds the spin control. SPIN0 removes the spin control.
TXTCONVERT	Causes entry values to the Registry to be written as strings instead of binary.

END PART

The END PART keyword defines the end of a control list.

Example:

```
PART   MPL Length   NUMERIC REQUIRED
       MIN 1 MAX 8 DEFAULT 3
       VALUENAME MinPedLen
END PART
```

POLICY

The POLICY keyword defines the policy within a category. Policy names that include spaces must be enclosed in quotation marks.

END POLICY

The END POLICY keyword denotes the end of a policy and all its components.

Example:

```
POLICY     policy
     PART  Part EDITTEXT
          VALUNAME  User Profiles
     END PART
END POLICY
```

VALUEON

The VALUEON keyword defines the Registry action to be taken when the policy is checked. This takes precedence over the default ON action for a CHECKBOX control.

Example:

```
PART !!TileWallpaper    CHECKBOX  DEFCHECKED
     VALUENAME          "TileWallpaper"
     VALUEON     "1"
     VALUEOFF    "0"
END PART
```

VALUEOFF

The VALUEOFF keyword defines the Registry action to be taken when the policy is not checked. This takes precedence over the default OFF action for a CHECKBOX control.

The example for the preceding VALUEON also serves as an example for VALUEOFF.

KEYNAME

The KEYNAME keyword is used to specify the full path of the Registry key. This is an optional key name to use with a category of policy. You do not need to specify the first part of the path through Hkey_Local_User or Hkey_Local_Machine as these are indicated by the CLASS statement.

Example:

```
KEYNAME     Security\Provider
```

NOTE If there is a KEYNAME value specified, it must be used by all child categories, policies, and parts. Any child categories, policies, or parts that define their own key name are excluded, but this rule extends to its child key words. ▪

VALUENAME

The VALUENAME keyword defines the Registry value entry name and is an optional modifier.

Example:

```
VALUENAME    "Control Speed"   "60"
```

This setting sets the mouse key Control Speed entry in the Registry.

VALUE

The VALUE keyword is an optional field defining the Registry value to apply to the VALUENAME keyword.

Example:

```
VALUENAME    ActiveBorder    VALUE    "174 168 217 32"
```

This sets the ActiveBorder Registry entry to the value "174 168 217 32."

Looking at the Admin.adm Template File

Now that you have an understanding of all the tools, let's walk through a sample excerpt from the Admin.adm template file.

```
CLASS MACHINE
...
CATEGORY !!System
KEYNAME Software\Microsoft\Windows\CurrentVersion\Setup
```

```
POLICY !!EnableUserProfiles
        KEYNAME Network\Logon
        VALUENAME UserProfiles
END POLICY
POLICY !!NetworkSetupPath
        PART !!NetworkSetupPath_Path EDITTEXT REQUIRED
        VALUENAME "SourcePath"
        END PART
END POLICY
```

Let's break this down line by line to reinforce your comprehension of the tools involved. The first line, CLASS MACHINE, indicates the Registry key that can be edited. In this case, the Hkey_Local_Machine branch of the Registry is active for modification. Several lines separate line 1 from line 2 in the Admin.adm file. The second line in this excerpt, CATEGORY !!System, indicates that you will be working with the system category as seen in the System Policy Editor in Figure 16.1.

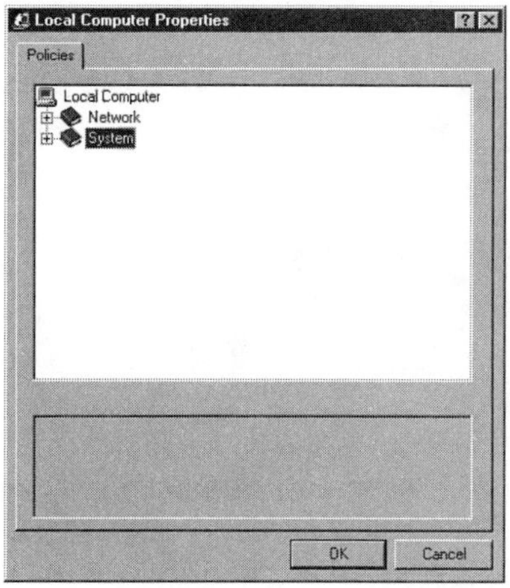

FIG. 16.1

The System Policy Editor view of the policy categories described in the Admin.adm file.

The third line, KEYNAME Software\Microsoft\Windows\CurrentVersion\Setup, indicates the full path of the Registry key you are working with. This key is shown from the Registry Editor in Figure 16.2.

The next four lines describe a policy setting in this subkey:

```
POLICY !!EnableUserProfiles
        KEYNAME Network\Logon
        VALUENAME UserProfiles
        END POLICY
```

The policy name is EnableUserProfiles, the KEYNAME is Network\Logon, and the VALUENAME is UserProfiles. This policy is viewed from the System Policy Editor in Figure 16.3.

FIG. 16.2

The Registry Editor view of the subkey Software\Microsoft\ Windows\ CurrentVersion\ Setup.

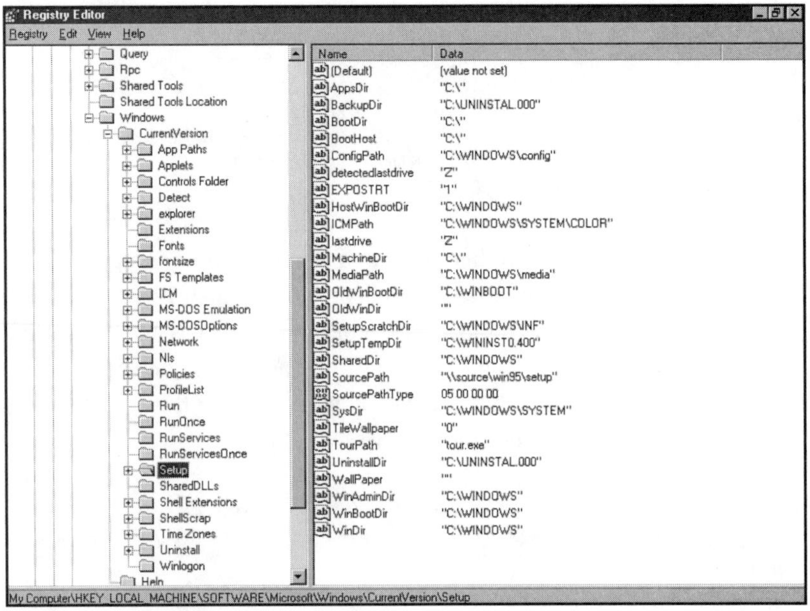

FIG. 16.3

The view of a specific policy configuration from the Admin.adm template as seen in the System Policy Editor.

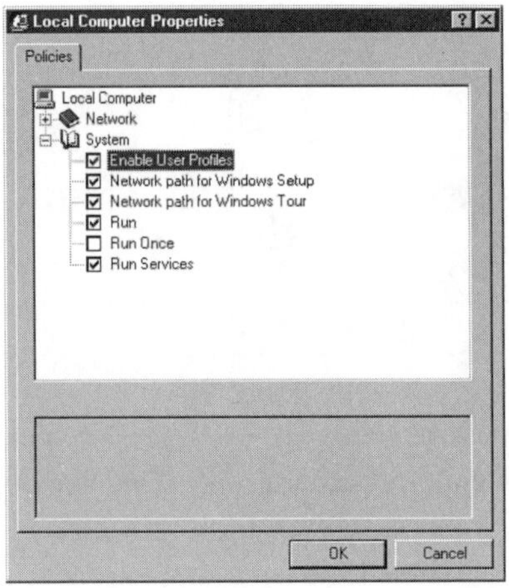

The next five lines go on to create another policy within the same category:

```
POLICY !!NetworkSetupPath
    PART !!NetworkSetupPath_Path EDITTEXT REQUIRED
    VALUENAME "SourcePath"
    END PART
END POLICY
```

The policy name is NetworkSetupPath. The PART statement defines the control used to set this policy value. In this case, the control name is NetworkSetupPath_Path. The EDITTEXT REQUIRED displays an edit field that requires the user to enter data in order to enable this policy. The next line, VALUENAME "SourcePath", defines the Registry value entry name. The next two lines indicate the end of the PART and POLICY procedures, respectively. Figure 16.4 shows the edit field in the policy as seen from the System Policy Editor. Figure 16.5 shows the associated field in the Registry Editor.

Part

III

Ch

16

FIG. 16.4

The policy as viewed from the System Policy Editor.

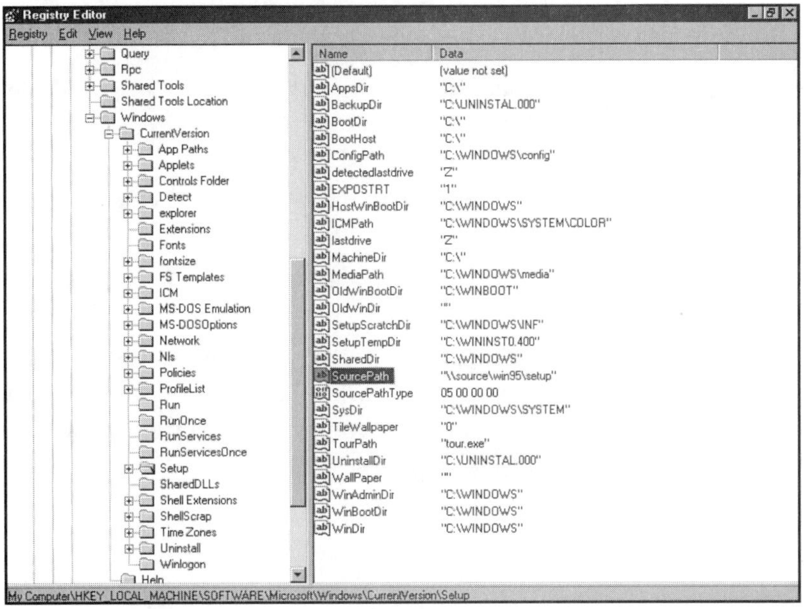

FIG. 16.5

The Registry view of the policy being edited.

This should help build your understanding, as well as your confidence in working with templates. It is a good idea to open the Admin.adm file in a text editor, like WordPad, and familiarize yourself with the syntax of the keywords and associated part values. After reviewing the Admin.adm template file, you should be comfortable manipulating the keyword in the Admin.adm file to create custom templates for your specific needs.

Creating a Template—A Business Example

What if your company is interested in creating templates using policies not included in the Admin.adm template? This is when you will test your understanding of this section. Let's go through a hypothetical example.

TIP It is often helpful to start with the Admin.adm file as the base for your custom template. To customize the Admin.adm template, first copy the file and name it something different. This ensures that you will always be able to go back to the Admin.adm file as a reference. Then you can edit the copy to customize it for your specific needs.

Suppose that the Admin.adm template meets nearly all of your policy needs. In fact, you use the same policy that was based on the Admin.adm template for all the end users. There is one big exception to the effectiveness of the Admin.adm template for your needs. Your company, Blue Print, Inc., has developed a niche in the market. They are known for the fact that all paper correspondence from them has blue colored text. It started out as a bit of a joke, but now it helps differentiate your company in a competitive market.

Your job as the systems administrator is to ensure that all end users in your company use a blue colored font in all their Microsoft Word applications. Your company recently converted to an exclusively Microsoft Desktop Operating System environment. Around 90 percent of the clients use Windows 95 and the remaining 10 percent use Microsoft NT 4.0 Workstation. What can you do?

Let's analyze this situation. A few things are quickly visible. First, some kind of network-wide system policy seems like a good way to ensure that everyone always initiates Word with a blue font. With that in mind, let's dig a little deeper. Because the Admin.adm template meets most of your needs, using it as the foundation for the new template is a good choice. Another issue is that application-based policies are effective only for applications that can read the Registry. Luckily, Microsoft Word 7.0a is the version your company uses on all the client machines, and it can read the Registry.

The next thing you should be aware of is that policies must be created separately for Windows 95 and Windows NT. This is intuitive, considering that the Registries in NT and 95 are not compatible. They do not implement policies in the same way, so you cannot create policies across both platforms with the same code.

So, what should be your plan of action:

1. Create a template called Blue.adm and NtBlue.adm from the Admin.adm and NtAdmin.adm templates. (Just copy and rename it.)

2. Determine the Registry change required to make this change (the blue font).

3. Incorporate this Registry change into a custom policy statement in the Blue.adm template.

4. Apply this policy to all your clients.

You now have the basic skills required to control any settings in both the Hkey_Local_Machine and Hkey_Local_User branches of the Registry. These tools can be used to create a group of system policies that can help you manage your entire local or wide area network as described in Chapter 15, "Using the Policy Editor to Administer the Registry." The full power of Registry customization and the tools to do it are expanded in Part IV of this book, "Programming the Windows Registry." ●

Part
III

Ch
16

P A R T

IV

Programming the Windows Registry

CHAPTER 17

Programming to the Standards

by Rich Kennelly

It takes just a few program calls and your application is quickly integrated with the Windows NT and Windows 95 Registry. After working with the Registry, you discover that it's easier and more manageable than the old INI file architecture.

This chapter introduces you to the Registry entries from a programmer's perspective. You learn which Registry keys an application may need to update. You also learn when to make the necessary changes to the Registry at installation, first execution, or upon exiting your application. The final section provides a Registry checklist to use when designing and developing your application. ■

Windows logo requirements

Explore the technical and marketing benefits of conforming to the "Designed for Windows NT and Windows 95" Logo requirements.

Learn how to change the Registry

Learn where and when your application should change the Registry.

Integrate your application with Windows

Using facilities such as Shell Extensions and OLE, the data produced by your application can become tightly integrated with Windows shell programs and other applications.

Shared components

Components shared across a number of applications are now installed in a single location, and a list of the shared system components is maintained within the Registry.

The "Logo Handbook for Software Applications"

Microsoft offers a "Designed for Windows NT and Windows 95" Logo. The Logo is licensed from Microsoft to help users identify software and hardware that are compatible with Windows NT and Windows 95 and are designed to take advantage of the benefits of these two advanced operating systems. The Logo is available only to applications that are certified by VeriTest, a third-party testing company.

Microsoft has a Web page from which you can download the "Designed for Microsoft Windows NT and Windows 95 Logo Handbook for Software Applications." We strongly recommend that you visit this page and download the handbook.

ON THE WEB

Information on the requirements for the Logo are available on the Internet at:

http://www.microsoft.com/windows/thirdparty/winlogo/default.htm

Besides listing the specific requirements for a Logo, the Logo Handbook also lists the many differences between the Windows NT and Windows 95 operating systems. Updated versions of the Logo Handbook are published on the Microsoft Developer's Network and as part of the Windows NT Workstation Resource Kit—Version 4.0 or higher.

Once licensed to use the "Designed for Windows NT and Windows 95" Logo, your organization can display the logo on product packaging, advertising, and other marketing materials. This can be a valuable tool to differentiate your products in a competitive environment.

Obtaining a Logo for Your Application

As mentioned previously, VeriTest performs the product testing for Logo qualification. To submit your product, you need to follow the steps listed in the aforementioned "Logo Handbook for Software Applications."

ON THE WEB

http://www.veritest.com   The VeriTest Web site.

You can forward any questions concerning the test process to **logolab@veritest.com**.

A summary of the submission steps follows:

1. Obtain a Pretest Kit from Microsoft.

ON THE WEB

The pretest kit is available on the Internet at **http://www.microsoft.com/windows/thirdparty/ winlogo/.htm**.

You can obtain a physical copy by sending an e-mail request to **winlogo@microsoft.com**.

2. Submit your product to VeriTest. You need to include the following:
   - Your software
   - Step-by-step instructions for using your software
   - Vendor questionnaire
   - VeriTest testing agreement
   - Windows NT and Windows 95 Logo License Agreement

3. You should receive test results from VeriTest within eight business days.

4. Once you are certified, VeriTest forwards the license agreement you submitted to Microsoft.

Part
IV

Ch

17

Logo Requirements

This section describes the most important requirements for obtaining the Logo license. Refer to the official Microsoft documents for full details. Much of the information described here was obtained from the "Logo Handbook for Software Applications" mentioned previously.

Operating System Requirements

To obtain the "Microsoft Designed for Windows NT and Windows 95" Logo, your application must run on both Windows 95 and the Windows NT Workstation. Also, your application must run in a Windows NT 4.0 environment—3.51 is not enough. There is no Logo for just NT applications, but you can apply for the "Designed for Windows 95" Logo if your application runs only in Windows 95.

32-Bit Requirements

Applications must be compiled with a 32-bit compiler and use the Win32 programming interface. With a few exceptions, all executable files and DLLs must be 32-bit.

Installation

The product must have a fully automated installation program with a graphical setup interface. Products distributed on CD-ROM must use the AutoPlay feature, which causes the install to run automatically when the CD-ROM is installed. On floppy disk, the install program must provide the ability to launch the install from the File, Run menu, or the Add/Remove Programs in the Control Panel. The product must recognize the version of Windows 95 or Windows NT and install the proper executable.

The following sections describe the required Registry changes that must be made at installation. You can find more details in "Putting Registry Entries in Their Place," later in this chapter.

Common Program Settings   Create Registry entries for your application's common program settings. Common program settings are defined as those values that would be common across all the users of a single application. Perhaps an entry identifying the application's directory would be a good example. Create a Registry key using the following format:

HKEY_LOCAL_MACHINE\SOFTWARE*Company Name**Product Name**Version*

Reference the "Common Program Settings" section later in this chapter for more details.

Register File Extensions   Create a Registry entry for unique data files. For example, if your application creates files with the extension .ADR, then your application must register the "ADR" file extension with Windows. Figure 17.1 illustrates a Registry entry created for the ADR file type. To register unique data files, add Registry entries for each file type using the following format:

HKEY_CLASSES_ROOT\.*<file extension>*

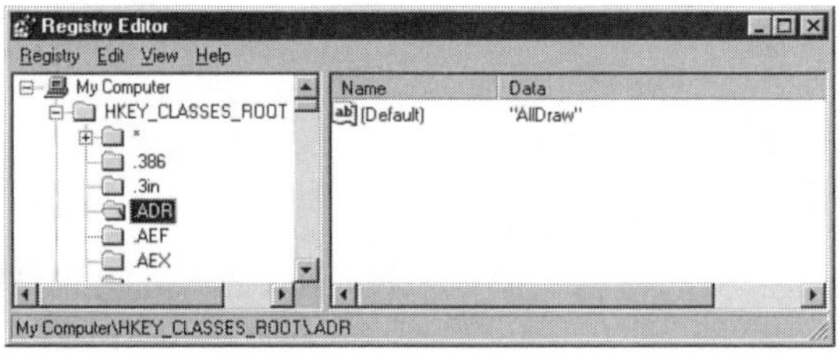

FIG. 17.1
The file extensions
subkey for the "ADR"
file type.

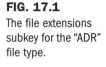

For more information on registering file extensions, see the "Integrating Your Application with Windows" section later in this chapter.

Register File Definitions   Register a file definition subkey for each file system object type created by your application. The File definition subkey defines the commands supported by Windows shell programs and OLE. Add a file definition subkey to the Registry using the following format:

HKEY_CLASSES_ROOT*<Class Definition Name>*

For more information on file definition subkeys, reference the section "Integrating Your Application with Windows" later in this chapter.

Register Shared Components   You need to register the shared components of your application. Shared components are those that are used across multiple applications and are installed to a common location. The most common example of shared components is DLLs. For example, if your application uses CTL3D32.DLL, as do many applications, you must register the file with Windows. These components are registered under the following subkey:

> HKEY_LOCAL_MACHINE\SOFTWARE\Microsoft\Windows\CurrentVersion\
> SharedDLLs

For more information on shared components, refer to the "Installing Shared Components" section later in this chapter.

Uninstall Registration   The uninstall procedure for your application must be properly registered and available from the Add/Remove Programs Icon in the Control Panel. To register your application, changes must be made to the following Registry subkey:

> HKEY_LOCAL_MACHINE\SOFTWARE\Microsoft\Windows\CurrentVersion\
> Uninstall\
> *Your Product Name*

For more information on registering the Uninstall procedure reference, see the "Uninstall Information" section later in this chapter.

Uninstall Procedure

Your application must provide a fully automated uninstall procedure that removes files, folders, and Registry entries. The uninstaller must remove any shortcuts it created and decrement the refcount for any removed shared components. The uninstall application must be accessible through the Add/Remove Programs Icon in the Control Panel.

User Interface

Your application must use system metrics for sizing. System metrics identify the attributes of the current system display, such as monitor resolution, pixels, and more. The system metrics allow an application to create and position properly the application windows, based on the attributes of the system on which it executes.

OLE

Your application must be an OLE 2.0 container or object server. There are some exceptions to this requirement, so consult the Microsoft documentation for details. Mostly, exceptions are limited to utility and other specialized applications.

UNC/LFN Support

The application must support the Universal Naming Conventions, which allow connections to network devices without a specific reference to a drive letter. In addition, products must support Long File Names. Long File Names can be as long as 260 characters.

Putting Registry Entries in Their Place

Although it may not appear so at first, Windows NT and Windows 95 Registry technology can greatly simplify the setup and maintenance of your application. The Registry improves and further standardizes the way each application manages its own data, communicates with system facilities, and supports multiuser environments.

This chapter identifies the Registry keys and values that your application needs to modify. Details of why, when, and how to modify each Registry subkey are provided. Many Registry entries should sound familiar from the previous Logo requirements discussion in this chapter. The final section includes a checklist you can use when designing your application.

Adding Program Settings to the Registry

Every application stores and retrieves its own program settings, such as setup information, user preferences, program data, and so on. These settings are often initialized at installation and modified by the application as it executes.

In Windows NT and Windows 95, program settings are primarily stored in the Registry. Settings that previously might have occupied their own section of an INI file, or their own INI file altogether, are now stored in designated Registry locations.

Windows NT and Windows 95 support a multiuser environment. As such, a single copy of your application may find itself being executed by a number of different users. Each user expects the settings they chose during their last session to be preserved the next time they log on to the system. Luckily, the Registry makes it reasonably easy to support this multiuser architecture. Program settings are separated into two distinct types of data, with two separate storage locations within the Registry:

- Common program settings
- User preferences

When determining where to store program settings, you must first determine if the information is common to all users of an application, or specific to each user.

Common Program Settings Common program settings are common to every user of an application. There is only one copy of common program settings, and they are initialized at program installation or setup time. If any user makes changes to the common program settings, those changes are propagated to every user on that system.

Your application should create a location in the Registry to store common program settings. The information should be stored in a Registry subkey created with the following format:

HKEY_LOCAL_MACHINE\SOFTWARE*company**product**version*

Figure 17.2 illustrates the common program settings that have been stored for the Microsoft Internet Explorer. Notice how the values stored in this location are common types of data (such as the program's caching directory, the default URL page, and so on) that are common among most users.

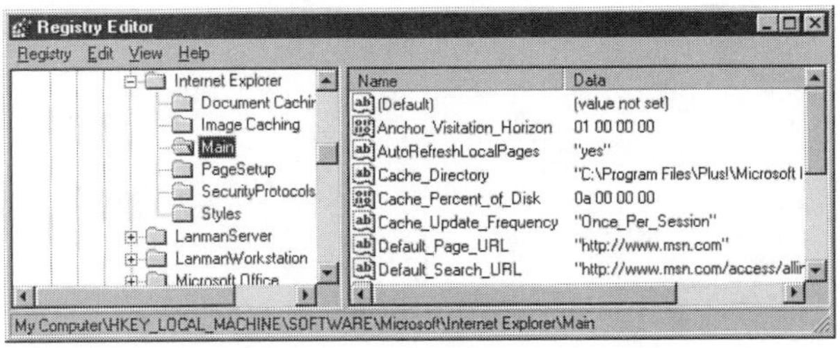

FIG. 17.2
Microsoft Internet Explorer common program settings.

N O T E Many applications use CurrentVersion for the version subkey. Others choose not to create a version subkey at all, providing only the product-level subkey. ▪

User Preferences User preferences are the program settings specific to each user of an application. There is a copy of user-preference data for each user that runs an application. The default values for the user preferences are set the first time an application is run by a new user. If a user makes changes to the user settings, other users are not affected.

Examples of user preferences for a word processor might include the author name, default font, and default spell checker settings. Figure 17.3 illustrates the user preferences for the Microsoft Internet Explorer. Notice how the subkey contains items that are specific to each individual user, such as whether to display the toolbar or status bar.

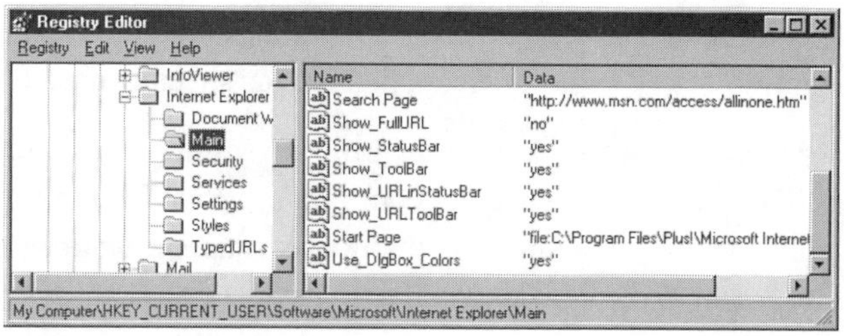

FIG. 17.3

Microsoft Internet Explorer user preferences.

User preferences are stored under the HKEY_CURRENT_USER root key using the same syntax used for the common program settings:

HKEY_CURRENT_USER\SOFTWARE*company**product**version*

The following listing illustrates AllDraw.C, the source code for initializing default values from HKEY_CURRENT_USER:

```
// Check if settings exist for AllDraw
if( RegCreateKeyEx( HKEY_CURRENT_USER,     // Handle of an open key
        "Software\\AllDraw",               // Subkey
        0,                                 // Reserved
        "AllDrawObject",                   // class string (ignored 95)
        REG_OPTION_NON_VOLATILE,           // Always non-volatile in 95
        KEY_ALL_ACCESS,                    // Access rights to the key
        NULL,                              // Gets default attributes
        lpphkYourApp,                      // Returned key
        lpdwDisposition)                   // Disposition - created or opened
        == ERROR_SUCCESS   )
    {
    if( dwDisposition == REG_CREATED_NEW_KEY )
        {
        // No current default - create in HKEY_CURRENT_USER key
        // Set default data for preloading AllDraw file
        RegSetValueEx(phkYourApp,          // Handle of an open key
            "PreLoad",                     // Value Name
            0,                             // Reserved
            REG_BINARY,                    // Binary data
            lpbPreLoadAllDraw,             // Pointer to data
            sizeof(bPreLoadAllDraw));      // Size of data
        }
    else
        {
        // Read default data which already exists for this user
        cbDataSize=1;
        RegQueryValueEx(phkYourApp,        // Handle of an open key
            "PreLoad",                     // Value Name
            0,                             // Reserved
            lpdwValueType,                 // Address of value type
```

```
            lpPreLoadAllDraw,              // Pointer to data
            lpcbDataSize );                // Pointer to size of data
    }
    // Close the key we opened or created
    RegCloseKey( phkYourApp );
    }
```

As noted earlier, the Windows Registry makes it easier to handle the multiuser environment. As illustrated in the preceding source listing, each time an application executes, the HKEY_CURRENT_USER key is set to point to the data of the currently executing User. This greatly simplifies a program's architecture.

If your application finds no user preferences in the existing HKEY_CURRENT_USER\ SOFTWARE subkey, a program can assume the user is running the application for the first time. The application should go ahead and create and initialize the default user values for the new user. If user-preference data already exists, the program can load the existing user preferences and set them accordingly. If you don't completely understand the specifics of the code, refer to Chapter 18, "Programming with the Win32 Registry API," for the details of the different calls.

Integrating Your Application with Windows

Windows NT and Windows 95 provide excellent facilities for integrating your application with Windows and other applications. Using facilities such as Shell Extensions and OLE, the data produced by your application can become tightly integrated with Windows shell programs and other applications.

A simple example is the task of double-clicking a file from within the Windows Explorer program. Using a few simple links you create in the Registry, a user's selecting your application's data file causes your application to be invoked automatically and the selected data file loaded. Other powerful features, such as OLE, allow a user to edit an object that was created by one application from inside another application.

Your application can quickly take advantage of these integration features by making a few subtle changes to the Registry. In some cases, minor changes to your application's command-line interface may be necessary, as well. All required changes focus on two subkeys of the HKEY_CLASSES_ROOT key:

- File Definition subkeys
- File Extension subkeys

Part
IV

Ch
17

File Definition subkeys contain information and commands for supporting features such as shell extensions and OLE. Your application needs to create a File Definition subkey for each file system object you want integrated with Windows, shell programs, or other applications. The name of the File Definition subkey is typically some combination of the program name and version number. For example, a File Definition subkey for a Microsoft Word 6.0 document is Word.Document.6 (see Figure 17.4).

FIG. 17.4

Microsoft Word 6.0
File Definition subkey.

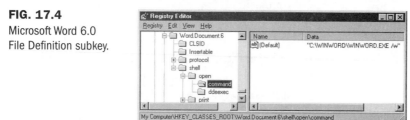

File Definition subkeys contain standard and custom command strings for Windows shell programs and OLE actions. To support these features, your application needs to add these commands during installation.

File Extension subkeys associate file types with a specific application or File Definition subkey. Figure 17.5 shows the File Extension subkey for a .DOC file on a system with Microsoft Word 6.0 installed.

FIG. 17.5

Microsoft Word 6.0
File Extension subkey
for a .DOC file.

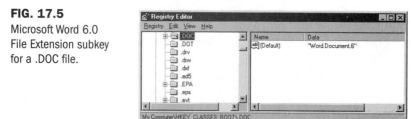

Your application needs to create a File Definition subkey, and in most cases a File Extension subkey, to provide any of the integration features discussed in this section. Creating these subkeys and values requires the use of two standard Win32 API calls: RegCreateKeyEx() and RegSetValue(). Chapter 18, "Programming with the Win32 Registry API," has more information on these calls.

Shell Extensions Shell extensions are features added to Windows shell programs such as the Windows Explorer or File Manager. These features allow your application to tightly integrate its files with Windows shell programs.

File Associations File associations, a type of shell extension, define which application should execute when a user double-clicks a particular data file. It also defines the application that should execute when a user requests that a certain file type be printed. For example, Figures 17.4 and 17.5 illustrate the Registry entries necessary for Microsoft Word 6.0 to provide file associations for the .DOC files. In Figure 17.5, the File Extension subkey creates a mapping of .DOC files to the File Definition subkey Microsoft.Word.6. The File Definition subkey defines the actions to be taken for the file type.

You can quickly provide file associations for your application with two simple steps:

1. Create a File Extension subkey under the HKEY_CLASSES_ROOT root key. Create a subkey titled ".*XYZ*," where *XYZ* is the extension of the data file your application creates. Set the default value string to the name of the associated File Definition subkey.

2. Create a File Definition subkey under the HKEY_CLASSES_ROOT root key. Create the subkey \Shell\Open\Command, setting its value to the command that should execute when a user double-clicks your application's data file from within a Windows shell program. Go ahead and try this using the Registry Editor to create these entries manually.

The same simple approach for creating file extensions can work for printing, as well as for opening a data file. Following the model of the file associations, an application can quickly provide automatic print support from a Windows shell program by creating a\Shell\Print\Command entry. The command then executes when a user wants to print a file directly from a shell program. Of course, your application has to support these commands. Figure 17.6 illustrates the Print command definition for a Microsoft Word 6.0 document.

FIG. 17.6

The Microsoft Word 6.0 Print command.

Context Menus Context menus display when a file system object is clicked with the right mouse button from within a Windows shell program. You can update the File Definition subkey so your application adds menu entries to the context menus of different file types.

Part

IV

Ch

17

For example, let's say you wanted to add the option "Enhance It" to a Word document file. Upon selecting this menu option, a program called ENHANCE.EXE executes, passing it the chosen file system object. Figure 17.7 shows the resulting context menu after a user clicked with the right mouse button while selecting a .DOC file.

FIG. 17.7
Enhance It context-menu command.

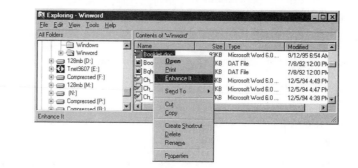

To add a context-menu entry, you must update the File Definition subkey of the desired file type. Figure 17.8 illustrates the changes necessary to the Registry to implement the "Enhance It" command. The entries define the menu-entry name and the command to be executed when the menu entry is selected.

FIG. 17.8
"Enhance It" Registry entries.

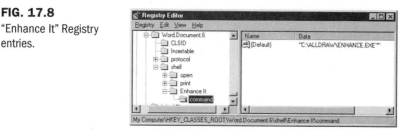

When adding a context-menu entry, there are a few things to keep in mind. Certain commands, known as *canonical verbs*, are automatically localized for a system. Any other command must be localized by the application. The standard canonical verbs are open, print, explore, find, opens, and properties.

Advanced Shell Extensions Windows NT and Windows 95 support features known as *advanced shell extensions*. These extensions combine changes to the Registry with the creation of a shell extension DLL to provide advanced integration with the shell programs. These advanced shell extensions have the power to create instance-specific icons, add pages to property sheets, modify right-click context menus, and more. These types of extensions are beyond the scope of this book, but an excellent article in the Microsoft Development Library entitled "Win32 SDK: Prog Guide to Win95, Extending the Win95 Shell" is a great place to start.

OLE Support   OLE (object linking and embedding) enables applications to share data in a seamless manner. Using OLE, a user can edit data belonging to one application while working inside a second application. Editing a picture from a Word for Windows document is an example of OLE. The Microsoft Draw application allows a Draw object to exist within a Word document and performs a seamless edit of the picture when the user double-clicks it. The user is left unaware that the data was created and modified using an entirely different application.

OLE is a complex subject, with large books dedicated solely to its use. For the purpose of this book, we focus on the integration of OLE with the Registry. OLE support requires the use of commands. These commands instruct Windows shell programs and applications how to communicate with and manage the data of another application.

OLE commands are stored in the application's File Definition subkey. The commands should be created at installation time and removed during the uninstall procedure. Table 17.1 illustrates a few basic OLE commands and the subkeys in which they are stored.

Part
IV
Ch
17

Table 17.1   Registry Subkeys for OLE Commands

Subkey	OLE Command
\protocol\StdFileEditing\server	Command line for opening an application
\protocol\StdFileEditing\handler	File name for handler DLL
\protocol\StdFileEditing\verb	Play or edit verb

Installing Shared Components

Previously, applications have had difficulty keeping control of the versions of software components installed on a system. Often, an application would install a DLL to a system only to have it overwritten by an older version of the component by a subsequent installation. Many times multiple copies of the same DLL would wind up on a system, with only luck controlling which version would be the one that was loaded. This random management of shared components caused many problems for users, including General Protection Faults, system hangs, and more.

To eliminate this ugly problem, Microsoft has introduced the concept of "shared components" with Windows NT and Windows 95. These components, shared across a number of applications, are installed in a single location. A list of the shared system components is maintained within the Registry. Included in the list is a reference number—often referred to as refcount—which identifies the number of applications on the system using the shared DLL. The shared components are listed under the HKEY_LOCAL_MACHINE\ SOFTWARE\Microsoft\Current Version\SharedDLLs subkey.

Figure 17.9 shows an example of a Windows 95 Registry's SharedDLLs subkey. Notice how the common component ctl3d32.dll has a reference count of 5, indicating five applications on the system are using the shared component. If one of those applications should uninstall itself, the reference count should be decremented by one. If the reference count is set to 0, the file should be removed by the uninstall procedure.

FIG. 17.9

SharedDLL Registry entries.

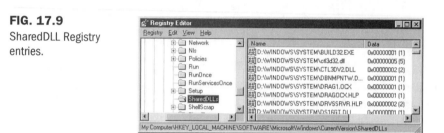

During installation, your application is responsible for properly installing shared components. To do so, an application should first check whether any of the required shared components are already installed on the system. If so, the installation should verify that the shared component is the required minimum version. If the component is acceptable, the installation should update the reference count for the component, indicating that it too will be using the shared component.

If the required shared component does not exist on the system, the installation should copy the file into a shared location. Using Registry API described in the next chapter, the Registry SharedDLLs list should be updated to include the component and the reference count should be set to 1.

Much like the install procedure must update the shared component information, your uninstall procedure must manage the shared component information affected by removing the application. When uninstalling, the reference count of any shared components that are being removed should be decremented by one. If the value of the reference count goes to zero, the file should be deleted. If all applications follow this procedure, shared components will exist on a system only as long as applications that use them are installed.

Uninstall Information

It is a Microsoft Logo requirement that each application provide an uninstall procedure. The uninstall procedure should remove all program files, Registry entries, link files, and other data that were created during the program installation or execution.

Users request that an application should be removed by selecting the Add/Remove Programs Icon from the Control Panel. The user is presented with a list of applications available for uninstall. Upon selection, the uninstall procedure for the selected application executes, removing all traces of the application from the system.

To make an uninstall procedure for an application available to users, the Registry must be updated with the name and location of the uninstall procedure. Luckily, the Registry updates are straightforward. Figure 17.10 illustrates the required subkeys and values for a sample program, AllDraw.

FIG. 17.10

AllDraw uninstall
Registry entries.

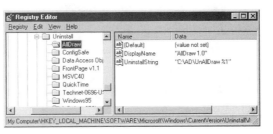

Part

IV

Ch

17

The uninstall procedure is available to all users because it is defined under the HKEY_LOCAL_MACHINE key. The uninstall information should be added to the Registry at installation. Designing the uninstall procedure itself is left as a task for the application developer and is beyond the scope of this book.

Summary: Required Steps for Registry Integration

Now that you know where all the information in the Registry is stored, and which information you need to provide or update in the Registry, you are ready to integrate your application with the Windows NT and Windows 95 Registry. To help you, this last section provides a list of steps for Registry integration. Make sure that you have addressed each of these items, even if you decide not to implement the feature immediately.

At Installation   Use the standard Windows NT and Windows 95 installation procedures to copy the required files to the system. Then perform the following steps from within your installation procedure:

1. Register shared DLL components.

   Create or modify shared DLL entries under the HKEY_LOCAL_MACHINE\SOFTWARE\Microsoft\Current Version\SharedDLLs subkey. For files that are already registered, update the reference count value.

2. Create a common program settings entry.

Create or update the Registry entries for common program settings under the HKEY_LOCAL_MACHINE\SOFTWARE\ *Your Company\Your App* subkey.

3. Create File Extension subkeys.

   Create or modify Registry entries for file extensions under the HKEY_CLASSES_ROOT subkey. Create a File Extension subkey for each supported file type.

4. Create File Definition subkeys.

   Create or modify the File Definition subkeys under the HKEY_CLASSES_ROOT root key. Add the necessary entries for file associations, context menus, OLE support, and the other Windows integration features.

5. Register the uninstall procedure.

   Register your application's uninstall procedure by adding the required Registry entries under the key HKEY_LOCAL_MACHINE\SOFTWARE\Microsoft\Windows\Current Version\Uninstall

Set User Preferences upon First Execution   Supporting the multiuser environments of Windows NT and Windows 95 requires that user preferences be set the first time an application executes. If the currently executing user is running the application for the first time, set the default values under the HKEY_CURRENT_USER\Software subkey. If the user has run the program before, load the default values from the HKEY_CURRENT_USER\Software subkey. ●

CHAPTER 18

Programming with the Win32 Registry API

by Rich Kennelly

This chapter provides the programming details necessary to integrate your application with the Registry. Look for hints on how to change the Registry, add keys and values, scan subtrees, and more. Along the way you learn how to avoid common Registry programming pitfalls and be warned about the differences between Windows NT and Windows 95. ■

Win32 interface

Learn how the Microsoft Win32 API provides a standard interface to the Registry across the family of Microsoft Windows 32-bit operating systems. Discover backward compatibility to Windows 3.1x systems with the Win32s interface.

Registry structure

Familiarize yourself with the file structures and differences between the Windows NT and Windows 95 Registries.

Using the Win32 Registry API

Get specifics on using the Win32 Registry APIs to manipulate the Registry.

Win32 Interface

Access to the Registry is provided through the Microsoft Win32 API (Application Programming Interface). Design your code to the Win32 interface to make it more "portable" across the Microsoft Windows family of 32-bit operating systems.

The 32-Bit Standard

Windows NT and Windows 95 include Win32 API support. Most compilers automatically include and recognize the Win32 API set when you build a 32-bit application.

The Win32 API provides approximately 25 Registry-related API calls. These functions, listed in Table 18.1, provide all the functions you'll need to read, write, delete, add, or open Registry keys and values. Utility functions enable you to back up the Registry, connect and view remote Registries, and more. Although Win32 is supported in both Windows NT and Windows 95 environments, there are differences that you need to consider when writing your program.

Table 18.1   Win32 Registry Functions

Function	NT	95	Win32s
RegCloseKey	Y	Y	Y
RegConnectRegistry	Y	Y	N
RegCreateKey	Y	Y	Y
RegCreateKeyEx	Y	Y	Y
RegDeleteKey	Y	Y	Y
RegDeleteValue	Y	Y	N
RegEnumKey	Y	Y	Y
RegEnumKeyEx	Y	Y	N
RegEnumValue	Y	Y	Y
RegFlushKey	Y	Y	N
RegGetKeySecurity	Y	N	N
RegLoadKey	Y	Y	N
RegNotifyChangeKeyValue	Y	N	N
RegOpenKey	Y	Y	Y
RegOpenKeyEx	Y	Y	Y

Function	NT	95	Win32s
RegQueryInfoKey	Y	Y	N
RegQueryValue	Y	Y	Y
RegQueryValueEx	Y	Y	Y
RegReplaceKey	Y	Y	N
RegRestoreKey	Y	N	N
RegSaveKey	Y	Y	N
RegSetKeySecurity	Y	N	N
RegSetValue	Y	Y	Y
RegSetValueEx	Y	Y	Y
RegUnLoadKey	Y	Y	Y

Win32s

Now you know about these great 32-bit calls you can make to manage the Registry and other Windows resources. But, you're wondering, "How can I maintain a single, or at least similar, source base for my Windows 3.1x and Windows for Workgroups customers?" The answer is Microsoft Win32s. Win32s is a subset of the Microsoft Win32 API designed to run on Windows 3.1x systems.

Design your application to use only calls supported by Win32s, and your Windows NT or Windows 95 application can run native in a Windows 3.1x environment. As a matter of fact, applications enjoy a number of added benefits when using Win32s in a Windows 3.1x environment:

- Performance benefits of 32-bit operation on the Windows 3.1x Operating System
- Similar source base for your Windows NT, Windows 95, and Windows 3.1x versions of software
- Full support for 16- and 32-bit OLE

The "s" in Win32s refers to *subset*. One downside to this solution is that not all of the Win32 APIs are available in a Win32s environment. An application must be constructed carefully to use only those features supported in every environment. Table 18.1 illustrates the environments that support each Registry function.

The Windows 3.1x operating systems do not include the Win32s components. Each application requiring Win32s must install the components if they are not already on a system. Microsoft was nice enough to provide the necessary setup program and binary files for Win32s in the SDK. The required files are provided in the following list. For more details of the Win32s installation, consult the "Win32s Programmer's Reference" (Win32.HLP), which is included with the Win32 SDK.

Win32s Required Files

advapi32.dll	netapi32.dll	w32skrnl.dll
comdlg32.dll	ntdll.dll	w32sys.dll
crtdll.dll	olecli.dll	win32s.exe
c_1252.nls	olecli32.dll	w32s16.dll
c_437.nls	olesvr32.dll	winmm.dll
c_850.nls	sck16thk.dll	winmm16.dll
gdi32.dll	shell32.dll	winspool.drv
kernel32.dll	unicode.nls	user32.dll
lz32.dll	version.dll	
mpr.dll	w32s.386	

Understanding the Registry

The Registry is a hierarchical structure made up of keys and values. Each key in the Registry structure can contain values and may also contain subkeys. In this way, keys are analogous to directories and values are analogous to files. Values can be used to store information of various types such as strings or binary data.

To view or change the Registry, use the Registry Editor tool provided with Windows 95 and Windows NT. Figure 18.1 illustrates how the Registry Editor displays the keys and values contained in the Registry.

FIG. 18.1
REGEDIT displays
Registry keys and
values.

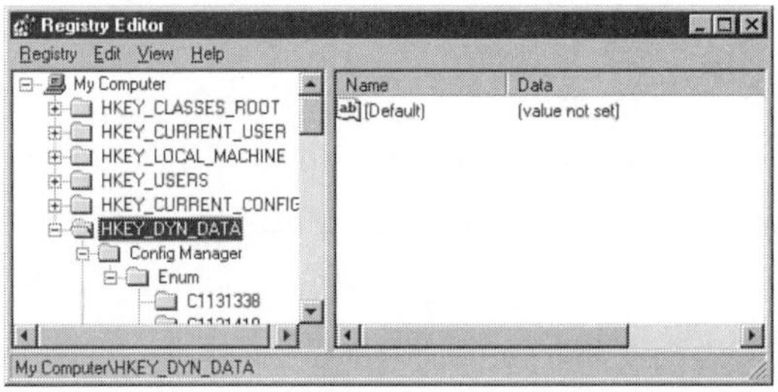

Registry File Structure

Behind the scenes, the values and keys that make up the Registry are maintained in an in-memory database. The initial Registry database is partially built from files stored on the system. Other parts of the Registry are built dynamically. For example, Windows 95 builds the information in the key HKEY_DYN_DATA\Config Manager each time the system boots. The specific files and build procedures for the Registry are different, depending on whether the system is running Windows NT or Windows 95.

For the most part, you won't be affected by the physical differences in the Windows NT and Windows 95 Registry files. If you venture into backing up and restoring portions of the Registry from within your application, however, you'll want to pay particular attention to these details.

Windows 95 Registry Files   The Windows 95 Registry is contained in two files called USER.DAT and SYSTEM.DAT. SYSTEM.DAT contains the standard system information that is common across all users and contained in the HKEY_LOCAL_MACHINE root key. USER.DAT contains user-specific information, such as User Policy information, desktop settings, and more.

Backup copies of the Registry files are stored in SYSTEM.DA0 and USER.DA0 files. Each time the system successfully boots, Windows stores copies of the Registry into these files. These can be used to Restore the Registry if it becomes corrupt.

Windows NT Registry Files   Windows NT uses a different and somewhat more complex scheme to store Registry information. The Windows NT Registry is stored as a group of *hives*. A single hive contains all of the information for each key at the top of the Registry hierarchy. By default, the hives that make up HKEY_LOCAL_MACHINE, illustrated in Figure 18.2, are stored in the SYSTEM32\CONFIG subdirectory of the Windows directory. The keys and their associated hive files are listed in Table 18.2.

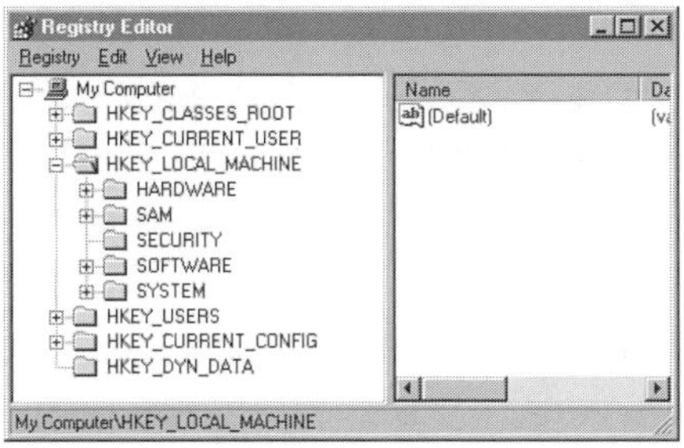

Part
IV

Ch
18

FIG. 18.2
NT Registry Root
Keys.

Table 18.2 HKEY_LOCAL_MACHINE Registry Hives

HKEY_LOCAL_MACHINE Key	Hive File	Log File
\SAM	SAM	SAM.LOG
\SECURITY	SECURITY	SECURITY.LOG
\SOFTWARE	SOFTWARE	SOFTWARE.LOG
\SYSTEM	SYSTEM	SYSTEM.LOG
		SYSTEM.ALT

A hive is stored as two files: a hive file, which has the same name as the hive that it contains; and a log file, which is a record of updates to the hive. The log file is used in case an update to the hive file is interrupted by a system crash. In this instance, the system uses the log file to recreate the changes to the hive that had not yet been stored in the hive file.

The system hive has an additional safety mechanism that ensures its integrity in case of a system crash during a flush. The system hive is stored in two separate files—SYSTEM and SYSTEM.ALT—that ensure one file remains uncorrupted in case of an interrupted flush. The system will use the uncorrupted file as the source of the system hive. The associated log file SYSTEM.LOG is also maintained.

User profile hives, which make up HKEY_USERS, are stored in user-specific subdirectories of the Windows PROFILES directory. Each hive is stored in the file NTUSER. DAT, in a unique subdirectory, with an associated log file of NTUSER.DAT.LOG. There is one exception: the hive that contains the default user profile is stored with the system hives in the SYSTEM32\CONFIG directory, using the names DEFAULT and DEFAULT.LOG.

Registry Data

Periodically, both Windows NT and Windows 95 flush the in-memory Registry database to the associated Registry files. At regular time intervals, or before exiting Windows, the Registry is written to disk. Applications can request the Registry be flushed by calling `RegFlushKey()`.

The in-memory Registry database contains two possible types of data—volatile and non-volatile. *Volatile keys* are keys that are not written from the in-memory Registry to the associated Registry files during a flush. The information is lost when the user shuts down and restarts Windows. *Non-volatile* information is always written to the proper Registry file during a flush. Windows 95 supports only the creation of non-volatile entries.

Windows NT allows you to create volatile keys and Registry subtrees. Volatile keys can be used to store temporary data, as they will disappear the next time Windows is invoked.

Using the Win32 Registry Calls

When you develop your application, use the Microsoft Win32 Registry calls to integrate with the Registry. There are six major types of Registry functions, as listed in Table 18.3. Typically, every application will require the Key Management and Value Management Registry functions. These two groups perform the most basic level of Registry services such as adding, deleting, or changing Registry keys and values. Each function call is described in detail in Appendix A.

Table 18.3   Registry Calls

Group	Definition
Key Management	The basic key functions for creating, deleting, opening, and closing Registry keys. Used by all applications, these functions are the backbone for the most basic Registry integration.
Value Management	The basic functions for managing Registry values. These functions are used for setting, deleting, and reading the values associated with a Registry key.
Enumeration	Return details of each Registry key, including values and descendants. These functions are used to traverse and analyze the Registry hierarchy, including Registry keys and their descendants.
Backup/Restore	Advanced functions that back up and restore portions of the Registry. These functions allow applications to write portions of the Registry to a file, and if necessary, restore those entries at a later time.
Utility	A set of calls that perform functions such as forcing a write of the in-memory Registry to disk, notifying an application when a certain Registry class changes, and connecting to a remote Registry.
Security	Security functions, available only on NT, which manage the security values associated with an NT Registry key.

Part
IV

Ch
18

Choosing Your Functions

As do many things in life, the Win32 API has evolved with time. Therefore, a number of functions actually have duplicates. For example, the functions RegSetValue() and

`RegSetValueEx()` both set a Registry key value. The difference is, the `RegSetValueEx()` function creates any number of values or types for a Registry key. The `RegSetValue()` function can set only the default value of a Registry key, supporting only strings as the data type. The `RegSetValueEx()` function provides greater features.

The Win32 API includes a number of functions that provide more extensive services than a previous function. These are typically named the same as the function they replace, with a post-fix of "Ex". When coding your application, use the advanced functions whenever possible. The original functions are included for backward compatibility.

Get a Handle on It

Like many things in Windows, Registry keys are accessed via a handle. When you open or create a Registry key, you are returned a handle to that key. Subsequent calls to analyze the key or create values require that you pass a key handle to the function.

Windows provides predefined reserved handles for the root level keys. When accessing a root level key, pass the common handle, as shown in the following list. There is no need to open or close the root keys—they are always open, accessible using the default key handle.

Reserved Root Key Handles

HKEY_CLASSES_ROOT

HKEY_CURRENT_USER

HKEY_LOCAL_MACHINE

HKEY_USERS

Key Management

The most basic Registry integration requires the use of key management functions. Opening, creating, or closing Registry keys are the fundamental calls for manipulating Registry data.

To access a Registry key, you first must call the `RegOpenKeyEx()` or `RegCreateKeyEx()` function. Both functions will open an existing Registry key, but `RegCreateKeyEx()` will create the key if it did not already exist. Both calls require a handle to an existing key and the name of the desired subkey. Listing 18.1 provides an example of how to call `RegCreateKeyEx()`.

Listing 18.1 Example: RegCreateKeyEx() Function

```
RegCreateKeyEx( HKEY_CURRENT_USER,     // Handle of an open key
    "Software\\AllDraw",               // Subkey
    0,                                 // Reserved
    "AllDrawObject",                   // class string (ignored 95)
    REG_OPTION_NON_VOLATILE,           // Always non-volatile in 95
    KEY_ALL_ACCESS,                    // Full access rights
    NULL,                              // Default security attributes
    lpphkey,                           // Returned Handle
    lpdwDisposition)                   // Disposition - created or opened
```

Initially, your open or create request will pass the handle of one of the root keys, as listed in Table 18.4, and the name of the subkey to open. The subkey name should use the format SUBKEY1\SUBKEY2\SUBKEY3, noting that there is no initial backslash on the subkey name. After the key has been opened successfully, a handle to the key is returned to the application.

Table 18.4 Registry Key Management Functions

Function	Definition
RegCloseKey()	Closes the specified Registry key, freeing the handle.
RegCreateKey()	Opens the specified key or subkey. If the key does not exist, RegCreateKey() will attempt to create it. This function is provided for backward compatibility only—all Win32 applications should use RegCreateKeyEx().
RegCreateKeyEx()	Opens the specified key or subkey. If the key does not exist, RegCreateKeyEx() will attempt to create it. The return value indicates whether the key was opened or created. A handle is returned for further access and closing the key.
RegDeleteKey()	Deletes the specified Registry key from the Registry. You cannot delete a root key.
RegOpenKey()	Opens the specified key or subkey. This function is provided for backward compatibility only—all Win32 applications should use RegOpenKeyEx().
RegOpenKeyEx()	Opens the specified key or subkey. A handle is returned for further access. Each key that is opened should be closed using the RegCloseKey() function.

Part
IV
Ch
18

When creating or opening a Registry key, an application specifies the desired access rights known as SAM (Security Access Mask). These rights control the type of access the application will have to the key. By default, your application should use the KEY_ALL_ACCESS rights. The different access rights are listed in Table 18.5.

Table 18.5   Access Rights

Name	Description
KEY_ALL_ACCESS	Combines the permissions of KEY_CREATE_LINK, KEY_CREATE_SUB_KEY, KEY_ENUMERATE_SUBKEYS, KEY_NOTIFY, KEY_QUERY_VALUE, and KEY_SET_VALUE.
KEY_CREATE_LINK	Right to create a symbolic link.
KEY_CREATE_SUB_KEY	Right to create a subkey.
KEY_ENUMERATE_SUB_KEYS	Right to scan (emumerate) subkeys.
KEY_EXECUTE	Right to read the key.
KEY_NOTIFY	Right to obtain notification upon changes to the key.
KEY_QUERY_VALUE	Right to query the values of the key.
KEY_READ	Combines rights of KEY_QUEREY_VALUE, KEY_ENUMERATE_SUB_KEYS, and KEY_NOTIFY.
KEY_SET_VALUE	Right to set value data.
KEY_WRITE	Combines the permissions of KEY_SET_VALUE and KEY_CREATE_SUB_KEY.

Keys created using the RegCreateKeyEx() function are by default non-volatile in a Windows 95 environment. Despite including a parameter for the volatility settings, Windows 95 ignores the parameter, setting all data to non-volatile. Non-volatile Registry information is written to disk during a Registry flush, while volatile data is not.

After the application is done using a Registry key, the key must be closed. RegCloseKey() closes the key, freeing the handle for re-use by the system. After a key is closed, the handle becomes invalid, so don't try to use it again.

The code in Listing 18.2 demonstrates how an application would open or create a key, perform the processing it requires, and then close the key. Pay particular attention to the dwDisposition value, which indicates if the key already existed and was opened, or was created by the application.

Listing 18.2   ALLDRAW.C—Example: Creating and Closing Registry Keys

```
if( RegCreateKeyEx( HKEY_CURRENT_USER,    // Handle of an open key
    "Software\\AllDraw",         // Subkey
    0,                           // Reserved
    "AllDrawObject",             // class string (ignored 95)
```

```
REG_OPTION_NON_VOLATILE,  // Always non-volatile in 95
KEY_ALL_ACCESS,           // Access rights to the key
NULL,                     // Gets default attributes
lpphkYourApp,             // Returned key
lpdwDisposition)          // Disposition - created or opened
== ERROR_SUCCESS     )
{
if( dwDisposition == REG_CREATED_NEW_KEY )
   {
...// New key created - do processing
   }
else
   {
...// Existing key opened
   }
// Close the key we opened or created
RegCloseKey( phkYourApp );
}
```

After a key is created, most applications want to read or set values in the key or look at its subkeys. Performing these tasks is quite easy and is discussed in the "Value Management" and "Enumerating Registry Keys and Values" sections later in this chapter.

`RegDeleteKey()` removes a key and its values from the Registry. Perhaps your application wants to uninstall itself, or has found outdated information from a previous version of software in the Registry that it needs to remove. `RegDeleteKey()` takes only two parameters—the handle of the parent key, and the name of the key itself.

If only it were so easy. Thanks to differences between Windows 95 and Windows NT, your application will need to be intelligent when deleting a key and its descendants.

> **CAUTION**
>
> `RegDeleteKey()` will fail in a Windows NT environment if the specified key has any subkeys. You must delete the subkeys first before deleting the key.

Windows NT requires that all subkeys be deleted before the actual key can be removed. This requires your code to traverse the descendants of a Registry tree to the bottom, deleting each subkey individually, working its way back up the list. On the other hand, Windows 95 will delete a key and all its subkeys.

There are a few things to keep in mind when using the Key Management functions:

- Registry keys may not be created at the root level. Only the predefined keys exist at the root and top level of the Registry.
- Windows 95 has demonstrated difficulties if an application fails to close a Registry key before a user shuts down the system.

■ Volatile data, supported only in an NT environment, is an excellent way to create temporary data for your application. After the system shuts down, the data is erased automatically.

Value Management

Every Registry key can have values associated with it. Comprised of many types of data, the values retain important pieces of information, while the keys help organize the information into specific areas.

Value Types   Windows NT and Windows 95 support a number of value types. These values, managed with the Value Management Functions, enable applications to store data in a number of formats. From strings to DWORDs, applications select where the data needs to go and how it should be stored. If an application has more than 2K of data for a single value, it is suggested that the information be stored outside the Registry, using a Registry value to point to the data file.

Table 18.6 lists the value types for Win32.

Table 18.6   Value Types

Value	Description
REG_BINARY	Binary data.
REG_DWORD	Double word equalling 32-bits.
REG_DWORD_LITTLE_ENDIAN	32-bit number in little-endian format. The most significant byte of a word is the high-order word.
REG_DWORD_BIG_ENDIAN	A 32-bit number in big-endian format. The most significant byte of a word is the low-order word.
REG_EXPAND_SZ	A null-terminated string. Contains references to environment variables such as "%TEMP%".
REG_LINK	A Unicode symbolic link.
REG_MULTI_SZ	Defines an array that contains Null terminated strings. The array is terminated by two successful Null terminating characters.
REG_NONE	No defined value type.
REG_RESOURCE_LIST	A device-driver resource list.
REG_SZ	A Null-terminated string. The most common format for storing strings.

When creating a value with `RegSetValueEx()`, the application provides the type of data and a pointer to that data. The most common data types are REG_BINARY, REG_DWORD, and REG_SZ. Using just these three types, your application can store any type of binary data, such as structures, 32-bit values, and strings.

N O T E The Windows 3.1x Registry supported only a single value type, the default, which was the REG_SZ value type. ■

Value Management Functions Value Management functions, as listed in Table 18.7, enable you to add, change, or delete the values associated with a Registry key. Most applications will either read or write values into the Registry. All functions require a handle to the desired Registry key, which can be obtained from a call to the `RegOpenEx()` or `RegCreateKeyEx()` functions discussed in the "Key Management" section.

Table 18.7 Registry Value Management Functions

Function	Definition
RegDeleteValue()	Deletes the value from the specified Registry key.
RegQueryValue()	Returns the data for the first value stored in a Registry key, commonly known as the *default data*. This function is provided for backward compatibility with Win32s. Applications that require access to more than just the default key value should use the `ReqQueryValueEx()` function.
RegQueryValueEx()	Returns the data and data type for the indicated Registry value.
RegSetValue()	Sets the value for the default data associated with a Registry key. Newer applications, or those wanting to set values other than the default value, should use the `RegSetValueEx()` function.
RegSetValueEx()	Sets the data and data type for the specified Registry key value. If the value does not exist, it will be created.

Reading values from the Registry is performed using the `RegQueryValueEx()` function. This function takes the handle of the desired key and the value name and returns the value data, data size, and data type. To access the key and read value information, the key must be opened with KEY_QUERY_VALUE access rights, which are contained in the KEY_ALL_ACCESS rights. Listing 18.3 illustrates the proper syntax for calling the `ReqQueryValueEx()` function.

Listing 18.3 Example: *RegQueryValueEx() Function*

```
RegQueryValueEx( hKey,           // Handle of an open key
        lpszValueName,           // Pointer to the value name
        lpdwReserved,            // Reserved - not used
        lpdwType,                // Returns value type
        lpbData,                 // Returns data in this buffer
        lpcbDataSize);           // Returns size of value data in bytes
```

It is true that the `ReqQueryValueEx()` function requires that the application already know the names of the values it is looking for. Many applications will be reading and setting values they already know exist. But, if your application is looking to analyze a key whose value names it does not know, it should use the `RegEnumValueEx()` function described in the "Enumerating Registry Keys and Values" section. The `RegEnumValueEx()` returns a new value for a subkey each time it is called, until there are no more unique values to return.

Writing and creating values is performed with the `RegSetValueEx()` function, as illustrated in Listing 18.4. This function takes a handle to the key as input, along with a value name, data, data size, and data type parameter. Your application calls this function when it wants to set or change the data in a value. A key must be opened with KEY_SET_VALUE rights for the application to get access.

Listing 18.4 Example: *RegSetValueEx() Function*

```
RegSetValueEx( hKey,             // Handle of an open key
        lpszValueName,           // Pointer to the value name
        lpdwReserved,            // Reserved - not used
        dwType,                  // Value type
        lpbData,                 // Data buffer
        cbDataSize);             // Data size
```

TIP If the data type is REG_SZ, REG_EXPAND_SZ, or REG_MULTI_SZ, the data length field must include a byte for the terminating character of the string.

Values are removed from a Registry key using the `RegDeleteValue()` function. The key must have been opened using the KEY_SET_VALUE access rights to succeed.

Enumerating Registry Keys and Values

For your application to analyze the Registry, it will most likely need to scan the Registry keys and values. To do this, the Win32 API includes a group of Registry functions commonly known as *enumeration functions*. These functions, listed in Table 18.8, enable an application to analyze the values or subkeys of a key. Specifically, these functions allow an application to:

- Retrieve Registry key details, including the maximum value and subkey sizes.
- Retrieve a list of the subkeys of a Registry key.
- Retrieve a list of the values of a Registry key.

Table 18.8 Registry Enumeration Functions

Function	Description
RegQueryInfoKey()	Returns information about the Registry key. Information includes the class name, number of subkeys, longest subkey name, number of values, longest value name, longest value data, security descriptor length, and the time of the last write.
RegEnumKey()	Returns detailed information about the subkeys of a Registry key. Applications should use RegQueryKeyEx() unless they require compatibility with Win32s.
RegEnumKeyEx()	Returns detailed information about the subkeys of a Registry key. RegEnumKey() also provides information about Registry keys.
RegEnumValue()	Each call to RegEnumValue() returns information about another value of a key. This is an excellent call for retrieving all the values of a key and the associated data and data types.

Part

IV

Ch

18

For example, say that you were writing a utility to track or analyze the values of each key in the Registry. Your application would need to perform a number of steps:

1. Open the Registry key to be tracked.
2. Read and analyze the key's values.
3. Perform steps 1 and 2 recursively for each descendant key, until the values of all subkeys have been analyzed.

Listing 18.5 lists pseudocode for traversing a Registry hive. The example illustrates how the enumeration functions can be used to scan the entire Registry hierarchy. Initially, the re-entrant code opens the primary Registry key using a call to the RegOpenEx() function.

After a key is open, the application uses the RegQueryInfoKey() to learn if the key has any subkeys or values. Valuable information, such as the longest subkey name and longest value string, is returned. This information allows an application to allocate buffers large enough to handle the maximum sizes.

The application then loops, making calls to RegEnumValue(). Each time the call is placed another value, its length and type are returned. After the function returns

ERROR_NO_MORE_ITEMS, all values have been retrieved. The application can then analyze each value, or store the values for later use.

Listing 18.5   Traversing a Registry Hive

```
ScanKeys(HKEY hKeyRoot, LPCTSTR KeyName)
    {
    .
    .
    .

    // Open the key
    retCode = RegOpenKey(hKeyRoot, KeyName, &hkey);

    // Gather information about subkeys and values
    retCode = RegQueryInfoKey (
        hkey,                // handle of key to query
        lpszClass,           // address of buffer for class string
        &cchClass,           // address of size of class string buffer
        &dwReserved,         // reserved
        &cSubKeys,           // address of buffer for number of subkeys
        &cchMaxSubkey,       // address of buffer for longest subkey name
        length               //
        &cchMaxClass,        // address of buffer for longest class string
        length               //
        &cchValues,          // address of buffer for number of value entries
        &cchMaxValueName,    // address of buffer for longest value name length
        &cchMaxValueData,    // address of buffer for longest value data length
        &cbSecurityDescriptor, //buffer address for security descriptor length
        &ftLastWriteTime     // address of buffer for last write time     )

    // Analyze the Key Values
    if (cchValues > 0)
        {
        while ((rtncode = RegEnumValue(hkey, iValue, valuename, &valueSize,
            &dwReserved, &datatype, pdata_buffer, &datasize))
            != ERROR_NO_MORE_ITEMS)
            {
            }
        }

    // Analyze subkeys
    if (cSubKeys > 0)
        {
        // Recursively process each subkey
        while ((rtncode = RegEnumKeyEx(hkey, iSubkey, subkeyname,
            &cchMaxSubkey,&dwReserved, classname, &cchMaxClass,
            &ftLastWriteTime))    != ERROR_NO_MORE_ITEMS)
            {
            // Recursively analyze each subkey
            ScanKeys(hkey, lpszNextKey);
            }
        }
    }
```

With each value accounted for, the application then descends the Registry tree, analyzing each subkey. The list of subkeys is obtained using the `RegEnumKeyEx()` function. Each call to the `RegEnumKeyEx()` function returns the next subkey in the tree, its class type, and the last time the key was written to. Each subkey is then analyzed calling the `ScanKey()` function recursively.

The `RegQueryInfoKey()` function provides detailed information about a Registry key, including the number of values and subkeys, and the maximum size of the value data buffers and class strings. Using this information, applications know the required size of the buffers they are allocating and whether there are subkeys that need to be analyzed. `RegQueryInfoKey()` can only analyze keys that have been opened with the KEY_QUERY_VALUE access rights, which are included with the KEY_ACCESS ALL privileges.

`RegEnumValue()` returns the value name, type, and data size of the specified value. `RegEnumValue()` returns information about one value on each call—the value referenced by the index number. Use `RegQueryValueEx()` to retrieve the total number of values. Then call `RegEnumValue()` repeatedly, first using a `dwIndex` of 0, then incrementing the index until all values have been retrieved, or the code ERROR_NO_MORE_ITEMS is returned. `RegEnumValue()` requires a key be opened with REG_QUERY_VALUE() access rights. Listing 18.6 illustrates the proper syntax for calling `RegEnumValue()`.

Listing 18.6   Example: *RegEnumValue()* Function

```
RegEnumValue( hKey,             // Handle of an open key
        dwIndex,                // Index of value to query
        lpszValueName,          // Returns value name
        lpcchValueName,         // Address of length of value name buffer
        lpdwReserved,           // Reserved value type
        lpdwType,               // Address of value type buffer
        lpbData,                // Data buffer
        lpcbDataSize);          // Address of Data size buffer
```

N O T E   When calling `RegQueryInfoKey()` in a Windows NT environment, the value returned for the `MaxValueData` field is not always accurate. To work around this, allocate a large data buffer on the `RegEnumValue()` call, then monitor the return code. If the return code indicates the buffer was too small, increase the size of the buffer and recall the function. Start with a buffer of 16 bytes, and then double the size of the buffer each time you get a failure on the data buffer size.

`RegEnumKeyEx()` returns information about subkeys of a Registry key. Applications use this call to retrieve the names of the subkeys and the last time they were modified. This function works similar to the `RegEnumValue()` function, returning information about one subkey on each call. `RegQueryInfoKey()` provides the total number of subkeys. Use the value to set up a loop, calling `RegEnumKeyEx()` with a different index until all the subkey information has been retrieved. It is important to note that the length of the subkey name does not include the Null terminating character.

Backup/Restore Functions

Registry backup functions, as listed in Table 18.9, store and retrieve all or portions of the Registry to a file. The system Registry has become the central nervous system of 32-bit Windows, making intelligent backup and recovery a must. From this need has grown an assortment of products that do Registry backup and restore. These products guarantee that a user can restore their Registry should it become corrupted. Other products, such as ConfigSafe from imagineLAN, Inc., track and identify all changes to the Registry as well.

Table 18.9   Registry Backup/Restore Functions

Function	Definition
`RegLoadKey()`	Retrieves information from a file and loads it into a subkey in the Registry. The information must have been saved with `RegSaveKey()`. This function loads subkeys at any level under HKEY_LOCAL_MACHINE or HKEY_USER only.
`RegReplaceKey()`	Retrieves information from a file and loads it into the Registry. This function works only on the immediate descendants (root hives) of the HKEY_LOCAL_MACHINE and HKEY_USER keys.
`RegRestoreKey()`	Retrieves information from a file and copies it over the specified key. Restore key does not delete any subkeys that exist in the current Registry, but not in the restored subtree unless it is restoring the entire HKEY_LOCAL_MACHINE or HKEY_USERS tree. This function is not available on Windows 95.
`RegSaveKey()`	Saves a key and its subkeys to the specified file.

Even applications that aren't backup-and-restore products will find these functions useful. For example, an application might want to store a subtree of information to a file, to be re-read later when a user selects a different option. Other applications might want to make backups of portions of the Registry at installation, or at other critical moments in their product's execution. Having these copies enables their support organization to restore those portions of the Registry if necessary, or compare current to previous settings.

Determining which Registry Backup Function to use can be very confusing. The calls your application will use depend on a number of items:

- The platforms on which your application will run
- The keys that will be stored or retrieved (root level or subkey)
- The volatility of your data (volatile or non-volatile)

RegSaveKey() is the only method for creating a Registry backup file. You could, of course, write the backup and restore functions yourself, storing and retrieving the Registry data in your own format. But, the RegSaveKey() function will perform this task quite admirably for you. Listing 18.7 illustrates the proper syntax for calling RegSaveKey().

Listing 18.7   Example: *RegSaveKey() Function*

```
RegSaveKey( hKey,          // Handle of key
      lpctFileName,        // Pointer to the file name
      lpSecurity );        // Pointer to security attributes
```

RegSaveKey() writes the specified Registry key and its descendants to the indicated file. The file then can be used by Registry restore functions such as RegLoadKey(), RegReplaceKey(), and RegRestoreKey(). The process calling RegSaveKey() must have SEBackupPriviledge for the call to succeed.

Part

IV

Ch

18

CAUTION

RegSaveKey() writes the Registry information to the specified file. If the file already exists on the system, the call will fail with the return code 1010. Make sure your application deletes the output file, if it already exists, before calling RegSaveKey().

Restoring the Registry presents an interesting dilemma. There are a number of functions available to restore all or part of the Registry. The trouble is that they each have their own set of limitations.

RegLoadKey() restores information from the specified file into the Registry. Any subkey at the hive level can be recreated by a call to RegLoadKey(), as long as the information had been stored using RegSaveKey(). Information restored using RegLoadKey() is volatile. That means the next time the system reboots, any information restored using this function will be lost. Think of this function as a temporary restoration of data. Before using RegLoadKey(), your application must delete the existing copy of the key and its descendants. Listing 18.8 illustrates the proper syntax for calling the RegLoadKey() function.

Listing 18.8   Example: *RegLoadKey() Function*

```
RegLoadKey( hKey,          // Root key
      lpszSubKey,          // Subkey name
      lpszFile );          // Pointer to the file name to store registry
```

RegReplaceKey() restores Registry hives by replacing the existing Registry key and its descendants with information from a new hive file. Windows does this by replacing the old hive file with the new hive file at Windows startup. Only keys that are at the root of a hive may be replaced using this function. The replacement hive files must have been created using the RegSaveKey() function. Listing 18.9 illustrates the proper syntax for calling RegReplaceKey().

Listing 18.9   Example: *RegReplaceKey()* Function

```
RegReplaceKey( hKey,    //
     lpszSubKey,        // Pointer to subkey
     lpszNewFile,       // Pointer to new file
     lpszBackupFile);   // Pointer to backup file.
```

When information is replaced in the Registry, a copy of the old information is stored in the file pointed to by lpszBackupFile. The application issuing the RegReplaceKey() request must have SE_RESTORE_NAME privileges.

CAUTION

RegReplaceKey() will replace a Registry hive with the replacement file. It will then delete the replacement file. So be aware that your application may need to recreate the file each time it expects to do a restore.

RegRestoreKey() is an excellent function for restoring all or portions of the Registry. For those of you looking to do this in both a Windows NT and Windows 95 environment, this call is only supported under Windows NT. Simply specify the key, source file, and options, and the Registry key and its descendants are updated. RegRestoreKey() overwrites the existing information in the Registry with the information from the file. The syntax for calling RegRestoreKey() is illustrated in Listing 18.10.

Listing 18.10   Example: *RegRestoreKey()* Function

```
RegRestoreKey ( hKey, // Key handle to begin restore
     lpszFile,        // Pointer to the file.
     fdwOptions );    // Optional flags
```

The fdwOptions field lets the application specify if the data restored to the Registry is volatile or non-volatile. Volatile data is lost when the system shuts down. Non-volatile data is stored in the Registry files, being restored the next time the system boots. Windows 95 only supports non-volatile data, so this flag is ignored. The application calling RegRestoreKey() must have SE_RESTORE_NAME privileges in order to succeed under Windows NT.

Selecting the proper restore function for the Registry depends on your application, the type of data (volatile or non-volatile), and the Windows operating system on which it will run. Read the small print on these functions closely in the reference material; it is this small print that will affect your application's functioning.

Utility Functions

Table 18.10 lists the Registry Utility Functions provided by the Win32 API. The first, `RegConnectRegistry()`, allows an application to connect to the Registry on a remote system.

Table 18.10   Registry Utility Functions

Function	Definition
`RegConnectRegistry()`	Connects a system to the Registry on a remote system. Only the two root keys, HKEY_LOCAL_MACHINE and HKEY_USERS, can be accessed in a remote Registry.
`RegNotifyChangeKeyValue()`	Provides notification when the specified Registry object changes.
`RegUnloadKey()`	Removes the specified Registry key, and all of its descendant keys, from the Registry. The Registry keys are only removed from the in-memory Registry, not the memory that resides on disk. This function is excellent for temporarily removing Registry trees from the Registry and replacing them with other trees.

Part
IV

Ch
18

`RegConnectRegistry()` operates much like `RegOpenKeyEx()`, returning a handle to a remote Registry key. The syntax for calling `RegConnectRegistry()` is illustrated in Listing 18.11. Using this function, applications can analyze and set values in a remote system's Registry database. Specify the remote computer name along with the root key to analyze. The only valid root keys for remote connectivity are HKEY_LOCAL_MACHINE and HKEY_USERS. Once connected and a Registry key is open, the normal functions can be used on the remote machine as if it were local. Pretty powerful stuff!

Listing 18.11   Example: RegConnectRegistry() Function

```
RegConnectRegistry( lpszComputerName,   // Remote computer name
                    hkey,               // Registry key
                    phkResult )         // Pointer to resulting handle
```

`RegNotifyChangeKeyValue()`, as illustrated in Listing 18.12, notifies an application when a change is being made to a Registry key or its subkeys. Based on the filter specified, the function watches for changes to the key names, attributes, last-write value, or security.

Your application can be notified via an event, or simply poll inside the function call until a change occurs.

Listing 18.12 Example: *RegNotifyChangeKeyValue()* Function

```
RegNotifyChangeKeyValue(   hkey,        // Key handle
                   bSubTree,            // Track Subkeys (T/F)
                   dwFilter,            // Indicates type of changes
                   hEvent,              // Event generated on change
                   bAsync );            // Notification option
```

`RegUnloadKey()` removes the specified key and subkeys from the Registry. The keys are removed only from the in-memory copy of the Registry, not from the actual file. This function is quite powerful when combined with the `RegLoadKey()` function. Because `RegLoadKey()` requires a key and its descendants be removed before it will restore a new key, the `RegUnloadKey()` function performs a very valuable function. The application calling this function must have the SE_RESTORE_NAME privilege. Listing 18.13 illustrates the proper calling syntax for the `RegUnloadKey()` function.

Listing 18.13 Example: *RegUnloadKey()* Function

```
RegUnLoadKey( hkey,    // Key handle
      lpszSubKey)      // Name of subkey to unload.
```

Registry Security

Key level security exists only on Windows NT. Windows 95 does not provide key level security. So, it is not surprising that the security functions listed in Table 18.11 are only supported on Windows NT.

Table 18.11 Registry Security Functions

Function	Definition
RegGetKeySecurity()	Retrieves security information for the specified key.
RegSetKeySecurity()	Sets the security information for the specified key.

Windows NT security is a complex issue. The Registry Security Functions can change the user-group and system-level securities assigned to a Registry entry. However, most applications will work just fine leaving security to the operating system, and taking the default values for security.

Security in an NT system is object-based. Each object, such as a Registry entry, has security attributes. Table 18.12 illustrates the basic types of security attributes.

Table 18.12   Security Information

Type	ID	Definition
Owner	OWNER_SECURITY_INFO	Identifies the primary owner of an object.
Group ID	GROUP_SECURITY_INFO	Identifies the primary group to which the object belongs.
DACL	DACL_SECURITY_INFO	Discretionary ACL (Access Control List) describes the access-specific owners or groups have to an object.
SACL	SACL_SECURITY_INFO	System ACL (Access Control List) describes the system level security an object has associated with it. If an object has system-level security, an administrator can perform an audit of any attempts to gain access to the object.

`RegGetKeySecurity()` and `RegSetKeySecurity()` enable an application to set and retrieve the security information for each Registry key. The security attributes are for keys only, values do not have security attributes.

Parameters to the security functions include the structure SECURITY_INFORMATION. This structure identifies the type of security information being set or requested.

Security functions also require a SECURITY _DESCRIPTOR buffer. This structure contains information, either provided or retrieved, about the object. The type of information would be relevant to the SECURITY_INFORMATION type. The structure may contain pointers to a Discretionary ACL, System ACL, owner information, or more. These structures are quite complex and won't be covered in any greater detail here. Suffice it to say that each type of data, as listed in Table 18.13, can be set and retrieved using the Registry Security Functions in combination with other Windows security calls. ●

Part

IV

Ch

18

CHAPTER 19

Programming the Registry Using C++

by Bernard Farrell

If you've followed the previous chapters, you're ready to start really playing with the Registry in your code. This chapter gives you everything you need to manipulate any aspect of the Registry and make it a useful and integral part of your application.

This chapter is *not* a tutorial on C++ programming, developing a C++ class, or using existing Microsoft Foundation Classes. It is assumed that you're already reasonably comfortable with Windows programming and using the MFC facilities. Although the chapter is geared towards C++, you can use much of the code to show you how to access the Registry from C. You can take advantage of what you learn to develop DLLs, or Console applications, in C.

All the example code in this chapter has been developed using Visual C++, version 4.20. If you don't have a Visual C++ subscription edition, then you may be using Visual C++ 4.0, or even an earlier version. Esoteric features within version 4.20 were not used, so you should not have any problems using the examples with an earlier version of Visual C++. No additional OCXs or add-on libraries were used in writing this code. ■

How to use the CWinApp functions

You'll look at the built-in member functions that give you limited access to the Registry and where these are appropriate.

How to handle existing Registry entries

The Registry contains a wealth of important values for a Windows application. Here you'll learn how to find and use these settings to your advantage.

How to save settings for any application

You can make any program more user-sensitive by storing user preferences, and other values, in the Registry for later use.

Other ways to manipulate the Registry

If you want to maintain information to help tailor your application, you'll need to know how to create and delete keys and values for your application.

Visual C++ Provided Functions

If you're using—or learning to use—Visual C++, you probably will take advantage of the MFC classes. One of the most important classes you use is the CWinApp class. This class has more than 40 member functions that deal with a number of areas of interaction between your application and the system. Table 19.1 lists several of these functions that deal with handling Registry values for your application.

Table 19.1   CWinApp Registry-related Member Functions

Function Name	Purpose
SetRegistryKey	Establishes a Registry key for use by your application. This *must* be called before using any of the Get or Set functions.
GetProfileInt	Reads an integer value from the Registry.
SetProfileInt	Creates and/or sets an integer value in the Registry.
GetProfileString	Reads a string value from the Registry.
SetProfileString	Creates and/or sets a string value in the Registry.

The names of the functions are somewhat misleading. They appear to refer to Profile settings. If you do not call SetRegistryKey, then these calls work on a profile file whose name is defined by your application name. Therefore, you *must* call SetRegistryKey before doing anything else in your application. Note that all of these calls use the data member fields m_pszRegistryKey and m_pszProfileName to determine where in the Registry your values belong.

Establishing Yourself in the Registry

The Windows logo standards require that your application occupy a place in the Registry that is defined by

> Your Company Name
>
> Your Application Name
>
> Your Application Version number

Specifically, the required "place" in the Registry for your application is

```
[HKEY_LOCAL_MACHINE]\SOFTWARE\Your Company Name\Application Name\Version
Number
```

To ensure that this happens, you should have a call in your CWinApp::InitInstance member function that establishes the correct Registry settings. Your code should be something like:

```
BOOL CRegOpenCloseApp::InitInstance()
{
    // Standard initialization
    // If you are not using these features and wish to reduce the size
    // of your final executable, you should remove from the following
    // the specific initialization routines you do not need.

#ifdef _AFXDLL
    Enable3dControls();                 // Call this when using MFC in a
                                        //shared DLL
#else
    Enable3dControlsStatic();       // Call this when linking to MFC
                                    // statically
#endif

    CString sCompanyName  = "Macmillan";

    //  The sSection is really the equivalent of the Version number.
    CString sSection       = "1.00";

    SetRegistryKey(sCompanyName);

    BOOL bResult = WriteProfileString(sSection, "Registered User", "Bernard
Farrell");
    bResult = WriteProfileString(sSection, "Company Name", "Directed
Solutions");

    int nTopPosn, nLeftPosn;

    nTopPosn  = (int) GetProfileInt(sVersion, "Top", -1);
    nLeftPosn = (int) GetProfileInt(sVersion, "Left", -1);

    LoadStdProfileSettings(0);  // Load standard INI file options
                                // (including MRU)

    ......

    // Dispatch commands specified on the command line
    if (!ProcessShellCommand(cmdInfo))
        return FALSE;

    return TRUE;
}
```

After this execution, your Registry should look something like Figure 19.1.

FIG. 19.1

Registry values
established with
CWinApp calls.

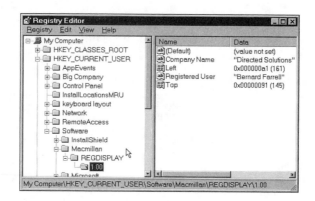

You must pass an argument into the `SetRegistryKey()` function. If you make this a zero
length string, the Registry entry should look like this:

```
[HKEY_LOCAL_MACHINE]\SOFTWARE\Application Name\Version Number
```

N O T E   The application name is derived from the name you gave your application when you
originally generated it (usually, the name of your project workspace), assuming you're
using MFC AppWizard. If you don't call `SetRegistryKey`, then the INI file name is derived from
the name of your EXE file. ▤

The string used for the section name in an INI file is used for the version number in the
Registry key. If you pass an empty string into the `WriteProfile...()` calls, then the entry
is written as a value under the application name key.

T I P   Because you will probably have to access Registry values elsewhere in your application besides
`CWinApp::InitInstance`, you should place the version information somewhere that is readily
available. You may want to add a public data member to your CWinApp derived object, say

```
LPCTSTR m_pszVersion;   // Program version used in Registry
```

You can then establish this value in `CWinApp::InitInstance`, making sure to call
`SetRegistryKey()`, and referring to the version from anywhere else in the application in the
following way:

```
CWinApp* pApp = AfxGetApp();

int nValue = (int) pApp->GetProfileInt( pApp->m_pszVersion,

             "Top", -1 );
```

By using these five CWinApp member functions, you are able to store and retrieve
values specific to your program via the Registry. You cannot retrieve values previously

established by Windows or other applications. You are restricted to the use of string and integer values, but these are sufficient for most purposes.

N O T E Be careful when using the `GetProfileInt` call outside of your CWinApp-derived class. If you omit the pointer to your CWinApp, you end up using the `GetProfileInt` call that handles *only* the INI files, *not* the `CWinApp::GetProfileInt` call. These calls take the same parameters, and you may think a value is not present because the call returns the default value. In fact, your application is trying to read from a nonexistent INI file. ■

Dealing with Existing Registry Values

At this stage in the book, you hopefully have read about the types of information contained in the Registry and you're itching to use some of these settings in your application. Given how much data is already available in the Registry, I want to start by looking at the different types of data values and how they can be safely read.

The rest of this chapter gives examples of how you can use the functions by showing parts of a program that enable you to move around the Registry displaying keys and their values. The source code for this program is located on the Web site. The dialog box for this program is shown in Figure 19.2.

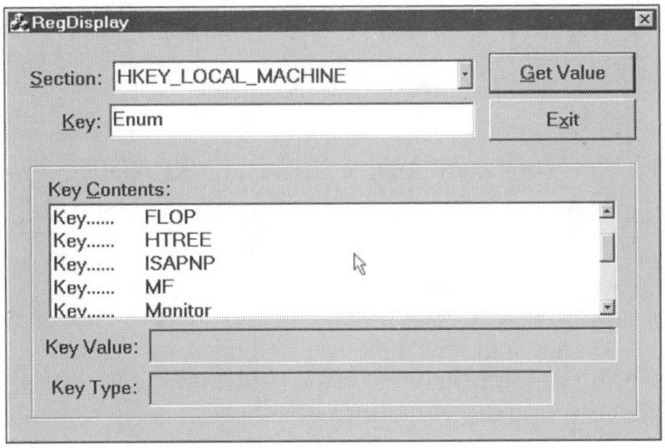

FIG. 19.2
RegDisplay—Registry Value Display dialog box.

Part IV Ch 19

You'll see how many of the functions were used in developing this application.

Declaring Win32 Functions for C++

If you're a C++ purist, you may not have had to access existing C code from within your program. This doesn't include the C runtime library, where Microsoft provides you with the declarations for the constants, data types, and functions, so you don't have to sweat the details. To get at the Registry calls directly, you may have to wrap the C interfaces up a little so C++ doesn't get too upset by them.

To handle the Registry from C++ or C, you need declarations for:

- Constants, including error return values
- Data types used as parameters and return values
- The Registry calls themselves

These declarations are fairly obvious. They're listed because you must either build a header file of your own that includes all the declarations you are interested in using, or you can use the Microsoft-provided files.

Choosing the Microsoft-provided files is probably a better idea, as the files are definitive, and they bear the effort of maintaining them. In that case, you need some or all of the following:

- Constants: WINREG.H and WINERROR.H
- Data types used as parameters and return values: WINREG.H and WINNT.H
- The Registry calls themselves: WINREG.H

N O T E   I determined that this was the appropriate set of header files by using the Find in Files command in the File menu for Visual C++ to look for some of the Registry calls (for example, `RegCreateKeyEx` and `RegQueryValueEx`) in the header files in the MSDEV\include directory. I then used the same command to look for some of the needed Constants (for example, REG_BINARY, ERROR_SUCCESS, and HKEY_CLASSES_ROOT).

If you decide to create your own header file—call it REGDEFS.H—with the appropriate parts from each of these, then you have to wrap the C functions in an `extern` statement:

```
extern "C"{
/*All your C stuff goes here ... */
}  /*  End of extern C  */
```

You can do this in the header file you create, but that means the header file won't work in C. So you either can make it more like

```
#ifdef __cplusplus
extern "C"{
#endif

/*All your C stuff goes here ... */
#ifdef __cplusplus
}  /*  End of extern C  */
#endif
```

or simply wrap the include line in your C++ code as follows:

```
extern "C"{
#include "regdefs.h"
}  /*  End of extern C  */
```

> **TIP**
>
> It's useful to look at the contents of WINREG.H. You can see how Microsoft has separated the Registry function calls into ANSI and Unicode versions of each using #ifdef facilities.
>
> You also can see how the newer Registry calls are defined for where the Windows version is at least 4.0. Look at RegQueryMultipleValues, for example.

It is assumed that you're developing an application for use in the ANSI space. Although developing programs using Unicode requires a lot more effort because of wide-byte strings and internationalization, it shouldn't affect how your code uses the Registry except for the changed data types (LPCSTR values become LPCWSTR and LPSTR are replaced by LPWSTR). You'll end up making the same calls, and the #define macros will map each call that involves strings to an ..A (for ANSI) or a ..W (for Wide) call, depending on whether you're using ANSI or Unicode.

> **NOTE**   If you're also working in Visual Basic, this is why you see the Alias for each Win32 call that uses strings defined with an A at the end. For example, the call to RegCreateKeyEx in Visual Basic is mapped to the function RegCreateKeyExA. Visual Basic does not handle Unicode. For more information about programming the Registry using Visual Basic, see Chapter 20, "Programming the Registry Using Visual Basic." ▪

Part

IV

Ch

19

Getting All the Information About a Registry Entry

Existing values in the Registry enable you to get information about your system configuration, user information, and so on. Even if the values that you're reading are those used in your own application, they probably have already been established as part of the installation script. Later, you'll see how to actually create new Registry entries when your application is working.

Before doing anything with the Registry, you must open the key. This gives your application a Handle to the key (normally a subkey fairly far down in the Registry tree) that makes it faster to subsequently manipulate the contents of that Registry key. If you've done any amount of Windows programming, then you should already have used handles for things such as bitmaps, fonts, and allocated memory.

> **CAUTION**
>
> As with other objects in Windows programming dealt with by means of Handles, your application must release all Registry handles before it exits. Therefore, your application *must* close all Registry keys that it has opened.
>
> If your application fails to close all Registry keys—perhaps because of an application crash during debugging—you may corrupt the Registry. It's *important* to back up the Registry frequently, perhaps each time you start a development session while debugging your application.
>
> And remember, you are most likely to forget to close an open Registry key when you detect an error in some part of your application and exit a function call before your code reaches the RegCloseKey() call. For more information about fixing the Registry, see Chapter 5, "Fixing a Broken Registry." For more information about backing up the Registry, see Chapter 9, "Using ConfigSafe to Track Down Settings."

Because of the nature of change, it's best to avoid using hard-coded strings for Registry keys. Use an initialized CString variable instead, and share it across your application if it's required in more than one place. Your code might look like this:

```
LONG           lRegCallResult;
REGSAM      samWanted;
HKEY           hSearchKey;

samWanted = KEY_ALL_ACCESS;
lRegCallResult = RegOpenKeyEx( hOpenKey,
               m_sKeyName,
               0,
               samWanted,
               &hSearchKey );

if (lRegCallResult != ERROR_SUCCESS)
{
    //  Display an error message...
    return;
}

CString        sStringValue;
LPTSTR         szBuffer;
DWORD          dwCheckType;

lRegCallResult = RegQueryValueEx( hSearchKey,
                 sValueName,
                 NULL,
                 &dwCheckType,
                 NULL,
                 &dwValueLength );

if (lRegCallResult != ERROR_SUCCESS)
{
    //  Display message...
    lRegCallResult = RegCloseKey( hSearchKey );
    return ;
```

```
    }

    //  This code only handles String values
    if (dwCheckType != REG_SZ)
    {
        //  Display message...
        lRegCallResult = RegCloseKey( hSearchKey );
        return ;
    }

    szBuffer = sStringValue.GetBuffer( dwValueLength+1 );

    lRegCallResult = RegQueryValueEx( hSearchKey,
                            sValueName,
                            NULL,
                            &dwCheckType,
                            (LPBYTE) szBuffer,
                            &dwValueLength );

    sStringValue.ReleaseBuffer( );

    if (lRegCallResult != ERROR_SUCCESS)
    {
        //  Display message
        lRegCallResult = RegCloseKey( hSearchKey );
        return ;
    }

    //  At this stage, the key value is in sStringValue...

    lRegCallResult = RegCloseKey( hSearchKey );
```

N O T E If you want to retrieve the contents for the value without two calls to
RegQueryValueEx, you should allocate a buffer that you believe is large enough and
pass it into the first call, along with its length. If it is too short, you get an ERROR_MORE_DATA
return value instead of the ERROR_SUCCESS value. Of course, you also miss the chance to
confirm that the data type is still REG_SZ, or whatever you expected. ▨

TIP When constructing key names, remember that the subkey names are separated by a backslash
character (\), and that this is an escape character in C and C++. So to specify the key name

HKEY_CURRENT_USER\Software\Microsoft

you must initialize a string to hold this key with the value

HKEY_CURRENT_USER\\Software\\Microsoft

This is a common coding error when dealing with Registry keys in C or C++.

Most applications store values in the Registry as strings (REG_SZ) or longs
(REG_DWORD). In fact, 11 different types of Registry data are supported. The #define
values for them are in WINNT.H.

While certain key values are well-defined and unlikely to change, your application should be able to deal correctly with any of the different types of data by using a combination of two calls to `RegQueryValueEx`. The first call gets the value type and its length, the second gets the value itself using information returned by the first call.

The sample application shows how to deal with some of the other data types, and displays them in the dialog box. Refer to Figure 19.3 to see what happens when you select a particular value.

Reading a Registry Key or Value

Whenever you open a key in the Registry, the handle returned by the `RegOpenKey()` call is not required to do anything more with the key itself. As the Registry is structured like a directory tree, the key you open may have subkeys, or values, or both. So once you open a key, you need a means to determine what information is contained within that key.

You do this using the `RegQueryInfoKey()` function. This call gives you information about the subkeys, values, size of the largest value, and so on. You'll find the function very useful when writing any application that traverses the Registry tree. In the sample application, when you choose a key, all the subkeys and values contained within that key are listed. You can choose a key and go deeper into the Registry, or you can choose a value and display its contents. Figure 19.3 shows what the display looks like with a key selected that contains subkeys and values below it.

FIG. 19.3
Displaying subkeys and values.

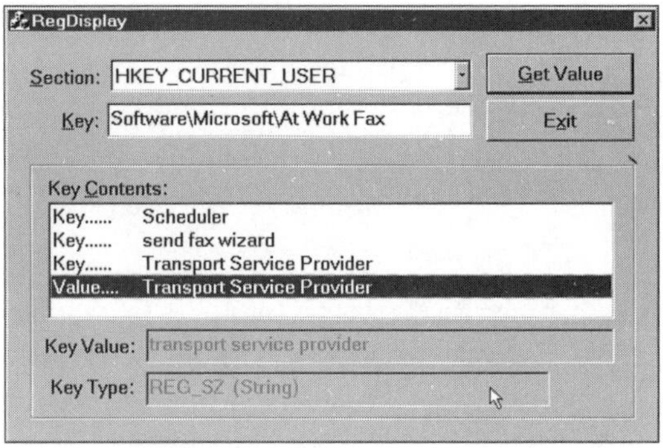

The following code shows the call and how you use it. Assume that the key being queried has already been opened successfully.

```
DWORD      dwSubKeyCount, dwValueCount, dwClassNameLen;
DWORD      dwMaxSubKeyName, dwMaxValueName;
DWORD      dwMaxValueLength;
FILETIME     ftLastWritten;
LONG        lResult;
```

```
CString    sClassName;
LPSTR      szClassBuffer = sClassName.GetBuffer(CLASS_NAME_LEN);


// Determine the number of subkeys and values
dwClassNameLen = CLASS_NAME_LEN;
lRegCallResult = RegQueryInfoKey( hSearchKey,
                    szClassBuffer,      // Class Name
                    &dwClassNameLen, // Name buffer length
                    NULL,               // Reserved
                    &dwSubKeyCount,  // Number of subkeys
                    &dwMaxSubKeyName,
                    NULL,               // Longest Class String
                                        // length
                    &dwValueCount,      // Number of values
                    &dwMaxValueName,
                    &dwMaxValueLength,
                    NULL,               // Security Descriptor
                    &ftLastWritten );

if (lRegCallResult != ERROR_SUCCESS)
{
    // Display a message...
    lResult = RegCloseKey( hSearchKey );
    return;
}

// Traverse the subkeys
DWORD          dwCount;

for (dwCount = 0; dwCount < dwSubKeyCount; dwCount++)
{
    // ... Do something with each of the subkeys
}


// Traverse the values for the opened key
for (dwCount = 0; dwCount < dwValueCount; dwCount++)
{
    // ... Do something with each of the values
}
```

In a situation like this, where there's an open key with a number of subkeys or values that you want information about, you can use the RegEnum...() calls to visit each subkey or value in turn and get information about it.

N O T E When you have a RegQueryInfoKey() followed by one or both of the RegEnum...() calls, you need to get the summary information about the sub-elements. The maximum length of each subkey name is useful for determining string storage needs, and the maximum length of each value is useful for determining value storage needs. In this case, you can't allocate a single value type because you have to allow for different kinds of values. ▪

`RegEnumKeyEx()` enables you to get each subkey in turn. In this example, you add the list of subkeys to the list box before each value.

```
//  Traverse the subkeys
DWORD          dwCount, dwSubNameLen;
CString         sKeyName;
LPSTR          szNameBuffer = sKeyName.GetBuffer( dwMaxSubKeyName + 20 );
CListBox       *pclContents = (CListBox *) GetDlgItem( IDC_LIST_CONTENTS );

for (dwCount = 0; dwCount < dwSubKeyCount; dwCount++)
{
    dwSubNameLen = dwMaxSubKeyName + 1;
    lResult = RegEnumKeyEx( hSearchKey,
                        dwCount,
                        szNameBuffer,
                        &dwSubNameLen,
                        NULL,      // Reserved
                        NULL,      // Class Name buffer
                        NULL,      // Size class name buffer
                        NULL );    // Last write time

    sKeyName.ReleaseBuffer( );

    if (lResult == ERROR_SUCCESS)
    {
        // sKeyName now contains the subkey name

    }
    else if (lResult == ERROR_NO_MORE_ITEMS)
    {
        //  There are no more subkey values.
        //  Because of the count in the for loop, this
        //  code should never get called.
        break;
    }
    else
    {
        //  Display an error message
        lResult = RegCloseKey( hSearchKey );
        return;
    }
}  //  for (dwCount...)
```

The `RegEnumValue()` call is a combination of the `RegEnumKeyEx()` and `RegQueryValueEx()` functions. In this case, you can get the contents of each of the values for the open key. In the case of the example application, you just obtained the value name and its data type. You also could get the value contents, but your code would end up doing a lot more work with a generic buffer pointer to ensure that you can properly handle all value types. It's much easier to program using the two calls to `RegQueryValueEx()` outlined in the previous section.

```
//  Traverse the values
for (dwCount = 0; dwCount < dwValueCount; dwCount++)
```

```
    {
        dwSubNameLen = dwMaxValueName + 1;
        lResult = RegEnumValue( hSearchKey,
                    dwCount,
                    szNameBuffer,
                    &dwSubNameLen,
                    NULL,          // Reserved
                    &dwValType,    // Value Type Code
                    NULL,          // Address for value data
                    NULL );        // Len of value data buffer

        if (lResult == ERROR_SUCCESS)
        {
            // szNameBuffer contains the name of the value,
            // and dwValType the type for the value...
        }
        else if (lResult == ERROR_NO_MORE_ITEMS)
        {
            // There are no more subkey values.
            // Because of the count in the for loop, this
            // code should never get called.
            break;
        }
        else
        {
            // Display an error message
            lResult = RegCloseKey( hSearchKey );
            return;
        }
    } // for (dwCount...)
```

 Remember in both of these calls, you must allocate space for the null terminator at the end of the name strings. You must also remember to pass the length of the string *including* this additional character into the call. Otherwise, you get a truncated name back, and ERROR_MORE_DATA instead of ERROR_SUCCESS as a status.

If your application is intended for Windows NT 4.0 *only*, then you can also use the RegQueryMultipleValues() call to get information about more than one value for an open key. Apart from being limited to use on NT, this call has some limitations in terms of the maximum amount of data it can return. It also is hard to establish the parameter values for the call because of the need to populate an array of VALENT entries. This structure is shown in the following example and must contain information, including name and data buffer pointers of the right size for each value that is needed.

```
typedef struct value_ent {
    LPTSTR  ve_valuename;  // Name of value to retrieve
    DWORD   ve_valuelen;   // Length of valueptr area
    DWORD   ve_valueptr;   // Buffer to populate with value
    DWORD   ve_type;       // Value type
} VALENT;
```

N O T E I have not yet used the `RegQueryMultipleValues()` call in an application. Because `RegQueryMultipleValues()` returns the values in a single, atomic call, it is likely to be most useful when you expect a set of values being queried to change if you get them as a series of `RegQueryValueEx()` calls. Otherwise, given the amount of code you need to develop to populate the VALENT fields for each required entry, using the `RegQueryValueEx()` call in some type of loop is still the best approach. ▪

Changing an Existing Registry Value

You can change the value of any existing Registry entry using the `RegSetValueEx()`. You should be careful with any changes that you make, in case your application causes problems with the rest of the system. In general, it's best to stick with Registry entries that are created for your application. A typical example is to store the location of the main window for your application when the user exits, so you can restore it later. You can use the same approach to store other state information.

In the sample code, the CWinApp call stores the Top value for the window, and the `RegSetValueEx()` stores the Left value. You can use this to compare the approaches. The code that uses `RegSetValueEx()` is shown in the following example:

```
//  Store the Left position using the Win32 Registry Calls
HKEY     hSearchKey;
REGSAM   samWanted;
long     lRegCallResult;

samWanted = KEY_ALL_ACCESS;
lRegCallResult = RegOpenKeyEx( HKEY_CURRENT_USER,
                    "Software\\Macmillan\\REGDISPLAY\\1.0",
                    0,
                    samWanted,
                    &hSearchKey );

if (lRegCallResult == ERROR_SUCCESS)
{
    lRegCallResult = RegSetValueEx( hSearchKey,
                "Left",
                NULL,
                REG_DWORD,
                (CONST BYTE*) &wpInfo.rcNormalPosition.left,
                sizeof(DWORD) );

    if (lRegCallResult != ERROR_SUCCESS)
    {
        // Display an error message...
    }

    lRegCallResult = RegCloseKey( hSearchKey );
}
```

Other Registry Functions

The preceding sections deal with the Registry calls that cover most of your application needs. This section deals with some of the remaining Registry calls that are available and how you might use them in your application.

You may want to skip this section if you're just starting with the Registry. Come back to it when you get a bit more experience, or you want to write some tools for manipulating the Registry itself.

Creating a New Registry Key and Value

There are many examples of applications that maintain some kind of status or context information, such as the list of files that have been recently opened. The Registry is an ideal location for this type of information. The RegCreateKeyEx() function is used to maintain this kind of information within the Registry. If you are considering using this function, make sure that you have correctly classified the type of data you plan to store—for example, computer-specific versus user-specific—and from that determine the correct part of the Registry to use.

▶ **See** "Putting Registry Entries in Their Place," **p. 306**

This sample code shows how you would store a new value in the Registry:

```
//  Store the file name (szFileName) in the registry
HKEY    hSearchKey, hNewKey;
REGSAM  samWanted;
long    lRegCallResult;
DWORD   dwDisposition;

samWanted = KEY_ALL_ACCESS;
lRegCallResult = RegOpenKeyEx( HKEY_CURRENT_USER,
                    "Software\\Macmillan\\REGDISPLAY\\1.0",
                    0,
                    samWanted,
                    &hSearchKey );

if (lRegCallResult == ERROR_SUCCESS)
{
    lRegCallResult = RegCreateKeyEx( hSearchKey,
                "Files",
                NULL,
                NULL,
                REG_OPTION_NON_VOLATILE,
                KEY_ALL_ACCESS,
                NULL,
                &hNewKey,
                &dwDisposition );
```

Part

IV

Ch

19

```
        if (lRegCallResult != ERROR_SUCCESS)
        {
            // Display an error message...
        }
        else
        {
            if (dwDisposition == REG_CREATED_NEW_KEY)
            {
                //  New key was created
            }
            else
            {
                //  Disposition is REG_OPENED_EXISTING_KEY
                //  'New' key already existed
            }

        lRegCallResult = RegSetValueEx( hNewKey,
                            "File 1",
                            NULL,
                            REG_SZ,
                            szNewFileName,
                            strlen( szFileName ) );

        lRegCallResult = RegCloseKey( hNewKey );

        }
        lRegCallResult = RegCloseKey( hSearchKey );
        }
```

Creating a key always opens it. This is true whether the key is actually created or already exists. If you want to make sure that it did not previously exist, then you need to check the value returned in the disposition parameter to determine what action occurred in the `RegCreateKeyEx()` call.

N O T E   If your application is maintaining some type of most recently used (MRU) list, then you would normally create a set of keys either at installation time, or when the user changes the size of this list. Then each time a new object is used, you would simply rotate values in the pre-existing list. ■

Removing a Registry Key or Value

Normally, you don't delete a Registry key or value. The values used by your application are usually established using an installation script and removed by the uninstall script that you provide. You must at least do this to conform to the Windows logo requirements.

However, you may want to keep track of some information, such as a list of objects in the Registry, and allow the user to remove it via some type of purge action in your application, as shown in the previous example. In that case, you use one or both of the `RegDeleteKey()` and `RegDeleteValue()` calls.

NOTE RegDeleteKey() works differently, depending on whether your application is running on Windows NT 4.0 or Windows 95. In the case of Windows NT, the function does *not* delete a key that contains any subkeys. To ensure that your application works properly on both systems, you can write a recursive key deletion function. ▨

If you are going to delete a key or some of its values, you must make sure that you open the key with appropriate permissions. Using KEY_WRITE allows you to do either operation on the key. Assuming that your key does not have any subkeys, your code would look like:

```
//  Delete a value and a key
HKEY     hSearchKey;
REGSAM   samWanted;
long     lRegCallResult;

samWanted = KEY_WRITE;
lRegCallResult = RegOpenKeyEx( HKEY_CURRENT_USER,
                        "Software\\Macmillan\\REGDISPLAY\\1.0",
                        0,
                        samWanted,
                        &hSearchKey );

if (lRegCallResult == ERROR_SUCCESS)
{
    //  First remove one of the values...
    lRegCallResult = RegDeleteValue( hSearchKey,
                    "Left" );

    if (lRegCallResult != ERROR_SUCCESS)
    {
        // Display an error message...
    }
    lRegCallResult = RegCloseKey( hSearchKey );

    //  Then remove the key itself...
    lRegCallResult = RegDeleteKey(HKEY_CURRENT_USER,
                "Software\\Macmillan\\REGDISPLAY\\1.0");

    if (lRegCallResult != ERROR_SUCCESS)
    {
        // Display an error message...
    }

}
```

Part
IV

Ch
19

TIP In the preceding example, you can see that the key to delete does not have to be open. In this case, only the last subkey is removed. After the deletion is complete, the key HKEY_CURRENT_USER\Software\Macmillan still exists.

> **N O T E**   The issues around handling change notification for Registry keys,
> `RegNotifyChangeKeyValue`, are probably too advanced for most users and would
> only work correctly in Windows NT. Therefore, they are not covered here. ▪

Other Source Code

You might learn more by looking at working examples of source code. In the case of the Registry, you can definitely pick up some useful tips by looking at as much code as you can find. Apart from the samples for this chapter, Microsoft has provided some useful examples that use the Registry.

There are two examples of programs, written in C, that access the Registry to display performance data. The programs also allow connection to remote machines. They can be found on the Microsoft Developer Network CD. Look for PERFMON and PVIEWER under the Windows NT samples section of the Product Samples. Full source code is provided, but you have to create a Project Workspace to build these applications.

On the Visual C++ installation disk, you'll find these two applications and another specifically for traversing the Registry. It's called Monkey, because you can use it to climb up and down the Registry tree. It's also a C application and can be found at: \MSDEV\Samples\SDK\Win32\Registry\.

Third-Party Products

Stingray has a product out on the market, called the Objective Toolkit. It's expensive, but you may like it for its Registry class and all the other classes it provides your application with, such as the additional document interface classes.

ON THE WEB

http://www.stingsoft.com/   You can download some sample code and decide whether you like the classes provided. I have no experience in using these classes myself, but a client company of mine has used the classes extensively and finds them very useable.

Windows NT Perl is an alternative programming language—a port of the UNIX Perl language—that provides an alternative means of developing applications on NT. Version 5 of the Windows NT port of Perl has several Registry interface functions.

ON THE WEB

http://www.perl.com/perl/index.html   This site is a place where you can get lots of information about Perl.

ftp://ftp.intergraph.com/pub/win32/perl/   Here you can download a copy of Version 4 for Windows NT.

ftp://ntperl.hip.com/ntperl/perl5.001m/CurrentBuild/   Version 5 is available at this site.

CHAPTER 20

Programming the Registry Using Visual Basic

by Bernard Farrell

Visual Basic is an extremely popular, user-friendly computer language. It's quick and easy to implement things using this language. You don't have to know the names of Windows messages or how to route them to the appropriate part of your application. You can try the program out without a lengthy compilation cycle, and Visual Basic comes with various VBXs and OCXs. You can take more than one approach to implementing an application, and if you don't like it, you're not losing thousands of lines of code. If Visual Basic doesn't allow you enough flexibility or speed, you can make direct Windows API calls to accomplish specific tasks.

When it comes to manipulating the Registry in Visual Basic, you can use these Visual Basic benefits to develop applications that take advantage of the Registry, or even write tools to handle the Registry.

In this chapter, you learn how to use standard Visual Basic calls to manipulate a small part of the Registry. You also see some third-party products that make it easier to play with any part of the Registry.

Visual Basic built-in functions

Visual Basic 4 comes with some simple functions for doing basic Registry manipulation. You learn reasons for not using them.

What third-party products are available

These can make accessing the Registry a lot easier, with some restrictions.

How to use the Win32 calls

You can use most of the Win32 calls very easily from Visual Basic, once you understand the rules.

Building a simple Registry class

You can use Visual Basic 4.0 to create a class for incorporation into different software you build.

You'll spend most of the time, however, working directly with Win32 calls from within Visual Basic. It's simple after you get the hang of it, but you can expect a lot of learning pains along the way. Hopefully you've already read about how easy it is to break your system by making changes to the Registry, and you'll bear this in mind as you experiment. ■

Warning: Using Visual Basic and Win32 Can Be Dangerous for Your System's Health

If you've been using Visual Basic for a while, you already know that it's a great product for building prototypes and full-featured software. However, you may not have used it before to directly access the power of Win32 functionality—a power that has its price.

It's hard to build a Visual Basic application that will cause system problems. When you use the Win32 calls, it can be like inserting a probe into the system's brain: Sometimes you'll get the desired effect; sometimes you'll tickle an unexpected nerve; and sometimes the system will die without warning.

So, before running your Visual Basic application, make sure you've saved all the source code. If the system crashes, you're less likely to lose everything.

TIP You can set the Visual Basic options to save the source code for you each time you run the application. Select the Tools menu's Options... command, and the Options dialog box will appear. On the Environment tab, select the Save Before Run, Don't Prompt button in the File Save frame. Click OK to close the dialog box.

Using Visual Basic Built-in Functions

Visual Basic provides four functions that enable you to create, retrieve, and delete settings in the Registry. The problem is that these functions allow only manipulation of values within the HKEY_CURRENT_USER\Software\VB and VBA Program Settings\ key. It's difficult to be completely consistent with Windows logo requirements using only these settings.

The error handling for the provided calls is also completely inadequate. You won't crash your system, but you may get unexpected results and you will need to add Visual Basic error handlers to deal with some situations. Understand that many expert users suggest avoiding these calls altogether, but if you decide to go ahead and use them anyway, there are some other issues you need to take into account.

Documentation Issues

The documentation for some of these calls is incorrect. In the Visual Basic documentation, SaveSetting and DeleteSetting are shown as function calls. They are actually procedures with named arguments. The documentation for these calls is incorrect.

> **TIP** Simply add the word **Call** in front of the examples for the SaveSetting and DeleteSetting procedures and the code as shown will work. For example,
>
>   DeleteSetting("MyApp", "MySection")
>
> should be shown as
>
>   Call DeleteSetting("MyApp", "MySection")

> **NOTE** Microsoft has a Knowledge Base problem note about this, which refers to the SaveSetting call for Microsoft Access. See the Knowledge Base article: "SaveSetting" Example in Help Has Incorrect Syntax. PSS ID Number: Q145657.

The examples in the documentation may lead you to believe that you can store both strings and numeric values in the Registry. You can, but the numeric values are actually stored as strings. This won't cause problems if you are saving and getting settings from within Visual Basic, but be careful when trying to read values saved with Visual Basic from other languages or tools.

The Calls Themselves

You can refer to the Visual Basic documentation for details on the syntax and arguments for each of these calls. This is only an overview of issues you'll want to be aware of when using any of these calls.

SaveSetting   This call allows you to store a Registry section and associated keys. Because it accepts named arguments, you can actually give the arguments in a different order if that helps you. You cannot omit any of the arguments.

You also cannot use a null string as the Key argument to try and store in the default value for a section.

> **TIP** If you get pretty much any part of these Registry calls incorrect, including trying a null string, you'll get a Visual Basic run-time error. This is run-time error 5: Invalid Procedure call.
>
> See the Visual Basic documentation for information about writing error handlers.

Remember that this is a procedure call, so the documentation examples are wrong.

> **T I P**   You can use the `SaveSetting` call to create nested keys. To do this, specify the key nesting in the section parameter.
>
> For more details, consult the Knowledge Base article: SaveSetting & GetSetting Allow Nested Settings. PSS ID Number: Q145694.

GetSetting   This call allows you to read a Registry setting established previously from within a Visual Basic program. Remember that this call only allows you to get to values within the HKEY_CURRENT_USER\Software\VB and VBA Program Settings\ key.

This call does not allow you to check for the existence of a key. If the combination of the arguments yields a Registry key that does not exist, then you can use only the (optional) default argument to flag that something is wrong.

> **T I P**   You can use this call before making a SaveSetting call to check whether a key exists. If you don't do this, then `SaveSetting` will overwrite any existing key value.

GetAllSettings   This call allows you to get all key values within a given section. If the appname or section parameters are incorrect, or do not exist, then the result will be an uninitialized variant.

> **T I P**   You can use the `IsEmpty()` call to check whether the result returned by `GetAllSettings` has been initialized.

DeleteSetting   Remember to use **Call** in front of the documentation examples for this call to work.

The documentation says this call does nothing if the specified section or key does not exist. What actually happens is that you will get a run-time error 5 again.

> **T I P**   The documentation shows that the key parameter is optional. However, the section parameter also seems to be optional. If you call this function with only an appname parameter, then the whole subtree for the application is deleted from the Registry.

There do seem to be some limitations to this.

> **N O T E**   There are some limitations to this behavior where you have used `SaveSetting` to create nested keys. See the Knowledge Base article: VB Registry Functions Are Limited with Nested Settings. PSS ID Number: Q149038. ▪

A Small Example

When you try to use these calls, you'll probably find that the example code given in the Visual Basic documentation helps very little. As mentioned earlier, it's also wrong. This section provides a small example illustrating how to use each of the main functions to get at the Registry.

The program is useful in that it keeps track of the size and location of the main window. When you start the program the first time, the size is based on the values established at design time, as shown in Figure 20.1.

FIG. 20.1
Accessing the Registry with VB Functions window on first run.

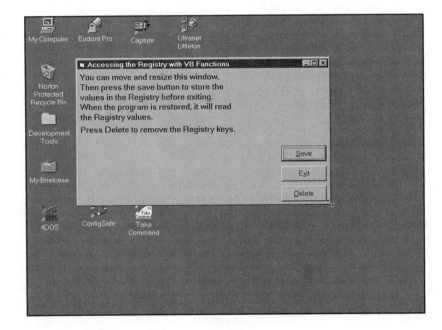

You can then resize or move the application window around. When you click on the <u>S</u>ave button, the Registry keys are set up with the values I'm interested in tracking for this window. My save code looks like this:

```
Private Sub cmdSave_Click()
    Dim sAppName As String

    sAppName = APP_NAME & "\" & APP_VERSION

    Call SaveSetting(sAppName, APP_SECTION, _
                     APP_WIN_TOP_KEY, frmVBMain.Top)
    Call SaveSetting(sAppName, APP_SECTION, _
                     APP_WIN_LEFT_KEY, frmVBMain.Left)
    Call SaveSetting(sAppName, APP_SECTION, _
                     APP_WIN_WIDTH_KEY, frmVBMain.Width)
```

```
Call SaveSetting(sAppName, APP_SECTION, _
                    APP_WIN_HEIGHT_KEY, frmVBMain.Height)
Call SaveSetting(sAppName, APP_SECTION, _
                    APP_WIN_STATE_KEY, frmVBMain.WindowState)

End Sub    '  cmdSave_Click
```

 TIP Rather than using strings for the various parameters in the SaveSetting call, I'm using CONSTs defined at the start of my program. This makes it easier to change the application name, version, and so on.

Notice how the name parameter includes a version string. You may want to do this to separate settings for different versions of your program.

You move and change the position of the window, and end up with the appearance shown in Figure 20.2.

FIG. 20.2
Saving the new
window settings.

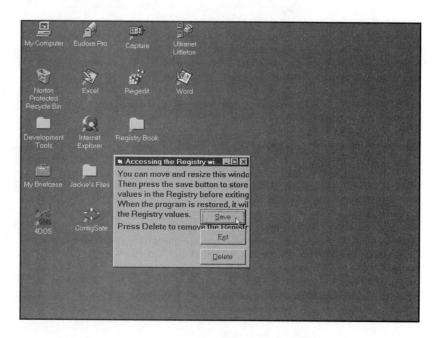

When you restart the application, you can recall the values from the Registry in the Form_Load() function. Of course, you have to allow for the fact that the values may not be found, and then you revert to the design time settings.

```
Private Sub Form_Load()
    Dim sAppName As String

    sAppName = APP_NAME & "\" & APP_VERSION
```

```
'  Try to read any available values from the Registry.
'  If a value is not found, use the appropriate value that was
'  established when we designed the form.
gWindowTop = GetSetting(sAppName, APP_SECTION, _
                        APP_WIN_TOP_KEY, -1)
If gWindowTop = -1 Then
    gWindowTop = frmVBMain.Top
End If

gWindowLeft = GetSetting(sAppName, APP_SECTION, _
                        APP_WIN_LEFT_KEY, -1)
If gWindowLeft = -1 Then
    gWindowLeft = frmVBMain.Left
End If

'  ...similar code removed

frmVBMain.Top = gWindowTop
frmVBMain.Left = gWindowLeft
frmVBMain.Height = gWindowHeight
frmVBMain.Width = gWindowWidth
frmVBMain.WindowState = gWindowState

'  Now Reposition the buttons.
ArrangeButtons

End Sub  '  Form_Load
```

As mentioned already, the values in the Registry are stored in subkeys under HKEY_CURRENT_USER\Software\VB and VBA Program Settings\. Figure 20.3 shows the Registry Editor with the settings established on my machine after running this program. You can see how these are stored under the VB and VBA Program Settings subkey.

FIG. 20.3
Registry settings for VB Registry Example.

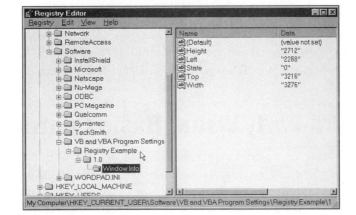

You have to add some error handling to the code that gets called when you click on the Delete button. You must allow for the fact that the Registry keys may already have been deleted, and you must remember to remove all traces of your application. This takes a total of three DeleteSetting calls.

```
'  Remove all the keys from the Registry
Private Sub cmdDelete_Click()
    Dim sAppName As String

    sAppName = APP_NAME & "\" & APP_VERSION

    On Error GoTo ERROR_HANDLER

    Call DeleteSetting(sAppName, APP_SECTION)

    '  This gets rid of the APP_VERSION subkey
    Call DeleteSetting(sAppName)

    '  This gets rid of the APP_NAME key
    Call DeleteSetting(APP_NAME)

    On Error GoTo 0
    Exit Sub

ERROR_HANDLER:
    If Err.Number = 5 Then
        '  This error is because the key was not found.
        Resume Next
    End If

End Sub  '  cmdDelete_Click
```

Look at the full set of source code (only about 150 lines) to see how the whole application fits together. You'll see that storing and using the values is fairly easy, with the major restriction being that you're forced to stay within one small section of the Registry.

The only call you haven't seen covered is the GetAllSettings call. This is left as an exercise to do on your own time. (Takes you back to academic life, doesn't it?)

Using Third-Party Visual Basic Controls

You're probably convinced that manipulating the Registry with Visual Basic procedures is a bad idea. Right now, you may not be ready to tackle the Win32 API directly. (Later, you'll see how easy this can be.) But, your boss is demanding that you provide her with an application that satisfies the Windows Logo requirements, so what do you do?

Fortunately, there are a small number of third-party products that allow you to play with the Registry. These also have some limitations, but are a *big* improvement on the Visual Basic functions. This section gives you a basic summary of the two products available. It's a sure bet that you'll see more products before too long, so keep that Web search engine actively scanning for more add-ons.

StorageTools

This product provides the ability to manipulate both the Registry and other OLE-structured storage. As the Registry is a small subset of the functionality it provides, it may be a little costly for just these calls. Given the reliability of other products by this company, you'll probably grow to depend on StorageTools.

Added Value Items   Besides the normal calls that allow you to create, edit, and delete values within the Registry, StorageTools provides some very useful properties in its control, and a large number of additional methods.

In the Registry control, you can set the root and key values for the Registry control and immediately get a count of the number of subkeys, and a list of their names and values. You can also get the default value for a given subkey, which is not possible from within the Visual Basic supplied calls.

This control also makes it easier to get and save different types of values. As you'll see later, storing or retrieving string and long (double word) values is fairly easy using Win32 calls; manipulating some of the other Registry data types is a lot harder from within Visual Basic.

StorageTools provides different methods to search for particular keys, subkeys, or values within a specified root section of the Registry. You can make this search perform matching against a full key name or value, or a partial match. You can also control whether case is used in matching.

The StorageTools Registry control also has better error messages and error handling. For simple manipulation of the Registry, using Win32 directly is still probably the best way to go. However, if you intend to develop some tools for working with the Registry, then StorageTools will likely be a good addition to your Visual Basic programming toolkit.

Desaware gives you a pretty reasonable help file. It's missing an example code, but they do give you a full-featured example application. They also have some sections in the help file that tell you some more about the Registry itself. Of course, as you're reading this book, you probably already know all the Registry-related information in this help file.

Using StorageTools   Given that you can use the extra methods in the Registry control to do some fairly powerful things, the next example enables the user to search for a particular key in the Registry and displays some information about it. Figure 20.4 shows the user interface for this application.

FIG. 20.4
The StorageTools
Example screen.

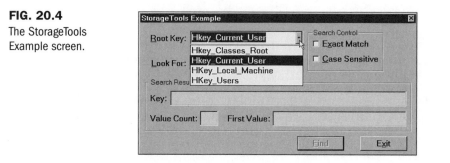

You can take direct advantage of some of the parameters able to be passed into the find functions provided by StorageTools. You can specify whether this is the entire key, and whether case should be used when matching.

After spending days designing the incredible user interface shown, the bulk of the work done in this code is extracted from the cmdFind_Click() routine.

```
If chkCaseSensitive = 1 Then bCase = True
If chkExactMatch = 1 Then bExact = True

'  Display an hourglass in case this takes a long time
frmSTTMain.MousePointer = 11
If txtFoundKey = "" Then
    bResult = rgCtl.FindFirstKey(txtLookFor.Text, _
                                 bCase, _
                                 bExact, _
                                 False)
Else
    bResult = rgCtl.FindNextKey()
End If

frmSTTMain.MousePointer = 0

If bResult Then
    '  Setup the current key so we get the full scoop
    '  on the key values
    rgCtl.CurrentKey = rgCtl.FindResultKey

    txtFoundKey.FontItalic = False
    txtFoundKey = rgCtl.FindResultKey
    txtValueCount = rgCtl.NumOfValues
    If rgCtl.NumOfValues > 0 Then
        txtFirstValue = _
            rgCtl.GetValueData(rgCtl.ValueNameArray(0), _
                               True)
    Else
        txtFirstValue = ""
    End If
Else
    txtFoundKey.FontItalic = True
    txtFoundKey = "Couldn't find " & txtLookFor.Text
```

```
        txtValueCount = ""
        txtFirstValue = ""
    End If
```

With very little extra work, you can decide whether to search on from the previous match, and you can get the data for a given value simply by setting the CurrentKey property for the Registry control.

The result of doing a search for a particular string is shown in Figure 20.5.

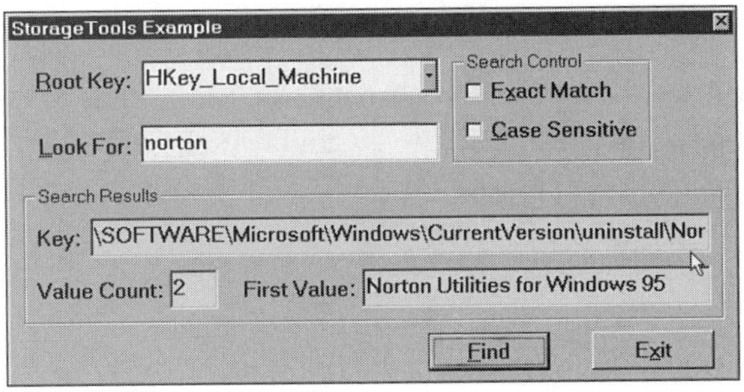

FIG. 20.5
StorageTools result with a case-insensitive search.

In this case, the Norton key displayed was about the sixth key containing the word *norton* under the HKEY_LOCAL_MACHINE root. Clicking the Find button multiple times allows you to get to the next one.

N O T E The entire source code for this example is included with the other examples for the book. Naturally, you'll need StorageTools to make it work. But even without a copy of StorageTools you can examine the code for its sheer beauty, or to decide whether the StorageTools Registry control will give you the kind of access to the Registry that you want. ▪

Missing Features   Currently, it appears that the StorageTools Registry control does not provide any means to use the Registry on another machine on the network. While it does make some allowances for differences between the various versions of Windows, it does not provide any facilities to allow for getting or setting security values for Registry entries.

Although this is an OCX, there's no documentation to show you how to use the Registry control from other languages such as Visual C++ or Access.

Price, Contact, and Other Details   Applications written using StorageTools can be freely distributed. When installed, you have the option of loading either a 16-bit or 32-bit version, or both. StorageTools comes with sample code for a Registry Browser. This is essentially a Visual Basic replacement for REGEDIT.

Part
IV
Ch
20

Assuming that you use only the Registry functions, and you're not producing a 16-bit version, you have to add only a total of three files to your product installation. These are dwReg32.ocx, msvcrt40.dll, and mfc40.dll. The total, uncompressed, size of these files is 1.27M.

> **N O T E** Depending on the other Visual Basic add-ons you have in your application, you may already be including the Microsoft DLLs. The size of the Desaware OCX itself is only 87Kb, which is a relatively small size penalty for what you get in return. ■

StorageTools is available directly from Desaware and other Visual Basic tools providers, and has a street price of about $115 at the time of this writing. Desaware is on the Web at **http://www.desaware.com/**, and can be contacted by e-mail at **74431.3534@compuserve.com.** They are located in Campbell, California at (408) 377-4770.

Wright Registry Control

With this control, there's good news and bad news. The good news is that a low-cost Visual Basic control is available and that it works. The bad news is that it's somewhat restrictive in terms of the features it provides; for most people this will not be an issue.

This product allows you to access more of the Registry than the standard Visual Basic calls, without actually having to learn how to deal with Win32. It has some additional features and is probably a good value for the money.

In the example in this section, you'll see how to look for all occurrences of a particular value name under the HKEY_CURRENT_USER section of the Registry and display the value contents. You can then edit some or all of these values and save the changes to the Registry. Figure 20.6 shows the example application window after performing a search.

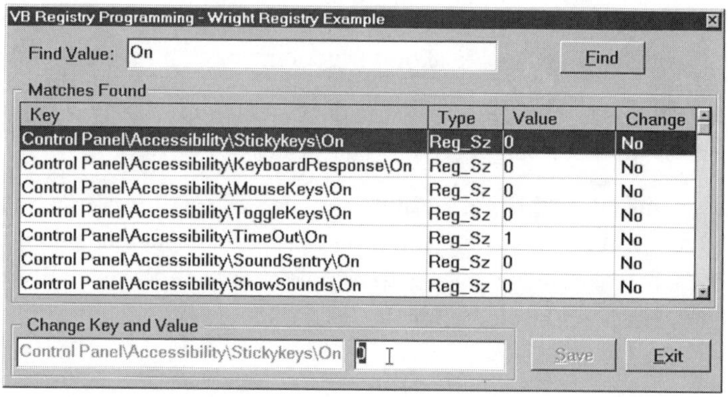

FIG. 20.6
The Wright Registry Control example application after finding all On values in HKEY_CURRENT_USER.

Type the name of the value you want to find, and click the Find button. All subkeys that contain the value are displayed, and you can then change particular ones and save the new values. Figure 20.7 shows what the window looks like after several values have been changed.

FIG. 20.7
The Wright Registry Control example application with two changed values.

Key	Type	Value	Change
Control Panel\Accessibility\Stickykeys\On	Reg_Sz	234	Yes
Control Panel\Accessibility\KeyboardResponse\On	Reg_Sz	0	No
Control Panel\Accessibility\MouseKeys\On	Reg_Sz	1023	Yes
Control Panel\Accessibility\ToggleKeys\On	Reg_Sz	0	No
Control Panel\Accessibility\TimeOut\On	Reg_Sz	1	No
Control Panel\Accessibility\SoundSentry\On	Reg_Sz	0	No
Control Panel\Accessibility\ShowSounds\On	Reg_Sz	0	No

The code uses recursion to look up all values contained within each subkey. In the Wright Registry control, you can get all keys and values under a given subkey name simply by assigning the subkey name. The keys and values are stored as collections, so your code can readily count how many of each there are under a subkey. The initial call into the recursive routine uses this approach to pass on the name of all subkeys that are on the current level in the Registry. This is shown in the following code sample:

```
If rgCtrl.Keys.Count > 0 Then
        '  Store the key names and recurse
        ReDim sKeyNames(rgCtrl.Keys.Count)
        For nCt1 = 1 To rgCtrl.Keys.Count
            sKeyNames(nCt1 - 1) = rgCtrl.Keys.Item(nCt1).Name
        Next nCt1

        Call FindValues(rgCtrl.Subkey, sKeyNames, rgCtrl.Keys.Count)
    End If
```

The Keys.Count value is automatically established for the Keys collection, as well as the name for all the keys, after you assign a Subkey string to the Registry Control. In the recursive call, FindValues(), you can see how one of the Wright functions, ValueExists(), is used to look for the value. This is shown in the following example:

```
If rgCtrl.ValueExists(txtFind.Text) Then
        grdMatches.Row = grdMatches.Rows - 1

        grdMatches.Col = COL_KEY
        grdMatches.Text = rgCtrl.Subkey & "\" & txtFind.Text
        AssignTypeValue (rgCtrl.Values(txtFind.Text).Type)
        grdMatches.Col = COL_VAL
```

Part
IV

Ch
20

```
                    grdMatches.Text = rgCtrl.Values(txtFind.Text).Value
                    grdMatches.Col = COL_CHANGED
                    grdMatches.Text = " No"

                    grdMatches.Rows = grdMatches.Rows + 1
        End If
```

After you know that the value is actually present in this subkey, you can use the name as a direct reference into the Values collection and get the type and value contents directly. The previous code stores these into the display grid. Note that the subkey name and value name are being cached into the grid. These are used later when updating the Registry contents.

The Wright Registry control makes it easy to change an existing value. In the example program, this is done in the code called when the user clicks the Save button. The relevant routine follows:

```
Sub UpdateRegVal(sFullName As String, sNewValue As String)
    Dim sSubKey As String, sValName As String, nSP As Integer

    For nSP = Len(sFullName) To 1 Step -1
        If Mid$(sFullName, nSP, 1) = "\" Then
            sSubKey = Left$(sFullName, nSP - 1)
            sValName = Right$(sFullName, Len(sFullName) - nSP)
            Exit For
        End If
    Next nSP

    rgCtrl.Subkey = sSubKey
    rgCtrl.Values(sValName).Value = sNewValue

End Sub
```

The code splits the name into a subkey and value name part. The subkey is loaded into the Subkey property of the Registry control, and the value is used to index into the Values collection and assign the new value specified by the user.

This example is somewhat limited, but could be extended to allow the user to rename a certain set of values, or even delete them. This code would be somewhat harder to implement, but using the Wright Registry would certainly make the Registry manipulation part of this fairly easy.

Missing Features   This product provides only a 32-bit version, as an OCX. This means that you should also be able to use it from within Visual C++, but there's no documentation provided to help you do this. Given what it provides you, continue using it within Visual Basic.

Using this control, you can access only four of the available root keys: HKEY_CLASSES_ROOT, HKEY_CURRENT_USER, HKEY_LOCAL_MACHINE, and HKEY_USERS. The control also only deals with a subset of possible Registry data types.

For the average user, this is probably more than enough for your typical kind of Registry manipulation.

This OCX does not provide integrated help, so pressing F1 while on a property or method for this control does not jump you into the related help topic. There appear to be some errors raised under certain conditions, but these are not documented in the provided help file.

You get the same feature set whether you're working on Windows 95 or Windows NT. Like StorageTools, there are no security-related features.

Price, Contact, and Other Details   The product can be downloaded from **http:// wrightfutures.com/download/wreg.zip**. At the time of this writing, this zip file is about 1.2M. This includes the help file and a sample application. Wright Futures provides only a 32-bit version of the product, best accessed from Visual Basic 4.0. The cost to register the product is $19.95, and this gets rid of that annoying reminder dialog box.

The only file you'll need to include with your application is WREG.OCX. This is about 65M, so it won't add much to your installation disk set.

The company that makes the Wright Registry control is Wright Futures, Inc. You can get more information about the company at **http://wrightfutures.com/**. You can also contact them by e-mail at **lpwright@aol.com** or on CompuServe at **74001,2244**.

Using Win32 Calls Directly from Visual Basic

Finally, the moment you've been waiting for. A chance to do some real coding using the Win32 calls to the Registry directly. If you've heard that you need to be an Einstein to do this, and take several months of C and Assembly language coding classes, relax. The next example shows you all that you need to know.

> **T I P** Coding with Win32 can get very addictive. If you *really* get into it, a great resource is the book *Visual Basic Programmer's Guide to the Win32 API.* This is a big and expensive book, so don't buy it unless you have an expense account and a well-constructed book shelf.

The next example gives you some of the features found in the Tweak UI application and shows you how to use many of the essential Registry calls from within Visual Basic. The biggest hurdle to successfully making calls to the Win32 library from within Visual Basic is correctly defining the functions and procedures you want to use. You may also have to define certain structures as parameters to and from these calls.

Part
IV

Ch
20

Given the sheer number of calls in Win32, this can be a huge amount of work. Microsoft does offer some help, providing you files in the WinAPI directory (see Table 20.1) under your Microsoft Visual Basic installation directory.

Table 20.1   Microsoft-Provided WinAPI Definition Files

File Name	Contents
WIN31API.TXT	Constants, declarations, and data types for Win16
WIN32API.TXT	Constants, declarations, and data types for Win32
WINMMSYS.TXT	Constants, declarations, and data types for Win 3.1 multimedia API calls

N O T E   The WIN32API.TXT file contains much useful information about the declarations and data types for Win32. This file is patched together from a number of sources, including WINNT.H, many of which are included with Visual C++. The comments may give you more insight into the meaning of certain important constants. ■

Ultimately, you want all of the Registry-related functions contained within WIN32API.TXT. Eventually, you may also include definitions for other functions. In the example code I've written, the ExitWindowsEx function is used if I need to restart Windows 95.

T I P   You can't just rename the WIN32API.TXT file into a Visual Basic .BAS module. Use the System Definitions.BAS file included with the examples for this book; it's a lot smaller (around 25Kb versus over 600Kb for the WIN32API.TXT file), and it works.

Extracting Information from Definition Files

To help you get parts of a large definition file out into more useful chunks, Microsoft provides a Text API Viewer application called APILOD32 with the Professional Edition of Visual Basic. This is also contained in the WINAPI subdirectory under your Visual Basic installation directory. There is some help for this application in the file APILOD.TXT.

This program scans the file selected and presents a list box with items divided into API type categories: Constants, Declares, and Types (see Figure 20.8).

You can add items into the Selected Items list box by double-clicking them in the Available Items list box. You can remove them from the Selected Items box by double-clicking them there.

After you've selected a subset of the definitions you're interested in, you can click the Copy button. This places the items into the Clipboard. You can then paste them from there into your Visual Basic module.

In the example shown, the following lines are inserted into the file. They've been broken down with Visual Basic continuation markers so that they show properly in the book.

```
Declare Function RegCloseKey Lib "advapi32.dll" _
    Alias "RegCloseKey" (ByVal hKey As Long) As Long
Declare Function RegCreateKey Lib "advapi32.dll" _
    Alias "RegCreateKeyA" (ByVal hKey As Long, _
    ByVal lpSubKey As String, phkResult As Long) As Long
Declare Function ExitWindowsEx Lib "user32" _
    Alias "ExitWindowsEx" (ByVal uFlags As Long, _
    ByVal dwReserved As Long) As Long
Type SECURITY_DESCRIPTOR
        Revision As Byte
        Sbz1 As Byte
        Control As Long
        Owner As Long
        Group As Long
        Sacl As ACL
        Dacl As ACL
End Type
Public Const REG_CREATED_NEW_KEY = &H1    ' New Registry Key created
Public Const REG_DWORD_BIG_ENDIAN = 5     ' 32-bit number
```

As you can see, most comments present in the input file are lost in the process. This is still a useful way to get small parts out of the WIN32API.TXT file.

If you're going to be doing this often, convert the input file into a Jet database file. APILod32 will prompt you to do this if you change the API type setting more than a few times.

FIG. 20.8
The list box lists available items.

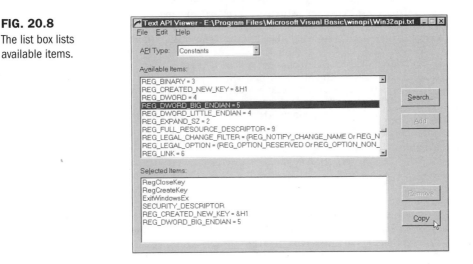

Opening the Registry and Reading Values

When you start the Win32 example, the Programming the Registry dialog box appears, as shown in Figure 20.9.

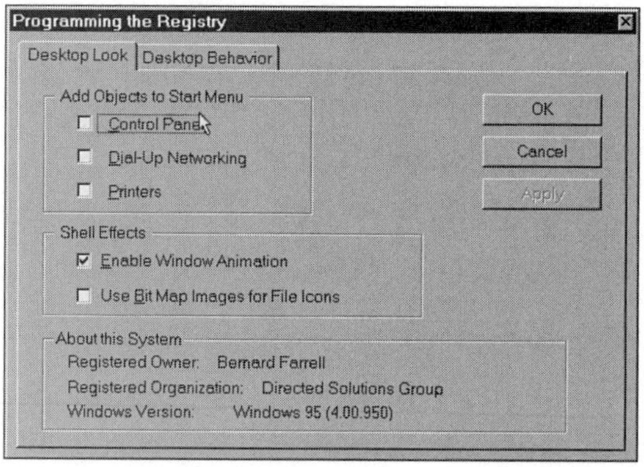

FIG. 20.9
Win32 Programming
the Registry main
screen on startup.

Immediately, you can see the result of getting certain values from the Registry. These are
displayed in the About This System frame at the bottom of the dialog box. You could write
the code to get the first of these values like this:

```
Dim hKeyUserHandle As Long, lResult As Long
Dim lValueType As Long, lNumChars As Long, sValue As String

lResult = RegOpenKeyEx(HKEY_LOCAL_MACHINE, _
               "Software\Microsoft\Windows\CurrentVersion", _
               0, KEY_READ, hKeyUserHandle)
If lResult = ERROR_SUCCESS Then
    ' First get the length of the string
    lResult = RegQueryValueExNULL(hKeyUserHandle, _
                      "RegisteredOwner", _
                      0&, lValueType, 0&, lNumChars)

    ' Then the string contents themselves
    If lResult = ERROR_SUCCESS Then
        ' Make a string big enough to hold the entire value
        sValue = String(lNumChars, 0)
        lResult = RegQueryValueExString(hKeyUserHandle, _
                          "RegisteredOwner", _
                          0&, lValueType, sValue, lNumChars)
    Else
        ' Some error, let the user know...
    End If
End If

If Len(sValue) > 0 Then
    ' Strip the null character from the end of the string
    sValue = Left(sValue, Len(sValue) - 1)
End If

' Remember to always close the key
lResult = RegCloseKey(hKeyUserHandle)
```

You can wrap this call up into a function—GetRegistryString—that is used throughout your code. This enables you to add more error handling in the Registry access. Even here, you've not done enough, but you can always go back and add more in the function.

This piece of code shows how to access the RegOpenKeyEx, RegQueryValueEx, and RegCloseKey calls. It's very important to remember to close the Registry key as soon as you're finished with it. If your program crashes while it's being tested and the key is left open, you may have problems with your Registry.

TIP You can see that there are two different versions of the RegQueryValueEx call. You use one to get general information such as a value type and value length from the Registry.

The other one gets you the contents of a string. This is defined as:

```
Declare Function RegQueryValueExString& Lib "advapi32.dll" _
    Alias "RegQueryValueExA" _
        (ByVal hkey As Long, _
         ByVal lpszValueName As String, _
         ByVal lpdwRes As Long, _
         lpdwType As Long, _
         ByVal lpDataBuff As String, _
         lpDataSize As Long)
```

The ByVal in front of the lpDataBuff parameter makes Visual Basic do all the work to convert the string it gets back from Win32—which is in C format, with an ASCIZ null character terminator—into a format that it can handle.

By comparing the parameters in one of the Registry calls, you can see that parameters defined as pointers need no work in Visual Basic. Normally, Visual Basic passes parameters into function calls by reference. The caller gets the address of the parameter value and decodes this to get the value itself.

If the routine being called expects to get the actual value—call by value—then you must have the ByVal keyword in front of the parameter when you declare it for Visual Basic.

The string that follows the Lib keyword tells Visual Basic what DLL contains the routine. If the DLL is located in the Windows System directory, then a name like "advapi32.dll" is enough. Otherwise, you would have to give the fully qualified name. I don't recommend this because it makes it very hard to move your application around.

NOTE You cannot change the Lib location at runtime. It's much easier if you use a simple file name and make sure that any DLLs you need are in the Windows System area. ▪

All of the Registry calls are contained in AdvAPI32.DLL, which is already loaded in the Windows System directory, so you don't have to worry about this file not being found.

Part
IV

Ch
20

The Alias keyword allows you to use any name you want within your Visual Basic program, and tells it what routine to actually call in the DLL. This is what you use to have more than one RegQueryValueEx... routine.

Changing the Registry

If you click any of the check boxes on the first property sheet, the Apply button, shown earlier in Figure 20.9, is enabled. When you've made all the changes you want, you can click the Apply button and have the changes written to the Registry. The following routine does all the work of writing values into a Registry string. The example shows how to do this with other value types.

```
Function SetRegistryString(hRootKey As Long, _
                           sKeyName As String, _
                           sValueName As String, _
                           sValueContents As String) _
                       As Integer
    Dim lResult As Long, hNewKey As Long

    lResult = RegOpenKeyEx(hRootKey, sKeyName, 0&, _
                           KEY_ALL_ACCESS, hNewKey)
    If lResult = ERROR_SUCCESS Then
        lResult = RegSetValueExString&(hNewKey, sValueName, _
                                       0, REG_SZ,
                                       sValueContents, _
                                       Len(sValueContents)+1)

        lResult = RegCloseKey(hNewKey)
    Else
        Dim sMessage As String, sTitle As String
        Dim nStyle As Integer, nResponse As Integer

        '  Display an appropriate error
        sMessage = "Error " & lResult & _
                   " when attempting to create " & sKeyName & _
                   " in Key Handle " & hRootKey

        nStyle = vbOKOnly + vbExclamation
        sTitle = "SetRegistryString Error"

        nResponse = MsgBox(sMessage, nStyle, sTitle)
    End If

    SetRegistryString = lResult
End Function ' SetRegistryString
```

TIP The Len() function in Visual Basic gives you the number of characters in a string. The Registry RegSetValueEx call will end up writing the contents of the string and a ASCIZ null character terminator at the end, so you must make sure to pass Len(StringVal)+1 in as the length parameter.

Again, the `RegSetValueEx` call is aliased to `RegSetValueExString`, so that Visual Basic converts the string into a C string type.

With this routine, it's assumed that the key already exists. If you need a more robust routine, you may want to replace the `RegOpenKeyEx` call with one to `RegCreateKeyEx`. `RegCreateKeyEx` will create a key only if one does not already exist.

Restarting Windows

In the example application, certain Registry changes don't take effect unless you restart Windows. You can do this by using the `ExitWindowsEx` routine provided in Win32. If you click the Apply button after making one of these changes, the program tells you that you need to restart windows for the changes to take effect, and asks if you want to do this (see Figure 20.10).

FIG. 20.10
Confirming that you want to restart Windows.

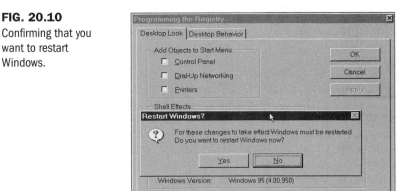

If you click the Yes button, then the following Visual Basic code actually does the work:

```
Dim sMessage As String, sTitle As String
Dim nStyle As Integer, nResponse As Integer

sMessage = "For these changes to take effect"
sMessage = sMessage & " Windows must be restarted."
sMessage = sMessage & Chr$(10)
sMessage = sMessage & "Do you want to restart Windows now?"

nStyle = vbYesNo + vbQuestion + vbDefaultButton2

sTitle = "Restart Windows?"

nResponse = MsgBox(sMessage, nStyle, sTitle)
If nResponse = vbYes Then
    nStatus = ExitWindowsEx(EWX_LOGOFF, 0&)
End If
```

Part
IV

Ch
20

Doing a logoff forces the Windows shell to restart, and is much quicker than rebooting the system.

Getting a Set of Key Values

It is easy to use the RegEnumValue call to get a set of values contained within a single Registry subkey. The second page provides you with a means to change the messages that are displayed as Tip of the Day Messages (see Figure 20.11) when you restart Windows. The combination of a RegEnumValue call with a List Box control gives you a reasonably intuitive interface with which to change values.

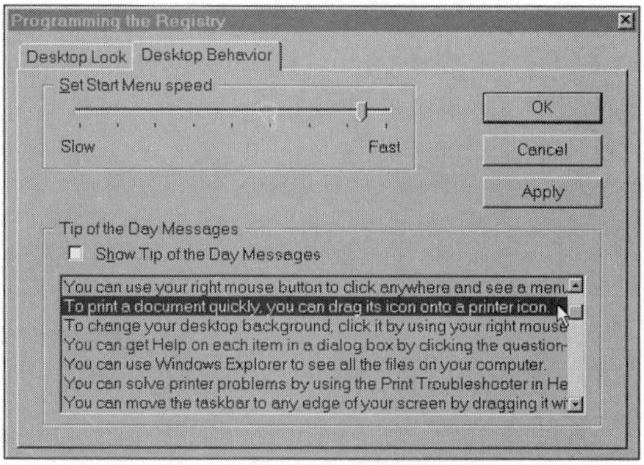

FIG. 20.11

Showing the Tip of the Day Messages.

In this case, the call to RegEnumValue wasn't encapsulated into a function because dealing with possibly different value types would make the interface fairly complex. You load the List Box using the following code:

```
'   Now open the tips value key and enumerate
'   all of the sub keys until we've got the text
'   of the system tips.
'   Notice how the security access includes
'   KEY_ENUMERATE_SUB_KEYS, so I can walk
'   the subkey values.
lResult = RegOpenKeyEx(HKEY_LOCAL_MACHINE, TIPS_VALUES_KEY, _
                        0, KEY_ALL_ACCESS, hKeyUserHandle)
If lResult = ERROR_SUCCESS Then
    For nStringCt = 0 To MAX_NUMBER_TIPS - 1
        asTipKeys(nStringCt) = String(TIPS_VALUES_MAX_LENGTH, 0)
        asTipValues(nStringCt) = _
                        String(TIPS_VALUES_MAX_LENGTH, 0)
        abTipChanged(nStringCt) = False

        '   Note the use of ByVal in the asTipValues()
        '   parameter to make sure that the VB string
        '   is correctly converted.
        lNumChars = TIPS_VALUES_MAX_LENGTH
```

```
            lResult = RegEnumValue(hKeyUserHandle, nStringCt, _
                          asTipKeys(nStringCt), _
                          lNumChars, _
                          0&, 0&, _
                          ByVal asTipValues(nStringCt), _
                          lNumChars)

        If lResult = ERROR_SUCCESS Then
            asTipKeys(nStringCt) = _
                StripNulls(asTipKeys(nStringCt))
            asTipValues(nStringCt) = _
                StripNulls(asTipValues(nStringCt))
        Else
            ' Presumably, no more keys
            asTipKeys(nStringCt) = ""
            asTipValues(nStringCt) = ""
        End If

    Next nStringCt

End If
```

Here you've created three associated arrays—one holds the keys and one holds the corresponding value for each key. The last array contains a Boolean set if the value is changed by the user. These arrays are used directly to load the List Box so you can see what Tip of the Day Messages are on your system and change them to something more useful.

If you double-click a line in this list box, a dialog box appears that enables you to type in a new message to replace the Tip message at that value. Typing a new Tip in the Change To text box and clicking OK causes the change to be made in the list box. The changes aren't written back to the Registry until you click the Apply button.

```
Dim nStringCt As Integer, lResult As Long

For nStringCt = 0 To MAX_NUMBER_TIPS - 1
    If asTipValues(nStringCt) = "" Then
        ' No more tips left, so exit
        Exit For
    End If

    If abTipChanged(nStringCt) Then
        lResult = SetRegistryString(TIPS_VALUES_ROOT, _
                        TIPS_VALUES_KEY, _
                        asTipKeys(nStringCt), _
                        asTipValues(nStringCt))

        If lResult <> ERROR_SUCCESS Then
            ' Add some error handling here
        End If

        abTipChanged(nStringCt) = False
    End If
Next nStringCt
```

Part
IV

Ch
20

If you examine the complete set of source code, you will be able to deal with almost anything that the Registry can present to your Visual Basic application. In the examples, there isn't any comprehensive error checking code. This is important for a production application and requires that you have a good knowledge of error handlers in Visual Basic.

And remember, the thing that will help you the most is remembering to save your source code and back up your Registry before tackling anything too ambitious.

Cleaning Up After Yourself

Microsoft provides an application called RegClean with the Visual Basic 4.0 Professional and Enterprise editions. This is contained in the PSS directory of your installation CD. The current version is RegClean 3.0, and the self-extracting version can also be found on the Microsoft FTP site (**ftp.microsoft.com**) in Softlib/Mslfiles/REGCLN.EXE.

When you first start RegClean, it performs a detailed scan of the Registry looking for errors. After this, you'll see the OLE Automation Correction Wizard screen (see Figure 20.12).

If you decide that you really want to get specific, you can click on the Options button and then deal with a host of ways to specify tuning. You'll get a dialog box, one page of which looks like Figure 20.13.

You can freely distribute this utility with your applications. So be good and share it with your friends.

FIG. 20.12
RegClean OLE
Automation Correction
Wizard Screen.

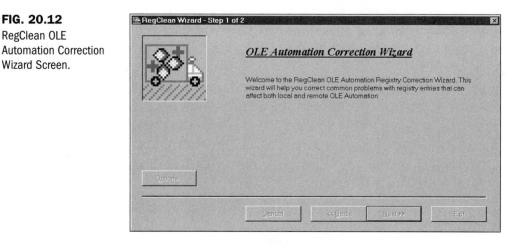

FIG. 20.13
The RegClean
Correction Options
screen, with the
Typelibs tab activated.

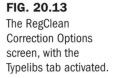

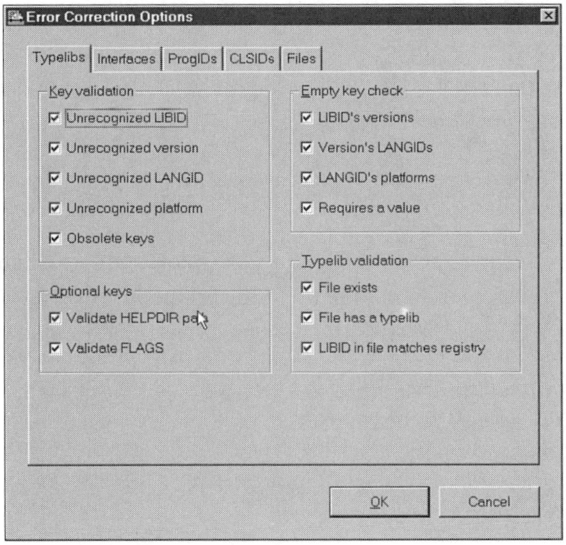

What's Missing

Probably the hardest call to deal with from within Visual Basic is the
`RegistryNotifyChangeKeyValue`. This requires some tricky Visual Basic coding
involving events and timers that are beyond the scope of this book.

N O T E   One suggested approach for dealing with Registry notifications is given in the article
"Hacking the Windows Registry" by Keith Pleas in the March 1996 issue of *Visual
Basic Programmers Journal*. ▦

More Example Visual Basic Code

There are two other examples of Visual Basic code that work with the Registry. In both
cases, the source is provided so you get an opportunity to learn more about getting at the
Registry from Visual Basic.

WinMag Tattler   This code is from an article in the May 1996 issue of *Windows Magazine*.
You can get it on the Net at the Windows site. The application itself simply gets some
values from a few Registry locations and displays them in a dialog box. Figure 20.14
shows the Tattler dialog box when the program is run on my system.

Part
IV

Ch
20

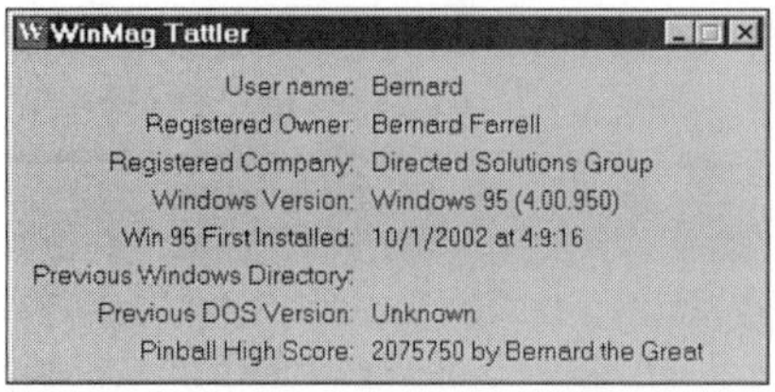

FIG. 20.14

The Tattler dialog box.

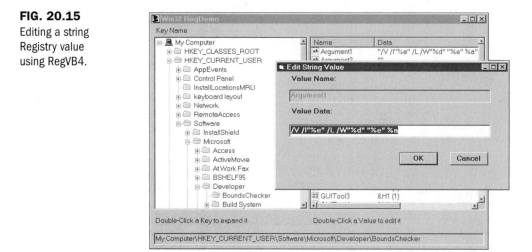

RegVB4   This code is almost a full-featured replacement for REGEDIT. It was written by Don Bradner and has been placed in the public domain. He is careful to point out that it's not meant to be a replacement for the Microsoft-provided Registry editors. However, it works rather well.

Figure 20.15 shows RegVB4 being used to edit a value for an existing Registry entry.

FIG. 20.15

Editing a string Registry value using RegVB4.

The version as distributed only allows editing of REG_SZ and REG_DWORD entries. It can be found on the Web at: **http://www.redshift.com/~arcatpet/vb.html**. This Zip file is about 28K, so it doesn't take long to download. ●

Appendixes

The Registry API

by Jerry Honeycutt

Program the Registry Using the API

Can't remember all those functions you learned in Chapters 17 through 19? Use this reference as a quick guide.

The Registry API is fully documented in the Win32 SDK and in the Microsoft Developer Network. As well, you learned how to use these functions in Chapters 17 through 19. This handy reference section is a bit more concise. It serves as a quick reminder of how to call each Registry function. Go ahead—rip these pages out of the book and keep them by your computer while you're hacking on the Registry. ■

You find a section for each Registry function in this chapter. Each section contains the following information:

> Summary
>
> C language function prototype
>
> Description of each parameter
>
> Description of the function's return value
>
> Overview of what the function does

RegCloseKey

RegCloseKey releases the handle of an open key.

```
LONG RegCloseKey( HKEY hKey )
```

Parameters

Parameter	Description
hKey	Handle of the open key to close

Return Values

Value	Description
ERROR_SUCCESS	RegCloseKey was successful
error value	RegCloseKey failed

Description

You can't count on RegCloseKey to immediately write your changes to the Registry. It could take several seconds before Windows flushes the cache. If you need to make sure your changes are written to the Registry immediately, use RegFlushKey.

CAUTION

Don't use hKey after you close it; it won't be valid.

RegConnectRegistry

RegConnectRegistry connects to a predefined key on another computer.

```
LONG RegConnectRegistry( LPTSTR lpMachineName, HKEY hKey, PHKEY phkResult )
```

Parameters

Parameter	Description
lpMachineName	Address of the string containing the name of the remote computer (for example "\\Computer")
hKey	Predefined handle: HKEY_LOCAL_MACHINE HKEY_USERS
phkResult	Address of buffer to receive the handle

Return Values

Value	Description
ERROR_SUCCESS	Successful
error value	Failed

Description

Use RegCloseKey to close a handle returned by RegConnectRegistry.

RegCreateKey

RegCreateKey creates a key or opens an existing key. Win32 programs should use RegCreateKeyEx, instead.

```
LONG RegCreateKey( HKEY hKey, LPCTSTR lpSubKey, PHKEY phkResult )
```

Parameters

Parameter	Description
hKey	Handle of an open key or one of the following reserved handles: HKEY_CLASSES_ROOT HKEY_CURRENT_USER HKEY_LOCAL_MACHINE HKEY_USERS
lpSubKey	Address of the string containing the subkey's name to create under hKey
phkResult	Address of the buffer for the new handle

Return Values

Value	Description
ERROR_SUCCESS	Successful
error value	Failed

Description

You can use RegCreateKey to create subkeys several levels deep in the hierarchy. You can create a new key under HKEY_LOCAL_MACHINE called **new1\new2\new3**, for example.

You must open the key identified by hKey with KEY_CREATE_SUB_KEY access.

If the string that lpSubKey points to is empty, RegCreateKey opens and returns the key pointed to by hKey.

RegCreateKeyEx

RegCreateKeyEx creates a key or opens an existing key.

```
LONG RegCreateKeyEx( HKEY hKey, LPCTSTR lpSubKey, DWORD Reserved, LPTSTR
lpClass, DWORD dwOptions, REGSAM samDesired, LPSECURITY_ATTRIBUTES
lpSecurity Attributes, PHKEY phkResult, LPWORD lpdwDisposition )
```

Parameters

Parameter	Description
hKey	Handle of an open key or one of the following reserved handles: HKEY_CLASSES_ROOT HKEY_CURRENT_USER HKEY_LOCAL_MACHINE HKEY_USERS
lpSubKey	Address of the string containing the subkey's name to create under hKey
Reserved	Must be zero
lpClass	Address of string that specifies the class name of this key
dwOptions	Options for this key (see Table A.1)
samDesired	Security for this key (see Table A.2)
lpSecurityAttributes	Address of SECURITY_ATTRIBUTES
phkResult	Address of the buffer for the new handle
lpdwDisposition	Address of buffer to receive disposition value (see Table A.3)

Return Values

Value	Description
ERROR_SUCCESS	Successful
error value	Failed

Description

You can use RegCreateKeyEx to create subkeys several levels deep in the hierarchy. You can create a new key under HKEY_LOCAL_MACHINE called **\new1\new2\new3**, for example.

You must open the key identified by hKey with KEY_CREATE_SUB_KEY access.

If the string that *lpSubKey* points to is empty, *RegCreateKey* opens and returns the key pointed to by *hKey*.

Table A.1 describes the possible values for *dwOptions*.

Table A.1   Values for *dwOptions*

Value	Description
REG_OPTION_VOLATILE	This is ignored in Windows 95. In Windows NT, this value indicates that the contents of this key will not be written to disk.
REG_OPTION_NON_VOLATILE	The contents of this key will be written to disk.

Table A.2 describes the possible values for *samDesired*.

Table A.2   Values for *samDesired*

Value	Description
KEY_ALL_ACCESS	Combination of KEY_QUERY_VALUE, KEY_ENUMERATE_SUB_KEYS, KEY_NOTIFY, KEY_CREATE_SUB_KEY, KEY_CREATE_LINK, and KEY_SET_VALUE access
KEY_CREATE_LINK	Permission to create symbolic link
KEY_CREATE_SUB_KEY	Permission to create subkeys
KEY_ENUMERATE_SUB_KEYS	Permission to enumerate subkeys
KEY_EXECUTE	Permission to read
KEY_NOTIFY	Permission for change notification
KEY_QUERY_VALUE	Permission to query subkeys
KEY_READ	Combination of KEY_QUERY_VALUE, KEY_ENUMERATE_SUB_KEYS, and KEY_NOTIFY
KEY_SET_VALUE	Permission to set data
KEY_WRITE	Combination of KEY_SET_VALUE and KEY_CREATE_SUB_KEY

Table A.3 describes the possible values for *lpdwDisposition*.

Table A.3 Values for *lpdwDisposition*	
Value	**Description**
REG_CREATED_NEW_KEY	New key was created
REG_OPENED_EXISTING_KEY	Key existed and was opened

RegDeleteKey

RegDeleteKey deletes a key.

```
LONG RegDeleteKey( HKEY hKey, LPCTSTR lpSubKey )
```

Parameters

Parameter	**Description**
hKey	Handle of an open key or one of the following reserved handles: HKEY_CLASSES_ROOT HKEY_CURRENT_USER HKEY_LOCAL_MACHINE HKEY_USERS
lpSubKey	Address of the string containing the subkey's name to delete

Return Values

Value	**Description**
ERROR_SUCCESS	Successful
error value	Failed

Description

RegDeleteKey removes the given key from the Registry and all of its value entries. Note that this function can't remove a key that has subkeys. The key must be opened with RegCreateKeyEx or RegOpenKeyEx.

RegDeleteValue

RegDeleteValue removes a value entry from the given key.

LONG RegDeleteValue(HKEY *hKey*, LPCTSTR *lpValueName*)

Parameters

Parameter	Description
hKey	Handle of an open key or one of the following reserved handles: HKEY_CLASSES_ROOT HKEY_CURRENT_USER HKEY_LOCAL_MACHINE HKEY_USERS
lpSubKey	Address of the string containing the value entry's name

Return Values

Value	Description
ERROR_SUCCESS	Successful
error value	Failed

Description

The key identified by *hKey* must be opened with HKEY_SET_VALUE access.

RegEnumKey

RegEnumKey enumerates the subkeys of an open key. It returns the name of a subkey each time you call it. Win32 programs should use RegEnumKeyEx instead.

LONG RegEnumKey(HKEY *hKey*, DOWRD *dwIndex*, LPTSTR lpName, DOWRD cbName)

Parameters

Parameter	Description
hKey	Handle of an open key or one of the following reserved handles:
	HKEY_CLASSES_ROOT
	HKEY_CURRENT_USER
	HKEY_LOCAL_MACHINE
	HKEY_USERS
dwIndex	Index of the subkey to return (0 based)
lpName	Buffer to hold the name of the subkey
cbName	Size of the buffer to hold the subkey name

Return Values

Value	Description
ERROR_SUCCESS	Successful
ERROR_NO_MORE_ITEMS	No subkeys remaining
error value	Failed

Description

The first time you call RegEnumKey, *dwIndex* should be 0. Then increment *dwIndex* with each successive call until RegEnumKey returns ERROR_NO_MORE_ITEMS.

The key identified by *hKey* must be opened with KEY_ENUMERATE_SUB_KEYS access. You must also use the RegCreateKeyEx or RegOpenKeyEx functions.

Note that the maximum buffer size required for *lpName* is MAX_PATH + 1.

> **CAUTION**
>
> While you're enumerating subkeys, don't call other Registry functions that might cause the order of the subkeys to change.

RegEnumKeyEx

RegEnumKeyEx enumerates the subkeys of an open key. It returns the name of a subkey each time you call it.

```
LONG RegEnumKeyEx( HKEY hKey, DOWRD dwIndex, LPTSTR lpName, LPDOWRD
lpcbName, LPDWORD lpReserved, LPTSTR lpClass, LPDWORD lpcbClass, PFILETIME
lpftLastWriteTime )
```

Parameters

Parameter	Description
hKey	Handle of an open key or one of the following reserved handles: HKEY_CLASSES_ROOT HKEY_CURRENT_USER HKEY_LOCAL_MACHINE HKEY_USERS
dwIndex	Index of the subkey to return (0 based)
lpName	Buffer to hold the name of the subkey
lpcbName	Buffer to hold the size of the subkey name
lpReserved	Must be NULL
lpClass	Buffer to hold the class of the subkey
lpcbClass	Buffer to hold the size of the class name
lpftLastWriteTime	Last time the subkey was written to

Return Values

Value	Description
ERROR_SUCCESS	Successful
ERROR_NO_MORE_ITEMS	No subkeys remaining
error value	Failed

Description

The first time you call RegEnumKeyEx, dwIndex should be 0. Then increment dwIndex with each successive call until RegEnumKey returns ERROR_NO_MORE_ITEMS.

The key identified by *hKey* must be opened with KEY_ENUMERATE_SUB_KEYS access. You must also use the RegCreateKeyEx or RegOpenKeyEx functions.

Note that the maximum buffer size required for *lpName* is MAX_PATH + 1.

> **CAUTION**
> While you're enumerating subkeys, don't call other Registry functions that might cause the order of the subkeys to change.

RegEnumValue

RegEnumValue enumerates the value entries for a registry key.

```
LONG RegEnumValue( HKEY hKey, DWORD dwIndex, LPTSTR lpValueName,
LPDWORD lpcbValueName, LPDWORD lpReserved, LPDWORD lpType, LPBYTE lpData,
LPDWORD lpcbData )
```

Parameters

Parameter	Description
hKey	Handle of an open key or one of the following reserved handles: HKEY_CLASSES_ROOT HKEY_CURRENT_USER HKEY_LOCAL_MACHINE HKEY_USERS
dwIndex	Index of the value entry (0 based)
lpValueName	Buffer to hold the name of the value entry
lpcbValueName	Buffer to hold the size of the name
lpReserved	Must be 0
lpType	Buffer to receive the value entry's type (see Table A.4)
lpData	Buffer to hold the data for the value entry
lpcbData	Size of the buffer to hold the data

Return Values

Value	Description
ERROR_SUCCESS	Successful
ERROR_NO_MORE_ITEMS	No subkeys remaining
error value	Failed

Description

The first time you call RegEnumValue, *dwIndex* should be 0. Then increment *dwIndex* with each successive call until RegEnumValue returns ERROR_NO_MORE_ITEMS.

The key identified by *hKey* must be opened with KEY_QUERY_VALUE access. You must also use the RegCreateKeyEx or RegOpenKeyEx functions.

To determine the maximum size of the buffer for the name and data, use RegQueryInfoKey.

> **CAUTION**
>
> While you're enumerating value entries, don't call other Registry functions that might cause the order of the value entries to change.

Table A.4 describes the possible values for *lpType*.

Table A.4   Values for *lpType*

Value	Description
REG_BINARY	Binary data
REG_DWORD	32-bit number
REG_DWORD_LITTLE_ENDIAN	32-bit number in little-endian form
REG_DWORD_BIG_ENDIAN	32-bit number in big-endian form
REG_EXPAND_SZ	Null-terminated string the contains a reference to an environment variable
REG_LINK	Unicode symbolic link
REG_MULTI_SZ	Array of null-terminated strings
REG_NONE	No data type specified
REG_RESOURCE_LIST	Device-driver resource list
REG_SZ	Null-terminated string

RegFlushKey

RegFlushKey writes all of your changes to the Registry.

```
LONG RegFlushKey( HKEY hKey )
```

Parameters

Parameter	Description
hKey	Handle of an open key or one of the following reserved handles: HKEY_CLASSES_ROOT HKEY_CURRENT_USER HKEY_LOCAL_MACHINE HKEY_USERS

Return Values

Value	Description
ERROR_SUCCESS	Successful
error value	Failed

Description

It's generally not necessary to call RegFlushKey, as Windows will flush the Registry to disk automatically.

> **CAUTION**
> Calling RegFlushKey too often can have a significant impact on your program's performance.

RegGetKeySecurity

RegGetKeySecurity returns a copy of the security descriptor for an open Registry key.

```
LONG RegGetKeySecurity( HKEY hKey, SECURITY_INFORMATION SecurityInformation,
PSECURITY_DESCRIPTOR pSecurityDescriptor, LPDWORD lpcbSecurityDescriptor )
```

Parameters

Parameter	Description
hKey	Handle of an open key
SecurityInformation	Indicates the requested security information
pSecurityDescriptor	Address of buffer to receive the security descriptor
lpcbSecurityDescriptor	Address of variable to receive the size of the security descriptor

Return Values

Value	Description
ERROR_SUCCESS	Successful
ERROR_INSUFFICIENT_BUFFER	Buffer is too small
error value	Failed

Description

If the size of buffer specified in *pSecurityDescriptor* is too small, this function returns ERROR_INSUFFICIENT_BUFFER and stores the number of bytes required in *lpcbSecurityDescriptor*.

The calling process must have READ_CONTROL (KEY_READ, KEY_WRITE, KEY_EXECUTE) access or be the owner of the key. The calling process must also have the SE_SECURITY_NAME privilege to read the system access-control list.

RegLoadKey

RegLoadKey imports the Registry information contained in a hive. If you're not sure about hives, see Chapter 2, "Inside the Windows Registry."

```
LONG RegLoadKey( HKEY hKey, LPCTSTR lpSubKey, LPCTSTR lpFile )
```

Parameters

Parameter	Description
hKey	Handle created by RegConnectRegistry, or a pre-defined handle: HKEY_LOCAL_MACHINE HKEY_USERS

lpSubKey	Address of string that contains the name of the key to create under *hKey*
lpFile	Address of string that contains the name of the file containing the hive

Return Values

Value	Description
ERROR_SUCCESS	Successful
error value	Failed

Description

The file containing the hive must have been created by RegSaveKey. The calling process must have the SE_RESTORE_NAME privilege.

RegNotifyChangeKeyValue

RegNotifyChangeKeyValue indicates when a key or any of its subkeys have changed.

```
LONG RegNotifyChangeKeyValue( HKEY hKey, BOOL bWatchSubtree, DWORD
dwNotifyFilter, HANDLE hEvent, BOOL fAsynchronous )
```

Parameters

Parameter	Description
hKey	Handle of an open key or one of the following reserved handles: HKEY_CLASSES_ROOT HKEY_CURRENT_USER HKEY_LOCAL_MACHINE HKEY_USERS
bWatchSubTree	Reports changes to subkeys if TRUE, otherwise only reports changes to the key

dwNotifyFilter	Specifies the flags that control what should be reported: REG_NOTIFY_CHANGE_ANEM REG_NOTIFY_CHANAGE_ATTRIBUTES REG_NOTIFY_CHANGE_LAST_SET REG_NOTIFY_CHANGE_SECURITY
hEvent	Identifies the event to raise if *fAsynchronous* is TRUE
fAsynchronous	Changes are reported by signaling *hEvent* if TRUE, otherwise RegNotifyChangeKeyValue doesn't return until a change is made

Return Values

Value	Description
ERROR_SUCCESS	Successful
ERROR_INVALID_HANDLE	Key is on remote computer
error value	Failed

Description

RegNotifyChangeKeyValue doesn't work with handles to keys on remote computers.

RegOpenKey

RegOpenKey opens an existing key. Win32 programs should use RegOpenKeyEx, instead.

LONG RegOpenKey(HKEY *hKey*, LPCTSTR *lpSubKey*, PHKEY *phkResult*)

Parameters

Parameter	Description
hKey	Handle of an open key or one of the following reserved handles: HKEY_CLASSES_ROOT HKEY_CURRENT_USER HKEY_LOCAL_MACHINE HKEY_USERS

lpSubKey	Address of the string containing the subkey's name to open under *hKey*
phkResult	Address of the buffer for the new handle

Return Values

Value	Description
ERROR_SUCCESS	Successful
error value	Failed

Description

RegOpenKey doesn't create the given key if it doesn't exist.

If the string that *lpSubKey* points to is empty, RegCreateKey opens and returns the key pointed to by *hKey*.

RegOpenKeyEx

RegOpenKeyEx opens the given key.

```
LONG RegOpenKeyEx( HKEY hKey, LPCTSTR lpSubKey, DWORD ulOptions, REGSAM
samDesired, PHKEY phkResult )
```

Parameters

Parameter	Description
hKey	Handle of an open key or one of the following reserved handles: HKEY_CLASSES_ROOT HKEY_CURRENT_USER HKEY_LOCAL_MACHINE HKEY_USERS
lpSubKey	Address of the string containing the subkey's name to open under *hKey*
ulOptions	Must be 0
samDesired	Security for this key (see Table A.5)
phkResult	Address of the buffer for the new handle

Return Values

Value	Description
ERROR_SUCCESS	Successful
error value	Failed

Description

RegOpenKeyEx doesn't create the subkey if it doesn't exist.

Table A.5 describes the possible values for *samDesired*.

Table A.5   Values for *samDesired*

Value	Description
KEY_ALL_ACCESS	Combination of KEY_QUERY_VALUE, KEY_ENUMERATE_SUB_KEYS, KEY_NOTIFY, KEY_CREATE_SUB_KEY, KEY_CREATE_LINK, and KEY_SET_VALUE access
KEY_CREATE_LINK	Permission to create symbolic link
KEY_CREATE_SUB_KEY	Permission to create subkeys
KEY_ENUMERATE_SUB_KEYS	Permission to enumerate subkeys
KEY_EXECUTE	Permission to read
KEY_NOTIFY	Permission for change notification
KEY_QUERY_VALUE	Permission to query subkeys
KEY_READ	Combination of KEY_QUERY_VALUE, KEY_ENUMERATE_SUB_KEYS, and KEY_NOTIFY
KEY_SET_VALUE	Permission to set data
KEY_WRITE	Combination of KEY_SET_VALUE and KEY_CREATE_SUB_KEY

RegQueryInfoKey

RegQueryInfoKey returns information about a key.

App
A

```
LONG RegQueryInfoKey( HKEY hKey, LPTSTR lpClass, LPDWORD lpcbClass, LPDWORD
lpReserved, LPDWORD lpcbSubKeys, LPDWORD lpcbMaxSubKeyLen, LPDWORD
lpcbMaxClassLen, LPDWORD lpcbValues, LPDWORD lpcbMaxValueNameLen, LPDWORD
lpcbMaxValueLen, LPDWORD lpcbSecurityDescriptor, PFILETIME lpftLastWriteTime )
```

Parameters

Parameter	Description
hKey	Handle of an open key or one of the following reserved handles: HKEY_CLASSES_ROOT HKEY_CURRENT_USER HKEY_LOCAL_MACHINE HKEY_USERS
lpClass	Address of buffer to receive the class name
lpcbClass	Address of the size of lpClass
lpReserved	Must be NULL
lpcbSubKeys	Buffer to receive number of subkeys
lpcbMaxSubKeyLen	Buffer to receive length of longest subkey
lpcbMaxClassLen	Buffer to receive length of longest class name
lpcbValues	Buffer to receive number of value entries
lpcbMaxValueNameLen	Buffer to receive length of longest value entry name
lpcbMaxValueLen	Buffer to receive length of longest value entry data
lpcbSecurityDescriptor	Buffer to receive length of the key's security descriptor
lpftLastWriteTime	Pointer to a FILETIME structure

Return Values

Value	Description
ERROR_SUCCESS	Successful
error value	Failed

Description

You must open the key identified by hKey with KEY_QUERY_KEY_VALUE access. Note that KEY_WRITE includes KEY_CREATE_SUB_KEY.

RegQueryMultipleValues

RegQueryMultipleValues returns the type and data for a key's list of value entries.

```
LONG RegQueryMultipleValues( HKEY hKey, PVALENT val_list, DWORD num_vals,
LPTSTR lpValueBuf, LPDWORD idwTotsize )
```

Parameters

Parameter	Description
hKey	Handle of an open key or one of the following reserved handles: HKEY_CLASSES_ROOT HKEY_CURRENT_USER HKEY_LOCAL_MACHINE HKEY_USERS
val_list	Address of an array of VALENT structures
num_vals	Contains the number of elements in val_list
lpValueBuf	Address of buffer to receive the data for each value
idwTotsize	Contains the size of lpValueBuf in bytes

Return Values

Value	Description
ERROR_SUCCESS	Successful
ERROR_CANTREAD	Can't read the given key
ERROR_MORE_DATA	lpValueBuf is too small
ERROR_TRANSFER_TOO_LONG	Data is greater than 1MB
error value	Failed

Description

RegQueryMultipleValues can be used with keys on remote computers.

RegQueryValue

RegQueryValue returns the data value of a key's default value entry.

```
LONG RegQueryValue( HKEY hKey, LPCTSTR lpSubKey, LPTSTR lpValue, PLONG
lpcbValue )
```

Parameters

Parameter	Description
hKey	Handle of an open key or one of the following reserved handles: HKEY_CLASSES_ROOT HKEY_CURRENT_USER HKEY_LOCAL_MACHINE HKEY_USERS
lpSubKey	Address of the string containing the subkey's name to query
lpValue	Buffer to receive default value entry
lpcbValue	Buffer to receive size of lpValue

Return Values

Value	Description
ERROR_SUCCESS	Successful
ERROR_MORE_DATA	lpValue isn't large enough
error value	Failed

Description

If the size of lpValue isn't large enough to receive the data, RegQueryValue returns ERROR_MORE_DATA. If lpValue is NULL, RegQueryValue returns ERROR_SUCCESS and stores the length of the value in lpcbValue.

The key identified by hKey must be opened with KEY_QUERY_VALUE access.

RegQueryValueEx

RegQueryValueEx returns the data value of a value entry.

```
LONG RegQueryValueEx( HKEY hKey, LPTSTR lpValueName, LPDWORD lpReserved,
LPDWORD lpType, LPBYTE lpData, LPDWORD lpcbData )
```

Parameters

Parameter	Description
hKey	Handle of an open key or one of the following reserved handles: HKEY_CLASSES_ROOT HKEY_CURRENT_USER HKEY_LOCAL_MACHINE HKEY_USERS
lpValueName	Address of the string containing the value entry's name
lpReserved	Must be 0
lpType	Type of data (see Table A.6)
lpData	Buffer to receive the data
lpcbData	Buffer to receive the size of the data

Return Values

Value	Description
ERROR_SUCCESS	Successful
ERROR_MORE_DATA	lpData isn't large enough
error value	Failed

Description

If the size of lpData isn't large enough to receive the data, RegQueryValueEx returns ERROR_MORE_DATA. If lpData is NULL, RegQueryValueEx returns ERROR_SUCCESS and stores the length of the value in lpcbData.

The key identified by hKey must be opened with KEY_QUERY_VALUE access.

Table A.6 describes the possible values for lpType.

Table A.6 Values for *lpType*

Value	Description
REG_BINARY	Binary data
REG_DWORD	32-bit number
REG_DWORD_LITTLE_ENDIAN	32-bit number in little-endian form
REG_DWORD_BIG_ENDIAN	32-bit number in big-endian form
REG_EXPAND_SZ	Null-terminated string the contains a reference to an environment variable
REG_LINK	Unicode symbolic link
REG_MULTI_SZ	Array of null-terminated strings
REG_NONE	No data type specified
REG_RESOURCE_LIST	Device-driver resource list
REG_SZ	Null-terminated string

RegSetKeySecurity

RegSetKeySecurity sets the security of an open key.

```
LONG RegSetKeySecurity( HKEY hKey, SECURITY_INFORMATION SecurityInformation,
PSECURITY_DESCRIPTOR pSecurityDescriptor )
```

Parameters

Parameter	Description
hKey	Handle of the open key to close
SecurityInformation	Indicates the contents of the security descriptor
pSecurityDescriptor	Address of the security attributes

Return Values

Value	Description
ERROR_SUCCESS	Successful
error value	Failed

Description

Setting a key's owner or group requires the calling process to have WRITE_OWNER permission or have the SE_TAKE_OWNERSHIP_NAME privilege. Setting a key's discretionary access-control list requires the calling process to have WRITE_DAC permission or own the key. Setting a key's system access-control list requires the calling process to have SE_SECURITY_NAME privileges.

RegReplaceKey

RegReplaceKey replaces the file containing a hive with another file.

```
LONG RegReplaceKey( HKEY hKey, LPCTSTR lpSubKey, LPCTSTR lpNewFile, LPCTSTR
lpOldFile )
```

Parameters

Parameter	Description
hKey	Handle of an open key or one of the following reserved handles:
	HKEY_CLASSES_ROOT
	HKEY_CURRENT_USER
	HKEY_LOCAL_MACHINE
	HKEY_USERS
lpSubKey	Handle to one of the predefined root keys:
	HKEY_LOCAL_MACHINE
	HKEY_USERS
lpNewFile	Address of string containing the name of the new file
lpOldFile	Address of string containing the name of the file to replace

Return Values

Value	Description
ERROR_SUCCESS	Successful
error value	Failed

Description

The calling process must have the SE_RESTORE_NAME privilege.

RegRestoreKey

RegRestoreKey imports the Registry entries from a file and replaces the specified key.

LONG RegRestoreKey(HKEY *hKey*, LPCTSTR *lpFile*, DWORD *dwFlags*)

Parameters

Parameter	Description
hKey	Handle of an open key or one of the following reserved handles: HKEY_CLASSES_ROOT HKEY_CURRENT_USER HKEY_LOCAL_MACHINE HKEY_USERS
lpFile	Address of the string containing the name of the file to import
dwFlags	Indicates if the key is volatile: REG_WHOLE_HIVE_VOLATILE

Return Values

Value	Description
ERROR_SUCCESS	Successful
error value	Failed

Description

If any subkeys of *hKey* are open, RegRestoreKey fails. The calling process must have the SE_RESTORE_NAME privilege. RegRestoreKey replaces the entire sub-tree with the new sub-tree imported from *lpFile*.

RegSaveKey

RegSaveKey saves the specified key and subkeys to a file.

```
LONG RegSaveKey( HKEY hKey, LPCTSTR hKey, LPSECURITY_ATTRIBUTES
lpSecurityAttributes )
```

Parameters

Parameter	Description
hKey	Handle of an open key or one of the following reserved handles: HKEY_CLASSES_ROOT HKEY_CURRENT_USER HKEY_LOCAL_MACHINE HKEY_USERS
lpFile	Address string that contains the name of the file into which the key and its subkeys are saved
lpSecurityAttributes	Security descriptor for the new file

Return Values

Value	Description
ERROR_SUCCESS	Successful
error value	Failed

Description

The calling process must have the SE_BACKUP_NAME privilege.

RegSetValue

RegSetValue sets the default value entry for a key. Note that your Win32 program should use RegSetValueEx.

```
LONG RegSetValue( HKEY hKey, LPCTSTR lpSubKey, DWORD dwType, LPCTSTR lpData,
DWORD cbData )
```

Parameters

Parameter	Description
hKey	Handle of an open key or one of the following reserved handles: HKEY_CLASSES_ROOT HKEY_CURRENT_USER HKEY_LOCAL_MACHINE HKEY_USERS
lpSubKey	Address of the string containing the subkey's name
dwType	Must be REG_SZ
lpData	Address of a null-terminated string
cbData	Length of the string in lpData

Return Values

Value	Description
ERROR_SUCCESS	Successful
error value	Failed

Description

If the key specified by lpSubKey doesn't exist, RegSetValue creates it.

You must open the key identified by hKey with KEY_SET_VALUE access.

N O T E If you're writing more than 2,048 bytes of data to a value entry, consider writing the data to a file and storing the file's name in the Registry. ▪

RegSetValueEx

RegSetValueEx sets the data for a value entry.

```
LONG RegSetValueEx( HKEY hKey, LPCTSTR lpValueName, DWORD Reserved, DWORD
dwType, CONST BYTE *lpData, DWORD cbData )
```

Parameters

Parameter	Description
hKey	Handle of an open key or one of the following reserved handles:
	HKEY_CLASSES_ROOT
	HKEY_CURRENT_USER
	HKEY_LOCAL_MACHINE
	HKEY_USERS
lpValueName	Address of the string containing the value entry's name
Reserved	Must be 0
dwType	Specifies the value entry's data type (see Table A.7)
lpData	Address of the value entry's data
cbData	Size of the value entry's data

Return Values

Value	Description
ERROR_SUCCESS	Successful
error value	Failed

Description

If the key specified by *lpSubKey* doesn't exist, *RegSetValue* creates it.

You must open the key identified by *hKey* with KEY_SET_VALUE access.

N O T E   If you're writing more than 2,048 bytes of data to a value entry, consider writing the data to a file and storing the file's name in the Registry. ■

Table A.7 describes the possible values for *dwType*.

Table A.7   Values for *dwType*

Value	Description
REG_BINARY	Binary data
REG_DWORD	32-bit number
REG_DWORD_LITTLE_ENDIAN	32-bit number in little-endian form

Value	Description
REG_DWORD_BIG_ENDIAN	32-bit number in big-endian form
REG_EXPAND_SZ	Null-terminated string the contains a reference to an environment variable
REG_LINK	Unicode symbolic link
REG_MULTI_SZ	Array of null-terminated strings
REG_NONE	No data type specified
REG_RESOURCE_LIST	Device-driver resource list
REG_SZ	Null-terminated string

RegUnLoadKey

RegUnLoadKey unloads the given key and subkeys from the Registry.

```
LONG RegUnLoadKey( HKEY hKey, LPCTSTR lpSubKey )
```

Parameters

Parameter	Description
hKey	Handle created by RegConnectRegistry, or a pre-defined handle: HKEY_LOCAL_MACHINE HKEY_USERS
lpSubKey	Address of string containing the name of the subkey to unload

Return Values

Value	Description
ERROR_SUCCESS	Successful
error value	Failed

Description

The calling process must have the SE_RESTORE_NAME privilege. The key indicated by lpSubKey must have been created by RegLoadKey. ●

Internet Resources for Windows

by Jerry Honeycutt

Windows is hot. Not just Windows 95, but Windows NT, too. Thus, the amount of information and programs that becomes available each day is staggering. If you don't want to wait for the next Windows super book or next month's magazine (they're three months out of date anyway), you have to go online to get that information. You can get a lot of it through commercial online services such as CompuServe, America Online, or The Microsoft Network. You'll find more variety, and potentially more useful information, on the Internet, however.

That's where this appendix comes in. It points you to some of the best resources on the Internet for Windows information, help, and programs. Keep in mind that there are hundreds of other Internet sites for each site that you find in this appendix. I don't include most of them because they contain nothing more than links to the other sites. The result is an empty Web of Windows pages, all linked together, that contain nothing but useless links. ■

FTP servers

FTP servers contain huge collections of Windows 95 and NT shareware programs that you can use.

Mailing lists

You can engage other folks in lively conversations about your favorite flavor of Windows.

UseNet newsgroups

Newsgroups are the place to look for quickly changing information and to find help for Windows.

World Wide Web

There's little doubt that the Web is the hottest resource on the Internet, especially for Windows.

ON THE WEB
You can find shortcuts to the Internet addresses described in this appendix on my Web site at
http://rampages.onramp.net/~jerry.

FTP Servers

The FTP servers in this section contain large collections of Windows shareware programs. They are all well organized, just like your own hard drive, so you can quickly find
the type of program for which you're looking. Note that most of these sites are indexed by
Shareware.com. See "Shareware.com," later in this chapter, for more information.

T I P If you don't have an FTP client, you can use your Web browser to access FTP servers. Type **ftp://**
followed by the FTP address in your Web browser's address bar.

Dr. CD-ROM

FTP address: **ftp.drcdrom.com**

Hot! That sums up this FTP site. It contains the complete WinWite and SimTel software
archives. The WinSite archive is in the WinSite-CICA folder, and the SimTel archive is in
the SimTel folder. In case you're not sure what files you're going to find in these archives,
take a look at this:

WinSite	WinSite is considered to be the largest collection of shareware and freeware on the Internet. It contains both Windows 95 and Windows NT programs.
SimTel	SimTel is the Coast to Coast Software Repository. It also con- tains both Windows 95 and Windows NT programs. In SimTel/ nt/Registry, for example, you'll find a variety of Windows NT Registry tools.

ON THE WEB
http://www.drcdrom.com is this FTP site's companion Web site.

Microsoft

FTP address: **ftp.microsoft.com**

This is the place to look for updated drivers, new files for Windows, and sometimes free programs. My favorite part of this FTP site is the Knowledge Base articles that answer common questions about most of Microsoft's programs. If you're having trouble finding your way around, look for a file called DIRMAP.TXT, which tells you what the different folders have in them. Here's what you find under each of the folders on this site:

/BUSSYS	Files for business systems, including networking, mail, SQL Server, and Windows NT.
/DESKAPPS	Files for all of Microsoft's desktop applications, including Access, Excel, PowerPoint, Project, and Word. You can also find information for the Home series, including games and Works.
/DEVELOPR	The place to look if you're a developer. There are folders for Visual C++, Visual Basic, various utilities, the Microsoft Developer Network, and more. If you subscribe to the *Microsoft Systems Journal*, check here to find the source code for articles.
/KBHELP	Microsoft's Knowledge Base folder. A *knowledge base*, in this context, is a help file that contains common questions and answers about Microsoft products. This folder contains one self-extracting, compressed file for each Microsoft product. The Windows 95 Knowledge Base files are under yet another folder called WIN95. If you're having difficulty with a Microsoft product, download the appropriate file, decompress it, and double-click it to load it in Help.
/MSDOWNLOAD	This folder contains all of Microsoft's latest Internet clients. Each client is in its own sub-folder. For example, Internet Explorer is in a sub-folder called ie3.
/SOFTLIB	The folder to check out if you're looking for updated drivers, patches, or bug fixes. This folder contains more than 2,200 files, though, so you need to check out INDEX.TXT to locate what you want.

/PEROPSYS	For personal operating systems. If you're looking for back issues of WINNEWS, look in the WIN_NEWS folder. There are other folders relating to all versions of Windows, MS-DOS, and Microsoft hardware.
/SERVICES	Contains information about TechNet, Microsoft educational services, sales information, and so on.

N O T E Many of the folders on the Microsoft FTP site have two files that you should read: README.TXT and INDEX.TXT.

README.TXT describes the type of files you find in the current folder and any subfolders. It also may describe recent additions and files that have been removed.

INDEX.TXT describes each file in the folder. It's a good idea to search for the file you want in INDEX.TXT before trying to pick it out of the listing. Note that Microsoft's site is constantly changing, so you'll want to check back there often. ▨

▶ **See** "Microsoft's Knowledge Base Online," **p. 436**

Walnut Creek

FTP address: **ftp.cdrom.com**

I consider myself lucky to get on this FTP site. It's incredibly popular. Walnut Creek sells CD-ROMs that are packed with freeware and shareware programs. Files from these CD-ROMs are available from the Walnut Creek FTP site, too. You find Windows 95 programs in /pub/win95 and Windows NT programs in /pub/winnt.

 This site is usually very crowded. If you get on to this site, don't let yourself get disconnected by taking a coffee break—it could be a while before you get on again.

 You can also access this site on the Web. Open **http://www.cdrom.com** in your favorite Web browser.

WinSite (Formerly Known as CICA)

FTP address: **ftp.winsite.com**

This archive used to be managed by the Center for Innovative Computing Applications (CICA) at Indiana University. They've created a new group called *WinSite* to manage the archive.

This could be the only FTP site that you need. It is one of the largest collections of freeware and shareware programs on the Internet. It's the Internet equivalent of CompuServe's WinShare forum (a forum on CompuServe that contains shareware Windows programs). You'll find Windows 95 programs in /pub/pc/win95 and Windows NT programs in /pub/pc/winnt.

ON THE WEB

http://www.winsite.com is this FTP site's companion Web site.

App

B

TROUBLESHOOTING

I've tried over and over to log onto the WinSite FTP server. A very large number of Internet users look for files at this FTP site. So you'll find it's very crowded most of the time. Keep trying. If you still can't get on to it, look at the log file that your FTP client program displays to find a *mirror site* (FTP servers containing the exact same files) near you.

Mailing Lists

Windows-related mailing lists keep your mailbox full of messages. I've received more than 100 messages a day from WIN95-L, for example. There's a lot of noise generated by these lists, but you can find a lot of gems, too. This section describes six of the most popular ones: **DevWire**, **WinNews**, **NT-USERS**, **WinNTnews**, **WIN95-L**, and **WINNT-L**.

Microsoft DevWire

This is for Windows programmers. You'll find news and product information, such as seminar schedules and visual tool release schedules. To subscribe, send an e-mail to **DevWire@microsoft.nwnet.com** with **subscribe DevWire** in the body of your message.

Microsoft WinNews

This weekly newsletter keeps you up-to-date on the latest happenings at Microsoft. You also find product tips and press releases. To subscribe, send an e-mail to **enews99@microsoft.nwnet.com** and type **subscribe winnews** in the body of your message.

NT-USERS

The Trade Unit of the Organization of American States provides this mailing list to discuss Windows NT. To subscribe, send an e-mail to **listserv@www.sice.oas.org** and type **join nt-users** in the body of your message.

WinNTnews

This is another regular newsletter similar to **WinNews**. It keeps you up-to-date on the latest and greatest with Windows NT. To subscribe, send an e-mail to **winntnews-admin@microsoft.bhs.com** and type **subscribe winntnews** in the body of your message. Note that this mailing list isn't maintained by Microsoft.

WIN95-L

The WIN95-L mailing list is more like a forum. A subscriber posts a message to the list, and the list forwards the message to the other subscribers. Using this mailing list, you get Windows 95 help much faster than you can through a support line or commercial online service. The answers are usually better, too. To subscribe, send an e-mail to **listserv@peach.ease.lsoft.com** and type **subscribe WIN95-L** *your name* in the body of your message.

> **CAUTION**
>
> WIN95-L floods your mailbox with hundreds of messages each day. If you want to receive four or five messages each day that contain 30 to 40 posts in each message (called a digest), send an e-mail to **listserv@peach.ease.lsoft.com** with the text **set win95-l digest** in the body of your message.

WINNT-L

WINNT-L is just like **WIN95-L** except that it's for Windows NT. To subscribe to this mailing list, send an e-mail to **listserv@peach.ease.lsoft.com** and type **subscribe WINNT-L** *your name* in the body of your message.

UseNet Newsgroups

You'll find plenty of Windows 95 and Windows NT newsgroups available on UseNet. Most of them are under the **comp.os.ms-windows** hierarchy. Microsoft has moved most of their support forums to UseNet under the **microsoft.public** hierarchy. Get a load of these newsgroups:

comp.os.ms-windows.advocacy

comp.os.ms-windows.announce

comp.os.ms-windows.apps.*

comp.os.ms-windows.networking.*

comp.os.ms-windows.programmer.*

comp.os.ms-windows.win95.*

comp.os.ms-windows.nt.*

microsoft.public.win95.*

microsoft.public.windowsnt.*

microsoft.public.win32.programmer.*

Get Help from UseNet

Some of the best information you can find on the Internet is available from other users, such as yourself, who've answered questions on UseNet. You have to be careful about naively listening to all of it, but for the most part you'll find good information.

So how do you get to all this information on UseNet? Deja News, that's how. Deja News is a search tool like Yahoo and AltaVista. It doesn't search the Web, though, it searches the UseNet newsgroup postings. Open **http://www.dejanews.com** and you'll see a Web page that looks like the one shown in Figure B.1.

FIG. B.1

You can use Deja News to find specific articles or newsgroups in which people discuss a topic.

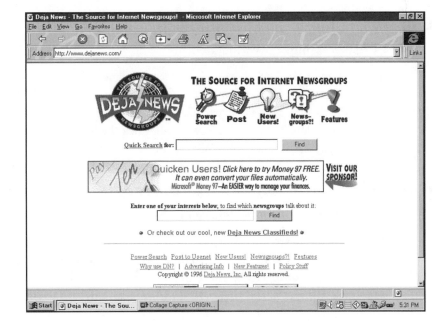

continues

continued

To search Deja News for postings about a particular subject, type your keywords in the first text box, and click the Find button next to it. Deja News returns a list of postings that match those keywords. Subject lines that begin with RE: are the best messages to open because they contain replies to questions.

To find a newsgroup in which people frequently discuss a particular topic, type your keywords in the second text box and click the Find button next to it. Deja News returns a list of newsgroups in which it frequently finds those keywords.

World Wide Web

The explosive growth of Windows 95 and Windows NT Web pages is evident if you search for the keywords **Windows 95** or **Windows NT** using Yahoo, WebCrawler, Excite, Lycos, or your own favorite search tool. You can find thousands of Web pages dedicated to Windows, some from the corporate community such as Microsoft or Symantec. Many more exist from individuals who want to make their mark on the world by sharing what they know about Windows.

The Web pages in this section are only a start. Each one contains links to other Windows sites. Before you know it, your Windows hot list will grow by leaps-and-bounds.

BugNet

URL address: **http://www.bugnet.com**

If you're not getting anywhere with that support line, try out this Web site. It documents all the latest bugs and sometimes offers solutions or workarounds. You can report a bug to this site as well. This site is particularly useful to check out the stability of a product before you fork out your hard-earned cash. Click the Win NT Bug List to open the Windows NT bug list, or click the Win95 Bug List.

Dylan Green's Windows 95 Starting Page

URL address: **http://www.dylan95.com**

Not only is Dylan Green's Web page packed with graphics, frames, and Java applications (see Figure B.2), but it's also packed with useful information about Windows 95, too. You find links for FAQs, troubleshooting, setting up your dialup connection, and shareware libraries at this site.

FIG. B.2
To get the full benefit of the Windows 95-like menus, you need to use Internet Explorer 2.0 or Netscape Navigator 2.0.

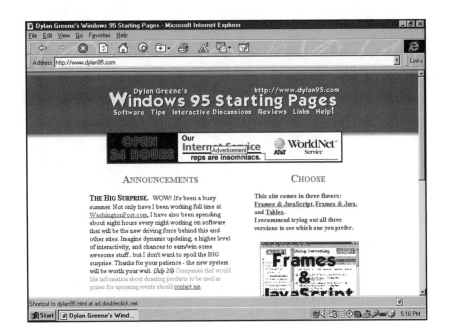

Exploring Windows NT Home Page

URL address: **http://www.cobb.com/ewn/index.htm**

The Cobb Group has put their monthly Windows NT journal on the Web for you to enjoy. You'll find a handful of NT tips and you can preview each issue on the home page shown in Figure B.3.

FedCenter

URL address: **http://199.171.16.49/fedcenter/fw95.html**

This Web page is sponsored by The InterFed Group (an organization dedicated to helping government employees participate in the Internet). It contains information about Windows 95 events and shareware programs, as well as links to numerous other Windows 95 Web pages.

Frank Condron's Windows 95 Page

URL address: **http://www.conitech.com/windows/**

This Web site was chosen as a ClubWin Web site. *ClubWin* is a collection of Web sites that have been recognized by Microsoft as providing outstanding Windows 95 support and information on the Web. This page fits the bill. It has updated drivers, software, hints, and links to other ClubWin sites.

FIG. B.3

Scroll down and click Back Issues to preview back issues of Windows NT.

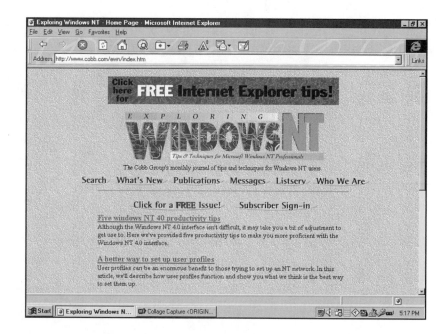

Getting the Most from the Windows 95 Registry

URL address: **http://www.usa.net/~rduffy/registry.htm**

This Web page contains a basic introduction to the Registry. It also has some tips that involve editing the Registry.

Inside the Windows Registry

URL addresses:

http://www.zdnet.com/~pcmag/issues/1418/pcm00083.htm

http://www.zdnet.com/~pcmag/issues/1419/pcm00116.htm

http://www.zdnet.com/~pcmag/issues/1501/pcm00121.htm

These three Web pages represent a three-part series from *PC Magazine* about the Registry. If you're looking for concise information about the Registry, check these out.

Jerry Honeycutt

URL address: **http://rampages.onramp.net/~jerry**

My Web page. Besides the usual boasting that you might expect, you find useful tips for Windows and the Internet. You also find any updates to this and other books you need to know about.

Microsoft Corporation

URL address: **http://www.microsoft.com**

Microsoft's Web site contains an amazing amount of information about its products, services, plans, job opportunities, and more (see Figure B.4). Not bad for a company that almost completely missed the Internet. Lately, most of it is dedicated to the Internet, but you can still find plenty of information about Windows. You can find the two most useful Windows 95 Web pages by clicking the Products link or the Support link.

FIG. B.4
Click Search to find exactly what you're looking for on the Microsoft Web site.

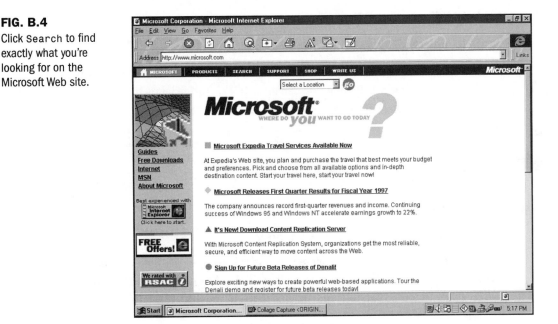

Here's what you find when you open each Web page:

■ *Products link.* This Web page contains links for most Microsoft products, including Windows 95. You find links to Microsoft pages for Windows 95, Office, BackOffice, Windows NT, and more. The bulletin board on this page also contains the latest information about Microsoft products.

■ *Support link.* The Support Desktop Web page provides access to the Microsoft Knowledge Base, which you can use to search for articles based on keywords that you specify. It also contains links to the Microsoft Software Library and Frequently Asked Questions (FAQ) Web pages.

▶ **See** "Microsoft Knowledge Base Online," **p. 436**

ON THE WEB

http://www.microsoft.com/devonly is Microsoft's For Developers Only Web site.

PC World's Windows 95

URL address: **http://www.pcworld.com/win95**

Wow! This Web page has links to almost everything you need for Windows 95. It has articles about Windows 95 that you can search. *PC World* claims to have the largest collection of Windows 95 shareware on the Internet. They may be right.

TIP   Click the `Tip-a-Day` to sign up for a free subscription to the Windows 95 Tip-of-the-Day mailing list.

Que Corporation

URL address: **http://www.mcp.com/que/**

This appendix wouldn't be complete without at least one reference to Que's Web site. Que's site contains information about all of the books Que publishes. Many times, you can even read electronic versions of Que's best-selling books while you're online.

Shareware.com

URL address: **http://www.shareware.com**

Shareware.com is a hot Web site that indexes shareware and freeware products on the Internet. You can search for products by platform, category, and so on. You can also look up the top products based on the number of downloads or recent submissions. If you're looking for a shareware product, you don't need to log on to an online service anymore; you can find it here (see Figure B.5).

FIG. B.5
Click Subscribe to join the Shareware Dispatch mailing list— a weekly mailing list that keeps you informed about the latest shareware programs.

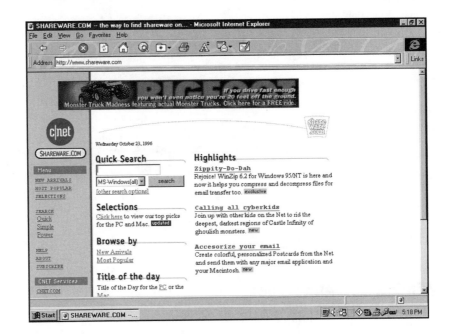

Stroud's CWSApps List

URL address: **http://www.cwsapps.com**

This Web site contains every Windows Winsock program available on the Internet. You find World Wide Web, FTP, e-mail, IRC, and UseNet client programs. You also find HTML editors and communication suites. In addition to the standard Winsock programs, this site contains all of the essential utilities that you need for Windows 95, such as WinZIP 95 and ViruScan for Windows 95.

Figure B.6 shows the easy-to-use interface for this Web site. Click a category to see a list of shareware programs for that category.

FIG. B.6
Click the 32-bit
Apps button to see a
huge list of Windows
95 and NT programs.

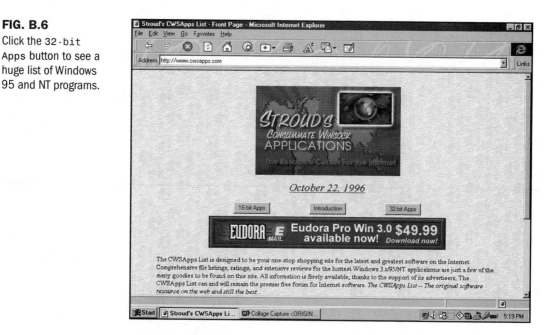

Windows 95 Annoyances

URL address: **http://www.creativelement.com/win95ann**

Just like the name implies, this site is dedicated to all the annoying features in Windows
95. The authors of this site don't just gripe about them, however. They offer solutions. If
you don't like the desktop icons, for example, you learn how to change them at this site. If
you're having trouble with networking in Windows 95, you can find information here that
just might help you. Figure B.7 shows you the Web page's sleek user interface.

Windows95.com

URL address: **http://www.windows95.com/**

Windows95.com is another graphically intensive page. It contains lots of links to other
Windows 95 sites, but you also find that it has useful information in its own right, such as
plenty of 32-bit shareware—particularly for new users.

FIG. B.7
Click one of the icons to learn more about that topic. Click Getting to know the Registry for information about the Windows 95 Registry, for example.

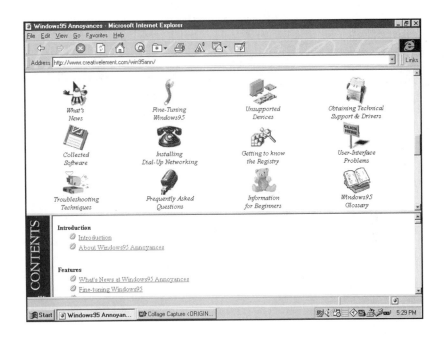

TIP Be sure to check out the Internet Hyperglossary, which defines some of the Internet terminology that escapes us all.

ZD Net Software Library

URL address: **http://www.zdnet.com/zdi/software**

Ziff-Davis's Software Library is the best collection of shareware and freeware on the Internet. I have absolutely no reservations making that statement. It contains thousands of files that you can search and download. They don't stop there. They actually review and rate each of the programs so that you know exactly what you're getting before you start downloading. Figure B.8 shows you what the ZD Net Software Library looks like.

ON THE WEB

Point your Web browser to **http://www.yahoo.com/Computers_and_Internet/ Operating_Systems/Microsoft_Windows** on Yahoo and click your favorite flavor of Windows. You'll find hundreds of links to a variety of Windows 95 and Windows NT Web pages.

FIG. B.8

Don't miss the `Remote Control` link at the bottom of the page, which lets you search the software library from a secondary browser window.

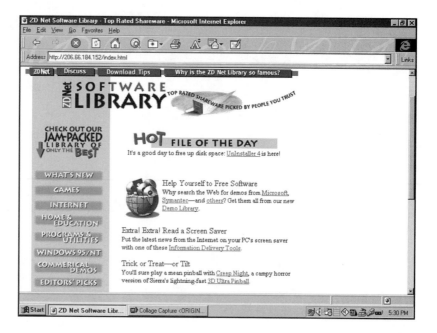

Technical Resources for Windows

by Jerry Honeycutt

**Y**our job is hard enough without having problems getting support or, for that matter, the information you need. Learning about the Registry is even tougher without the benefit of Microsoft's sage Registry wisdom. Fortunately, Microsoft recognizes the value of useful and timely information, so they provide many ways to get it.

If the Internet is your thing, you can get great support information through the Knowledge Base. Prefer stuffing CD-ROMs into your hungry computer? Try out Technet or Developer Network. If you haven't given your fax machine a workout in a while, check out Microsoft's FastTips. ■

Microsoft's Knowledge Base Online

Don't waste your time with Microsoft's help line; you can solve your problem here.

Microsoft Technet

Microsoft Technet is like having a full-time support engineer by your side.

Microsoft Developer Network

If you're a Windows developer, you can't possibly live without the Developer Network.

Microsoft FastTips

You can get the most common Knowledge Base articles delivered directly to your fax machine.

Microsoft's Knowledge Base Online

Microsoft's Knowledge Base contains thousands of articles, each of which provides information about a specific problem. Each article describes the problem's symptoms, causes, resolution, and, sometimes, status. For example, you might learn that the reason your desktop redraws so painfully slow is because the video driver has a bug that you can repair by changing a setting in the Registry. Open **http://www.microsoft.com/kb** in your Web browser and you'll see Microsoft's Knowledge Base as shown in Figure C.1.

FIG. C.1

You can get support from the Knowledge Base for any of Microsoft's products, including Windows 95 and NT.

Choose a product

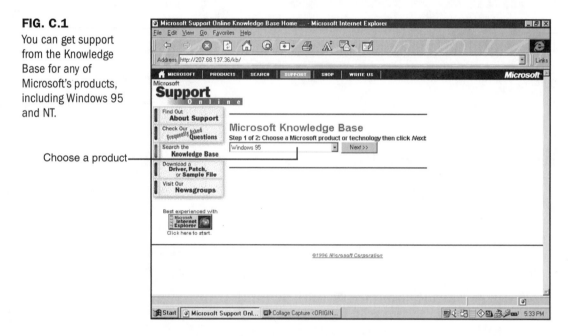

The types of articles that the Knowledge Base contains are quite impressive. Here are the categories that you can find at the time of this writing:

    Application Notes Available

    Confirmed Bugs

    Display (video, monitor, resolution) Issues

    Documentation Errors

    Environment and Configuration Issues

    Error Message Follow-Up Information

    Files Available for Download

    Fixed Bugs

General Programming Issues

Hardware

Interaction Between Microsoft Products

Interactions with 3rd Party Products

Multimedia, Including Programming Issues

Networking, Including Programming Issues

OLE, Including Programming Issues

Product Features or Functionality

Printing, Including Programming Issues

Problems Not Classified as Bugs (Features?)

Sample Code

Sample Macros

Setup and Installation Issues

Step-by-Step Procedures for Tasks

Sound (Audio) Issues

Tools, Utilities, Wizards, etc.

Troubleshooting Information

User Interface, Including Programming Issues

Microsoft TechNet

Microsoft TechNet is a must-have resource for folks who are in a position to support Microsoft products such as Windows 95 or NT. It's a CD-ROM that Microsoft distributes to subscribers on a monthly basis. It contains information you need to plan your projects, execute your plans, and solve problems. It'll make a hero out of you. Here's what you'll find on the CD-ROM:

- Technical information, such as product evaluations and implementation guides.
- The Microsoft Knowledge Base, which contains answers to more than 50,000 technical questions.
- Microsoft Resource Kits for products such as Windows, Microsoft Office, and Microsoft Mail.
- Conference notes taken from shows such as Tech-Ed and DevCon.
- Updated drivers and patches, which contain the latest files in the Microsoft Software Library.

To subscribe to Microsoft TechNet, call (800) 344-2121. The cost is $299 for a single user and $39.95 for each additional user. You can get a server-unlimited user license for $699.

Microsoft Developer Network

Microsoft Developer Network (MSDN) is very similar to TechNet except that it's for Windows developers. You can always point out a serious Windows developer because they have the Development Library stuffed into their CD-ROM (see Figure C.2). Like TechNet, you subscribe to MSDN to receive quarterly updates. Unlike TechNet, MSDN has different subscriptions depending upon how many goodies you need (and can afford):

Library	The Library subscription gets you the Development Library, which is a CD-ROM that contains over 1.5G of documentation, articles, samples, and the Developer Knowledge Database. You also get the Developer Network News and a discount on Microsoft Press books. Cost? $199 per year.
Professional	The Professional subscription gets you everything in the Library subscription, as well as the Development Platform, which is a set of CD-ROMs that contain all of the software development and device driver kits, Windows and Windows NT Workstation operating systems, and premium shipments of important system releases. The professional subscription is $499 per year.
Enterprise	The Enterprise subscription gets you everything in the Professional subscription, plus the BackOffice Test Platform, which contains the latest server components of Microsoft BackOffice. The enterprise subscription is $1,499 per year.
Universal	The Universal subscription is the ultimate Subscription level. It contains everything in the Enterprise level. It also includes all of the Microsoft Visual Tools (Visual Basic and Visual C++, for example), Microsoft Office products, and upcoming development tools. The Universal subscription will set you back a whopping $2,499 per year.

You can subscribe to the Microsoft Developer Network by calling (800) 759-5474. Note that if you already subscribe to one of the subscription levels, Microsoft offers a reasonable upgrade fee to one of the higher levels.

FIG. C.2
You'll see a lot of
Microsoft InfoViewer
because it's used
for a number of
Microsoft's developer
and support
databases.

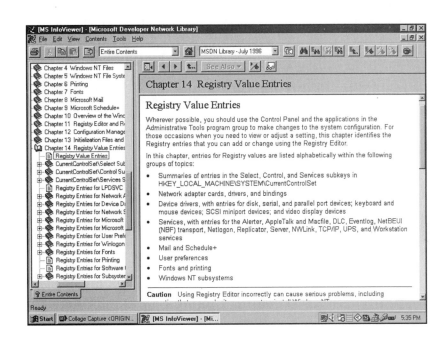

Microsoft FastTips

Microsoft FastTips is a free, automated service that you can use to get answers to some of the more common problems Microsoft has recorded. The way it works is that you call FastTips, provide your fax number, order an item, and FastTips faxes you the article. Call the number in Table C.1 that most closely matches the type of information you need.

Table C.1 FastTips 1-800 Numbers

For tips about:	Call:
Desktop applications	(800) 936-4100
Personal operating systems	(800) 936-4200
Development tools products	(800) 936-4300
Business systems	(800) 936-4400

TIP Get a FastTips Map before you use this service so that you can more easily find your way around. Call one of the numbers in Table C.1. Then, choose 1, 2, and 1. Follow the instructions that the automated attendant gives you along the way.

Index

I-J

icons
  bitmap icon images, 138-139
  caches, expanding, 133
  class-definition subkeys, 108-109
  Control Panel submenus, 135-136
  data types, 61
  desktops
    changing, 129-130
    removing, 138, 178-179
    Tweak UI settings, 178-179
  folders, 139
  shortcut icon arrows, 137
    Tweak UI settings, 178
  subkeys, 138

importing
  changed files into Windows Explorer, 68
  line command parameters, 69-70
  REG files, /c switch, 70
  Registry, 268
    line command parameters, 69-70
    restoring Registry, 90-91

INF files, 28, 260-263
  DefaultInstall section, 261
  distributing, 264-266
    e-mail, 265
    login scripts, 266
    Web pages, 264
  Registry sections, 261-263
  Version section, 261

INI files, 32-33, 36
  IOS.INI, real-mode drivers, 216
  SYSTEM.INI,
    see SYSTEM.INI file
  WIN.INI, 205-209

InprocServer32 subkeys (CLSIDs), 118-119

InstallLocationsMRU subkey (Windows 95), HKEY_USERS, 46

integrating applications, 309-313, 315-316
  File Definition subkeys, 310
  File Extension subkeys, 310
  installation, 315-316
  OLE support, 313
  setting user preferences, 316
  shell extensions, 310-312
    advanced, 312
    context menus, 311-312
    file associations, 311
  see also programming

IntelliPoint
  MouseKeys custom settings, (Windows 95), 152
  NUMLOCK key, (Windows 95), 153

IntelliType 1.1, MouseKeys custom settings, (Windows 95), 152

Internet Explorer
  default protocol, changing, 129
  EXE files, preventing automatic opening, 150
  reassocating file extensions, 87
  search engine default, setting (Tweak UI), 177
  troubleshooting, 150
    Unable to Create Folder messages, 152

Internet Registry resources, 419-420
  FTP servers, 420-423
    Dr. CD-ROM, 420
    Microsoft, 421-422
    Walnut Creek, 422
    WinSite (formerly CICA), 422-423
  mailing lists, 423-424

  shortcuts, 420
  UseNet newsgroups, 424-426
  World Wide Web, 426-433
    BugNet, 426
    Dylan Green's Windows 95 Starting Page, 426
    FedCenter, 427
    Frank Condron's Windows 95 page, 427
    Getting the Most from the Windows 95 Registry, 428
    Inside the Windows Registry, 428
    Internet resource shortcuts, 420
    Jerry Honeycutt (author), 429
    Microsoft Corporation, 429-430
    PC World, 430
    Que Corporation, 430
    Shareware.com, 430-431
    Stroud's CWSApps List, 431
    Windows 95 Annoyances, 432
    Windows NT home page, 427
    Windows95.com, 432-433
    ZD Net Software Library, 433

IO.SYS file (Windows 95), 193, 202-203

IOS.INI file, real-mode drivers listing, 216

IOS.LOG file, MS-DOS compatibility mode, 220-221

IP routing, disabling (Windows 95), 149-150

IsShortcut value, removing, 137

Check out Que® Books on the World Wide Web
http://www.mcp.com/que

As the biggest software release in computer history, Windows 95 continues to redefine the computer industry. Click here for the latest info on our Windows 95 books

Make computing quick and easy with these products designed exclusively for new and casual users

xamine the latest releases in vord processing, spreadsheets, perating systems, and suites

The Internet, The World Wide Web, CompuServe®, America Online®, Prodigy® —it's a world of ever-changing information. Don't get left behind!

ind out about new additions to ur site, new bestsellers and ot topics

In-depth information on high-end topics: find the best reference books for databases, programming, networking, and client/server technologies

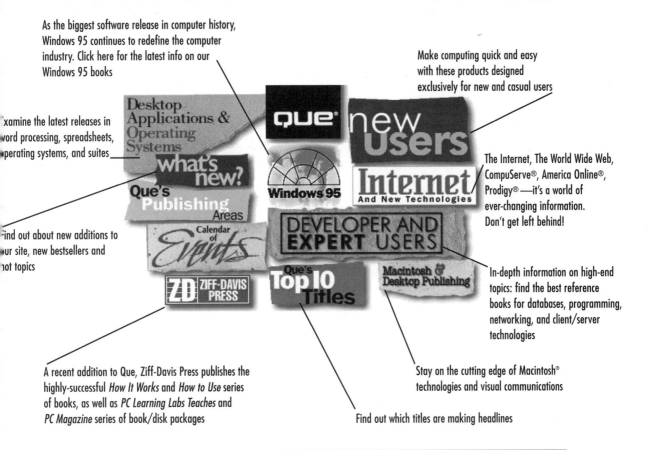

A recent addition to Que, Ziff-Davis Press publishes the highly-successful *How It Works* and *How to Use* series of books, as well as *PC Learning Labs Teaches* and *PC Magazine* series of book/disk packages

Stay on the cutting edge of Macintosh® technologies and visual communications

Find out which titles are making headlines

With 6 separate publishing groups, Que develops products for many specific market segments and areas of computer technology. Explore our Web Site and you'll find information on best-selling titles, newly published titles, upcoming products, authors, and much more.

- Stay informed on the latest industry trends and products available
- Visit our online bookstore for the latest information and editions
- Download software from Que's library of the best shareware and freeware

Copyright © 1996, Macmillan Computer Publishing-USA, A Viacom Company

Complete and Return this Card
for a *FREE* Computer Book Catalog

Thank you for purchasing this book! You have purchased a superior computer book written expressly for your needs. To continue to provide the kind of up-to-date, pertinent coverage you've come to expect from us, we need to hear from you. Please take a minute to complete and return this self-addressed, postage-paid form. In return, we'll send you a free catalog of all our computer books on topics ranging from word processing to programming and the internet.

☐   Mrs. ☐   Ms. ☐   Dr. ☐

ne (first) [ ] (M.I.) [ ] (last) [ ]

dress [ ]

[ ]

y [ ] State [ ] Zip [ ]

ne [ ] Fax [ ]

npany Name [ ]

nail address [ ]

'lease check at least (3) influencing factors for urchasing this book.

nt or back cover information on book .... ☐
cial approach to the content .... ☐
npleteness of content .... ☐
hor's reputation .... ☐
olisher's reputation .... ☐
ok cover design or layout .... ☐
ex or table of contents of book .... ☐
e of book .... ☐
cial effects, graphics, illustrations .... ☐
er (Please specify): _____ ☐

low did you first learn about this book?

v in Macmillan Computer Publishing catalog .... ☐
ommended by store personnel .... ☐
v the book on bookshelf at store .... ☐
ommended by a friend .... ☐
eived advertisement in the mail .... ☐
v an advertisement in: _____ ☐
d book review in: _____ ☐
er (Please specify): _____ ☐

low many computer books have you urchased in the last six months?

s book only .... ☐   3 to 5 books .... ☐
ooks .... ☐   More than 5 .... ☐

4. Where did you purchase this book?

Bookstore .... ☐
Computer Store .... ☐
Consumer Electronics Store .... ☐
Department Store .... ☐
Office Club .... ☐
Warehouse Club .... ☐
Mail Order .... ☐
Direct from Publisher .... ☐
Internet site .... ☐
Other (Please specify): _____ ☐

5. How long have you been using a computer?

☐ Less than 6 months   ☐ 6 months to a year
☐ 1 to 3 years   ☐ More than 3 years

6. What is your level of experience with personal computers and with the subject of this book?

	With PCs	With subject of book
New	☐	☐
Casual	☐	☐
Accomplished	☐	☐
Expert	☐	☐

Source Code ISBN: 0-7897-0842-6

7. Which of the following best describes your job title?

Administrative Assistant .... ☐
Coordinator .... ☐
Manager/Supervisor .... ☐
Director .... ☐
Vice President .... ☐
President/CEO/COO .... ☐
Lawyer/Doctor/Medical Professional .... ☐
Teacher/Educator/Trainer .... ☐
Engineer/Technician .... ☐
Consultant .... ☐
Not employed/Student/Retired .... ☐
Other (Please specify): _____ ☐

8. Which of the following best describes the area of the company your job title falls under?

Accounting .... ☐
Engineering.. ☐
Manufacturing .... ☐
Operations.. ☐
Marketing .... ☐
Sales .... ☐
Other (Please specify): _____ ☐

Comments: _____

9. What is your age?

Under 20 ....
21-29 ....
30-39 ....
40-49 ....
50-59 ....
60-over ....

10. Are you:

Male ....
Female ....

11. Which computer publications do you read regularly? (Please list)

_____
_____
_____
_____
_____
_____
_____
_____
_____
_____

Fold here and scotch-tape to r